STAKEHOLDERS IN THE LAW SCHOOL

This collection brings together a distinguished group of researchers to examine the power relations which are played out in university law schools as a result of the different pressures exerted upon them by a range of different 'stakeholders'. From students to governments, from lawyers to universities, a host of institutions and actors believe that law schools should take account of a vast number of (often conflicting) considerations when teaching their students, designing curricula, carrying out research and so on. How do law schools deal with these pressures? What should their response be to the 'stakeholders' who urge them to follow agendas emanating from outside the law school itself? To what extent should some of these agendas play a greater role in the thinking of law schools?

Stakeholders in the Law School

Edited by
FIONA COWNIE

·HART·
PUBLISHING
OXFORD AND PORTLAND, OREGON
2010

Published in North America (US and Canada) by
Hart Publishing
c/o International Specialized Book Services
920 NE 58th Avenue, Suite 300
Portland, OR 97213-3786
USA
Tel: +1 503 287 3093 or toll-free: (1) 800 944 6190
Fax: +1 503 280 8832
E-mail: orders@isbs.com
Website: http://www.isbs.com

Hart Publishing Ltd, 16C Worcester Place, Oxford, OX1 2JW
Telephone: +44 (0)1865 517530 Fax: +44 (0)1865 510710
E-mail: mail@hartpub.co.uk
Website: http://www.hartpub.co.uk

British Library Cataloguing in Publication Data
Data Available

ISBN: 978-1-84113-721-6

Typeset by Compuscript Ltd, Shannon
Printed and bound in Great Britain by
CPI Antony Rowe Ltd, Chippenham, Wiltshire

Contents

List of Contributors

Rosemary Auchmuty is Professor of Law at the University of Reading. She is a feminist historian and legal scholar and has written on property law, legal education and legal history as well on as many aspects of gender and sexuality and law, and on popular culture, especially girls' school stories. Her books include *A World of Girls* and *A World of Women*. She has contributed to several of the *Feminist Perspectives on Law* series (Routledge-Cavendish) and is a member of the Feminist Judgments Project. Her most recent work has been on early women law students and legal academics in the UK.

David Bamford is Dean of Flinders Law School, South Australia. He brings extensive experience as a senior political adviser, solicitor and barrister to his academic work. His primary teaching has been in the area of litigation, dispute resolution and regulation of politics. His research has focused on the workings of the civil and criminal justice system and he has been engaged in commissioned research for state and federal governments in Australia on bail and custodial remand, restorative justice, and court evaluations.

Andrew Boon is Dean of Law at the University of Westminster. He originally worked as a solicitor before lecturing at South Bank Polytechnic. He works on all aspects of the legal profession, particularly work, ethics and regulation, and has been consultant to the Law Society of England and Wales and the General Council of the Bar of England and Wales on their recent training framework review, and on legal education matters generally. He is currently Vice-Chair of the Bar Standards Board Education and Training Committee. In addition to numerous articles he has written books on legal skills, notably advocacy, and with Professor Jenny Levin (University of Wales, Swansea) co-authored *The Ethics and Conduct of Lawyers in England and Wales*, now in its second edition. He is currently a member of the ISA/RCSL Working Group on Legal Professions and the editorial board of *Legal Ethics*.

Anthony Bradney is Professor of Law at Keele University, having previously held chairs at the University of Leicester and the University of Sheffield. His research interests include law and religion, law and popular culture, and legal pluralism. He has also written extensively about the nature and practice of university legal education. His publications include *Religions, Rights and Laws* (1993), *Teaching Legal System* (with Fiona Cownie,

1999), *Living Without Law: An Ethnography of Dispute Avoidance and Resolution in the Religious Society of Friends* (with Fiona Cownie, 2000), *Conversations, Chances and Choices: The Liberal Law School in the Twenty-First Century* (2003) and *Law and Faith in a Secular Age* (2008). He is also the co-author of two textbooks, *How to Study Law*, which is now in its fifth edition, and *The English Legal System in Context*, which is now in its fourth edition.

Richard Collier is Professor of Law at Newcastle University, UK. His primary research interests concern questions around law and gender, with a particular focus on issues surrounding men and masculinities, ranging from family law and social change to legal education, crime and criminology. He has published widely in these and other fields and has recently completed the research project 'Fathers' Rights and Law Reform' (2008), funded by the British Academy/Leverhulme Trust Thank-Offering to Britain Fellowship. His books include *Masculinity, Law and the Family* (1995), *Masculinities, Crime and Criminology: Men, Corporeality and the Criminal(ised) Body* (1998), *Fathers' Rights Activism and Law Reform in Comparative Perspective* (edited with Sally Sheldon) (Hart Publishing, 2007), *Fragmenting Fatherhood: A Socio-Legal Study* (with Sally Sheldon, Hart Publishing, 2008) and *The Man of Law: Essays on Law, Men and Gender* (Routledge-Cavendish, 2009). Richard has presented a wide range of international plenary and keynote addresses and is an editorial board member of *Social and Legal Studies*.

Fiona Cownie is Professor of Law at the University of Keele, UK. She is a specialist in legal education, and her published work includes *Legal Academics: Culture and Identities* (2004) as well as numerous journal articles and contributions to edited collections. Her most recent legal education monograph is *A Great and Noble Occupation: The History of the Society of Legal Scholars* (with Professor Ray Cocks) (Hart Publishing, 2009). Professor Cownie is the convenor of the international group of scholars whose latest project forms the subject-matter of this collection of essays. This group is part of the Working Group on the Legal Professions, which is affiliated to the International Sociology Association's Research Committee on the Sociology of Law.

Andrew Goldsmith is Professor of Law and Executive Director, Centre for Transnational Crime Prevention, University of Wollongong, Australia. Until 2008 he was Professor of Law and Criminal Justice at Flinders University. Prior to that, he worked in clinical legal education at Monash University. His research interests for more than a decade have included legal education and legal professionalism as well as transnational security issues, particularly crime, law enforcement, counter-terrorism and rule of law reform. He currently heads an Australia Research Council Linkage Project with the Australian Federal Police International Deployment Group, entitled *Policing the Neighbourhood*, which is examining Australian police peace-keeping and capacity-building contributions in recent years to Papua New Guinea, Solomon Islands and Timor-Leste. His most recent book is *Crafting Transnational Policing: Police Capacity-Building and Global Policing Reform* (with James Sheptycki) (Hart Publishing, 2007). He was formerly Editor in Chief of *Legal Education Review*.

Rob Midgley is Deputy Vice-Chancellor: Academic Affairs and Research at the University of Fort Hare, South Africa, and a former professor and Dean of Law at Rhodes University. He is a member of the Academy of Science of South Africa (ASSAf) and a past President of both the Society of Law Teachers of Southern Africa and the South African Law Deans' Association. His research interest concentrates on the South African law of delict (torts) and he has authored numerous articles and two books, *Lawyers' Professional Liability* (Juta & Co, 1992) and *Principles of Delict* (with JC van der Walt, 3rd edn (LexisNexis Butterworths, 2005), which, with minor revisions, was also published as 'Delict' in *The Law of South Africa* (2005). He is also an experienced facilitator, focusing on environmental monitoring.

Benjamin J Richardson is a Professor at Osgoode Hall Law School, Canada, and previously held positions at the law schools of the Universities of Manchester (UK) and Auckland (New Zealand). He teaches and researches environmental law and aboriginal law, and is the author or editor of several books, including *Indigenous Peoples and the Law* (Hart Publishing, 2009), *Socially Responsible Investment Law* (Oxford University Press, 2008) and *Environmental Law for Sustainability* (Hart Publishing, 2006). Among his faculty responsibilities, Professor Richardson has been the Chair of the LLB admissions committees at Osgoode Hall and the University of Manchester School of Law. At Osgoode Hall, he is presently the Director of the Graduate Program in Law.

Julian Webb is Professor of Legal Education at the University of Warwick, and Director of the Higher Education Academy UK Centre for Legal Education. He has previously held chairs at the Universities of Westminster and the West of England. Julian is the co-author/editor of five books, including *Learning Legal Rules: A Student's Guide to Legal Method and Reasoning* 6th edn (Oxford University Press, 2006) and *Lawyering Skills and the Legal Process* (with Caroline Maughan) 2nd edn (Cambridge University Press, 2005). Professor Webb has published over 40 chapters and peer-reviewed papers, mostly on legal education policy and pedagogy, legal ethics, and the sociology of law.

Avis Whyte is a senior research fellow and senior lecturer at the University of Westminster, having joined the university after the completion of her LLM at the University of Leicester. She researches in the field of the legal profession, particularly in relation to legal aid, barristers and work done *pro bono publico*. Avis is also a Fellow of the Higher Education Academy.

Introduction: Contextualising Stakeholders in the Law School

FIONA COWNIE

'STAKEHOLDERS'

THE THEME WHICH permeates this collection of essays is, put simply, the notion that there are many different 'interest groups', all of which have differing ideas about the purpose of a university law school and the legal education it offers. Acknowledging the continuing debate around the fact that the legal academy is subject to differing, and often conflicting, pressures from many of these groups, whether they are students and their parents, the legal profession, the state in its various forms, business and commercial interests or even legal academics, the project upon which this book is based took shape. Our purpose was to offer some in-depth analysis of what the consequences might be for law schools and legal education of these 'stakeholder' pressures.

The term 'stakeholder' has enjoyed increasing currency within the academic world: Bradney's chapter opens with examples of its use by the Quality Assurance Agency in the UK as well as by universities in the US, New Zealand and Australia. During the course of his discussion he uncovers many other instances of its persistent appearance in higher education discourse. In several of the essays in this collection, the use of the term 'stakeholder' to describe all the groups who have an interest in determining the path taken by the legal academy is a convenient abbreviation; the use of the term itself, as opposed to some other term such as 'interest groups', does not add significantly to the analysis; the interest lies in considering what pressures exist and in debating what the reaction of the legal academy should be to their existence. However, as Bradney points out in his chapter, the term 'stakeholder', with its origins in the literature of business management and business ethics, could signal some problematic and perhaps unintended consequences for the legal academy, and his essay analyses at length both the term itself and the potential difficulties its continuing use could cause. In addressing this conceptual issue, Bradney throws new light on the politics which underpin the relationship between the legal academy and society.

THE UNDERLYING DEBATE

There has long been a debate amongst observers of the legal academy about the purposes of legal education, and all the stakeholders discussed in this collection can be placed without too much difficulty somewhere along the continuum of that debate. Broadly, the question has been: do law schools exist to train lawyers or to offer a liberal legal education? To characterize the debate in its starkest terms, on the one hand are ranged those who think law schools are primarily about producing future lawyers, whose view of the curriculum is that it should reflect the needs of the legal professions, with time devoted to the traditional doctrinal analysis of law and that law schools should ensure that students learn the skills, such as mooting, which are clearly relevant to practice. On the other hand there are those who are clear that the function of a university law school, if it is to truly fulfill its role as part of the academy, is to offer a liberal education in law, resulting in a law school which Roger Brownsword has argued would have the following four features:

> In its most general terms the mission of the law school (in both its teaching and its research activities) is to work towards an understanding of the phenomenon, or practice, of law.
>
> The project of understanding law implies (a) a pervasive enquiring approach... and (b) a willingness to follow lines of inquiry into disciplines that contribute to our appreciation of the law.
>
> Law school discourse should be what Roberto Unger describes as 'a sustained conversation about our [socio-economic and political] arrangements'...
>
> Although there is no standard way in which the liberal model must be implemented... it is a *sine qua non* of this project that law school academics, whether in their role as teachers or researchers, should act as exemplars of the inquiring approach.[1]

This is a debate which has preoccupied legal scholars throughout the Common Law world. In the UK speeches delivered by successive Presidents of the Society of Legal Scholars provide evidence of the enduring nature of this debate, and illustrate its potency.[2] In 1960, Professor FH Lawson (University of Oxford) urged members of the Society to play a more active part in the making of law, not merely the teaching of it. During the course of his speech, he comments that:

> Academic law has had to compete with practice, whereas History can only be academic... Law teaching still appears to the outside world like the teaching of a

[1] R Brownsword 'Law Schools for Lawyers, Citizens and People' (1999) Chapter 2 in F Cownie (ed) *The Law School—Global Issues, Local Questions* (Aldershot, Ashgate) 27–28.

[2] The Society of Legal Scholars (formerly the SPTL—the Society of Public Teachers of Law) is the longest-established and largest professional association of legal academics in the UK and Ireland; see www.legalscholars.ac.uk.

> trade, or at best the transmission of a body of received doctrine, and that other faculties no longer regard as the prime task of a university.[3]

Professor Lawson's remarks were echoed in the following decade by Professor FR Crane (Queen Mary College, University of London), delivering his Presidential Address in 1976. In the course of discussing the teaching of land law Professor Crane reflected that:

> Every subject in a University law curriculum must have a substantial intellectual content... [because] Law Faculties in the United Kingdom are concerned to give a liberal education through the discipline of law. Such a statement, today and to this audience, is surely a platitude, yet the theme is asserted again and again in the pages of our Journal, at least until the present decade.[4]

However, it would appear that far from being a platitude, the assertion of law as an academic discipline was still a controversial statement, since law teachers were far from united in their views about the purpose of legal education, as Professor CF Parker (University of Exeter) commented in his Presidential Address the following year. Noting the wide range of topics which had formed the subject of Presidential Addresses, he went on:

> This wide range of topics reflects the many facets of university legal studies which, one is almost tempted to say, mean all things to all men. There is the law teacher who sees Law almost exclusively as a rigid academic discipline, with as little, or as much, relevance to actual life as the study of the Aeneid, another thinks essentially in terms of practice in the courts, the minutiae of cases and procedure; yet another sees Law as the expression of human rights, the key to Utopia. Indeed, it would be an unusual University Law Faculty where such a variety of views could not be found.[5]

Crossing the globe and looking at the contemporary situation, we find Professor Michael Coper, Dean of the Australian National University (ANU) Law Faculty, giving a talk as part of the deans and directors series of lectures at ANU. He concludes his remarks by saying:

> I gasp at the stereotypes I have encountered about law as a discipline, generally that it is a 'professional' or 'vocational' discipline, and therefore concerned primarily with the content of rules. The study of law, of the philosophy of law, and of the role of law in society, takes its proper place alongside the study of any of the wide range of cognate disciplines in the humanities and social sciences; but even for the professional, law cannot be just a study of the content of rules. The professional lawyer will be ill-equipped to discharge his or her professional role without the insights and reflectiveness inspired by Oliver Wendell Holmes, who,

[3] FH Lawson, 'The Academic Lawyer As Jurist' (1959–60) 5 *Journal of the Society of Public Teachers of Law* (NS) 182, 184.
[4] FR Crane, 'Presidential Address: Reflections on Land Law and Its Teaching' (1976–1979) 14 *Journal of the Society of Public Teachers of Law* (NS) 69.
[5] CF Parker, 'Presidential Address' (1976–1979) 14 *Journal of the Society of Public Teachers of Law* (NS) 3.

> after all, devoted his entire career, apart from a brief period as a professor at Harvard Law School, to the practice of his profession.[6]

The very fact that a distinguished Australian law dean, giving a public lecture in his own university in 2002, finds it necessary to spell out so clearly the fact that law is not merely a vocational discipline, suggests that the academic/vocational debate is alive and well. Similar examples could be drawn from all the other Common Law jurisdictions, and during the course of the essays which form this collection, readers will come across many references, explicit and implicit, to this long-running controversy.

STUDENTS AS STAKEHOLDERS

Factors affecting students can soon affect the law school. Discussing the state of Canadian legal education at the end of the 1990s, Harry Arthurs comments that in an era of economic downturn:

> Quite understandably, students have become very nervous about their future job prospects. Most try to make themselves more marketable by using their recently acquired power as 'consumers' to insist on courses, syllabuses and pedagogies which, in their perception, reinforce their survival skills... they are increasingly impatient with 'humane professionalism', the ethos of Canadian law schools since the 1960s, and they increasingly exercise their right to avoid 'purely academic' offerings. And this brings them into direct conflict with their already beleaguered professors, who confront heavier workloads, more rigorous performance measures, declining financial prospects—and now, it seems likely, intellectual frustration.[7]

In this book, it is the analysis of students as stakeholders which concerns Richardson, Boon and Whyte, and Goldsmith and Bamford. Richardson's chapter amply illustrates the way in which many aspects of the 'stakeholding' debate resonate across the Common Law world. He considers students as stakeholders in relation to the policies and procedures that govern admission to the law school, looking at five Common Law jurisdictions (US, Canada, UK, Australia and New Zealand) and focusing on the tensions between policies whose objective is to widen university access in order to achieve a more diverse student body, and the traditional methods of selecting students based on academic grades and test scores. Boon and Whyte explore the changing relationships between students and the academy brought about not only by the development of mass higher education and the widening participation agenda, but also by the increasing

[6] M Coper, 'The Path of the Law' (2002) 76(11) *Australian Law Journal* 716, 724.
[7] HW Arthurs, 'The Political Economy of Canadian Legal Education' (1998) 25.1 *Journal of Law and Society* 14, 31.

characterisation, at least in some institutions, of students as 'customers'. They argue that conceptualizing the student as 'stakeholder' rather than 'consumer' is preferable, because it is consistent with the idea that a student is a co-producer of their learning, and with that comes the possibility of authentic dialogue between students, legal academics and the legal academy. Goldsmith and Bamford examine the pressure from students for their legal education to be more 'practical'. They argue that offering practice-oriented opportunities within the academic legal curriculum does not signal the ascendancy of vocationalism or the defeat of a liberal model of legal education. Rather their view is that it is possible to engage with legal practice in the classroom in such a way as to foster a constructive engagement between the practical realm and the goals of breadth of vision and the ability to engage in critique which are commonly associated with academic knowledge and learning.

LEGAL ACADEMICS AS STAKEHOLDERS

Legal academics are clearly stakeholders in the sense that their professional lives are played out within the legal academy and they have much to lose (or gain) as their influence wanes or increases relative to all the other interest groups attempting to influence the nature of university law schools. Yet they continue to be an under-researched aspect of the law school, although in the UK particularly there has recently been more interest in examining aspects of legal academic life.

Clare McGlynn's work has been particularly useful in providing empirical evidence about the position of women in the legal academy, as well as offering insights into the 'private life' of the law school through the testimonies of some of the women who work there.[8] Richard Collier has written extensively about masculinity as it plays out in the legal academy, looking at the sexual politics of law teaching and the relationship between men and feminism, throwing light on the relationship of the power of law and the power of men and the values and practices which are part of the everyday life of the law school.[9] In '"Nutty Professors", "Men in Suits" and "New Entrepreneurs"' he went on to explore the relationship between the social production of heterosexual masculinities and the 'making of men' as practising lawyers and as legal academics, arguing that:

> [T]he sexed bodies of women and men are constituted at particular moments and settings as having differential access to 'knowledge' resulting from their embodied social locations in a gendered world… the constitution of 'professional'

[8] C McGlynn, *The Woman Lawyer: Making the Difference* (London, Butterworths, 1998).

[9] R Collier, 'Masculinism, Law and Law Teaching' (1991) 19 *International Journal of the Sociology of Law* 427.

masculine bodies and subjectivities can be seen as important factors in the production and maintenance of the continuing marginalization and discrimination of women.[10]

More recently, Collier has explored the situation of academics as 'new knowledge workers' within an increasingly corporatised working environment. Work which cannot be formally measured in terms of 'outputs' becomes invisible, and because the boundaries of academic work are so indeterminate, Collier argues that the effects of increased demands from the university are playing out differently for men and women.[11] Collier's work is complemented by that of Celia Wells, whose contribution to this area of research is a series of articles on women in the law school, exploring in that particular context some of the explanations for their position relative to men, as well as providing some interesting empirical evidence about the particular position of women law professors.[12] Recently, Spencer and Kent have focused on the practices surrounding sabbatical leave.[13] My own book on legal academics attempted to throw light on the professional identities of legal academics and the culture of academic law, and while it is the first sustained account to date of this area, it by no means contains the last word on the topics covered.[14] Rather it is intended to act as a stimulus to further research by drawing attention to some of the gaps in our knowledge. Work on legal academics is by no means confined to the UK. There is also work on this area in the US, including Philip Kissam's book *The Discipline of Law Schools*, which offers an extended analysis of the routine practices and habits of American law schools[15] and an extensive literature on gender and the law school.[16] In Australia Margaret Thornton has made a sustained

[10] R Collier, '"Nutty Professors", "Men in Suits" and "New Entrepreneurs": Corporeality, Subjectivity and Change in the Law School and Legal Practice' (1998) 7 *Social and Legal Studies* 27, 45.

[11] R Collier, 'The Changing University and the (Legal) Academic Career—Rethinking the Relationship Between Women, Men and the "Private Life" of the Law School' (2002) 22 *Legal Studies* 1, 22.

[12] C Wells, 'Working Out Women in Law Schools' (2001) 21(1) *Legal Studies* 116; C Wells, 'Exceptional Women or Honorary Men? Notes from the Women Law Professors Project' (2000) 53 *Current Legal Problems* 181; C Wells, 'Women Law Professors—Negotiating and Transcending Gender Identities at Work' (2002) 10 *Feminist Legal Studies* 1.

[13] M Spencer and P Kent, 'Perpetuating Difference? Law School Sabbaticals in an Era of Performativity' (2007) 27(4) *Legal Studies* 649.

[14] F Cownie, *Legal Academics: Culture and Identities* (Oxford, Hart Publishing, 2004).

[15] P Kissam, *The Discipline of Law Schools: The Making of Modern Lawyers* (Durham, NC, Carolina Academic Press, 2003).

[16] In 1999, for example, the Association of American Law Schools ran a workshop for women in legal education for which Robbins and Okonska compiled a 35-page bibliography, the majority of which is composed of material specifically relating to the legal academy; S Robbins and M Okonska, *Bibliography on Women in Legal Education* (1999) www.aals.org/wle99/biblio.html.

contribution to the literature in a series of articles which again have a focus on gender, as well as in a chapter in her book on the legal profession.[17]

In this collection, it is Collier who concentrates on legal academics as stakeholders as he focuses on the question of class as it affects legal academic identity, and suggests that there is much work to be done around the question of how class affects the ways in which legal academics are (or are not) able to function effectively as stakeholders in the law school. In particular, he examines the notion of 'belonging', and how that is affected by class origins. Is the 'stakeholder experience' of legal academics the same, regardless of their class origins? Do certain psycho-social consequences accompany the fact that some legal academics do not feel at ease in the middle-class milieu of the contemporary university law school? Setting these questions in the context of his previous work on the remodeling of the legal academic as 'new knowledge worker' Collier explores how we might better find out what it means to say that law schools are marked by significant effects of class in terms of their operational codes and cultures. He points to the use of auto-ethnography as a way to explore the ways in which questions of emotion inform the way class is understood and accounted for as having specific effects on academic cultures and experiences.

FEMINISTS AS STAKEHOLDERS

Throughout the Common Law world, the academic/vocational debate has often provoked heated exchanges between those holding differing, and often opposing, views of the purpose of legal education. The intensity of the debate was clearly visible in the United States in the exchanges provoked by the publication of Dean Paul Carrington's article 'Of Law and the River', in which he attacked those legal academics whom he characterized as teaching 'legal nihilism'.[18] The nihilists he had in mind were generally taken to be members of the Critical Legal Studies movement, but the thrust of the argument applies equally to what Arthur Austin characterized as the other 'outsider' groups, such as those adopting a feminist approach.[19] Carrington's elegantly written article draws on Mark Twain's *Life on the Mississippi* to explore the question of what is best practice in professional training (Carrington was interested in lawyers, Mark Twain in the training

[17] See, eg M Thornton, 'Technocentrism in the Law School: Why the Gender and Colour of Law Remain the Same' (1998) 36(2) *Osgoode Hall Law Journal* 369; M Thornton, *Dissonance and Distrust: Women in the Legal Profession* (Melbourne, Oxford University Press, 1996).

[18] P Carrington, 'Of Law and the River' (1984) 34 *Journal of Legal Education* 222.

[19] A Austin, *The Empire Strikes Back: Outsiders and the Struggle Over Legal Education* (New York, New York University Press, 1998). At page 1, Austin labels doctrinal scholarship as 'empire' and 'outsiders' as Crits, Feminists and Critical Race Theorists.

of steam boat pilots).[20] The main feature of Carrington's analysis is that he consistently criticises what he terms 'nihilism' and 'its lesson that who decides [the law] is everything and principle nothing but cosmetic'.[21] As for the nihilist teachers, he writes:

> The nihilist teacher threatens to rob his or her students of the courage to act on such professional judgment as they may have acquired. Teaching cynicism may, and perhaps probably does, result in the learning of the skills of corruption: bribery and intimidation. In an honest effort to proclaim a need for revolution, nihilist teachers are more likely to train crooks than radicals. If this risk is correctly appraised, the nihilist who must profess that legal principle does not matter has an ethical duty to depart the law school, perhaps to seek a place elsewhere in the academy.[22]

Unsurprisingly, the article provoked a wide-ranging debate; one of the contributors to that debate who disagreed with Carrington was Owen Fiss. His response focuses on the need to encourage, not stifle, debate:

> Law schools are professional schools, insomuch as they train people for a profession. But they are also academic institutions, and by that I mean they seek to discover the truth. We cannot shut off an avenue of inquiry, for fear that it would render the professional training pointless... Every law school should confront the question whether law exists, and it is of the essence of academic freedom to allow all sides to speak, even those who would answer that question in the negative and thus recommend that our doors be closed and resources used for other purposes.[23]

Fiss goes on to comment that the issue that divides him from Carrington goes right to the *idea* of a university law school. It is here in his conclusion that his response most clearly illustrates that it is the academic/vocational controversy which underpins the Carrington debate:

> Law professors are not paid to train lawyers, but to study law, and to teach their students what they happen to discover. The law school you and I are talking about is an integral part of the university, and by virtue of that membership and all the commitments it entails must be pure in its academic obligations.[24]

In her chapter on feminists as stakeholders, Auchmuty analyses the relationship of the legal academy and feminists, arguing that the attitudes of law schools in England and Wales towards feminists has shifted from hostility and the exclusion of women from the legal academy to a situation in which the balance of power has shifted significantly. She traces developments from

[20] Carrington, 'Of Law and the River' (1984) 224.
[21] Ibid 227.
[22] Ibid.
[23] Fiss' response is contained in PW Martin, '"Of Law and the River" and of Nihilism and Academic Freedom' (1985) 35 *Journal of Legal Education* 1, 24.
[24] Ibid 26.

the very early days of the 'Woman Movement' and the first occasions on which women were admitted to law schools, through the mid-twentieth century when women were present, but largely marginalized in the legal academy, to the emergence of a much stronger feminist critique. Auchmuty concludes by arguing that more recently feminist research, as well as the contribution of feminists as teachers and administrators, has come to be widely valued by the legal academy as a whole.

THE LEGAL PROFESSION AS STAKEHOLDER

It is probably the legal profession which springs to mind as the obvious subject of any discussion of stakeholding and the university law school. The tensions between professional practice and the legal academy are longstanding, and have their roots in the history of legal education as Law was introduced to the academy throughout the Common Law world. In England and Wales, for example, when law began to be taught in the universities towards the end of the nineteenth century, academic lawyers faced hostile challenges from practising lawyers, who could not see the point of an academic legal education, and would have preferred to have continued with the apprenticeship model of training which had existed hitherto. It is no accident that when the great constitutional lawyer, AV Dicey, delivered his inaugural lecture as the Vinerian Professor of Law at Oxford he entitled it 'Can English Law Be Taught At Universities?'.[25] His purpose, of course, was to demonstrate not only that it could, but that it *should*. The previous apprenticeship model of legal education, he argued, had offered little, if any, formal instruction, and students who sought to assist themselves by reading books would have found existing legal texts wholly inadequate; legal works were at best, said Dicey: '[A] mere accumulation of notes on detached points of curious rather than useful learning. They are deficient in all general principles, in all ideas of method.'[26]

University legal education could remedy all these defects and provide a systematic education, while the new legal academics could write clear, logical books, which could be used by both students and practitioners.[27] David Sugarman has argued persuasively that these early legal academics, struggling to establish their professional identities in the face of all this scepticism, devoted themselves to establishing Law as a discipline which involved the 'science of law'.[28] In doing so, however, Sugarman emphasises

[25] AV Dicey, *Can English Law Be Taught At Universities?* (London, 1883).

[26] Ibid 13.

[27] Ibid 19ff.

[28] D Sugarman, 'A Hatred of Disorder: Legal Science, Liberalism and Imperialsim' (1991) in P Fitzpatrick (ed) *Dangerous Supplements: Resistance and Renewal in Jurisprudence* (London, Pluto Press) 34, 36–38.

that the new law dons did not wish to trespass on the province of practising lawyers: 'Jurists, by an act of conscious self-limitation, refrained from criticizing, let alone meddling, with the content of the law. That was for others. Their skills resided in formal organization.'[29] They were generally very deferential to the bar and the bench, often dedicating their textbooks to judges, and writing very much with the profession in mind.[30]

The story of the relationship between the legal profession and legal academia in the UK has remained an uneasy one to this day. In his book on the contemporary English law school, *Conversations, Choices and Chances*, Bradney notes the difficulties surrounding the Joint Statement issued by the Law Society and the General Council of the Bar, which details certain subjects and skills which must be taught if a law degree is to be recognised for the purposes of entry to the legal profession.[31] The professional bodies can justify the Joint Statement by reference to their need to ensure that those entering the legal profession are properly qualified, but, as Bradney argues, its existence is problematic for law schools because it impinges on their autonomy. He quotes an interview given by Roger Smith shortly before he took up a post as Director of Legal Education and Training at the Law Society: 'There is a growing tension as HE [Higher Education] expands. HE institutions seek more autonomy and the profession may tend to have attitudes that might seem old-fashioned to those involved in the education world.'[32] Commenting on the way in which law schools and the professions have become embroiled in 'the somewhat mysterious processes that result in the continual writing and rewriting of the Statement', Bradney concludes: 'In principle the writing of a syllabus seems to be plainly a pedagogic matter best left to those who practice education. Nevertheless, in practice the construction of the Joint Statement is a political matter'.[33]

It is not only in England and Wales that the relationship between the law school and the legal profession is a somewhat difficult one. Discussing the history of American legal education, Stephen Feldman notes the longstanding tensions between legal practitioners and legal academics, commenting that:

> Especially in law, elite practitioners and university leaders pushed for different types of schools. Practitioners wanted law schools that emphasized legal practice, 'ideal law office' schools that combined 'theoretical instruction with a wide range of practice courses'. Meanwhile, university leaders sought to develop highly

[29] Ibid 41.

[30] Ibid 42.

[31] A Bradney, *Conversations, Choices and Chances: the Liberal Law School in the Twenty-First Century* (Oxford, Hart Publishing, 2003) 165.

[32] Ibid 165.

[33] Ibid 166.

> theoretical and academically selective law schools that would mirror the rest of the university.[34]

Feldman's basic argument is that over the decades, university law professors have traditionally conceived of themselves first and foremost as lawyers, teaching students about the law and about how to practice law, doing research whose main purpose was to reform and improve the law.[35] However, as the academic professionalisation of the legal academy progressed, law professors began to move away from their roots in legal practice and towards the heart of the academy, constructing their professional identity in terms of 'law professor' rather than 'lawyer'. Today, Feldman argues, the increasing tendency of law professors to engage in interdisciplinary scholarship 'underscores the acute tensions between academics and practitioners', because by drawing on the methods of other disciplines, from literary criticism to anthropology 'interdisciplinary legal scholars distance themselves ever further from the skills and concerns of practitioners'.[36] Feldman's conclusion echoes my own work on English legal academics, in which I argued that law is a discipline in transition, moving away from its doctrinal, practice-oriented roots towards the heart of the academy.[37]

This process of academic drift is also picked up by Boon and Webb in their chapter on the legal profession as stakeholder, and plays a significant part in the controversial conclusions they reach as they speculate about possible future developments in the relationship between the legal academy and the legal profession. Looking at the tensions between the legal academy and the legal profession, they argue that by transferring a significant amount of responsibility for the legal education of potential practitioners to the academy, the professional bodies have lost the ability to respond quickly to demands from their members for greater flexibility in the training regime. Meanwhile, they see dangers for the academy as it continues to experience academic drift and arguably a growing amount of autonomy. Their thesis is that if law degrees move too far away from the needs of the profession, we may reach a stage where possession of a law degree is no longer the usual path towards entry to the legal profession, and the academy may suffer a consequential decline in student numbers. Their other equally controversial conclusions provide a stimulating basis for debate, not only about the future of the legal academy in England and Wales,

[34] S Feldman, 'The Transformation of an Academic Discipline: Law Professors in the Past and Future (or Toy Story Too)' (2004) 54 *Journal of Legal Education* 471, 479; the quotations in Feldman's text are from WR Johnson, *Schooled Lawyers: A Study in the Clash of Professional Cultures* (1978).

[35] Ibid 472.

[36] Ibid 489.

[37] F Cownie, *Legal Academics: Culture and Identities* (Oxford, Hart Publishing, 2004) 58.

but also in other jurisdictions where the relationship between profession and academy is played out with local variations but with clearly similar common themes.

THE STATE AS STAKEHOLDER

In her article 'Privatizing the Universities', Jane Kelsey examined the convergence of the restructuring of tertiary education which has taken place around the world and its implications for law schools.[38] Kelsey's examination of the position of New Zealand law schools at the end of the twentieth century provides a clear example of the way in which that most powerful of stakeholders, the state, can affect the whole higher education system, including, of course, the law schools within it. She argues that the changes in the university system in New Zealand experienced during this period were an integral part of a broader neo-liberal experiment which had been taking place in New Zealand since the early 1980s.[39] The radical approach of the state, reflected in a Treasury briefing for the incoming government in 1987, made it clear that such traditional roles of universities as that of 'critical friend' or 'speaking truth to power' were to be marginalized:

> Historically universities may have acted as a key source of free information and discussion on political and other sensitive issues. In the information age this is no longer the case and the very multiplicity of information sources is itself a form of protection—as modern totalitarian states have found.[40]

The market driven approach of the government was reflected in a number of discussion documents which focused not on the inherent value of education, but on the need for education to take its place in the market like any other commodity:

> [A]cademics must demonstrate their utility to society by placing themselves in an open market and accordingly compete for students who will provide the bulk of core funding through tuition fees. If academic research has a value it can stand up to the rigours of competition for limited funds.[41]

In New Zealand, Kelsey argues, the changes to tertiary education during this period were dramatic, but 'compared to other areas of economic and social policy, however, progress towards the Treasury's vision was slow'.[42]

[38] J Kelsey, 'Privatizing the Universities' (1998) 25(1) *Journal of Law and Society* 51.

[39] Ibid 62.

[40] New Zealand Treasury, *Government Management: Briefing Papers to the Incoming Government* (1987) Vol 1 Ch 6 and Vol 2, quoted in Kelsey, n 38, 62.

[41] M Robinson, 'Governance of Tertiary Institutions' (New Zealand State Services Commission Paper to the Taskforce on Capital Charging of Tertiary Institutions, 18 August 1992, unpublished), quoted in Kelsey, n 38, 62.

[42] Kelsey, 'Privatizing the Universities' (1998) 63.

This resulted in the government bringing forward proposals designed to increase the rate of change. These proposals were expressed in terms of providers and funders operating in an international market for higher education, with an emphasis on regulatory mechanisms and accountability.[43] The implications for law schools, in Kelsey's view, included not only those consequences which would be experienced by the sector as a whole, such as decreased resources, increasing students numbers and so on, but in particular a threat to the future of legal research, since the competitive tendering process for receiving research funds is ill-suited to the lone-researcher library-based model of much legal scholarship.[44]

Kelsey regards New Zealand as an extreme example of the attempted privatization of the higher education sector, but she makes the point that moves towards a market-driven system are not unique to New Zealand:

> Seemingly unconnected changes to tertiary education policies across many countries display a remarkable congruity. This reflects a coherent policy agenda which is promoted through interlocking networks of international actors and agencies, which cross-fertilize with the officials, politicians entrepreneurs and commentators who influence policy at the national level.[45]

Whether we agree with Kelsey's analysis or not, her work provides a powerful illustration of the potential effects on the university law school of the state as stakeholder. In the underlying academic/vocational debate, a state which understands education as merely a commodity, primarily serving the needs of the economy by providing suitably skilled workers, clearly has a vocational focus, and is likely to have little sympathy with the idea of legal education which is primarily designed to produce independently-minded critical thinkers.

In this collection, it is Midgley who most directly addresses the issue of the state as stakeholder in the university law school, as he considers the case of South Africa. In the post-apartheid era, it is unsurprising that matters of law and of education were at the forefront of attempts to reform the status quo and build a new type of state. Sitting at the intersection of these institutions, university law schools in South Africa found themselves the subjects of considerable pressures to change, as both the Department of Justice and the Department of Education actively pursued a transformation agenda which profoundly affected the legal education landscape. Midgley's experience as part of this process is put to good use in his perceptive analysis of the extent to which the state has succeeded in achieving its objectives.

[43] Ibid 64.
[44] Ibid 68.
[45] Ibid 53.

CONCLUSION

The chapters in this collection represent an attempt by an international group of scholars who have a sustained interest in the legal academy to address the issues raised by the existence of 'stakeholders' or 'interest groups' who all have their own agenda and wish to 'encourage' the law school to move in a particular direction. Their analysis throws new light on the academic/vocational debate which has long preoccupied legal education scholars, as well as offering suggestions of particular issues which should concern all those who are interested in legal education around the Common Law world.

1

*Legal Academics as Stakeholders: Reconceptualising Identity and Social Class**

RICHARD COLLIER

In considering the lived experience of legal academia [class] is a factor which is too important to be overlooked.[1]

Social worlds are organised, structured and imbued with meaning by reference to what sort of people the protagonists are, that is their sense of their own social identity... lifestyles are reflexive projects: we (and relevant others) can see (however dimly) who we want to be seen to be through how we use the resources of who we are.[2]

INTRODUCTION

THERE EXISTS, IN a rich interdisciplinary literature concerned with the changing nature of higher education, a general consensus that we are, internationally, living in a new era for universities. The contours, themes and concerns of the debate about what has been termed the rise of the corporatised university have been discussed in detail elsewhere.[3] It has become a recurring theme in this work that there are a range of stakeholders in the law school, each of whom may have different, and by no means necessarily

* This chapter draws on themes also discussed in the forthcoming book: R Collier, *Men, Law and Gender: Rethinking the 'Man' of Law* (London, Routledge, forthcoming).

[1] F Cownie, *Legal Academics: Culture and Identities* (Oxford, Hart Publishing, 2004) 203.

[2] Ibid 37.

[3] This literature is voluminous. See, eg A Brooks and A Mackinnon (eds), *Gender and the Restructured University* (Buckingham, SRHE/Open University Press, 2001); J Currie and J Newson (eds), *Universities and Globalization* (London, Sage, 1998); S Marginson and M Considine, *The Enterprise University: Power, Governance and Reinvention in Australia* (Cambridge, Cambridge University Press, 2000); M Henkel, *Academic Identities and Policy Change in Higher Education* (London, Jessica Kingsley, 2000); M Kogan and S Hanney, *Reforming Higher Education* (London, Jessica Kingsley, 2000).

complementary, interests.[4] The history of legal education and scholarship in the UK has, equally, been the subject of a vast body of research.[5] A theoretically and methodologically diverse scholarship has explored many aspects of university law schools, and a convincing case has been made, not least within recent work concerned with women legal academics,[6] for taking the law school seriously. Again, many issues have been addressed: the practices and cultures of the legal academic community, pedagogical issues relating to law teaching, the changing experience and aspiration of law students and, my specific focus in this chapter, a growing engagement with what has been termed the 'private lives' of legal academics.[7]

Contributions elsewhere in this book chart diverse aspects of how political, economic and cultural change has impacted on understandings of stakeholders in the law school. Whatever the origins, development and use of the stakeholder terminology in higher education,[8] there is some agreement that the emergence of the stakeholder idea has ran alongside these shifts in understandings of what universities are 'for', as well as changes in the scope and nature of academic disciplines themselves. We must remember, at the outset, that there is no one type of university law school or legal academic. We cannot generalise about the effects of change in the field of higher education.[9] Law schools vary greatly in terms of institutional context, academic reputation and the function they are seen to have within distinctive legal, political, local and wider communities. Different jurisdictions and legal and university systems further mediate the ways in which higher education reforms are experienced. The academic community is made up of diverse groups: academic staff, porters, catering and security workers, undergraduate and postgraduate students, secretarial staff, librarians, researchers and so forth. The stakeholder body, meanwhile, is commonly interpreted as including (at the very least) students, their families and wider kin, business and commercial organisations (including, and not confined to, the legal profession), the local community/region, university staff, government and society itself. Recognising such diversity, this chapter focuses

[4] See Cownie, this volume; also Bradney, this volume.

[5] For a summary of this work and these debates see A Bradney, *Conversations, Choices and Chances: The Liberal Law School in the Twenty-First Century* (Oxford, Hart Publishing, 2003).

[6] See, eg C Wells, 'Working Out Women in Law Schools' (2001) 21 (1) *Legal Studies* 116; C Wells, 'Women Law Professors—Negotiating and Transcending Gender Identity at Work' (2002) 10 (1) *Feminist Legal Studies* 1; F Cownie, 'Women Legal Academics—A New Research Agenda?' (1998) 25 (1) *Journal of Law and Society* 102; F Cownie, 'Women in the Law School—Shoals of Fish, Starfish or Fish Out of Water?' in P Thomas (ed) *Discriminating Lawyers* (London, Cavendish, 2000).

[7] Cownie, n 1.

[8] See Bradney, this volume.

[9] It is also important to note that legal education and research into law and legal regulation take place in locations other than university law schools.

on one stakeholder group in the law school that has been the subject of increased attention within research in legal education but one which has, I shall argue, tended to be under-theorised: legal academics.

Studies of the restructured academy, less developed within legal studies than in some other fields of scholarship,[10] suggest significant changes may be under way in relation to ideas of organisational identity (what it means to identify *as* an academic).[11] In the discipline of law, different interpretations have emerged as to what these changes might mean for university law schools, legal education and, my focus here, research on legal academics, understood as one group of stakeholders in the law school.[12] In a recent study, McWilliam has argued that new organisational cultures and forms of governance have sought to remodel or refashion the academic subject in ways in keeping with the new world in which universities operate.[13] This has involved, she suggests, a prevailing culture of risk minimisation and audit, of individuals, institutions, departments and organisations, that has sought to engage 'all individuals within the university (managers and non-managers) in doing particular sorts of work on themselves, the work of turning themselves into "professional experts"'.[14]

It is not, and has not, been suggested that attempts to refocus and align the work of universities to service the needs of the economy and/or external stakeholders, whether in terms of the research they produce or students that they educate, is necessarily successful, a somehow fixed and finished product. Nor is it suggested these processes cannot be, and are not, resisted.[15] Part of the richness of the emerging literature, including work on stakeholders in the law school to which this book

[10] See, eg P Hillyard et al, 'Leaving a "Stain upon the Silence": Contemporary Criminology and the Politics of Dissent' (2004) 44 *British Journal of Criminology* 369; R Walters, 'New Modes of Governance and the Commodification of Criminological Knowledge' (2003) 12 (1) *Social and Legal Studies* 26.

[11] A Brooks, 'Restructuring Bodies of Knowledge' in A Brooks and A Mackinnon (eds), *Gender* (2001); E McWilliam, 'Changing the Academic Subject' in R Hunter and M Keys *Changing Law: Rights, Regulation, Reconciliation* (Aldershot, Ashgate, 2005).

[12] *cf* Bradney, above n 5; M Thornton, 'The Demise of Diversity in Legal Education: Globalisation and the New Knowledge Economy' (2001) 8 (1) *International Journal of the Legal Profession* 37; M Thornton, 'Among the Ruins: Law in the Neo-Liberal Academy' (2001) 20 *Windsor Yearbook of Access to Justice* 3; M Thornton, 'Technocentrism and the Law School' (1998) 36 (2) *Osgoode Hall Law Journal* 369; R Collier, '"We're All Socio-Legal Now?" Legal Education, Scholarship and the Global Knowledge Economy—Reflections on the UK Experience' (2004) 26 (4) *Sydney Law Review* 503; R Collier, 'Restructuring the Universities, Remaking the Legal Academy?' (2005) in R Hunter and M Keys (eds), *Changing Law* (2005); R Collier, 'The Changing University and the (Legal) Academic Career—Rethinking the "Private Life" of the Law School' (2002) 22 (1) *Legal Studies* 1; P Hillyard and J Sim, 'The Political Economy of Socio-Legal Research' in P Thomas (ed) *Socio-Legal Studies* (Aldershot, Dartmouth, 1997) 45.

[13] McWilliam, n 12.

[14] Ibid 7, my emphasis.

[15] R Collier, 'The Liberal Law School, The Restructured University and the Paradox of Socio-Legal Studies' (2005) 68 (3) *Modern Law Review* 475.

contributes, is the recognition of the co-existence of conflicting pressures, the complex and contradictory nature of developments.[16] Nonetheless, exploring how the idea of the private life of the law school has been deployed within a distinctive sub-genre of writing concerned with legal academics as stakeholders, the time is propitious to interrogate further the idea that the personal life of legal academics can be approached via a distinction between the public life of academic law and the private life of legal academia.[17]

I wish to consider therefore, more specifically, one aspect of how the legal academic has been approached as stakeholder in the law school and situated social subject—an interrogation of the relationship between social class and the idea of the private life of the law school. As Cownie observes:

> The 'identity matters' of gender, class, race and sexuality include some of the least explored areas of legal academia, yet this study provides evidence that *they have significant effects*, not only upon the professional identities of legal academics, but also on key aspects of the culture of academic law.[18]

What does it mean, however, in the context of the changes in higher education outlined above, to speak of these 'significant effects' of class upon the 'professional identities of legal academics and the culture of academic law'? In focusing on class, I do not wish to efface the intersectional nature of social categories, the multiple dimensions of discrimination and diversity in relation to experience. Nor do I wish, in any way, to downplay the importance of gender, race and sexuality. Rather, there is a need to reconsider how the legal academic has been conceptualised as a particular kind of *classed* individual, and how useful the idea of the private life of the law school is in seeking to progress understanding of legal academics as stakeholders.[19]

The argument is structured around three sections. First, I will explore how ideas of class have been deployed within recent research on the legal academy. In section two, I look more closely at a theme central to this work, the idea that working class experience can be understood in terms of a social mobility project. In section three I focus on some methodological questions around social experience underscoring this interpretation. There is, I shall argue, a pressing need to reassess theoretically and in terms

[16] See also A Bradney, 'Law as a Parasitic Discipline' (1998) 25 *Journal of Law and Society* 71; A Bradney and F Cownie, 'British University Law Schools in the 21st Century' in D Hayton (ed), *Law's Futures* (Oxford, Hart Publishing, 2000); A Bradney and F Cownie, *Transformative Visions of Legal Education* (Oxford, Blackwell, 1998).

[17] Cownie, n 1, 42.

[18] Ibid 203.

[19] Ibid 203.

of methodology the idea of the 'classed' subject in accounts of the legal academic as stakeholder in the law school.

CLASS, LEGAL ACADEMICS AND 'PRIVATE LIFE' OF THE LAW SCHOOL

Fiona Cownie's book *Legal Academics* presents a powerful connection between the cultures and practices of the legal academy and the development of the legal discipline in the UK.[20] Emphasising the analytic potential of an anthropological approach to legal education, developing 'an ethnography of the disciplines',[21] she suggests that 'the behaviour, values and attitudes of legal academics have implications for the future development of the discipline of law'.[22] The 'ways in which particular groups of academics organise their professional lives are intimately related to the academic tasks on which they are engaged'.[23] Linking this 'cultural approach to studying law'[24] to identity 'as a device for analysing the culture of academic law',[25] Cownie notes, with regard to earlier empirical surveys of the legal academy,[26] that 'although we can glean much information, both about the tribe of academic lawyers and their territory' from such work, it belongs to the 'public life' of academic law. What is required, in contrast, is a 'venture... into *the more private aspects* of legal academia'.[27]

Cownie's work is of particular significance in discussing class and legal academics. As a picture of how professional lives are organised, *Legal Academics* is the most sustained account to date of how the behaviour, values and attitudes of British legal academics interconnect with political, cultural and policy questions within a rapidly changing higher education sector. We find, for example, discussion of how audit, equity and anti-discrimination agendas can impact on the perceptions of legal academics, what it means for the individuals concerned to teach and research law. Further, Cownie's book, at least on the surface, appears to run against the grain of much of the recent work on the corporatisation of higher education.[28] Far from seeing a re-visioning of the commitments and aspirations of the academic subject

[20] Cownie, n 1.

[21] Cownie, n 1, 9. See also T Becher, *Academic Tribes and Territories: Intellectual Enquiry and the Culture of Disciplines* (Buckingham, Open University, 1989); T Becher and M Kogan, *Process and Structure in Higher Education*, 2nd edn (London, Routledge, 1992); P Trowler, *Academics Responding to Change: New Higher Education Frameworks and Academic Cultures* (Buckingham, Open University Press/SRHE, 1998).

[22] Cownie, 'Women Legal Academics' (1998) 103.

[23] T Becher, n 21, quoted in Cownie, ibid 109, my emphasis.

[24] Cownie, n 1 p 1, 9.

[25] Ibid 13–14.

[26] For discussion, ibid 41–42.

[27] Ibid 42, my emphasis.

[28] See also Bradney, n 5.

as occurring in ways in keeping with the imperatives of the new economy (broadly, a realignment of the legal academic as 'academic capitalist'),[29] Cownie presents 'considerable evidence' of

> the enduring nature of certain core aspects of the culture of academic law, which suggest that the professional identities of legal academics may be more resistant to pressure than some commentators have acknowledged. Their prime objective as teachers was to teach students to think; despite benchmarks, audit and other forms of quality assessment they did not talk in terms of 'transferable skills' or increasing the employability of their students.[30]

Whilst 'academic lawyers are subject to the changes taking place in higher education just as much as members of other "academic tribes"', therefore, the 'culture of academic law and the professional identities constructed within it display a great deal of resilience, retaining, importantly, a fundamentally academic orientation.'[31]

It is against the backdrop of these broader changes in higher education that *Legal Academics* engages explicitly therefore, as part of an interrogation of the 'identity matters'[32] of gender, race, ethnicity and sexual orientation, with the question of how social class relates to the working lives of legal scholars. What does it tell us about the legal academic as stakeholder in the law school?

SOCIAL CLASS AND LEGAL ACADEMICS

Drawing on the views of the respondents in her study,[33] Cownie notes that class background had 'little effect upon their professional identities', although 'half of them immediately qualified this by saying that in fact it had affected their research interests, or their desire to be involved in education'.[34] Additionally, she observes, a 'significant minority of respondents *did not feel at ease* in the middle-class milieu of the legal academy.' While

> rejecting the notion that class had any particular effects upon the culture, the reality appears to be that it is a significant factor for many academics working

[29] In addition to work cited above n 3, see S Slaughter and L Leslie, *Academic Capitalism: Politics, Policies and the Entrepreneurial University* (Baltimore, Johns Hopkins University Press, 1997); S. Cooper, J Hinkson and G Sharp (eds), *Scholars and Entrepreneurs: The Universities in Crisis* (Melbourne, Arena Publications, 1992); J Currie, B Thiele and P Harris, *Gendered Universities in Globalized Economies: Power, Careers and Sacrifices* (Lexington, Maryland, 2002).

[30] Cownie, n 1, 206.

[31] Ibid.

[32] Ibid 10.

[33] Cownie's study is based on interviews with 54 legal academics working in university law schools in England. For discussion of methods and access questions, n 1, 14–15.

[34] Ibid 203, my emphasis.

> in law schools... Being a legal academic was unequivocally regarded as being a middle class occupation.[35]

In seeking to unpack the apparent tension between these comments, it is necessary to look more closely at this relationship between class and the legal academy.

Class, of course, is a deeply contested concept.[36] It has been addressed within earlier discussions of universities[37] and it features, to a degree, in recent accounts of women legal academics. Socio-economic background, meanwhile, is an issue central to the policies of the present government around the expansion of higher education. Class concerns are, in addition, a prominent theme within diverse cultural representations of universities and academic life (for example, in novels, plays, films).[38] Cownie's study presents, however, a discussion of how class can impact in the contemporary legal academy and on the experience of legal academics. Drawing primarily on a sociological and occupational-based framework informed by ideas of social and cultural capital derived from the work of Bordieu,[39] a number of contradictions, we have seen, inform the perceptions of class on the part of Cownie's interviewees.

Class is described as having 'little effect' upon professional identity, whilst, at the same time, for 'half of them', it affected their chosen research interests and personal experience of higher education.[40] Intriguingly, this group 'contained almost no one with a middle class background' suggesting a correlation, for this 'significant minority',[41] between some aspects of having a working-class background and an experience of 'not feeling at ease' within the legal academy:

> About a fifth of the respondents did not feel that they wholly identified with the middle classes. This group was a mixture of people from working class and lower middle class backgrounds *who still felt distanced from the middle class milieu of the legal academy*.[42]

[35] Ibid.

[36] S Edgell, *Class* (London, Routledge, 1993).

[37] Eg AH Halsey, *Decline of Donnish Dominion: The British Academic Professions in the Twentieth Century* (Oxford, Clarendon Press, 1995)).

[38] As Cownie observes, n 1, 176: '[S]tereotypically, academia has a very middle-class image. The pages of academic novels, from *Lucky Jim* to *Changing Places* are littered with images of the middle-class milieu of the academic life.'

[39] P Bordieu, *Outline of a Theory of Practice* (Cambridge, Cambridge University Press, 1977); P Bordieu, *Homo Academicus* (Paris, Editions de Minuit, 1984); P Bourdieu, *Distinctions: A Social Critique of the Judgement of Taste* (London, Routledge, 1989). For critical discussion see L Adkins and B Skeggs (eds), *Feminism After Bordieu* (Oxford, Blackwell, 2004).

[40] Cownie, n 1, 203. It is suggested, for example, that these took 'a particular interest in subjects such as welfare law, criminal law or labour law'.

[41] Ibid 203.

[42] Ibid 180, my emphasis.

'Being' a legal academic is unequivocally seen by 'all the respondents' in Cownie's study as 'a middle class job'.[43] If legal academics 'unquestionably perceive their current status as inherently middle class', however, the reading suggests 'they do not all come to that position with the same cultural capital'.

Drawn 'from a slightly wider class background than the students they teach',[44] these observations broadly mirror those of scholars from other disciplines. They map to the picture emerging, for example, from within sociology and cultural studies, where recent research has been concerned to explore what it means to speak of a distinctive working-class subjectivity or experience in the context of universities.[45] In the next section I look more closely at this work, and explore how it can help to 'flesh out' the observations of the legal academics in Cownie's study, and make sense of some of these apparent contradictions.

ON 'BECOMING' MIDDLE-CLASS[46]

'Where Does Memory End and Imagination Begin?'[47]

> Within my working environment, it's middle class. *But in my home life, it's more of a mix.* I know I'm middle class in terms of career, but *I feel different—I don't have the same background as my middle class friends* so their families, and what they do when they go and visit them for the weekend and so on is very different. Their parents are well-educated, and mine are not, *so it makes a difference.* But not within my job. (lecturer, early career, female, new university)[48]

Recent discussions of working-class academics[49] are driven, in part,[50] by a perceived gap within earlier qualitative work on class in terms of its failure

[43] Ibid, 176. Note also observations by Wells, above n 6, 2001, 136.

[44] Cownie, ibid 180. The Law Society's longitudinal study, cited by Cownie, suggests only about 18% of law students' parents were engaged in 'working class occupations'; D Halpern, *Entry into the Legal Professions: The Law Student Cohort Study Years 1 and 2* (London, The Law Society, 1994) 21.

[45] See further p 31 and n 46, below.

[46] Such a term is, of course, problematic and in what follows I wish to resist a reifying of class in recognising the multidimensional and (temporal, spatial, cultural) contingent nature of class identification. Class itself is internally stratified along race, gender and ethnic lines and, on one level, it makes little sense to speak of a 'middle-class' or 'working-class experience'. See further discussion in S Munt (ed), *Cultural Studies and the Working Class: Subject to Change* (London, Cassell, 2000); Especially A Medhurst, 'If Anywhere: Class Identifications and Cultural Studies Academics', in Munt (ed), 19–36.

[47] T Davies, cited in P Farley, *Distant Voices, Still Lives: BFI Modern Classics* (London, BFI Publishing, 2006) 7.

[48] Cownie, n 1, 180.

[49] Eg Munt, n 46.

[50] It is also important to note how questions of social class have also been central to political and policy debates about schooling and the expansion of higher education (see below), with a growing interest in issues of gender, race and education providing further impetus to this work.

to adequately theorise the social subject and engage with the complex, and frequently contradictory, nature of social experience. As Carol Smart[51] argues in her book *Personal Life*, many traditional sociological engagements, whether in relation to families or employment, tended to ignore the significant affective dimensions of 'everyday' social relations, in so doing effacing the interconnectedness of the lives of women, children and men, erasing what she terms the 'real lives' of individuals.

This point has a particular bearing on attempts to engage with the experiences of legal academics via reference to the idea of the private life of the law school. 'Real lives' are mediated (inevitably) by a range of factors, such as age, class, geographical location, religion, ethnicity, sexuality, health and disability. Beyond the differences that exist between social groups, what it subjectively means to a particular individual to be a legal academic will vary enormously, depending not just on the institution in which one is employed but also the specificities of life history and biography, stage of life course, family and friendship networks and commitments, and the diverse social contexts that situate specific practices. One challenge in approaching the private life of the legal academy, therefore, is to avoid a form of analysis whereby 'real people and their lives ... become a kind of grist to a pre-existing theoretical mill ... reduced to ciphers for a culturally and historically specific knowledge-building industry'.[52]

In addressing these issues, and drawing attention to the affective domain in social relations, a number of studies have explored the potential of autobiography and use of cultural memory for developing an account of the emotional politics of class identity.[53] Questions of emotion, as Cownie's interviewees illustrate, are rarely far below the surface in discussions of the 'significant effects' of class. They are evident in the comments of several respondents in *Legal Academics* who report a sense of loss, dislocation and 'not belonging' in the process of 'becoming' middle class. Such a feeling of being 'out of place' has also been reported within sociological and cultural studies accounts of class mobility, denoting the sense of a 'half-and-half existence' marked by a dislocation with parental and wider family experience in the process of becoming middle-class. In ways mediated by generation, gender and race, such narratives of class mobility through education

[51] C Smart, *Personal Life: New Directions in Sociological Thinking* (Oxford, Polity, 2007).

[52] Ibid 190.

[53] See also B Skeggs, *Formations of Class and Gender: Becoming Respectable* (London, Sage, 1997); S Charlesworth, *A Phenomenology of Working Class Experience* (Cambridge, Cambridge University Press, 2000); Munt (ed.), n 46; B Skeggs, *Class, Self, Culture* (London, Routledge, 2003); P Devine, M Savage, J Scott and R Crompton (eds), *Rethinking Class: Cultures, Identities and Lifestyles* (Palgrave Macmillan, 2004); A Milner, *Core Cultural Concepts: Class* (London, Sage, 1999); T Edensor, 'A Welcome Back to the Working Class' (2000) 34 *Sociology* 805.

are, on one level, not dissimilar from that charted by Hoggart over fifty years ago in his book *The Uses of Literacy*.[54] We see here a process of status mobility that can be fraught and experientially powerful, marked by feelings of being uprooted, anxious, ever watchful and vigilant, of being 'neither here nor there'. It is a sense of distance and rupture evocatively captured in poetry (for example, in Tony Harrison's poem *Bookends*)[55] as well as in sociological writings and cinema.[56]

Cownie's study suggests, however, that it is also part of the lives of some legal scholars, who present a complex picture of the tensions involved in acceptable self-presentation in what can be experienced as an indeterminate class position. And, of particular importance to a discussion of the effects of class and capital on the legal academy, this process appears to have consequences for some individuals. As one of Cownie's respondents notes: 'Most of the students are from the same [middle class] background as me, *so it's no problem at all*... (reader, experienced, male, old university)'.[57]

Following Cownie in her adaptation of ideas of social and cultural capital derived from Bordieu, social confidence and familiarity with cultural codes around ways of speaking, dress, modes of participation and interaction can be associated with educational background in ways that inform such perceptions of success and status, whether it be of the self or the standing of the particular institution in which one studies or is employed. Perceptions of discrimination and disadvantage in career progression, meanwhile, can be linked to this sense of institutional belonging and ability to 'play the game', to ideas of cultural capital that, it is suggested, may privilege those from more established middle-class backgrounds familiar with certain cultural codes.

At the same time, sociological research suggests, classed cultures of consumption and lifestyle inform perceptions of commodity desire,[58] with a working-class background commonly associated with some distinctive

[54] R Hoggart, *The Uses of Literacy: Aspects of Working-Class Life With Special Reference to Publications and Entertainments* (London, Penguin, 1966). See also B Jackson and D Marsden, *Education and the Working Class: Some General Themes Raised by a Study of 88 Working-Class Children in a Northern Industrial City* (London, Routledge and Kegan Paul, 1962).

[55] 'Back in our silences and sullen looks, for all the Scotch we drink, what's still between's not the thirty or so years, but books, books, books'. T Harrison, 'Bookends' in *Collected Poems* (London, Viking, 2007).

[56] See, eg J Seabrook, *A World Still to Win: Reconstruction of the PostWar Working Class* (London, Faber, 1985). See generally M Pickering, *History, Experience and Cultural Studies* (London, MacMillan, 1997); A Milner, *Literature, Culture and Society* (London, UCL Press, 1996); J Bourke (ed), *Working Class Cultures in Britain 1890-1960: Gender, Class and Ethnicity* (London, Routledge, 1994).

[57] Cownie, n 1, 179.

[58] G McCracken, *Culture and Consumption* (Bloomington, Indiana University Press, 1990); S Edgell, K Hetherington and A Warde (eds) *Consumption Matters: The Production and Experience of Consumption* (Oxford, Blackwell, 1997); S Brown, AM Doherty and B Clarke (eds), *Romancing the Market* (London, Routledge, 1998). See also J Baudrillard, *The Consumer Society* (London, Sage, 1998).

personal characteristics (being driven or over conscientious, of feeling a 'need to prove' oneself in an alien environment).[59] Interlinked to the above, social class further mediates access to the cultural and material resources of previous generations in the form, for example, of advantages potentially provided by inheritance in terms of wealth transmission and life course planning, part of the material basis of these 'private lives'.

Class also, however, importantly, informs the structures of feeling and emotion referred to above, the cultural assessment of value and distinction of belonging or being seen as 'other'.[60] It would seem that feeling distanced from the middle-class milieu of the legal academy can come with certain psycho-social consequences. 'Passing' as middle class, intriguingly, it has been argued, involves far more than subjugating or amending accent and modes of expression, monitoring dress and deportment (or, as it was once put to me, 'holding the right cutlery at the formal dinner'). In a telling observation, Beverley Skeggs observes how, ultimately, class passing rarely works (whereas, for example, 'sexual passing' frequently does).[61] Rather, reflecting the extent to which assumptions about class can be embedded within institutional practices and cultures, as well as ingrained in lived experience, structures of feeling and cultural memory, the working-class man or woman, it is suggested, will eventually make themselves known as such, just as the middle-class subject can rarely get away with 'slumming it' (a point on which I defer to the astute observations of *Pulp's* 'Common People').[62]

Recent sociological work provides some further insights into what Andrew Sayer has evocatively termed the moral significance of class in British society.[63] Sayer suggests that emotions are themselves subject to moral judgements in ways informed by assumptions about class. Thus, following Sayer, the interlinking of social class, emotion and normative judgement appears present in a number of aspects in the discussion of everyday academic life under consideration by Cownie. And as Smart notes, in drawing on Sayer's work, everyday experiences of emotion such as anxiety and shame[64] can also be informed by issues of class. Classed dimensions

[59] A correlation between perceived lack of social and cultural capital and feelings of needing to work ever harder, being over conscientious for fear of being 'found out'. A 'relaxed', 'laid back' persona, in contrast, has been associated with high educational status, whereby established paper credentials (and in particular any association with Oxbridge) 'speak for themselves'.

[60] R Williams, *Marxism and Literature* (Oxford, Oxford University Press, 1997), 132: 'The term is difficult, but "feeling" is chosen to emphasise a distinction from more formal concepts of "world-view" or "ideology"... we are concerned with meanings and values as they are actively lived and felt... not feeling against thought, but thought as felt and feeling as thought'.

[61] B Skeggs, 'The Appearance of Class: Challenges in Gay Space', in Munt (ed), n 46, 142.

[62] *Pulp*, 'Common People' from *Different Class* (Island Records, 1999). 'But still you'll never get it right, cos when you're laid in bed at night, watching roaches climb the wall, if you call your Dad he could stop it all.'

[63] A Sayer, *The Moral Significance of Class* (Cambridge, Cambridge University Press, 2005).

[64] Smart, n 51, 140.

of experience may inform, for example, how individual women and men negotiate the organisational cultures and forms of governance discussed above that are seeking to remodel or refashion the academic subject. To refer back to the work of McWilliam, individual academics doing work 'on themselves', turning themselves into 'professional experts', 'academic capitalists' or, indeed, 'respected figures' in their field, do not work on a *tabula rasa*, but in a manner mediated by their negotiation of social formations and boundaries that are shaped by (amongst other things) class: 'If class position, like gender and race, fundamentally affects people's lives, disadvantaging and even injuring some while advantaging and empowering others, *then it affects the kind of people individuals become*.'[65]

Even a cursory look at the cultural norms and modes of interaction within different university law schools would reveal how deeply these classed codes and assumptions can be, informing, as Cownie suggests, dominant organisational cultures, the practices of staff and students alike and the inter-subjective policing of acceptable social boundaries:

> I've seen these academics, impeccable 'liberal' credentials all of them, freeze, look askance, in the prolonged company of someone from what is quite clearly (but never named as) a working-class background. They're happy with their own, for sure, and they are so polite to the face. But listen carefully to the way and where judgements are expressed, to opinions about clothing, an accent, the body presentation and, especially for women, anything at all related to being 'too' sexual. Don't tell me class doesn't inform that. (reader, experienced, male, old university: personal correspondence).[66]

The above discussion reflects on aspects of the narrative observed by some of Cownie's respondents of being 'cut' from the resources of generations gone before. This is just one example, however, of how class can be understood as an identity with significant effects in law schools, informing ways of feeling, judging, value and so forth. A rather different question concerns how, in the context of the changing university and expansion of higher education noted above, these effects of class may themselves be changing and now playing out in rather different ways.

CHANGING UNIVERSITIES: NEW FORMATIONS OF CLASS?[67]

Considering the significant effects of class referred to by Cownie it is important to note how social change has differential impact depending on the embodied, situated location of individuals.[68] The grammar school girl/boy

[65] Sayer, n 63, 206, my emphasis.
[66] Personal correspondence, copy with author.
[67] B Skeggs, 1997, n 53.
[68] A Medhurst, 'If Anywhere' in Munt (2000) 25.

mobility narrative has become, for example, a distinctive feature of the literature on legal academics ('I'm the first in my family to attend university')[69] as well as in broader cultural accounts of academic life. However, such mobility narratives must themselves be socially and historically contextualised as the product of a particular political, economic and cultural moment. Within a very different political and economic infrastructure, it would appear class identities and experiences of mobility may be playing out in different ways. In particular, in the context of the restructured (and re-gendered)[70] university, research suggests rather different structures of feeling and cultural encoding may now be informing the effects of class with regard to the law school and questions about access to economic, social and cultural capital.

I have argued elsewhere that the remodeling of the academic as new knowledge worker has involved, within an increasingly corporatised environment, a complex, and in many ways contradictory, shift in the dominant configurations of legal education and research (in relation, for example, to the gendered cultures of law schools and the status of contextual/socio-legal study).[71] There is reason to believe, however, that this model of performativity may have had 'special consequences for the class-mobile person in the academy'.[72] The reality of access to higher education for many working-class and ethnic-minority adults reveals certain paradoxes within national policy and institutional practice on widening participation.[73] A considerable evidence base suggests working-class groups have not only historically been but continue to be excluded from participation in higher education, notwithstanding the expansion of the system and policy drives towards greater inclusion.[74]

Further, research is emerging, drawing on both qualitative and quantitative data, concerned with the intersectional nature of social class, ethnicity and gender in the process whereby individuals choose which university to attend. In the case of law schools, much is known about how class can inform perceptions of career options, the status of institutions

69 See, eg interviews in C McGlynn, *The Woman Lawyer: Making the Difference* (London, Butterworths, 1998).

70 Brooks and Mackinnon, n 3.

71 Collier, n 12, 2004.

72 Cownie, n 1, 213, citing J Ryan and C Sackrey, *Strangers in Paradise: Academics from the Working-Class* (Boston, South End Press, 1984) 18.

73 M Bowl, *Non-Traditional Entrants to Higher Education: 'They Talk About People Like ME'* (Stoke, Trentham Books, 2003).

74 See, eg L Archer, M Hutchings and A Ross, *Higher Education and Social Class: Issues of Exclusion and Inclusion* (London, Routledge Falmer, 2002); G Paton, 'Number of Working Class Students Has Barely Increased' *Daily Telegraph* (London 25 June 2008); National Audit Office 2008, reporting that 'white working-class boys' are more likely to 'miss out' on higher education than any other group. On law, P Thomas (ed), *Discriminating Lawyers* (London, Routledge-Cavendish, 2000).

and subsequent experience of professional legal practice.[75] If the shift from elite to a mass system[76] has been accompanied by much political rhetoric about widening access and meritocratic equalisation, however, research suggests that the expansion is at best partial and may, in some respects, have deepened social stratification and generated new and different inequalities.[77]

It is important to reflect, therefore, in such a context, on what it means to state that university law schools are marked by 'significant effects' of class in terms of their operational codes and cultures. It remains possible, for example, if not without qualification, to broadly map the hierarchy of UK law schools and the career progression of their graduates to profiles of class and ethnicity, with higher concentrations of working-class and black and ethnic-minority staff and students well-documented in the 'new' universities and those outside the 'elite'. Participation in higher education among people from working-class groups remains, more generally, stubbornly low, with lower social classes and ethnic minorities seen by the present government as either not going into higher education in sufficient, politically acceptable, numbers or, if they do, not attending the higher status institutions.[78] This lends the above accounts of not (fully) 'fitting in' a particular salience in the present political and economic context. Moreover, legal academics generally, as members of a distinctive, segmented socio-spatial consumption group,[79] stand in an uneasy relation to 'private/corporate capital, knowledge-based activities' and new ideas of 'middle-class consumption'[80]

[75] Note M Shiner, 'Young, Gifted and Blocked! Entry to the Solicitor's Profession' in P Thomas (ed), *Discriminating Lawyers* (2000) 87–120; P Thomas and A Rees, 'Law Students—Getting in and Getting on' in P Thomas (ed), (2000) 33–37; D Halpern, *Entry Into the Legal Professions: The Law Student Cohort Study Years 1 and 2* (London, Law Society, 1994); M Shiner and T Newburn, *Entry Into the Legal Professions: The Law Student Cohort Study Year 3* (London, Law Society, 1995); M Shiner, *Entry Into the Legal Professions: The Law Student Cohort Study Year 4* (London, Law Society, 1997); M Shiner, *Entry Into the Legal Professions: The Law Student Cohort Study Year 5* (London, Law Society, 1999).

[76] Ministers have set a target to get 50% of young people into higher education.

[77] D Reay, M David and S Ball, *Degrees of Choice: Social Class, Race and Gender in Higher Education* (Stoke, Trentham Books, 2005).

[78] Ibid.

[79] See also P Chatterton and R Hollands, 'Theorising Urban Playscapes: Producing, Regulating and Consuming Youthful Nightlife City Spaces' (2002) 39 (1) *Urban Studies* 95, 109; R Collier, '"Be Smart, Be Successful, Be Yourself…": Representations of the Training Contract and the Trainee Solicitor in Advertising by Large Law Firms' (2005) 12 (1) *International Journal of the Legal Profession* 51.

[80] Chatterton and Hollands, 'Theorising' (2002) 97. See also on reformations of middle-class identity M Savage, P Dickens and T Fielding, *Property, Bureaucracy and Culture: Middle Class Formation in Contemporary Britain*, (London, Routledge, 1992); M. Savage and T Butler (eds), *Social Change and the Middle Classes* (London, UCL Press, 1995); R Crompton, 'Consumption and Class Analysis' in S Edgell, K Hetherington and A Warde (eds), *Consumption Matters: The Production and Experience of Consumption* (Oxford, Blackwell, 1996); T Butler, *Gentrification and the Middle-Classes* (Aldershot, Ashgate, 1997).

in ways that suggest that what it means to be and to identify *as* middle class are also shifting considerably.

In the light of the above it may be more accurate to suggest that, far from fading away, the significance of class has been reshaped and remodelled, and is playing out in different ways in the context of the changing university and the shifting narratives of class mobility discussed above. Broader economic and cultural changes are producing different kinds of engagements with the processes of aestheticisation and emotionalisation seen within sociology to be key features of (self) management within the performance cultures and consumption practices that mark the 'everyday' within late modernity.[81] It may be, for example, that ideas of academic vocation are themselves marked by classed distinctions between *having* a paid job (traditionally, a working-class identification) and *being* or embodying the job one does, divisions that are themselves becoming, in some contexts, increasingly blurred.

METHOD AND CLASS—RETHINKING THE PRIVATE LIFE OF THE LAW SCHOOL

Where does this leave us? There exists I suggest, notwithstanding institutional commitments to formal equality and diversity, a sense of awkwardness around class within parts of the legal academic community interlinked with the questions of emotion and feeling, self-identity and cultural positioning discussed in this chapter. In developing strategies to conserve collective and individual identities, not least perhaps around being a 'critical' scholar of law,[82] if not institutional outsider, issues of class background and a reflexive awareness of one's own cultural and economic capital may be, for some, understandably disquieting. What, after all, is the potential problem alluded to by one of Cownie's respondents in his observation that 'most of the students are from the same [middle class] background as me' so '*it's no problem at all*'?[83] As Skeggs observes, in a context where the working class have not had access to the 'legal, aesthetic or moral authority' which gives legitimacy to social positions, what processes of '(dis)identification' are at play here?[84]

Yet if class has been 'the ghost at the feast' of critical legal scholarship, how far is one to go in this 'venture... into the more private aspects

[81] See, eg and generally Z Bauman, *Consuming Life* (Oxford, Polity, 2007); Z Bauman, *Liquid Times: Living in an Age of Uncertainty* (Oxford, Polity, 2006); S M Lash and J Urry, *Economies of Signs and Space* (London, Sage, 1993).

[82] Note the reading of P Goodrich, 'The Critics Love of the Law: Intimate Observations on an Insular Jurisdiction' (1999) 10 (3) *Law and Critique* 343.

[83] Cownie, n 1, 179, my emphasis.

[84] Skeggs, n 53. See also the work of Sayer, n 63.

of legal academia'?[85] In his account of a 'flight to the elite' amongst UK critical legal scholars, Goodrich looks to the potential of an engagement with psychoanalysis that, it is suggested, might have analytic and political purchase for legal studies.[86] It is difficult to see, however, how the interlinking of social class and the complexity of the material and emotional structures in which career choice is exercised play out in this reading of career progression and personal advancement. Equally, in the accounts of the effects of class reported by Cownie in *Legal Academics*, seeing class as a 'significant factor for many academics working in law schools'[87] it is unclear what happens to the *experience* of loss and pain, pleasure and achievement discussed above, what it means to be one person in 'my working environment', another 'in my home life'. What we miss is precisely the richness, depth and emotional resonances of social experience central to recent sociological engagements with personal life. The affective domain appears to fade away at the very moment it is evoked as being of some (unspecified) political significance.

This raises the question, therefore, of methodology, the limits of ethnography and how 'private life' is theorised in this work. With regard to method, alternative explorations are emerging which point to new ways of engaging with questions of emotion and class in relation to academic cultures and experiences. In seeking to 'make the familiar strange',[88] Cownie's 'meso-qualitative'[89] study of legal academics explores 'how the social world is experienced by legal academics'. Deriving from an anthropological tradition of studying the 'other' ethnographically, it adopts the recognised qualitative research method whereby the researcher uses participant observation and/or interviews in order to gain a deeper understanding of a group's culture (in this case, legal scholars). The aim is to help understand and theorise modes of human behaviour within the group across different contexts (here, different law schools, within various universities in the sector, and across a diverse body of legal academics).

Emotion, we have seen, is rarely far below the surface in such readings of the effects of class. 'Identity matters', that is, are to the fore, identity itself seen as multiple and never unified, marked by a 'fragmentation of the self'.[90] Ethnographical work has well-documented limits, however, in taking forward understanding of the inter-subjective effects of class discussed above, and the precise nature of this fragmentation. Engaging with the question of

[85] Cownie, n 1, 42.
[86] Goodrich, n 82.
[87] Cownie, n 1, 203.
[88] S Delamont, 'Just like the Novels? Researching the Occupational Culture(s) of Higher Education' in R Cuthbert (ed), *Working in Higher Education* (Buckingham, SRHE and Open University Press, 1996), quoted in Cownie, n 1, 14.
[89] Cownie, ibid.
[90] Ibid 12.

the authenticity of voice, for example, where the researcher is her/himself a member of the group in question, we face the important problem of shared processes of self-inscription between researcher/researched. To refer back to the moral significance of class discussed by Andrew Sayer, above, this raises questions of how recognition and the multiple dimensions of interaction underscore the way features of social life are 'made visible' in contexts where 'actions, looks or expressions rather than words [can] convey the significant meaning'.[91]

It is in contrast to such an approach that recent work in the area of auto-ethnography has sought to engage with the meanings and uses of personal narrative in developing knowledge of how self-identity and social forms can be culturally constituted through biographical genre.[92] Whilst itself open to critique, this approach has informed a number of accounts seeking to explore the intersectional nature of social class, offering potential advantages over traditional ethnography in approaching the significant effects of class in the university law school. In particular, it opens up the emotional realm as a way of understanding the links between the social context under study and the processes whereby emotion is, or is not, then made visible. As developed by academics within cultural studies this approach, at times used interchangeably with personal narrative and autobiography, turns to life history as a way of providing insight into various dimensions of class experience.[93] Far from dismissing testimonies as introspective, subjective and unscientific, however, these auto-ethnographies can themselves be seen as political in nature, engaging readers to revalue the place of cultural memory and structures of feeling and requiring us to consider issues hitherto 'off the radar'.[94]

I wish to conclude with a question therefore.[95] What might an auto-ethnography of the middle-class legal academic—assuming that there is such

[91] Smart, n 51, 152.

[92] See, eg D Reed-Danahay (ed), *Auto-Ethnography: Rewriting the Self and the Social* (London, Berg, 1997); A Meneley and DJ Young (eds), *Auto-Ethnographies: The Anthropology of Academic Practices* (Peterborough, Ont, Broadview Press, 2005); NL Holt, 'Representation, Legitimation, and Autoethnography: An Autoethnographic Writing Story' (2003) 2 (1) *International Journal of Qualitative Methods*1: S Denshire, 'In Praise of Auto-Ethnography' (2006) 53 (4) *Australian Occupational Therapy Journal* 346.

[93] See, eg V Walkerdine, *Schoolgirl Fictions* (London, Verso, 1991); A Kuhn, *Family Secrets: Acts of Memory and Imagination* (London, Verso, 1995); A. Medhurst, n 46.

[94] Davies' observation 'Where does memory end, and imagination begin?' above thus captures how 'the past' can itself be present and active within cultural memory, a key element of autobiographical discourse, something that is not 'left behind' but which informs the commitments of the present. See further discussion in Smart 'Personal Life', 2007. The work of the film-maker Terence Davies in many way exemplifies this point: see *Of Time and the City: A Love Song and a Eulogy* (HanWay/BBC films, 2008).

[95] In evoking, for example, the fragmented nature of memory in focusing on how class has shaped the stories individuals tell about their lives and their relations with others, an engagement with writing as a way of understanding self in explorations of feeling.

a thing, given the conceptual identifications implicitly at play here—actually look like? Far from routinely pathologising working class experience, constituting it as the actual or potential analytic problem,[96] what would it mean to turn attention to the nature of these middle class cultures and norms in university law schools (for, implicitly, it is being claimed that there is such a thing) in a discursive attempt to stop the depiction of working class as Other?[97] To return to the work of Sayer, in considering how researchers seek to account for the actions of others, and to 'offer explanations for things that "other" people do' (other stakeholders), this raises the 'question of whether sociologists regard themselves as the exceptions when they speak or write about the lives of ordinary people'.[98]

If discussion of policy change in higher education has paid insufficient attention to the complexity of agency, what might emerge from the stories of those who have been positioned as the subjects of the structural changes detailed above? If an ethnography of the disciplines is to seriously engage with the effects of class, it will miss much if it fails to address the processes that 'constitute the subjectivity, defences and coping practices of most of the population... not taking apart, this fiction which functions in truth [it seems]... not to see the ways in which subjects cope, produce defences against.... conditions'.[99] How does that which falls beyond the conventional categories of academic identity (but undoubtedly within the 'personal' domain)—questions of intimacy and sexuality, desire and friendship, of health, sickness and ageing, of love, care and dependency, of jealously, dislike and, indeed, fear, ambition and inevitable disappointment[100]—connect to the cultures of academic law, and how are these situated experiences articulated and made sense of?

In a telling passage, Cownie notes how: '[A]wareness of gender issues is not very deeply embedded into the culture of academic law, and that most academic lawyers *have to be specifically directing their attention to the subject* before they readily identify gender as problematic.'[101] In writing this paper I have frequently asked myself whether many academic lawyers also have to be specifically directing their attention to the subject of class before they identify it as in any way problematic. Class, as Valerie Walkerdine and others have argued, is not something consigned to the past, that which is

[96] *cf* T Eagleton, *The Illusions Of Postmodernism* (Oxford, Blackwell, 1996).

[97] *cf* M Thornton, 'Neoliberal Melancholia: The Case of Feminist Legal Scholarship' (2004) 20 *Australian Feminist Law Journal* 7, 12.

[98] Smart, above n 51, 65.

[99] V Walkerdine, 'Subject to Change Without Notice: Psychology, Post-Modernity and the Popular' in S Pile and N Thrift (eds), *Mapping the Subject: Geographies of Cultural Transformation* (London, Routledge, 1995) 329.

[100] Cownie's study suggests that work-life balance, for example, 'is an issue which is intimately connected with the culture of academic law, and the ways in which legal academics construct their professional identities' above n 1, 118.

[101] Ibid, my emphasis.

'left' in the narrative of an individual mobility project, a journey of 'progress' to 'become' middle class (and to become respectable?).[102] It is always present and active to varying degrees, part of our life histories, of our cultural memory, that which is shared (with some) and, all too often, unsaid, seen as intensely personal. Yet 'naming class', it has been argued, can be seen not as an act of essentialism, but an assertion of pride and belonging (in family, education, community and regional culture), not a form of alienation and loss in the move to another class, but 'part of a narrative which allows me a place from which to struggle, a sense of belonging.'[103] As Sayer notes: 'Through both subtle and unsubtle differences in recognition of others, people are in varying degrees included or excluded, and allowed access to different opportunities.'[104]

This chapter has traced some ways forward in thinking about class in developing understanding of the legal academic as stakeholder in the university law school. We live in a time when discourses of social mobility and classlessness have become culturally powerful. To what extent, however, are myths about class still operating to ensure the perpetuation of existing inequalities? To what extent has class 'become an awkward part of the social jigsaw', the focus of heightened social stereotyping, political containment and marginalisation?[105] What new identifications are thrown up if, as some suggest, speaking of class is no longer seen as legitimate, if 'we're all middle class now'?[106] What would it mean, in developing further the study of legal academics, to rethink the concepts and methods through which class has been discussed, to reclaim class as a 'lost identity'? What new insights and hitherto silent voices might be revealed, and what stories of pain, and joy, might they speak?

102 Walkerdine, n 99. Also Skeggs, n 53.

103 V Walkerdine, 'Subject to Change" (1991) 158.

104 Sayer, n 63, 55.

105 I Jack, 'Working Class Has Come to Mean Beer Guts and White Vans' *The Guardian* (London, 1 December 2007) 36.

106 A particular theme within recent debates around working-class cultures and questions of race and ethnicity. See, eg M Collins, *The Likes of Us: A Biography of the White Working Class* (London, Granta, 2004); G Dench, K Gavron and M Young, *The New East End: Kinship, Race and Conflict* (London, Profile Books, 2006); Jack, 'Working Class' (2007) 36.

2

Feminists as Stakeholders in the Law School

ROSEMARY AUCHMUTY

TO CLAIM FEMINISTS as stakeholders in the law school may appear, at first sight, a contradiction in terms. The word 'stakeholder' implies a person in a position of influence, upon whose support the institution relies, and whom in consequence it tries to satisfy. In a law school this would mean someone who is both *appreciated* and *influential* in terms of the curriculum, research agenda, staffing and/or management of resources. Yet most law schools in England and Wales would not admit to having been much influenced by feminists, would not recognise any dependence on them, and have generally not made any special effort to please them. Feminists, on the other hand, have clearly had good reasons for wanting a stake in legal education. From the moment English university law schools admitted women, feminists targeted legal study in their quest to understand the mechanics of male dominance and female subordination, seeing the possession of a law degree as a tool to help them expose and challenge the gendered legal order. They can never have imagined how long it would take. Almost a century—from 1875 to 1971—was to pass between the admission of the first woman law student and the appointment of the first woman law professor in the UK,[1] and the gendered order is still far from dismantled. Hence the continued concern of feminists today about what goes on in the country's law schools.

Feminists have also recognised the importance of education in perpetuating the ideas and practices that sustain patriarchal power and keep women in their place. 'Law schools transmit the first messages about what is permissible in the law and about appropriate styles of lawyering,' Clare McGlynn points out.[2] They are also the place where such customs can

[1] R Auchmuty, 'Early Women Law Students at Cambridge and Oxford' (2008) 29 *Journal of Legal History* 68; C McGlynn, *The Woman Lawyer: Making a Difference* (London, Butterworths, 1998) 62.

[2] C McGlynn, 'Women, Representation and the Legal Profession' (1999) 19 *Legal Studies* 86.

be questioned, alternatives suggested and students empowered to expect change. This makes the law school an important place for feminists to be.

But what about the law schools' attitude to feminists? Stakeholding is a two-way relationship, and this chapter will consider whether there is any possibility that the feminist need for access to and influence upon legal education could be matched by the law schools' reliance on feminists. Given the resistance of the law schools to feminist input into the curriculum, let alone in their appointments, management practices or culture generally,[3] can such an argument be seriously entertained? This chapter will argue that it can. Feminists are so accustomed to failure, lack of progress and backlash that we sometimes lose sight of our successes and our power. (Non-feminists, of course, ignore them.) With the benefit of hindsight, however, we can now track the slow development of feminist influence from total exclusion to reluctant acceptance and, in many institutions today, actual dependence. The chapter will therefore take a historical approach, tracing the relationship of feminists to the law school in five stages: (1) in the nineteenth century, before women were admitted to the universities; (2) between the opening of the law schools and the opening of the legal professions to women; (3) between the first wave of feminism and the second; (4) with the advent of a feminist critique during the second wave of feminism; and (5) since the introduction of the Research Assessment Exercise in the 1990s when, I shall argue, the balance of power between the law schools and feminism decisively shifted and law schools were forced to accept their reliance on feminist research, teaching and management skills.

First, though, a few definitional points. The word 'feminist' was not in use until the 1890s but is now routinely employed by historians to describe supporters of the nineteenth-century 'Woman Movement' as well as those who in later decades were happy to apply the term to themselves.[4] I use the word in a broad and general sense to describe anyone who recognises the significance of gender in the organisation of society, who sees women as, at best, *unequal* and *discriminated against* and, at worst, *oppressed*, and

[3] A great deal has been written, particularly in the last 20 years, on the misogynist culture of UK law schools. See, eg R Collier, 'Masculinism, Law and Law Teaching' (1989) 9 *International Journal of the Sociology of Law* 477; R Collier, '"Nutty Professors", "Men in Suits" and "New Entrepreneurs": Corporeality, Subjectivity and Change in the Law School and Legal Practice' (1998) 7 *Social and Legal Studies* 27; McGlynn, 'Women, Representation and the Legal Academy' (1999) 19; C Wells, 'Working Out Women in Law School' (2001) 21 *Legal Studies* 116; C Wells, 'Women Law Professors—Negotiating and Transcending Gender Identities at Work' (2002) 10 *Feminist Legal Studies* 1; R Collier, 'The Caring University and the (Legal) Academic Career—Rethinking the Relationship Between Women, Men and the "Private Life" of the Law School' (2002) 22 *Legal Studies* 1; R Auchmuty, 'Agenda for a Feminist Legal Curriculum' (2003) 23 *Legal Studies* 377; F Cownie, *Legal Academics: Culture and Identities* (Oxford, Hart Publishing, 2004).

[4] P Levine, *Victorian Feminism 1850–1900* (London, Hutchinson, 1987) 14; B Caine, *Victorian Feminists* (Oxford, Oxford University Press, 1993) 7; R Delmar, 'What is Feminism?' in J Mitchell and A Oakley (eds), *What is Feminism?* (Oxford, Basil Blackwell, 1986) 8.

who wishes to improve the position of women. This definition includes men as well as women, though one is always mindful that *any* display of feminist sensibility by a man is liable to be over-praised on account of its rarity. However, there are huge differences of political analysis even among avowed feminists, male *or* female, so my definition will of necessity be an inclusive one.[5]

Equally, the concept 'law school' embraces a range of institutional structures with very different histories, goals and cultures.[6] This chapter will confine its discussion to the law schools of England and Wales, but even these are extraordinarily disparate, and changing. As Twining puts it:

> The scene in England and Wales has been characterized as diversity in respect of institutions, pluralism in respect of educational ideas and methods, fragmentation of stages of professional formation, relative diffusion of power, rapid expansion in a period of financial stringency, and continuous, but less rapid, change at a variety of levels.[7]

In particular, there remains a fundamental divide between the pre-1992 institutions and the post-1992 former polytechnics and colleges of higher education, and lesser divisions within each of these groups (even more so with the advent of a new clutch of universities in the 2000s). Significant differences include the rotating management of the 'old' universities, in contrast to the permanent heads of schools and deans of the 'new'; a stronger focus on research in the old, and on teaching (especially innovation in teaching) in the new, in large part due to their very different roots; the long-established commitment to *access* of the new universities, which manifests itself in the provision of (inter alia) part-time and vocational courses, as well as a more socially mixed student intake; and the greater importance attached to something called 'academic freedom' in the old universities, which makes the academic staff of those institutions less amenable to control and regulation, and the new universities correspondingly prompter to respond to external pressures and fashions.[8] These are generalisations, but insofar as they hold true for many institutions they presuppose very different environments for the reception of feminism.

[5] There are many textbooks that attempt to explain the different brands of feminist analysis. See, eg M Humm, *Feminisms: A Reader* (Hemel Hempstead, Harvester Wheatsheaf, 1992); V Bryson, *Feminist Debates: Issues of Theory and Political Practice* (Basingstoke, Macmillan, 1999).

[6] RL Abel, *The Legal Profession in England and Wales* (Oxford, Basil Blackwell, 1988) ch 17; F Cownie, *Legal Academics* (2004).

[7] W Twining, 'Thinking About Law Schools: Rutland Reviewed' in A Bradney and F Cownie (eds), *Transformative Visions of Legal Education* (Oxford, Blackwell, 1998) 7.

[8] The old universities, being the norm against which all newcomers are measured, have an extensive bibliography. On law schools in the new universities, see P Leighton, 'New Wine in Old Bottles or New Wine in New Bottles?' in Bradney and Cownie (eds), *Transformative Visions* (1998) 85.

Most English law schools date from the 1960s onwards, so any description of an earlier period will fit only the minority of older institutions, of which, in terms of law teaching (and most other things), Cambridge, Oxford and London were dominant.[9] It is worth noting, however, that even in this early period of legal education it was often the provincial universities who were more open to women and to radical ideas, perhaps because they were anxious to increase their student numbers.[10] This is shown by the way Victoria (later Manchester) University welcomed the suffragette leader Christabel Pankhurst as a law student in the early years of the twentieth century—as we shall see, below.

FEMINISM BEFORE THE OPENING OF THE LAW SCHOOLS TO WOMEN

The so-called 'first wave' of feminism lasted from the 1850s to the granting of the vote to women in 1918, challenging women's subordination across the whole spectrum of social and political life from education to employment, marriage, sexual morality and civil rights. As part of this movement, feminist critiques of English law long pre-dated women's entry into the universities.

For most of the nineteenth century, formal legal education was not open to women. Barred from the universities and from professional legal training, those who wished to understand the nature and form of their own legal disabilities, let alone to strategise around reform, had to educate themselves. And they did. Barbara Bodichon's *Brief Summary in Plain Language of the Most Important Laws Concerning Women* (1854) paved the way for the passing of the Married Women's Property Acts of 1870 and 1882.[11] Frances Power Cobbe's writings on 'Wife Torture in England' led directly to the Matrimonial Causes Act of 1878, which enabled battered wives to obtain separation orders against their husbands.[12] Josephine Butler's essays on prostitution and the injustice of the sexual double standard achieved the repeal of the Contagious Diseases Acts.[13] None of these women had any

[9] RL Abel, 'Comparative Sociology of Legal Professions' in RL Abel and PSC Lewis (eds), *Lawyers in Society III* (Berkeley, Harvard University Press, 1989) 89.

[10] C Dyhouse, *No Distinction of Sex: Women in British Universities 1870–1939* (London, UCL Press, 1995) 8.

[11] BLS Bodichon, 'A Brief Summary' in CA Lacey (ed), *Barbara Leigh Smith Bodichon and the Langham Place Group* (London, RKP, 1987) 23; L Holcombe, *Wives and Property: Reform of the Married Women's Property Laws in Nineteenth-Century England* (Toronto, University of Toronto Press, 1983).

[12] FP Cobbe, 'Wife Torture in England' in S Hamilton (ed), *'Criminals, Idiots, Women and Minors': Victorian Writing by Women on Women* (Peterborough, Ont, Broadview Press, 1995) 132; Caine, *Victorian Feminists* (1993) ch 4.

[13] J Butler, 'An Appeal to the People of England on the Recognition and Superintendance of Prostitution by Governments' (1870) and 'Letter to my Countrywomen, Dwelling in the

formal legal training, but each displayed a formidable knowledge of the relevant law and legal processes, and each had a clear and perceptive analysis of the social and political conditions that gave rise to the discriminatory and oppressive laws.

Even earlier than these, the novelist Caroline Norton was prompted by the real-life calamity of having her children taken from her by her husband to discover something which she (in common with most mothers) had never realised—that legitimate children belonged absolutely to their fathers—and to embark on the campaign that was to give separated women access to their children.[14] She researched, she wrote, she publicised her cause, and she succeeded. Later, the discovery that all her property belonged to her estranged husband too led her to campaign for separated women to be able to keep their own property.[15] Again, she researched, she wrote, and she won.

What made Norton's battle more than a mere personal quest for justice was her readiness to generalise from her own experience to that of all women in her situation and to seek a universal, not an individual solution. Though she (somewhat disingenuously) denied any feminist purpose, she clearly grasped the political nature of what she was doing in exposing the ways that men sought to control their wives by taking possession of both children and property and that the law institutionalised male power over women generally, all in the face of a rhetoric of 'protection' and the sanctity and safety of the home. Bodichon, Cobbe and Butler, in contrast, *were* self-identified feminists who consciously participated in several of the campaigns for women's rights that made up the first wave of the British women's movement. They addressed meetings, spoke to legal men and MPs and, above all, *wrote*—and, in the face of great hostility, were astonishingly successful in generating the necessary impetus for legal reform.

The experience of these first-wave campaigners illustrates how feminism is both an *analysis* (a way of understanding what is going on) and a *politics* (a form of activism). Although the academy is primarily concerned with the analytical side of feminism, many feminists would argue that analysis divorced from politics is meaningless, and particularly so in the case of law. The connexion between feminist thought and feminist action was certainly clear in nineteenth-century Britain, largely because of women's total exclusion from the formal political and legal processes.

Farmsteads and Cottages of England' (1871) in S Jeffreys (ed) *The Sexuality Debates* (London, RKP, 1987) 111; Caine, n 4, ch 5.

[14] P Stevenson [pseud C Norton], 'A Plain Letter to the Lord Chancellor on the Infant Custody Bill' (1839) in JO Hoge and J Marcus (eds), *Selected Writings of Caroline Norton* (Delmar, NY, Scholars' Facsimiles and Reprints, 1978); A Acland, *Caroline Norton* (London, Constable, 1948).

[15] C Norton, 'English Laws for Women in the Nineteenth Century' (1854) and 'A Letter to the Queen on Lord Chancellor Cranworth's Marriage and Divorce Bill' (1855) in Hoge and Marcus (eds), *Selected Writings of Caroline Norton* (1978).

When the Small Society for the Promotion of Legal Education for Women was formed in London in 1878, its aim was not to seek entry to legal education in the universities but to open the way for women's entry into the legal profession. Law was not a graduate profession at the time—the usual route was via the apprenticeship (articles or pupillage); in 1876, however, the professional bodies had instituted classes, and it was to these that women sought access. Nevertheless feminists felt it necessary to justify the attempt, which failed, in terms of fitting women for effective citizenship in an era of increasing rights. 'Women need such knowledge much more than formerly,' explained the *Englishwomen's Review*,

> precisely because they are more independent agents than formerly. Even when married they have acquired, by recent legislation [the Married Women's Property Acts of 1870 and 1874], rights and responsibilities apart from their husbands ... which it is of the greatest consequence they should understand.

Yet such was their anxiety to avoid the impression of trespassing on masculine preserves that a defensive tone crept in:

> At first sight the study of law does not seem so eminently feminine as the sister study of medicine... The tendency of court practice is to teach the lawyer accuracy, coolness, decision, clearness of thought; it does not necessarily harden or coarsen.[16]

Here the anonymous reporter shows awareness of the medical propaganda of the time claiming that too much of the wrong kind of education would 'masculinise' women. But is she also suggesting that legal learning made lawyers hard and coarse? If so, her analysis has much in common with today's feminist critics' claims of a hostile 'male culture' in law.

WOMEN ENTER THE LAW SCHOOLS, 1871–1920

Like law, education was a central plank of first-wave British feminism, and the opening of university courses to women was largely due to campaigning by Victorian feminists (including Bodichon, Cobbe and Butler) and their success in winning the sympathy of male academics. The first women's university college (at Hitchin, later Girton) was opened in 1869; its first woman law student commenced her studies in 1875. Oxford followed suit a decade later.[17] Meanwhile, a programme of special women's classes at University College, London, beginning in 1871, quickly led to integration into the male undergraduates' classes, enabling women to study a range of degree subjects including law. When London University opened its degrees to women in 1878, women became eligible to register for external

[16] (1878) 60 *Englishwomen's Review* 151.
[17] Auchmuty, n 1.

degrees, as did Eliza Orme, becoming England's first woman law graduate in 1888.[18]

A law degree then was not the same thing as a law degree now. Legal education in the universities had been in a parlous state, with little student interest in the academic discipline (and, for many years, no need to take examinations to obtain a BA or LLB). Largely focused on Roman law, it contained little of relevance to the intending lawyer.[19] Not that this mattered: most solicitors and barristers put their faith in their respective apprenticeship systems, scorning both academic learning and professional skills training. By the time the first women law students arrived at Cambridge, Oxford and London, the curriculum had been re-designed, with the addition of examinations and more English law content, and the university chairs were occupied by distinguished scholars like Dicey, Bryce and Maine who were reform-minded and sympathetic to higher education for women. But it was still an academic exercise, with no input from the professions. *Their* attitude was entirely different to that of the law professors: having been forced to institute professional training, the Law Society and the Bar Council refused to entertain requests from women (including Eliza Orme) to take their examinations.[20] From the 1880s, therefore, Englishwomen could obtain university law degrees (or at least take the examinations at Cambridge and Oxford, which did not grant women degrees until the twentieth century), but could go no further in law.

It cannot be said that the universities welcomed women with open arms. The ancient foundations of Cambridge and Oxford were particularly hostile to female students, whose formal marginalisation was to continue well into the twentieth century. Within this context, however, women *law* students were received with relative civility and even kindness. There were no angry demonstrations of the kind that faced women medical students,[21] an omission largely due to the fact that for 45 years after their admission to law school women remained unable to proceed to a career in law. Law was just an academic study like any other and extending it to women posed no particular threat to men.

The early women students had mixed motives for studying law, ranging from a desire for knowledge for its own sake, or to share in men's access

[18] MJ Mossman, *The First Women Lawyers: A Comparative Study of Gender, Law and the Legal Professions* (Oxford, Hart Publishing, 2006) ch 3.

[19] E Jenks, 'English Legal Education' (1935) 101 *Law Quarterly Review* 162; LCB Gower, 'English Legal Training' (1950) 13 *Modern Law Review* 137; JH Baker, 'University College and Legal Education 1826–1976' (1977) 30 *Current Legal Problems* 1; AH Manchester, *A Modern Legal History of England and Wales* (London, Butterworths, 1980) 54–63.

[20] Mossman, *The First Women Lawyers* (2006) 114–8.

[21] E Moberly Bell, *Storming the Citadel: The Rise of the Women Doctor* (London, Constable, 1953); A Sachs and JH Wilson, *Sexism and the Law: A Study of Male Beliefs and Legal Bias in Britain and the United States* (Oxford, Martin Robertson, 1978) 3–22.

to an intellectual life, to a wish to help others, particularly women.[22] This latter goal could have been a feminist, or simply a feminine, one: in a world of separate spheres it was sometimes hard to tell the difference. One way of justifying a move into a masculine field or occupation was to point to a specifically female constituency for your services, and this was Cornelia Sorabji's explanation: she intended to return (and in fact did return) to her native India to act as advocate for women in *purdah*, who were forbidden to speak to men.[23] As women doctors found, however, this reasoning also served to debar women from competition with men in the most prestigious professional specialisms, and most early women law students steered clear of any assumption that they would only work with women. With her conservative, pro-Empire attitudes, Sorabji—Oxford's first woman law student—makes an unlikely feminist, indeed would probably have rejected the label, yet she certainly understood the mechanics of male power and fought courageously to make a career in a man's world.

Even in those early days there were women who sought a legal education in order to have a legal career. Eliza Orme, the very first woman law student, was one of these: denied the possibility of becoming a solicitor, she set up her own law firm and did the work anyway. But Orme was also an active feminist; her whole family was involved in the suffrage movement, and it is difficult to avoid the conclusion that she undertook legal study in part to empower her to understand and challenge women's legal disabilities.[24] This was certainly true of Manchester's first woman law graduate, Christabel Pankhurst, who was persuaded to undertake a law degree because 'a knowledge of law might be useful in work for woman suffrage'—and 'useful it was indeed to prove'.[25]

Pankhurst's story deserves fuller attention because it illustrates the feminists' complex relationship to legal education, and to law itself. In 1903, shortly after Bertha Cave had applied to be admitted to Gray's Inn, Christabel Pankhurst applied to Lincoln's Inn. Both women were turned down.[26] Later that same year, Pankhurst entered the Victoria University of Manchester (now the University of Manchester) after a period of intensive coaching to bring her less than adequate girls' education up to matriculation standard.

[22] Auchmuty, n 1, 93–5.

[23] C Sorabji, *India Calling: The Memories of Cornelia Sorabji, India's First Woman Barrister* (New Delhi, Oxford University Press, 2001) 27; S Gooptu, *Cornelia Sorabji: India's Pioneer Woman Lawyer* (Oxford, OUP, 2006); Mossman, n 18, ch 5.

[24] E Crawford, *The Women's Suffrage Movement: A Reference Guide 1866–1928* (London, UCL Press, 1999) 479–80. See also Mossman, n 18, ch 3.

[25] C Pankhurst, *Unshackled* (London, Cresset, 1989 [1959]), 43.

[26] According to Elsie Lang, 'It was said that this refusal drove her into militancy; her father had been a well-known member of the Bar'. EM Lang, *British Women in the Twentieth Century* (London, T Werner Laurie, 1929) 146.

Like many mature students today (she was 23 years old when she embarked on her degree course), Pankhurst had many concerns in her life which prevented her from giving full attention to her studies. In the same month as she entered the university, her mother Emmeline Pankhurst founded the Women's Political and Social Union (WSPU), the militant branch of the movement for votes for women in Britain. Christabel was soon very active in the organisation, addressing public meetings, writing pamphlets and demonstrating at political gatherings. In October 1905 she was imprisoned for a week for refusing to pay a fine after her arrest at one such demonstration. Only her final examinations drew her temporarily from the cause. 'After the stir at the university and their friendly settlement at the time of my imprisonment,' she wrote later, 'it would be ungracious and, in the long run at any rate, be unwise to throw up my studies and the degree within a few months of the day'.[27] She graduated with first-class honours in July 1906.

It is interesting, and perhaps unexpected, to learn that the university was understanding about her political work and her brush with the law. It is also noteworthy that, in spite of all her distractions, Pankhurst achieved first-class honours, demonstrating that women were at least the intellectual equals of men. Indeed, the result is even more impressive when one considers the necessity for feminists of divorcing their political critique of the law from their academic study of it, a difficulty many later women law students have also had to overcome in order to demonstrate successful mastery of the objectivity prized in legal studies.

Pankhurst could not have emerged from her studies in any doubt that English law was designed by men for men. As for women's place in this grand design, she would have discovered that, in some areas of the law, their position was simply ignored, while in others, women 'enjoyed' different treatment from men which, though sometimes described as a 'privilege', in fact gave them fewer rights and less autonomy. What she would probably *not* have learned at law school, but would have known from her own experience, was the paralysing effect of the doctrine of 'uninterrupted usage', so often put forward to justify women's exclusion from public life. She had grown up with the story of her barrister father's failure to convince the court that women should be entitled to vote[28] and, though this had happened long before her birth, the irony must have struck her forcibly at law school as she learnt the rules of statutory interpretation: for *Chorlton v Lings* concerned the interpretation of two statutes, the one (Representation of the People Act, 1867) offering the vote to every 'Man' with ratable property, the other ('An Act for Shortening the Language used in Acts of

[27] Ibid 62.

[28] *Chorlton v Lings* [1868] 4 LR 374; see Sachs and Wilson, *Sexism and the Law* (1978) 22–5.

Parliament', 1850) passed to ensure that 'in all Acts Words importing the Masculine Gender shall be deemed and taken to include Females'. Yet in the Representation of the People Act, according to the court, 'Man' meant *man*, since there was no recorded instance of a woman voting in England since the sixteenth century. 'Uninterrupted usage' justified the continued withholding of the parliamentary franchise from women—and their exclusion from the legal profession.[29]

Pankhurst's legal studies would also have brought home to her the difficulty of women's having any influence at all on the law. Of course she knew that women were excluded from the parliamentary vote and the possibility of standing for parliament—that was why she had become involved in the women's suffrage campaign in the first place—and she was also well aware that they were barred from the legal professions of solicitor and barrister, for she herself had applied for membership of Lincoln's Inn and, despite the sponsorship of Lord Haldane, been refused. But at university she would have been reminded on a daily basis of the extent of women's isolation from the legal world. By the start of the twentieth century all British universities accepted women for their degree courses and all except Oxford and Cambridge granted them degrees. But at Manchester she was the only woman law student in the entire college. For three years she studied in classes without a single female colleague. All her teachers were, of course, male, and all her textbooks written by men. When she graduated, her appearance on the stage was met with a 'humorous hostile demonstration' (whatever that means) by her male fellow-graduands, as her sister Sylvia reported.[30]

Christabel Pankhurst had entered law school with faith in the rule of law: once, speaking at an Independent Labour Party conference, she had opposed a motion calling for direct action, arguing instead for obedience to the law, 'ordered propaganda' and the democracy of the ballot box.[31] Growing up with a lawyer father, she might have reasoned that, given a system as powerful and self-referential as law, only someone with insider knowledge and skills could hope to challenge and, ultimately, to change it. But she emerged from law school a militant, her belief in the potential of the law to reform itself exhausted. Under her direction, the militants adopted extra-legal tactics in desperation because more than half a century of peaceful campaigning had failed to secure the vote for English women.

So perhaps the most useful legacy Christabel Pankhurst took from her legal studies was an insight into the way the law worked. Feminists knew that women were discriminated against, and they knew why; but law school

[29] The same reasoning was employed in denying women the right to practise as solicitors. See *Bebb v Law Society* [1914] 1 Ch 286.

[30] S Pankhurst, *The Suffragette Movement* (London, Virago, 1977 [1931]) 214.

[31] Ibid 158.

gave Pankhurst an understanding of *how* this could happen in a legal system which professed justice and equality. A knowledge of substantive public and criminal law, though helpful as a guide to strategy, would not have proved as useful to the suffragettes as Pankhurst's grasp of how the legal processes worked in defence of men's interests. But perhaps even she was taken aback at the lack of legal protection the law offered to suffragettes apprehended by the police. Public opinion contended that violent actions deserved a violent response, but the suffragettes' heckling and assaults on property were met with much more vicious assaults on their persons. Women were seized by their breasts, dragged by their hair into waiting vans, force-fed with tubes pushed down their throats, while held down by prison guards—and the law did nothing to check this behaviour.[32]

As we know, the suffragettes' efforts helped secure the vote for (some) British women in 1918, and a year later, Parliament passed the Sex Disqualification (Removal) Act 1919, which obliged the Law Society and the Bar to admit women to their ranks. But, despite her brilliant degree, Christabel Pankhurst never entered legal practice. One cannot really be surprised. She stood once for Parliament, representing a 'Women's Party', was unsuccessful, and thereafter turned her attention to other crusades.[33] Other early women law students, however, persevered with the law. Even though some of them were now in their thirties or forties—Cornelia Sorabji was 54!—these persistent pioneers studied for the relevant professional examinations, registered their articles or joined their Inns and ate their dinners, simply in order to qualify and show that women—or they themselves—could do it. Some went on to practise; others not. Ivy Williams, the first English woman to be called to the Bar, became the first woman legal academic as tutor and lecturer at Oxford.[34]

In sum, then, this first stage of feminist involvement in the law schools was almost entirely one-way. Feminists looked to the law schools for the knowledge and skills they needed to understand the nature of the discrimination they suffered, and to help them to counter it. If the women accepted without question the conditions they were offered—institutional marginalisation, enforced ladylike behaviour, no influence whatsoever on curriculum or university customs, however alienating or discriminatory—this was because they simply could not afford to bite the hands that fed them. One must also bear in mind the *informal* education women university students would have obtained, in some ways even more useful than the formal

[32] R Fulford, *Votes for Women* (London, Faber, 1958); A Raeburn, *The Militant Suffragettes* (London, Michael Joseph, 1973); A Rosen, *Rise Up Women! The Militant Campaign of the Women's Social and Political Union, 1903–14* (London, RKP, 1974).

[33] Crawford, n 24.

[34] H Fox, 'Williams, Ivy' (2004) *Oxford Dictionary of National Biography*, www.oxforddnb.com; Auchmuty, n 1, 88–89.

instruction, such as the contact with a range of educated men and women with varying degrees of prejudice and politics, that enabled them to know their enemies as well as their friends, and the experience of communal life at the older universities in particular, with its comradeship and support, its freedom from family ties and burdens, and the college societies—the debating, the political, the mock parliament, the settlement work—that functioned not simply as diversion but as training for public life. All these gave those women who chose to work for women the confidence and ability to engage in the feminist struggle when they left college—as teachers, civil servants, MPs, businesswomen and, eventually, lawyers.

What the law schools got from the feminists seems, in contrast, minor. They benefited from a small number of dedicated, often very able students: of the first 12 students at Cambridge and Oxford, for example, five got firsts,[35] while at University College Eliza Orme carried off the Jurisprudence and Constitutional Law prizes.[36] Individual law teachers gave generously of their time and energies, but the institutions were content to contain any threat posed by the women students by denying them degrees or membership of the university at Cambridge and Oxford, where they also imposed quotas which continued until the 1950s;[37] other universities relied on the social obstacles to women embarking on law degrees, and the social pressure to conform to convention, to achieve the same limitations on feminist influence. What we see, in fact, especially at Cambridge and Oxford, is the control of any sympathetic individual members of the university (some of whom, like FW Maitland, fully deserve the label of 'feminist') by the most powerful stakeholders in the institution: the alumni, who dominated every quarter of British public life; the (male) undergraduate student body, many directly affected by and antagonistic to the female competition; and the body of academic staff, which included the usual quantity of conservatives and anti-feminists. As the secretary of the Oxford Society of [Women] Home Students observed in 1897:

> University men are not willing that women should share fully in the life of the universities. I don't mean to say they are not willing that women should go in for their examinations or have the advantages of the same education, because we know that they are, and since we began our work in Oxford we have all along been met with the greatest possible sympathy. But they are not willing that women shall share in the life of the University, or form part of the governing

[35] Auchmuty, n 1, 76–79.

[36] L Howsam, 'Orme, Eliza' (2004) *Oxford Dictionary of National Biography*, www.oxforddnb.com.

[37] H Hopkins, *The New Look: A Social History of the Forties and Fifties in Britain* (London, Secker & Warburg, 1964) 320.

> body, or be associated with men in all the higher work of the University… the fact remains that we are no more liked now than when we began.[38]

In short, the feminists needed the law schools, but the law schools did not need the feminists—yet.

CONTAINMENT AND MARGINALISATION, 1921–1970

With the opening of the legal profession to women in 1920, feminists entered a new stage in their relationship with the law schools. Though possession of a law degree was never a prerequisite for a career at law, it could at last lead to one, at least for those women law graduates with the necessary contacts; many were the fortunate daughters or sisters of lawyers who could obtain articles or pupillages for them.[39] As a consequence, more women began to enter law school, though only Cambridge, Oxford and London admitted significant numbers.[40] Even then, there were sufficiently few to ensure a tolerant acceptance that may have seemed idyllic in comparison with the hostility women met in the legal profession outside, but which was nonetheless uncomfortable. Evelyn Ellis, later professor of law at Birmingham, recalled that as late as the 1960s there were only eight women to about 200 male law students in her year at Cambridge; the education, she recalled, was superb, but the atmosphere distinctly unwelcoming.[41] Cambridge is notorious for its 10:1 quota for female students,[42] but other law schools almost certainly practised gender discrimination. Even allowing for parental or school discouragement of girls to apply to study law, had academic merit (that is, A-level grades, let alone any broader measure of ability) been the sole criterion for selection, there would have been many more women, probably a majority, in these years. Abel actually says as much: 'At first, much smaller proportions of women applicants than of men seem to have been accepted by university law departments, which is surprising, since women usually have better secondary school credentials.'[43]

To a feminist this is not at all surprising, since preference for male candidates is a normal feature of patriarchal societies, and even equal numbers of women can feel like 'too many' to threatened men. Clare

[38] Quoted in G Sutherland, 'The Plainest Principles of Justice: The University of London and the Higher Education of Women' in FML Thompson (ed), *The University of London and the World of Learning 1836–1986* (London, Hambledon Press, 1990) 43.

[39] Evidence from the College Registers of Cambridge and Oxford. Auchmuty, n 1, 91.

[40] Oxford, Cambridge and London between them accounted for about three-quarters of law students in the years before the Second World War. Abel, *The Legal Profession* (1988) 266.

[41] McGlynn, n 1.

[42] C Wells, 'The Remains of the Day: The Women Law Professors Project' in U Schultz and G Shaw (eds), *Women in the World's Legal Professions* (Oxford, Hart Publishing, 2003) 231.

[43] Abel, n 6, 276.

McGlynn reports anecdotal evidence that quotas of between ten and 25 per cent were routinely placed on female students.[44] As late as 1980 (that is, after the Sex Discrimination Act 1975 made it illegal), Ella Rule told the Association of Law Teachers that there was 'a tendency to discriminate against women on the ground that, if vacancies are in short supply, men should be favoured'.[45]

Women's participation in the law schools in this period is almost completely unresearched, largely because such male chroniclers as there have been have mostly failed to notice women's existence. As Carol Dyhouse has written: 'It is not so much that women's experiences were consciously edited out of history, rather that a whole dimension of women's separate experiences, history and traditions had never been fully visible to male observers.'[46] Anyone reading the literature of the interwar and immediate postwar decades will be struck by the repeated references to 'gentlemen' when speaking of lawyers and law teachers[47] and 'men' in the case of students.[48] Rick Abel's chapter of the growth of academic institutions in his 1988 book, *The Legal Profession of England and Wales,* notes that, despite the entry of women into law teaching, 'none of the recent empirical studies has thought to describe this important change'.[49] Guy Neave's chapter on the development of law in higher education between 1950 and 1986 gives no information on the proportion of women entrants into, or graduates from, UK law schools prior to 1970, when the figures were 23 per cent for entrants and 17.2 per cent for graduates.[50] The statistics were simply not available. We know, however, that the proportion of women students in English and Welsh universities as a whole actually *declined* between 1920 and 1939, from 24 per cent to 23 per cent of the student body, while that of women academics remained the same in the 1970s as it had been in the 1920s![51] Looking back, Katherine O'Donovan

[44] C McGlynn, 'The Status of Women Lawyers in the United Kingdom' in Schultz and Shaw (eds), *Women in the World's Legal Professions* (2003) 145.

[45] E Rule, 'The Prospects for Women Law Graduates' in M Slade (ed), *Law in Higher Education into the 1980s* (Bristol, Association of Law Teachers, 1980) 32.

[46] Dyhouse, *No Distinction of Sex* (1995) 245.

[47] The Society of Public Law Teachers was open to 'gentlemen' and, in fact, excluded women until 1948. Abel, n 6, 267; F Cownie and R Cocks, *'A Great and Noble Occupation': the History of the Society of Legal Scholars* (Oxford, Hart Publishing, 2009) 57–8, 67–8.

[48] Eg 'The great virtue of the tutorial system is that it teaches men to write.' PB Carter, 'Law at Oxford: Miscellaneous Comments' (1955) 5 *Journal of the SPTL* 126; 'It should be borne in mind that among the persons reading law would be some of the ablest young men in the country' CJ Hamson, 'Law Teaching Methods at Cambridge' (1955) 5 *Journal of the SPTL* 161.

[49] Abel, n 6, 267. Abel himself has always done his best to redress this lack.

[50] G Neave, 'From the Other End of the Telescope: Deprofessionalization, Reprofessionalization, and the Development of Higher Education, 1950–1986' in Abel and Lewis (eds), *Lawyers in Society III* (1989) 184, 18x.

[51] Dyhouse, n 10, 17, 138.

(later professor of law at Queen Mary College, London) recalled that she was never taught by a woman law teacher, nor ever met one.[52]

In the legal profession, too, women failed to make the expected progress. If the first-wave feminists had looked forward to a time when feminist legal reform would be led from within by women lawyers, they were quickly disappointed. As Pearson and Sachs point out, women soon discovered that '[t]he removal of legal impediments [to becoming lawyers] was not the same as creating equal opportunities'.[53] By the time of women's admission to the profession in 1920, feminism was in retreat, and it took all the new female lawyers' energies simply to keep their practices going in the face of a level of misogyny and professional discrimination that seems shocking today but was simply taken for granted then.

Unsurprisingly, then, the period between the end of the first wave of feminism and the start of the second wave in the late 1960s is generally considered a fallow period for feminism. The history of this half-century demonstrates how feminism, being an outsider movement, constantly has to re-invent itself; it has no stable, continuous history because its achievements never enter reproducible knowledge—they are, indeed, deliberately erased or reconstructed in safe, non-radical forms with the feminist agency removed.[54] Those of us who have lived through the second wave of feminism will recognise the features of a 'post-feminist' society such as those which followed the granting of the vote to women in 1918, since we are living in such a period today: the assumption, made by conservatives and feminists alike, that with full civil rights women are now 'equal' (or have even 'gone too far' and that *men* are now discriminated against); the mainstreaming of feminist activity in parliament, professional associations and other mixed-sex bodies; the faith in gradual progress and the 'trickle-up' effect—followed by slow disillusionment and the realisation that formal equality does not necessarily bring substantive equality in its train, that women's voices are all too easily drowned out and women's needs ignored in mixed settings, and that invisible, informal barriers are much harder to break down (even to recognise) than the open discrimination of the past. This picture describes both women's experience of higher education and their experience of the legal profession in the interwar and postwar period.

[52] McGlynn, n 1, 61.

[53] R Pearson and A Sachs, 'Barristers and Gentlemen: A Critical Look at Sexism in the Legal Profession' (1980) 43 *Modern Law Review* 405.

[54] We are often told, for example, that it was the government's appreciation of women's work in the First World War that won them the vote—not the feminist campaigns conducted so assiduously for over 60 years! For a more recent example, here is Mark Thompson, *Modern Land Law*, 3rd edn (Oxford, Oxford University Press, 2006) on the Married Women's Property Acts: '[P]ressure grew for the establishment of the principle of separate ownership of property between spouses. Success came with the enactment of the Married Women's Property Act of 1882' (269). No mention of where the pressure came from, or why.

Unfortunately, in the absence of an organised women's movement, there were no recognised alternative standards against which women could measure the shortcomings of the law school or professional experience, nor any easy way to validate any unarticulated alienation or discomfort they might feel.

Yet the interwar women lawyers still managed to keep feminism alive in small but significant ways. Unable to exert much influence on mainstream law, they saw their role as opening doors for other women, networking and political lobbying, and disseminating and demystifying legal knowledge to women and other outsider groups. We can see these goals in operation in the life and career of Helena Normanton. Admitted to Middle Temple 'within hours' of the passing of the Sex Disqualification (Removal) Act, she was called to the Bar in 1922, worked up a busy practice—'everything from divorce to murder'—and taught history part-time at the Universities of Glasgow and London.[55] Later, as President of the Married Women's Association, Normanton fought for the right of married women to keep their maiden name for professional purposes (as she herself had done) and for divorce law reform. This led to a break with the Married Women's Association in 1952 after some members accused her of an 'anti-man' policy. She thereupon set up the Council of Married Women. Separate professional bodies of this kind not only performed important support, mentoring and networking roles for women excluded from or marginalised in the male professional associations, but also acted as lobby groups and consultants for government inquiries and commissions seeking the 'woman's point of view'. This was the form that professional feminism took at the time and Normanton's legal training and status as a practising barrister equipped her well for the task. An Associate Grand Dame of the International Society of Women Lawyers, President of the Federation of Business and Professional Women, Normanton was an archetypal 'equal rights' feminist of the interwar and immediate postwar period.

Alongside networking and lobbying, the other form that legal feminism took between the wars was the dissemination of legal knowledge to women. Rather like a law school for the masses, this movement was characterised by articles in the women's pages of newspapers and magazines and a range of popular texts on how law affected women in their everyday lives. Although we never hear of them today, Maud I Crofts' *Women Under English Law*,[56] Helena Normanton's *Everyday Law for Women*,[57] Erna Reiss's *Rights*

[55] NA Franz, *English Women Enter the Professions* (Cincinnati, Ohio, privately printed, 1965) 282.

[56] MI Crofts, *Women Under English Law* (London, National Council of Women of Great Britain, 1925). As Maud Ingram, she had been one of the four litigants in *Bebb v Law Society* [1914] 1 Ch 286 challenging the Law Society's denial of admission to women.

[57] H Normanton, *Everyday Law for Women* (London, Ivor Nicholson and Watson, 1932).

and Duties of Englishwomen: A Study of Law and Public Opinion[58] and Florence Earengey's *A Milk-White Lamb: The Legal and Economic Status of Women*[59] were examples of volumes intended to instruct readers on the legal position on women (in the case of Normanton's book, on *everything* legal a woman needed to know, from the traffic laws to the trust), and to direct their attention to areas in need of reform. This dual goal put them in the same tradition as the writings of Bodichon and Norton and, like them, demonstrated the shortcomings of formal legal education as far as feminists were concerned. The difference was that these new works were written by women *lawyers* and intended to empower women, not to persuade the male voters and lawmakers upon whose support the Victorian feminists depended. This established a tradition, picked up again by the women's liberation movement later, of writing by women, for women, on women's legal position and rights, creating a separate legal culture because the real one was hostile and inaccessible.

THE RISE OF A FEMINIST CRITIQUE, 1971–1990

All this was to change when the coincidence of three developments in the late 1960s altered irrevocably the relationship of feminism to the law school. The first was the move, following increased numbers of applications to the professions of barrister and solicitor, to change them into *graduate* professions. The second was the expansion of higher education that began in the late 1960s and has continued inexorably to the present, the result of successive governments' wish to increase the pool of skilled labour in the UK.[60] The third, of course, was the rise of the women's liberation movement: the 'second wave' of feminism.

Other scholars have written in detail about the first two developments. Rick Abel notes that, as far as the law schools were concerned, the expansion from the late sixties up to the mid-eighties was almost entirely due to the increasing numbers of women students being admitted.[61] Where, in 1967, only 17 per cent of students coming into the university law schools were women, by 1978 this proportion had risen to 39 per cent and, by 1983, 45 per cent. The change in the polytechnics was even more dramatic, from 11 per cent female law students in 1967 to 46 per cent in 1983.[62]

[58] E Reiss, *Rights and Duties of Englishwomen: A Study of Law and Public Opinion* (Manchester, Sherratt and Hughes, 1934).

[59] F Earengey, *A Milk-White Lamb: The Legal and Economic Status of Women* (London, National Council of Women of Great Britain, 1949).

[60] V Coppock, D Hayden and I Richter, *The Illusions of 'Post-Feminism': New Women, Old Myths* (London, Taylor & Francis, 1995) 47–8.

[61] Abel, n 6, 277.

[62] Ibid 276.

Since 1988, there have been more women law students in England and Wales than men.[63] Today women make up two-thirds of all law students.[64] This transformation of the law student body has created a whole different set of conditions within which feminists must operate.

Rick Abel comments that '[t]he growth of academic legal education has had one unambiguous effect: it opened the profession to women. The academy, as an ostensibly meritocratic institution, has always been somewhat more cautious about engaging in explicit discrimination.'[65] On the contrary, as we have seen, what brought the discrimination in university admissions to an end was the need to expand higher education combined with a changing social climate about women's place, the latter being almost wholly due to feminist influence. After 1975, sex discrimination in education and employment was forbidden by law[66] though it could—and did—legitimately continue at the self-employed Bar, which was exempt from the legislation. In 1978 Helena Kennedy was driven to write a scathing condemnation of the 'no-women' policy of many Chambers, as well as the masculine culture that made life so difficult for those women who did manage to get in.[67]

In Britain the women's liberation movement made its first real impact with the publication of the first four demands in 1970.[68] In the following year, two central texts of the movement appeared: Kate Millett's *Sexual Politics*[69] and Germaine Greer's *The Female Eunuch*.[70] The feminist journal *Spare Rib* followed in 1972. By this time it was virtually impossible for a female undergraduate to remain untouched by feminism, whether she subscribed to its tenets or not. However conventional the law schools (and they *were* conventional), the wider social environment heightened women's consciousness to the extent that they could no longer accept the terms on which their presence had been tolerated for so long.

Hilary Mantel entered the London School of Economics in 1970. 'My course was law, and my burning desire for equity made me peculiarly unsuited to the subject,' was her ironic recollection.[71] The course was interesting, the teaching excellent; she did well in her first year. But what good was a law degree to a woman?

[63] McGlynn, n 1, 7.

[64] McGlynn, n 44, 145.

[65] Abel, n 6, 276.

[66] Sex Discrimination Act 1975.

[67] H Kennedy, 'Women at the Bar' in R Hazell (ed), *The Bar on Trial* (London, Quartet Books, 1978) 148.

[68] These were for equal pay, equal education and job opportunities, 24-hour childcare, and free contraception and abortion on demand.

[69] K Millett, *Sexual Politics* (London, Rupert Hart-Davis, 1971).

[70] G Greer, *The Female Eunuch* (London, Granada, 1971).

[71] H Mantel, *Giving Up the Ghost: A Memoir* (London, Harper, 2004) 154.

> I wanted to be a barrister. How was I to do this? The facts of life pressed in on me. I was female, northern and poor. My family would not be able to help me through my post-graduate studies, or my pupillage—that is to say, the barrister's apprenticeship. Women barristers were then in a small minority. A few brave women from unhelpful backgrounds had crashed the system. I had assumed I would be one of them. But now my resolve was undermined.[72]

In her second year she transferred to Sheffield to be near her boyfriend. There she encountered a very different learning milieu. At LSE there had been five women lecturers (out of 31) in the Law School, one of them the distinguished feminist Olive Stone. At Sheffield there were only two (out of 22).[73] She was taught by 'a bored local solicitor who made it plain that he didn't think women had any place in his classroom'. Looking back, she comments:

> Some people have forgotten, or never known, why we needed the feminist movement so badly. This was why: so that some talentless prat in a nylon shirt couldn't patronise you, while around you the spotty boys smirked and giggled, trying to worm into his favour.[74]

These were the years when women seeking legal work were routinely asked about their plans for marriage or 'starting a family',[75] when the Bar Council cheerfully admitted—even tried to justify—its members' discrimination against women.[76] Within the academic profession, however, these more blatant forms of discrimination had perforce to come to an end; yet women were still kept in their place by a range of subtle (and not so subtle) techniques including the private put-down, the public humiliation, the accidental overlooking, the deliberate ignoring, and the consistent undervaluing.[77] Women continued to be sexualised, stereotyped and excluded from what Angela Montgomery described as the 'male club'. In her first post: 'The Senior Common Room was like a public schoolboys' tea party: they would

[72] Ibid 157.

[73] *Commonwealth Universities Yearbook* (London, Association of Commonwealth Universities, 1970), entries for London School of Economics and University of Sheffield.

[74] Ibid 160.

[75] As Mantel found, ibid 161.

[76] 'Questions concerning matrimony and childbirth, when asked of potential pupils or tenants, inevitably give rise to bitter resentment, but they may only reflect the genuine anxiety of a Head [of] Chambers to avoid a sudden and disastrous exodus of established practitioners in later years. Such anxiety may even lead to a reluctance to offer tenancies to individual women so as to avoid a concentration of women at a given level in Chambers, or indeed to take on more than a specific number of women in total.' Statement by the Bar Council quoted by E Rule, 'The Prospects for Women Law Graduates', n 43, 35. Alas, this is not the place to deconstruct this tortuous and illogical piece of self-justification.

[77] For descriptions and analysis of these phenomena, see M Thornton, *Dissonance and Distrust: Women in the Legal Profession* (Melbourne, Oxford University Press, 1996) and Wells, n 3.

read the *Times* and it was clear they did not want to be joined and that this was definitely their territory.'[78]

This kind of discrimination was much more difficult to fight because it was covert, not overt. Contrasting her experience as a lecturer with her days as a law student, Montgomery noted:

> In my undergraduate department there was the clear acknowledgement of difference: women were different, black people were different. We were certainly marginalized, but at the same time our difference was recognized. In the department I then entered as a member of staff, they were so apparently 'right on' that there was no difference acknowledged, and this became more of a problem than the earlier marginalization had been.[79]

The invisibility of discrimination in a self-identified egalitarian setting continues to be a problem for women today.

In the early years of the second-wave women's movement legal feminism largely operated outside the established institutions, both in education and in law. Feminists united around the specific demands of the women's liberation movement, many of which were legal in form—equal pay, abortion law reform, an end to violence against women—in loosely organised, non-hierarchical and carefully targeted associations. The feminist theorising of this time was once again closely linked to feminist action (for example, in campaigns against rape and pornography) and practically all of it took place outside the law school, in women's groups or women's studies classes.[80] The latter, initially concentrated in the non-vocational adult education sector in Britain, began to enter higher education in the 1970s.[81] When some legal academics became involved in these interdisciplinary courses, they were taunted and 'accused of teaching knitting', recalled Katherine O'Donovan, who taught on the MA Women's Studies at Kent.[82] But for many such women, the admission of feminist critiques into their professional work was transforming. 'In the writings of the women's movement, I found a self who had long been suppressed,' wrote O'Donovan. 'It is difficult now to convey the sense that many of us had in reading that, "this is about me"'.[83] The next step was to incorporate these feminist understandings into disciplines. Cautiously, but with increasing deliberateness and confidence, feminist

[78] A Montgomery, 'In Law and Outlaw? The tale of a journey' in L Stanley (ed), *Knowing Feminisms: On Academic Borders, Territories and Tribes* (London, Sage, 1997) 59.

[79] Ibid 60.

[80] J Radford, 'History of Women's Liberation Movements in Britain: A Reflective Personal History' in G Griffin et al (eds), *Stirring It: Challenges for Feminism* (London, Taylor & Francis, 1994) 40; G Griffin (ed) *Feminism Activism in the 1990s* (London, Taylor & Francis, 1997).

[81] A Warwick and R Auchmuty, 'Women's Studies as Feminist Activism' in Griffin (ed) *Feminist Activism in the 1990s* (1997) 182.

[82] McGlynn, n 1, 62.

[83] Ibid.

academics began to use feminist ideas, content and analysis in literature, history, sociology and, eventually, law courses. Feminism at last entered the legal curriculum.

Law students had generally avoided women's studies; once it came to them, however, a small but eager minority snapped up the 'Women and Law' options that focused on ways law affected women in particular areas of their lives such as domestic violence and discrimination in the workplace. As the feminist critiques of law became more sophisticated, the courses moved on to problematising the construction of legal knowledge generally.[84] They drew on a range of other disciplinary tools, a radical departure for a subject so famous for its refusal to look beyond itself. Later 'gender' replaced 'women' as the operating principle and, in spite of fears to the contrary, the safer name did not mean that the scholarship lost its feminist edge.[85]

Feminist teachers were able to capitalise on the huge increase in female students in the legal academy. Between 1970 and 1988, four times as many additional women students entered universities as men.[86] Higher numbers do not pre-suppose greater receptivity to feminist ideas but they do make it easier to talk about women's experience and to justify doing so in the context of legal studies. An important group within this female influx were, moreover, feminist activists who, just as first-wave feminists like Christabel Pankhurst had done eighty years before, turned to the law school to obtain the knowledge or qualifications that would enable them to progress the feminist cause more effectively. I myself was one of these mature entrants; so too was Elizabeth Woodcraft, now Deputy Head of Tooks Chambers. An Essex girl from a working-class family, in the mid-1970s Woodcraft was a national co-ordinator for the Women's Aid Federation.

> I worked closely with Jo Richardson MP on her Domestic Violence and Matrimonial Proceedings Bill, which was a major breakthrough in legislation for women by permitting the police to become involved in the civil world of injunctions. I so much enjoyed this part of the work that instead of returning to teaching I decided to read for the Bar.[87]

Once qualified, as a criminal barrister Woodcraft represented women defendants including Greenham Common demonstrators and wives accused of beating their husbands, but eventually 'came to find crime an inhospitable

[84] A Bottomley, 'Feminism in Law Schools' in the *University College, London, Faculty of Laws Working Paper No 5* (London, UCL, 1987) 7.

[85] 'In the 1980s there has been a tendency for these courses to be watered down into "Gender and the Law" in some institutions.' JA Scutt, 'Women and the Law' in C Kramarae and D Spender (eds), The *Knowledge Explosion: Generations of Feminist Scholarship* (Hemel Hempstead, Harvester Wheatsheaf, 1993) 208.

[86] Wells, n 3, 8.

[87] McGlynn, n 1, 140.

area of law for me as a woman'.[88] She now works entirely in family law, which 'is often seen as the natural home or ghetto for women barristers,' she admits, 'but I made a positive, political choice to do this type of work'.[89]

For Elizabeth Woodcraft, as for Christabel Pankhurst, legal training was a means to a feminist end; a former Chair of the women's legal advice charity Rights of Women, she continues to see her role as a dual one: in court, representing women and children and trying to influence the law in feminist directions while, outside it, providing legal advice to rights organizations, being 'part of a wider process of changing things'.[90]

As the numbers of women law students increased, so too did the numbers of women law teachers, though much more slowly. The *Commonwealth Universities Yearbook* recorded a total of three women law lecturers in England and Wales in 1948; ten years later there were ten; by 1970 there were 36; and by 1975, by which time the first woman professor had been appointed, 62.[91] In 1981 women law teachers formed a support group to help deal with the frustration and alienation many felt in their male-dominated institutions.[92] Professor Nicola Lacey has paid tribute to the way the Women Law Teachers Group gave her an interest in issues of gender and law.[93] Angela Montgomery, however, left law teaching altogether. 'Things have got to change a very great deal for these to become safer institutions for women,' she wrote. 'Higher education is much more discriminatory against women than any other form of professional employment.'[94]

A SHIFTING BALANCE OF POWER, 1991 TO THE PRESENT

While developments in other jurisdictions were similar,[95] the English experience received a wholly unexpected boost in the 1990s with the advent of the Research Assessment Exercise (RAE). This involved the government undertaking an investigation, using senior academic assessors, of the quality of research in participating university departments, with significant financial rewards for those reaching the highest levels. Two factors in this exercise affected the incorporation of feminist ideas into the legal curriculum. The first was that the RAE refused to recognise a category of women's studies research. This meant that all those scholars engaged in inter-disciplinary

[88] Ibid.
[89] Ibid 141.
[90] Ibid.
[91] *Commonwealth Universities Yearbooks* (1948, 1958, 1970, 1975). The first woman law professor was Claire Palley at Kent (and previously at Queen's University, Belfast).
[92] Abel, n 6, 267.
[93] N Lacey, *Unspeakable Subjects: Feminist Essays in Legal and Social Theory* (Oxford, Hart Publishing, 1998) ix, 1.
[94] Montgomery, n 78, 71.
[95] See, eg Thornton, *Dissonance and Distrust* (1996).

feminist research were forced back into their subject-specific disciplines. The academic lawyers thus returned to legal research. The second was that departments set about attracting more active researchers in order to attract more funding from the government. Feminist legal scholars working unappreciated in some academic backwater, and feminist spokeswomen working outside the universities altogether, suddenly found themselves sought after. They rose quickly through the academic ranks. As Celia Wells noted:

> This new accountability, where public funding comes to be directly affected by teaching and research performance, meant that there were more powerful incentives to refine discriminatory practices. The very successful women who had not been promoted became suddenly valued by their own institutions or poached by others.[96]

The post-1992 universities were particularly open to feminist new blood, either not appreciating, or not caring, that they were welcoming highly radical influences into the fold: all that mattered was that the newcomers published a lot of good research. And it helped that many were experienced teachers and organisers as well. But 'old' universities, too, which might in earlier decades have preferred men as a matter of course, realised that they had more to gain from accepting the most talented applicants for lectureships even if they were women—*even* feminists. Professor Jo Shaw, for instance, wrote that she was 'plucked from obscurity and caught on the waves of market forces crashing against the bulwarks of tradition and convention in the universities as the impact of the RAE began to gather strength'.[97]

The effect of this legitimisation of feminist legal research cannot be overstated. If women's studies as a separate discipline was profoundly weakened, the energy which had gone into it was now channelled into feminist perspectives on the traditional disciplines. This forced a recognition of feminist scholarship on departments which had hitherto ignored it, including law schools. Research clusters sprang up, of which the first, Liverpool University's Feminist Legal Research Unit, was formed in 1993. In the same year, Britain's first feminist legal journal, *Feminist Legal Studies,* began publication from the University of Kent. A conference on Women and the Law was organized by Clare McGlynn at Durham in 1996. Also in 1996, Anne Bottomley's edited collection *Feminist Perspectives on the Foundational Subjects of Law*[98] inaugurated an ongoing 'Feminist Perspectives' series focusing on the whole range of areas taught on the law degree.

Feminist studies came late to the legal curriculum, but once arrived, they flourished. By 1996 15 law schools offered Women/Gender and Law

[96] Wells, n 3.
[97] Ibid 58.
[98] London, Cavendish Publishing, 1996.

courses; two years later, the figure was 24—one-third of all law schools in the country.[99] In 1996 the University of Hertfordshire recruited Professor Robyn Martin to set up the first LLM in Gender and Law, and the following year, the University of Westminster, which as the Polytechnic of Central London had pioneered postgraduate women's studies teaching in the early 1970s, instituted an LLM Women and Law. Some law schools became known precisely for their gender work: in the 1990s, for example, Keele developed an expertise in gender, sexuality and law that was to lead to an international reputation for first-class scholarship.

In spite of these achievements, by the late 1990s a sense of despair permeated feminist academe. Women remained marginalised in the curriculum and the institution itself, and nothing the feminists accomplished seemed to move them any closer to justice and equality. 'Despite the fact that half the "consumers" (as students are now termed) are female, the curriculum in many universities remains tuned to the person as male, and the core individual of western liberal higher education as the male citizen', wrote Mary Evans, a pioneer of women's studies at the University of Kent, in 1997.[100] The Hansard Society reported that 'the proportion of women in senior academic posts is derisory', singling out Oxford and Cambridge for particular attack: 'It is wholly unacceptable that the centres of modern academic teaching and excellence in Britain remain bastions of male power and privilege'.[101]

In the law schools, women might form an even higher proportion of the students, but the ratio was still not reflected in the staff, especially at senior level. In 1998 women made up 39 per cent of law school teachers, but only 14 per cent of professors.[102] This meant that if a law school had any woman law professor, she was probably the only one. There were 55 women law professors in 2000, most of whom would 'have spent their entire careers in this kind of isolated position',[103] wrote Celia Wells, speaking from personal experience; but 60 per cent of law schools had *never* had a woman chair. Nor had the curriculum changed in any fundamental way to take account of women's experiences and concerns. Almost uniquely in academic writing, the pronoun 'he' continued to do service for men *and* women in law textbooks; family law was still not compulsory; and the law school remained resistant to the findings of feminist scholarship. Certainly,

[99] McGlynn, n 1, 14.

[100] M Evans, 'Negotiating the Frontier: Women and Resistance in the Contemporary Academy' (1997) in L Stanley (ed), *Knowing Feminisms* 49.

[101] *The Report of the Hansard Society Commission on Women on Top* (London, Hansard Society, 1990) 10–11.

[102] McGlynn, n 1, 20. The national average of women professors in all disciplines was 8%, Wells, n 3.

[103] Wells, n 42.

women were not overlooked in the way they used to be—this would be difficult in classes that might number only one or two men—but

> we have not seen a fundamental reconceptualisation of the legal subject, from the ground up—from his lace-up shoes to his collar and tie. A century ago there was little doubt that he possessed masculine attributes: legal discourse was explicitly and unashamedly oriented towards men. Now the legal subject is also supposed to be a woman and yet the jurisprudence of the twenty-first century does not reflect this sex change.[104]

Although Ngaire Naffine tried to make a virtue out of feminists' outsider status, the prevailing tone of turn-of-the-century feminist legal writing was pessimistic, even desperate in tone. 'Women remain fringe-dwellers of the jurisprudential community almost a century after being "let in"', declared Margaret Thornton.[105]

Perhaps, however, this pessimism was but the darkness before the dawn. If we focus on the achievements of the last forty years instead of the deficits, it is possible to paint a much more hopeful picture. Women may not be equally represented yet among law teachers in the British universities but, glancing down the staff lists, one can see that very few law schools have remained untouched by feminist scholarship. Where in the 1990s we were thinly scattered across the country, today most institutions have a significant grouping of established feminist legal scholars, including many at the most senior level. Several of these women are, or have been, Heads of School or Department; the number of law professors with feminist credentials increases year on year, many to my knowledge having been head-hunted for their research and management or entrepreneurial skills. Women who produce feminist legal work now occupy the highest positions in professional bodies such as the Society of Legal Scholars, the Socio-Legal Studies Association and the Research Committee for the Sociology of Law. They edit top legal journals. They sit on the boards and panels of funding bodies such as the Arts and Humanities Research Council and the Economic and Social Research Council. They are members—indeed, Chairs—of RAE panels, the very arbiters of what constitutes high-quality legal research: Celia Wells was the Chair of the 2008 Law sub-panel. These roles are valued by law schools as markers of scholarly output; they count towards research excellence scores and consequently help to bring status and, perhaps most importantly, *money* to the institution. And should this catalogue of senior successes suggest that feminists are confined to the higher levels of the law school, and that feminism in the academy will die out when the current generation retires, note should be had of the Feminist Judgments project inaugurated in 2008 by Clare McGlynn, Rosemary Hunter and Erika

[104] N Naffine, 'In Praise of Legal Feminism' (2002) 22 *Legal Studies* 73.
[105] M Thornton, n 77, 3.

Rackley, whose participants number over 40 women of all age groups from universities across the UK.

The result is that law schools formerly uninterested in, or even hostile to, feminist work have been forced to put away their prejudices and appoint feminist scholars because their usefulness outweighs any personal distrust or distaste. The process that began with the first RAE of 1992 has accelerated beyond our wildest imagination. In particular, the invisible barrier of 'sufficient presence' seems to have broken down in many institutions: instead of calling a halt after one or two appointments, we see law schools like Keele and Kent building on their reputations for this kind of scholarship by adding feminist after feminist to the department. In 2003, the Arts and Humanities Research Council funded a Centre for Law, Gender and Sexuality—a joint enterprise between Keele, Kent and Westminster law schools—to the tune of a million pounds. From the time the Centre took up residence at Kent, no fewer than *five* feminist law professors have joined a department which already had one—which in the past would have been quite enough.

There can be no doubt that the influx of academics doing feminist work has been an unsettling process for many British law schools. Although there cannot be many institutions where feminists (or even women) are in a majority, nevertheless their presence *en bloc* has been known to cause resentment among some scholars doing conventional work. More commonly, however, resistance takes the form of simply ignoring the *content* of feminists' work, whilst accepting its institutional usefulness. This behaviour is widespread. Despite the prolific output of the feminists and its frequent high quality, mainstream legal scholarship often proceeds with barely a reference to it, or none at all. As I have remarked on earlier occasions, there is legal scholarship and there is *feminist* legal scholarship and, while the latter takes account perforce of the former, engagement in the other direction is rare—and always optional.[106] Nevertheless, though many mainstream scholars regard feminist work as marginal, partial or self-serving, Directors of Research could not afford to ignore the broad-based composition and guidelines of the RAE's law panel, which positively encouraged socio-legal and feminist work, or the experience of law schools like Keele, whose strong gender and sexuality submission won it a rare top score in the 2001 RAE. Law schools now realise that they must accept the feminist work even if they dislike it.

Perhaps the most significant victory for feminism has been the appointment in 2003 of the first woman Law Lord, Brenda Hale, a former legal academic *and a feminist*, co-author of one of the first second-wave studies

[106] Auchmuty, 'Agenda for a Feminist Legal Curriculum' (2003) 393.

of women and law.[107] Her judgments have already made a difference in the law, and her senior role means that her feminist analysis cannot simply be ignored. Perhaps her presence will help to erode the entrenched marginalisation of feminist scholarship in the academy which sits so oddly alongside the increasing institutional importance of feminists themselves. For feminists now provide a significant research contribution in most law schools. They occupy senior management posts in many. They design and teach innovative courses—and teach traditional courses in innovative ways—that are popular with an increasingly diverse, not to say increasingly *female*, student body. In order to sustain an argument that the modern law school needs feminists as much as feminists need law schools, one has only to ask: what would happen to the law schools if all the feminists were, at a stroke, removed? It's a prospect that would terrify most law school heads, if they ever thought about it.

CONCLUSION

This chapter has tried to demonstrate that feminists are indeed stakeholders in the law schools of England and Wales at the present time. We are essential to their successful operation in all aspects of their work: research, teaching, management and pastoral care. But in terms of *our* personal stake in the institution, we have an even more important role to play: as role-models and transmitters of the feminist message. We educate future generations of lawyers, judges and policy-makers, and some of us help to influence the law-making processes through our academic and policy writings and as members of strategic and consultative bodies. The law school provides us with valuable freedom to incorporate our politics into our work, and for this we must be grateful.

But much remains to be done to make law schools genuinely hospitable to feminists. First, they need to take on board what we are actually *saying*. It is shocking that mainstream legal scholarship—even legal textbooks for students—can continue to ignore feminist understandings and theories, yet still be regarded as 'excellent'. Feminism is not just a point of view, it is a critical analysis that demands consideration and engagement.

A second requirement of the law school is that it reform its workplace practices. A considerable body of evidence attests to the persisting discrimination against women in the legal academy in terms of appointments, pay, promotions, work allocation and, above all, *recognition*.[108] This must change if the law schools want our labour. Now that we are becoming invaluable to our institutions, we need to start flexing our muscles.

[107] S Atkins and B Hoggett, *Women and the Law* (Oxford, Basil Blackwell, 1984).
[108] See n 3.

Thirdly, law schools have yet to respond properly to the astonishing feminisation of the law student body in the last forty years. After a hundred years of marginalisation and containment, women's position in the legal academy has been completely reversed, so that today we teach a majority—in some institutions, a *huge* majority—of women students. Yet our successful female graduates planning to be lawyers will emerge from the law school into a professional world which, if not actually hostile to women, is still set in intolerant and discriminatory ways. Twenty years ago Rick Abel observed that, since female students got better degrees on average than men,[109] 'to the extent that women lawyers fail to attain the same professional rewards as men, the obstacles must be located in the post-academic stages of their careers'.[110] We need to prepare the women entrants to deal with the obstacles they will face. The 'egalitarian' law schools have ignored this problem up to now, by their complacency contributing to women's general disempowerment in law. In an era of greater accountability, they can no longer afford to do this: they must address the needs of their women graduates before the new culture of complaints and compensation catches them out. Feminists are undoubtedly best suited for the role of providing women students with the necessary tools of analysis and strategy; indeed, most of us are already engaged in this process.

I suspect, however, that the law schools will not change until the legal profession does. The law degree has the closest relationship to its eponymous profession of all university degrees, as Wells points out.[111] At present it is all too easy to justify perpetuation of the old 'core curriculum' of the law degree, or even to strengthen it with professional demands for *more* business law and the like, and *less* of the 'irrelevant' socio-legal and critical theoretical nonsense; and it is all too difficult for feminists and others to mainstream the latter, when students do not perceive it as necessary or even useful for legal practice. Fortunately, the professions do seem to be waking up to the importance of gender issues; the Bar has recognised the level of harassment and misogyny that aspiring women barristers face,[112] and the Law Society has made itself aware of the reasons why so many women solicitors 'drop out'.[113] The judiciary too is making strenuous efforts to move with the times, with the introduction of an appointments board to

[109] As they still do. McGlynn, n 44, 145.

[110] Abel, n 6, 279.

[111] Wells, n 3.

[112] See conclusions in J Shapland and A Sorsby, *Starting Practice: Work and Training at the Junior Bar* (Sheffield, Institute for the Study of the Legal Profession, 1995); and for comment, *New Law Journal* (May 1995) 621, 626, 665.

[113] See L Duff and L Webley, *Women Solicitors: Equality and Diversity* (London, Law Society of England and Wales, 2003), commissioned to explain this problem; and L Webley and L Duff 'Women Solicitors as a Barometer for Problems within the Legal Profession—Time to Put Values Before Profits' (2007) 34 *Journal of Law and Society* 374.

replace the old boys' network of personal recommendations, and compulsory education on sensitive matters like race, gender and sexuality.[114] These reforms have not simply occurred because the professions somehow became more tolerant and inclusive, though no doubt the official histories will represent them in this light; they were a response to the damning findings of feminist legal researchers like Clare McGlynn,[115] Hilary Sommerlad,[116] Kate Malleson,[117] Liz Duff and Lisa Webley.[118] The truth is that the legal profession needs feminists as much as the law schools do.

[114] K Malleson, 'Promoting Diversity in the Judiciary: Reforming the Judicial Appointments Process' in P Thomas (ed), *Discriminating Lawyers* (London, Cavendish Press, 2000) 221; K Malleson and F Banda, 'Factors Affecting the Decision to Apply for Silk and Judicial Office' (2000) Lord Chancellor's Department Research Series 2/00; K Malleson, 'Judging Judicial Review: Criteria for Judicial Appointment' in R Gordon (ed), *Judicial Review in the New Millennium* (London, Sweet & Maxwell, 2003) 19; K Malleson, 'Gender Equality in the Judiciary: Why Difference Won't Do' (2003) 11 *Feminist Legal Studies 1*; K Malleson, 'Prospects for Parity: The Position of Women in the Judiciary in England and Wales' in G Shaw and U Shultz (eds), *Women in the World's Legal Professions* (Oxford, Hart Publishing, 2003) 175; K Malleson, 'Rethinking the Merit Principle in Judicial Selection' (2006) 33 *Journal of Law and Society* 126; K Malleson, 'The Judcial Appointments Commission in England and Wales: New Wine in Old Bottles? in K Malleson and P Russell (eds), *Appointing Judges in an Age of Judicial Power: Critical Perspectives from Around the World* (Toronto, Toronto UP, 2006) ch 2.

[115] 'Soliciting Equality—the Way Forward' (1995) 145 *New Law Journal* 1065, 1070; 'Sex Discrimination at the Margins' (1996) 146 *New Law Journal* 379; 'Paying for Equality' (1997) 147 *New Law Journal* 568; 'The Business of Equality' in C McGlynn (ed) *Legal Feminisms: Theory and Practice* (Aldershot, Dartmouth, 1998) 101; 'The Business of Equality in the Solicitors' Profession' (2000) 63 *Modern Law Review*, 442; 'Strategies for Reforming the English Solicitors' Profession: An Analysis of the Business Case for Sex Equality' in U Schultz and G Shaw (eds), *Women in the World's Legal Professions* (2003) n 42; C McGlynn and C Graham, *Soliciting Equality—Equality and Opportunity in the Solicitors' Profession* (London, Young Women Lawyers, 1995).

[116] 'The Myth of Feminisation: Women and Cultural change in the Legal Profession' (1994) 1 *International Journal of the Legal Profession* 31; 'The Gendering of the Professional Subject: Commitment, Choice and Social Closure in the Legal Profession' in McGlynn (ed), *Legal Feminisms* (1998) 3; 'Women Solicitors in a Fractured Profession: Intersections of Gender and Professionalism in England and Wales' (2003) 10 *International Journal of the Legal Profession* 213; 'Can Women Lawyer Differently? A Perspective from the UK' in Schultz and Shaw (eds), *Women in the World's Legal Professions* n 42, 191; 'Becoming a Lawyer: Gender and the Processes of Professional Socialization' in S McIntyre and E Sheehy (eds), *Calling for Change: Women, Law and the Legal Profession* (Ottawa, University of Ottawa Press, 2005) 159; H Sommerlad and P Sanderson, *Gender, Choice and Commitment: A Study of Women Lawyers* (Aldershot, Ashgate, 1998).

[117] See n 114.

[118] L Duff and L Webley, n 113.

3

The Legal Professions as Stakeholders in the Academy in England and Wales

ANDY BOON AND JULIAN WEBB

THEORISTS OF THE Anglo-American professions see a symbiotic relationship with universities,[1] but the relationship is often problematic. The conventional view of disciplines reflecting professional practice is that knowledge is created by practitioners through work[2] and organised, analysed and theorised in the academy.[3] Defined as possession of an interest in an entity, this coalescence of interests around knowledge is the basis of the relationship between legal professions and the academy. But both also have different interests in the other, involving finance, status and, arguably, values. Our path follows the history of legal education and training in England and Wales and the contemporary relationships that this has produced. We consider in some detail the divergence of interests in the nature of legal education and training and the misunderstandings that flow from it. From this foundation, we speculate on the future of the academy and the legal profession, both independently and in terms of their relationship.

In respect of both the legal profession and the academy, it is important to recognise their fluid composition. The legal profession in England and Wales is usually conceived as comprising two branches, barristers and solicitors, represented by two professional bodies, the General Council of

[1] E Greenwood, 'Attributes of a Profession' (1957) 2 *Social Work* 45; T J Johnson, *Professions and Power* (London and Basingstoke, Macmillan, 1972); M S Larson, *The Rise of Professionalism: A Sociological Analysis* (Berkeley, University of California Press, 1972).

[2] A Abbott, *The System of Professions: An Essay on the Expert Division of Labour* (Chicago, University of Chicago Press, 1988); A Abbott, 'Jurisdictional Conflicts: A New Approach to the Development of the Legal Professions' (1986) 2 *American Bar Foundation Research Journal* 187.

[3] M Young (ed), *Knowledge and Control: New Directions for the Sociology of Education* (London, Collier-Macmillan Publishers, 1971).

the Bar for England and Wales and the Law Society respectively.[4] Both of these occupations have a major influence on the academy and a stake in the outcomes of legal education and training, through their professional bodies and on their own behalf as employers. The professional bodies are the main contact point between the academy and the world of practice and also a key protagonist with the universities in the negotiation of the initial stage of legal education and training. The legal market reflects diverse and increasingly divergent interests, which a function of the professional bodies is to harmonise. As the Law Society, in particular, has struggled to cope with increasing fragmentation of interests within the profession, some of these interest groups have broken ranks and sought direct influence on the education and training market.

There are well over 100 universities and university colleges in England and Wales and most offer law degrees. British universities are, however, extremely diverse, with divergent interests. While it is important to note this heterogeneity in discussing the legal academy, the organisation of universities and the way this affects culture is discussed elsewhere in this collection.[5] In this chapter, the main significance concerns the status of institutions, and particularly the former binary divide between the universities and the polytechnics. This distinction is important because universities are usually classified by reference to the era in which they were recognised as universities[6] and interests are to some extent defined by this. For our purposes, the 'new' universities, those created in 1992 by re-designating the polytechnics, are significant because, as a group, they have a distinctive relationship with the legal profession. By dint of scale and common perception, the universities constitute 'the academy'. In law, however, this is not the whole picture. There are large private colleges, the College of Law and Inns of Court School of Law, originally established by the Law Society and

[4] There are other groups providing legal services, but this piece deals with these two. Legal executives, licensed conveyancers and advice workers are at varying degrees of professionalisation and some have relationships with individual universities. They, however, probably have had less influence on the academy than the more traditional professional bodies and the major legal employers. It should also be noted that the Clementi reforms (discussed below, and now enshrined in the Legal Services Act 2007) have added a further layer of complexity as the professional bodies have now formally separated their representative and regulatory functions, with the latter now including much of the professional bodies' education and training activity.

[5] See Boon and Whyte, this volume.

[6] The medieval institutions, Oxford and Cambridge, have the highest status, followed by London and Durham, created in the early nineteenth century. The redbrick universities, including Birmingham, Bristol, Liverpool, Manchester and Sheffield, received Royal Charters in the late nineteenth and early twentieth centuries. In the rapid expansion post-war, Nottingham and Exeter were followed in the 1950s by the Colleges of Advanced Technology: Bath, Brunel, Loughborough. In the 1960s, seven 'campus universities', including York, Warwick, Sussex and Essex, were built on green field sites.

Bar respectively.[7] These two organisations dominated vocational education for many years, but have been joined more recently by BPP Law School, a private college that has established itself as a major competitor. In 2001 the Inns of Court School of Law was incorporated into City University, leaving the College of Law and BPP as the remaining private providers. Especially since both the College of Law and BPP have been granted degree awarding powers,[8] they can claim to be included in some notion of 'the legal academy' and will almost certainly have a significant role in how the relationship between the profession and academy plays out. To understand the relationships between these various conceptions of the academy and the profession, it is necessary to examine the nature of the universities and their changing relationship with law as a discipline.

INSTITUTIONAL RELATIONSHIPS BETWEEN THE LEGAL PROFESSION AND THE ACADEMY

The roots of English legal education and training are not in the academy, and it is these origins that are, for some, the source of current conflicts, confusions and misunderstandings.[9] Up until the mid-twentieth century the history of English legal education was largely dominated by the apprenticeship model. Whilst the Bar had become a predominantly graduate profession somewhat earlier, until the 1960s, significant numbers of solicitors still qualified by serving five-year articles of clerkship rather than by attending university. The professions had, from the 1870s gradually introduced exemptions from the professional examinations for graduates. The growth of graduate entry into the profession was not a product of professional policy and planning, but a consequence of the post-Second World War growth in university admissions, primarily among the middle classes. In short, the professions did not themselves choose to become graduate occupations, but

[7] The Law Society created its own School of Law in 1903 and in the early 1960s amalgamated with Gibson and Weldon, the largest of the private law tutors that had also prepared students for the solicitors' examinations, to create the College of Law. The Inns of Court School of Law was established to provide training to Bar students only in 1967, though lectures had been organised by the Inns of Court through the Council of Legal Education since the late 1850s. BPP Law School was established as an offshoot of BPP Professional Education, which started in 1976 as a corporate provider of accountancy training courses.

[8] The College of Law became the first private provider of legal education to be granted degree awarding powers under the more liberal regulatory regime introduced by government in September 2004. So far the College has used its powers only to award LLBs to students who complete both its GDL and LPC/BVC courses.

[9] See M Burrage, 'From Practice to School-Based Professional Education: Patterns of Conflict and Accommodation in England, France and the United States' in S Rothblatt and B Wittrock (eds), *The European and American University since 1800* (Cambridge, Cambridge University Press, 1993); also L Schwarz, 'Professions, Elites and Universities in England, 1870–1970' (2004) 47(4) *Historical Journal* 941.

were obliged, de facto, to adopt that position by virtue of the educational aspirations of their would-be entrants.[10] By the end of the 1960s, the law degree, built around a 'core' group of subjects that gave exemption from the first stage of professional examinations, had became the most popular route to qualification, and Law Society acquiescence to the Ormrod Report's recommendation that five-year articles should be phased out by 1980 was largely inevitable.[11] As Richard Abel has observed, this shift in control over the supply of trainees to the profession represented a not insignificant change in power relations between the profession and the academy.[12] The legal profession's influence on the initial stage of legal education came to depend increasingly on negotiation with the universities over the content of what came to be called 'qualifying law degrees'.

From the 1960s, the profession's requirement that graduates have a suitable platform for the vocational stage[13] transmuted into requirements for 'qualifying degrees' set out in the Joint Announcement of the Bar and the Law Society. This has undergone a number of iterations, and in its current manifestation is less prescriptive than it has ever been. The main requirement is that qualifying degrees include (in some form, not necessarily as discrete modules), seven conventional subject areas that the profession fancifully call the 'Foundations of Legal Knowledge'.[14] There are additional requirements, such as attention to communication skills and the various contexts in which the law is expected to be delivered, but it is not known how seriously these are taken on degree programmes. The emergence of a 'skills agenda' for undergraduate legal education in the 1980s itself reflected an unusual convergence of vocational and academic concerns, with wider student and state demands for 'practical relevance'. Building, in part, on the tradition of clinical legal education, and on the influence of new skills training programmes that were being developed for the vocational stage in a number of Commonwealth jurisdictions, discrete, skills-based, courses began to be developed in undergraduate programmes, particularly in the (then) polytechnic sector.[15] In 1986, a joint committee on the future of the legal

[10] Burrage, ibid,148.

[11] Mr Justice Ormrod (Chairman), 'Report of the Committee on Legal Education' (Cm 4595, 1971).

[12] RL Abel, *The Legal Profession in England and Wales* (Oxford, Basil Blackwell, 1988), notably at 63ff, 164ff, and 272.

[13] A Bradney *Conversations, Choices and Chances: The Liberal Law School in the Twenty-First Century* (Oxford, Hart Publishing, 2003) 165.

[14] 'Joint Statement on Qualifying Law Degrees' (London, Law Society and the Council of Legal Education, August 1999) www.sra.org.uk/documents/students/academic-stage/academicjointstate.pdf.

[15] See, eg N Gold, K. Mackie and W. Twining (eds), *Learning Lawyers' Skills* (London, Butterworths, 1989); C Maughan and J Webb, 'Introduction' in J Webb and C Maughan (eds), *Teaching Lawyers' Skills* (London, Butterworths, 1996); A Boon, 'History is Past Politics: A Critique of the Skills Movement in England and Wales' (1998) 25 *Journal of Law and Society* 151.

profession was set up by the Law Society and Bar, under the chairmanship of Lady Marre.[16] The Marre Committee is interesting, not so much for its impact, but for its status as virtually the last, relatively united, stand by the professions against the increasing challenges to their traditional privileges that culminated (at the time) in Lord Mackay's 1989 Green Papers.[17] The Committee's report dedicated three relatively short chapters to academic and vocational legal education. In the process, it rejected, on very pragmatic grounds, the possibility of combining the academic and vocational stages in a single four year university-based programme.[18] It did set out the first formal attempt by the professions to identify the range of academic and professional skills to be developed by legal education, and also, at the urging of the College of Law and Council of Legal Education, called on the law schools to address certain perceived inadequacies in the skills and knowledge developed at the academic stage. Such exhortations at the time were more aspirational, or even symbolic, than real, though the creation of 'Subject Benchmarks' in 1992 by the government-sponsored Quality Assurance Agency provided impetus to the 'skills agenda' and an expectation that interactive skills are addressed somewhere within the undergraduate law curriculum.[19]

Having ceded considerable authority to the universities, both branches of the profession focused their attention on the vocational stage, both to ensure that potential practitioners were properly prepared and to control entry. In the nineteenth century the profession had begun using examinations[20] as an essential tool of its gate-keeping function.[21] From the 1960s the pass rates in the various subjects that constituted the solicitors' vocational stage varied wildly, creating considerable mistrust of the processes. The other potential control mechanism, a formal apprenticeship of one year's pupillage for barristers and two year's article's of clerkship for solicitors, limited the size of the profession to the numbers of training opportunities available. During this period the legal profession also boosted the standing of the vocational stage. Formal training in the nineteenth century had been fairly haphazard, and both Law Society and Bar had come under pressure from government

[16] *A Time for Change: Report of the Committee on the Future of the Legal Profession* (London, General Council of the Bar and the Law Society, July 1988), hereafter the 'Marre Committee'.

[17] See the Marre Committee, n 16, paras 3.8–3.13; also Rick Abel's discussion of the background to the Green Papers in RL Abel, *English Lawyers Between Market and State: The Politics of Professionalism* (Oxford, Oxford University Press, 2003), chapter 2.

[18] Marre Committee, n 16, paras 13.30–13.34.

[19] See Bradney, n 13, 172–3.

[20] The Law Society instituted examinations in 1836 but passing an examination for the Bar only became compulsory in 1872 and the process leading to it was haphazard. E Cruikshank 'Building a Profession' (2003) 100 *Law Society's Gazette* 32.

[21] The Solicitors' Act 1860 introduced a three-tier examination, with the preliminary examination including Latin, at the beginning, middle and end of articles.

committees and other bodies to institute examinations and provide more consistent training. This they did slowly and, on the whole somewhat reluctantly.[22] The Bar at this time retained control over its vocational stage through the Inns of Court School of Law (ICSL) as a monopoly provider. This model of professional control resulted in vocational courses that were unimaginative in content and delivery, and widely derided as crammers for new subject matter often not covered on degrees. It did, however, sow the seeds of innovation by expanding the range of providers since, by the 1960s, the Law Society had licensed a number of the colleges of commerce (soon to become new polytechnics) to deliver tuition for 'Part I' and 'Part II' of the Solicitors Examinations. Although the courses were delivered externally, as well as at the College of Law, close control was retained over both the curriculum and the assessment process, whereby students sat a common externally set and assessed examination.

Two developments arguably began to change the profession's relationship with the academy; the first was the recognition of the polytechnics as universities. The 'elevation' of the polytechnics in 1992 doubled the number of university law schools and placed them in more direct competition for students and research funding. The polytechnics had been created to cater for more diverse, less elite groups, to be teaching-led rather than research-led and to be more orientated to industry, commerce and the professions. Their removal from local authority control delivered their governance from statutory control by elected local authority officials to the private business people who largely constituted their boards.[23] They were already more managerial and, with less collegial cultures than the old institutions, were, in some respects, more entrepreneurial and willing to engage with the graduate market. However, at the same time, the collapse of the binary divide undoubtedly reduced further the distinctiveness of the former polytechnics. While they have continued to deliver much of the provision of vocational legal education, most of them have expanded their activities also into the delivery of the LLMs and research degrees that were formally more the preserve of the pre-1992 universities.[24]

Mobility across the new/old divide has—at least for research active staff—we suspect, increased. Moreover with potential access also to government research funding through the Research Assessment Exercise (RAE), the new universities themselves came under competing pressures. Few of the former polytechnics could claim a strong research culture, and yet a growing number saw the RAE as a significant endeavour that created not

[22] See, eg Burrage, n 9, 144–45.

[23] M Rustin, 'Stakeholding and the Public Sector' in G Kelly, D Kelly and A Gamble (eds) *Stakeholder Capitalism* (Sheffield, Palgrave/Political Economy Research Centre, 1997) 79.

[24] P Leighton, 'New Wine in Old Bottles or New Wine in New Bottles?' (1998) 25 *Journal of Law and Society* 85, 93.

just the potential to generate research income per se, but would also have market consequences, particularly in the context of increasing competition for good quality undergraduate and (academic) postgraduate students. One early consequence of the new pressure to research was the development or expansion of research fields, reflecting new university scholars' backgrounds such as legal education, the legal profession and practical aspects of lawyering, which were not so deeply mined or dominated by the research-intensive universities. It is not entirely fanciful to suggest that, among other things, this has served to focus a more critically reflective, academic gaze on both the training and other functions of the professional bodies themselves[25] and, perhaps opened paths of communication between the two domains.

The second development affecting the profession's relationship with the academy was the adoption of a new model for vocational education that began to evolve in the 1990s, which was based more on a partnership with providers than had been the previous regime. This was required by a quite marked change of direction from the traditional, didactic teaching that had previously characterised the vocational courses. In 1989 the Inns of Court School of Law announced the revision of the Bar Final Course to incorporate a new emphasis on skills and transactions.[26] The Law Society quickly followed suit by announcing a new Legal Practice Course (LPC), but went further by inviting new providers to apply to offer the course. The number of LPC providers, previously limited to the College of Law and a select number of polytechnics, expanded rapidly until over thirty institutions had been validated. The Bar then also applied this principle to the new Bar Vocational Course (BVC), approving eight providers, including the Inns of Court School of Law and the College of Law. Both courses had a demanding curriculum, involving the assessment of performance. Perhaps more significant, however, was the fact that the validation regime of both courses involved intending providers proposing their own delivery methods within the broad ambit of the profession's course specification. This allowed scope for novelty and innovation that offered a break from the sterility and atrophy of the previous models. Despite an intrusive monitoring regime, initially conducted annually, this signalled possibilities for a new relationship of trust between the profession and the providers of legal education and training.

[25] The most obvious example would be the growing body of research into skills-based education in law which, with some notable exceptions—especially William Twining and Avrom Sherr—has been largely dominated by scholars writing from within the new university sector. Much of this literature has been highly critical of the instrumental approach to skills that dominated the professional training agenda in the 1990s.

[26] The new course was called the Bar Vocational Course to differentiate it from the old Bar Final Course, which was retained for a period as a recognised course of qualification for students intending to practice in jurisdictions outside England and Wales.

PROFESSIONS AS STAKEHOLDERS

Just as the profession was gaining a more significant foothold within the academy, through its vocational courses, the notion of stakeholding was gaining credence across the system. The concept was not new, having been used to described a right to suffrage based on property ownership,[27] a political rallying call in America's Great Depression[28] and, in the 1980s, as a label for the Conservative Party's vision of a property and share owning democracy. It was placed centre stage by New Labour with the idea of a 'stakeholder economy'[29] and by Tony Blair's speech in Singapore in 1996 setting out his vision of a political 'third way' between social and market orientations.[30] 'Stakeholder capitalism' envisaged a cluster of social reforms described as social partnership in civil society, recognition of the mutual rights and obligations of those engaged in business enterprises, from boardroom to shop floor,[31] and a balance of power in areas of public life hitherto considered unaccountable.[32] The notion of stakeholding did not create a new situation for either the academy or the professions, but it was a new way of describing a process, already ongoing, of ratcheting up the accountability of both.

One of stakeholding's main functions was constraining rampant market liberalism by making intermediate institutions, rather than the state, the locus of political and economic activity. This assertion of the superiority of culture over legislation[33] envisaged that inclusion, whether in companies or society, would encourage self-imposed social and ethical constraints in the interests of the wider community and self-respect (for example, for employees) based on the values of loyalty and trust and the long term view.[34] Both the universities and professions could be regarded as intermediate institutions, but the effect of stakeholding was not that they were used as such, but rather that *they* were held more accountable to those perceived to be *their* stakeholders. This was because both institutions were perceived to

[27] Rustin, n 23, 49.

[28] When General Electric identified four stakeholder groups: shareholders, employees, customers and the general public. E Jansson, 'The Stakeholder Model: The Influence of the Ownership and Governance Structures' (2005) 56 *Journal of Business Ethics* 1, 5.

[29] One 'in which everyone has the opportunity to succeed and everyone the responsibility to contribute.' T Blair, 'Introduction: My Vision for Britain' in G Radice (ed), *What Needs to Change: New Visions for Britain* (London, HarperCollins Publishers, 1996) 10.

[30] Ibid 12.

[31] W Hutton, 'An Overview of Stakeholding' in Kelly, Kelly and Gamble (eds), *Stakeholder Capitalism* (1997) 3.

[32] The scandals of privatisation, when coteries of public sector managers reaped profits while their industries' workers became unemployed, led to a desire for 'durable compromises between different social interests'. See Rustin, n 23, 81.

[33] J Plender, *A Stake in the Future: The Stakeholding Solution* (London, Nicholas Brealey Publishing, 1997) 258.

[34] Ibid 256–7.

be dysfunctional in terms of government's social and economic vision. The universities were failing to deliver more vocational higher education in the service of the economy and the professions were a barrier to 'affordable' legal services, a goal that became paramount with a public spending and legal aid crises in the 1980s, with government dissatisfaction focused on the distorting effects of professionalism on the market.

Record numbers of lawyers from the 1960s onwards did not significantly reduce the cost of legal services, with the increase supported by a booming conveyancing market and expanding legal aid budgets. By the 1990s both markets were in recession, the housing market crash in the early 1990s forcing many solicitors into legal aid work. The spiralling legal aid bill led to unpopular cuts in the budget. The profession embarked on a campaign defending legal aid from the government's attack. The government blamed the situation on solicitors milking legal aid by generating unnecessary work.[35] The government's resolve to cut the profession's power coincided with growing concern about access to the profession. Government evinced its determination to see equal opportunities policies realised in the face of the profession's indirect discrimination against working class and ethnic minority applicants. A more cynical view is that government aimed to create a more 'responsive' market for legal services by increasing the supply of lawyers willing to do legal aid and other low paid work, thereby reducing costs. The last move in this sequence was Sir David Clementi's review of the professional regulation of lawyers. This threatened, for a while, removal of the profession's regulatory powers,[36] but, as noted already, Clementi eventually settled on the separation of regulatory and representative functions, the former to be exercised under the supervision of a 'super-regulator', the Legal Services Board.

The universities also courted governmental disfavour because of their apparent disdain for the need for higher education to serve the economy. They were under pressure to expand to create a more educated workforce from the 1950s onwards. Thereafter, they also came under pressure to change the nature of the curriculum and the way it was delivered to respond to the implications of a widening participation policy. In the 1960s the Robbins Report presaged the first phase in a substantial programme of expansion which sought to achieve an increase in student numbers from 216,000 in 1963–64 to over half a million by 1980–81—a target that was nearly achieved.[37] Moreover, Robbins' emphasis on a modern version of the liberal

[35] AS Zuckerman, 'Lord Woolf's Access to Justice: Plus Ca Change...' (1996)59 *Modern Law Review* 773.

[36] Department of Constitutional Affairs, *Competition and Regulation in the Legal Services Market* (CP(R2)07/02) (2003); D Clementi, *Review of the Regulatory Framework for Legal Services in England and Wales: Final Report* (2004) (the Clementi Review).

[37] C Moser, 'The Robbins Report 25 Years After—and the Future of the Universities' (1988) 14 *Oxford Review of Education* 5, 6.

tradition, which saw higher education as possessing four complementary core objectives—first, to educate for specific skills and vocations, second, to produce 'not mere specialists but rather cultivated men and women',[38] thirdly, to advance scholarship and learning, and fourthly, to transmit a common culture and values—was largely accepted in political circles. This set the scene for many of the subsequent trends in English higher education policy. Perhaps because of the Report's predominantly academic 'voice', this continuity is easily overlooked, but there have also been important shifts in emphasis. While the Robbins Committee acknowledged the importance of skills and what we might now term 'employability', it treated this as a function that was, as Barnett argues, 'offered on the terms of, and firmly under the control of, the academic community'.[39]

In the 1960s the need for a more practical and vocational curriculum for a more diverse student body found its expression, first, in the government's construction of a binary policy for higher education with the creation of the polytechnics. The decision to accord the polytechnics university status in the early 1990s in turn was balanced by initiatives intended to increase responsiveness and accountability of the whole sector. This included the identification of potential stakeholders, such as the professional bodies, employers and students. This agenda was embraced by university management. In 1985 a report by vice-chancellors and others on the efficiency of the universities (The Jarratt Report) acknowledged that they must offer 'value for money' but suggested that 'the system can only work effectively if the Government states what it expects of the system and its constituent parts'.[40] Jarratt held the continuing relevance of Robbins' aims of higher education, but recommended that government provide long-term guidelines so that they could undertake long-term strategic planning.[41] The report also took a rather negative view of its own constituency, asserting that academic freedom was sometimes confused with licence[42] and adding that the academic tendency to rate professional and disciplinary affiliations equal with university membership represented a 'managerial challenge'.[43] Consequently, Jarratt favoured a far more managerial culture in the universities.

In the evolving higher education agenda, employers were seen as particularly important because of the perceived link between education, training

[38] 'Report of the Committee on Higher Education' (Cm 2154, 1963) (The Robbins Report), paras 24–26; Ormrod, 'Report of the Committee on Legal Education' (1971) para 106.

[39] R Barnett, 'The Coming of the Global Village: A Tale of Two Inquiries' (1999) 25 *Oxford Review of Education* 293, 304.

[40] Committee of Vice-Chancellors and Principals, *Report of the Steering Committee for Efficiency Studies in Universities* (CVCP, 1985) para 4.26 and 4.27.

[41] Ibid recommendation 5.1(a).

[42] Ibid para 4.2.

[43] Ibid para 2.7(b).

and the successful economy. Government funding and other initiatives, then and since, have sought to strengthen these ties.[44] This reflected a change in government strategy towards the universities, whereby recurrent funding was reduced and replaced, if at all, by marginal, non-recurrent funding for programmes shifting the orientation of the sector towards the economy. A parallel move was the ramping up of the powers of regulatory bodies such as the Quality Assurance Agency. This was legitimised by the perception that there is a social stake in higher education via the government's investment.[45] This shift, away from autonomy over academic quality, saw intellectual notions of fitness for purpose replaced by bureaucratic ones. For some, this has had the affect of making the universities more commercially orientated, public corporations. For many academics it also led to a shift in traditional activities, away from research to teaching and administration, that was both resented and resisted.[46]

THE PROFESSION AND THE ACADEMY—A CLASH OF INTERESTS?

The autonomy of both legal profession and law schools has been undermined by accountability. An accommodation between them might ease the pressure on each, but they do not see their interests as mutually compatible and, historically, their relationship has not been close.[47] The interest of the profession is to establish a form of legal education that is fit for purpose that responds effectively to increasing levels of specialisation, the demands of government and students for economy and to the need for regulatory efficiency. The profession is under steady pressure from its own constituency. One of the most vociferous sectors is the corporate/commercial law firms, which criticise the 'inadequate standards of legal education that all firms are seeing now, coming out of the academic stage'[48] and particularly

[44] See, eg the Enterprise in Higher Education initiative—A Boon 'Enterprise in Higher Education: A New Agenda for Institutional Change?' (1990) 24 *Law Teacher* 14; see generally the emphasis in the Dearing Report on orientating higher education more towards the economic needs of society and fitting higher education into a framework of 'lifelong learning'—R Dearing, *Higher Education in the Learning Society* (London, HMSO, 1997); this focus has been emphasised again in the Leitch Review of Skills' recent emphasis on 'employer engagement' in higher education—see *Prosperity for All in the Global Economy—World Class Skills: Final Report* (December 2006) paras 3.62, 4.38–4.39, available at www.dcsf.gov.uk/furthereducation/uploads/documents/2006-12%20LeitchReview1.pdf.

[45] The fact that quality assurance processes only examine whether an institution's quality assurance system is fit for purpose reflects a concern about value for public money, rather than the legitimate interests of stakeholders.

[46] S Bassnett, 'Anger and Outrage at the Corporate Model' *The Independent*, (London 26 January 2007) available at www.independent.co.uk/news/education/higher/susan-bassnett-anger-and-outrage-at-the-corporate-model-433501.html

[47] Boon, n 15, 156–7, 159–61.

[48] A Clarke, 'Student Angst' *Law Society's Gazette*, 20 July 2000, available at www.lawgazette.co.uk/news/student-angst.

trainees' writing skills, research skills and knowledge of law. This is a criticism of the content of law degrees, the balance struck in the curriculum between private, public and welfare subjects, and of its ordering, whereby basic contract law, the mainstay of commercial practice, is a first year subject largely forgotten by the time students enter a training contract. It is said to be a reason why the commercial law market shows a strong preference for graduates from non-law, conversion course diplomas rather than degree students, although the the fact that the conversion courses provide to an additional pool of elite university graduates is also a factor for recruiters.[49] Criticism of undergraduate courses compared with the vocational courses is also implicit. A warning for providers of first degrees is the fact that legal employers are wont to change even these courses, if given an opportunity to do so. At the other end of the scale, legal aid firms often struggle to recruit trainees scared off by the cost of qualifying and the threat of a future of penury.

THE PROFESSION'S INTERESTS

Professions are made up of diverse interest groups, sometimes making it difficult to achieve intra-professional consensus on regulatory issues. As is widely acknowledged, over the past thirty years, the legal profession has changed dramatically. Traditional professional monopolies have been removed, or at least substantially redrawn; an increasing gap in status (perhaps) and remuneration (definitely) has emerged between those serving corporate clients and those practising in areas of 'private plight'; the largest firms and chambers have grown almost exponentially, and the work itself has become increasingly stratified and specialised.

Change for the Bar has been largely about managing the rapid expansion of what was traditionally a small referral advocacy profession. While both sides of the profession have grown significantly since the 1970s, the pressures this has imposed on the Bar have, arguably, been proportionally greater. The Bar today has grown to about 11,500 practitioners in private practice.[50] But this is now in a context of increasing internal competition, caused by the loss of the monopoly over higher court advocacy rights, declining legal aid, and a slowly shrinking pool of pupillages.[51] In addition

[49] V Bermingham and J Hodgson, 'Desiderata: What Lawyers Want From Their Recruits' (2000) 35 *Law Teacher* 1.

[50] Lord Neuberger (Chair), *Entry to the Bar Working Party: Final Report* (London, General Council of the Bar, November 2007) (the Neuberger Report) para.6, available at www.barcouncil.org.uk/news/NeubergerMonitoringandImplementationGroup.

[51] Each year around 2000 students are completing the Bar Vocational Course, in pursuit of about 500 pupillages. idem para.15. The number of BVC diplomats has increased steadily since the Inns of Court School of Law (now part of City University Law School) lost its monopoly over the BVC in 1993; student numbers at the ICSL had peaked in 1992 at about 1,100—see Abel, n 17, 100.

the Bar has also come under increasing pressure to enhance access and increase the diversity of the profession.[52]

As regards education and training, these tensions have often left the Bar negotiating a passage between the proverbial rock and hard place. The interests of the established profession have, to an extent, lain in seeking to re-establish a higher degree of supply control over entry to the profession—and yet as the Bar Standards Board pointed out in its own response to the Interim Report of the Neuberger Working Party, limiting numbers for its own sake is not a feasible option.[53] Indeed, additional supply controls could have unintended and negative consequences for access and diversity. Similarly, while the preservation of the Bar as a specialist advocacy profession arguably depends on its ability to provide a higher level of advocacy training than its competitors,[54] BVC providers are also likely, given the continuing disparity between places and pupillages, to need to ensure that the course delivers a sufficient range of transferable skills to give their graduands 'added value' in the wider marketplace.[55]

Within the solicitors' profession, change has manifested most obviously in the increasing economic and political divergence of two significant power blocks: the City and commercial firms, and the high street and legal aid firms. These blocks tend to have strongly divergent views on education and training because of the requirements of their distinctive types of practice. The City and commercial firms favour training strong on commercial and transactional law, and on intellectual and research skills. Recruiting from social elites, and with many years before their lawyers are trusted with clients, they are less concerned with subjects like conveyancing or with 'soft skills'. The high street and legal aid firms, however, require lawyers familiar with litigation and a broad range of private and welfare law. Since their trainees usually have early exposure to clients and case handling, they also require a good grounding in the interpersonal legal skills, like interviewing and negotiation. The legal professional bodies, in setting education and training requirements, have to reconcile, or balance, the needs and wishes of these, and other, sectors.[56] The difficulty of achieving this balance is

[52] See, eg the data summarised in ch 4 of the (then) Department for Constitutional Affairs, Discussion Paper, 'Entry to, and Retention in, the Legal Profession', prepared for the Standing Conference on Legal Education, November 2004 (copy on file with the authors).

[53] Bar Standards Board, 'Response to the Interim Report of the Entry to the Bar Working Group' (May 2007) available at www.barstandardsboard.org.uk/news/pressarchive/489.html.

[54] This was undoubtedly part of the logic which saw the Elias Working Party (of which Julian Webb was a member) substantially enhance the advocacy component of the BVC in its review of the Course Specification, adopted in 2002.

[55] Note also in this context the recommendation of the Neuberger Report (2007) paras 158–60, that the BVC should be 'upgraded' to a Masters' qualification.

[56] The Legal Education and Training Group (LETG) represent the interests of the City and commercial firms and the Legal Aid Practitioners Group those of high street and legal aid firms. The LETG describes itself as 'an association of legal training and development professionals'

illustrated by the recent history of firms' involvement with the Legal Practice Course.

The critique of trainees by commercial firms, many paying prospective trainees' LPC fees, was that the generalist LPC represented a lost opportunity to remedy specific deficiencies and induct students into their firm. The 'City eight' consortium reached agreement with Nottingham, BPP and the Oxford Institute, a joint venture between Oxford University and Oxford Brookes, to deliver a City LPC to their prospective trainees. In 2004 Allen and Overy split from the eight and the remainder decided to drop Nottingham and BPP. Nottingham and the College of Law, which was initially rejected by the City firms, responded to being excluded from the City LPC by developing courses for bespoke delivery to individual firms.[57] In 2006, one firm launched an LPC in collaboration with the College of Law for only 25 students studying over a single semester.[58] The Law Society was left with little choice but to approve these arrangements incrementally, despite having earlier conceded a larger slice of the LPC curriculum to the City lobby. There was general disquiet that the 'common platform' of vocational preparation was being sacrificed, evoking direct, public criticism from Lord Woolf.[59] The professional body's concession to employer groups was an admission of uncertainty revealing the delicate threads by which the ideal of common professional training hung.

In addition to satisfying its constituencies, a profession has a strong interest in demonstrating regulatory competence. A key capacity is harmonising legislative requirements with professional policy, interests and preferences. Before the influence of the European legislation began to be felt, this was a relatively easy task. Parliament usually consulted directly on matters affecting professions. The 'Europeanisation' of English law, and particularly employment law, has, however, had direct impact on domestic arrangements that cannot be ignored. The EC drive to liberalise the employment market first began to impact on lawyers from 1977, when it became possible for services to be provided in another European state.[60] The next step concerned the right to practice in another country as an assimilated member of their profession. In 1988 professions were mandated to recognise

representing the interests of member firms to ensure 'quality in legal education and appropriateness in regulation of legal education and training to the profession's needs'. www.letg.org.uk.

[57] H Begum, 'Baker and McKenzie Signs Trainees up to College of Law's New Bespoke LPC' *The Lawyer* (26 June 2006) p.8; J. Parker, 'Fast Learners' *Lawyer 2B* (8 May 2006) (http://www.thelawyer.com/cgi-bin/item.cgi?id=120585&d=pndrpr&h=pnhpr&f=pnfpr).

[58] Berwin, Leighton Paisner. See J Parker, 'Fast Train to London Bridge' *The Lawyer* (13 March 2006), 16.

[59] A Mizzi, 'Lord Woolf Criticises City law Firms for Launching 'Elite' Training Consortium' *Law Society Gazette* 97 (25 June 2000) 4.

[60] EC Directive 77/249.

professional qualifications obtained in another European state and to provide aptitude tests designed to assess any subject matter deemed essential for practice in the host country.[61] These tests generally took the form of the final examination taken by professional entrants in the host country. This was often a difficult hurdle and was perceived as an exercise in protectionism by the legal professions of the member states. Finally, in 1988, qualified lawyers of one member state were entitled to practice in another member state under their title of origin, and to be admitted to membership under host country title after three years' 'effective and regular' practice there.[62] England is the most popular European destination for lawyers shifting jurisdiction.[63]

The fragility of domestic arrangements for accommodating lawyers from other jurisdictions was brought home by the European Court decision in *Morgenbesser*,[64] which held that a European legal profession cannot insist on its own specified qualifications when considering whether to enrol a trainee lawyer from another member state.[65] Rather, they must consider the equivalence of qualifications and experience gained in the other member state. It was a simple step to foresee that domestic students might make similar arguments, driving a coach and horses through existing requirements that they must have passed specified courses.

The Academy

Academics are socialised in and tend to organise around the protection and development of their discipline. The ideology and attitudes of the academy are, to some extent, shaped by its origins. Universities were formed in the early medieval period by scholars or students banding together in legal corporations, entering modernity distanced from the world by theological roots and the esoteric nature of learning. The impression of ivory towers left by this legacy has a powerful grip on the academic imagination, but the golden age is not well evidenced. From the seventeenth century onwards, the nascent universities were plagued by demands that they engage more with the everyday.[66] Prototype academics would probably recognise their successors' inclination to feel that the 'pragmatic compromise between

[61] EC Directive 89/48.

[62] EC Directive 98/5.

[63] K Gromek-Broc, 'The Legal Profession in the European Union—A Comparative Analysis of Four Member States' (2002) 24 *Liverpool Law Review* 109.

[64] *Christine Morgenbesser v Consiglio dell'Odine degli avvocati di Genoa (Case C-313/01)* [2003] All ER (D) 190 (Nov).

[65] Therefore, for example, they could not be required to take an LPC if parts of their experience were 'equivalent'.

[66] KR Minogue, *The Concept of a University* (London, Wiedenfeld and Nicholson, 1973) 27.

useful knowledge and education', often risks destroying education rather than improving it'.[67] They would probably also share an inclination to defend 'their' project, however conceived, from 'those who would take it over and bend it to their purposes'.[68] Both groups would be assisted by the wonderful ambiguity of the university concept and by the lack of convincing arguments for change. While new agendas for the universities are promoted as a necessary response to social need, there is generally no normative status to their ascribed functions. In modern times, government has tended to increase its voice and, particularly where funding strings are attached, its agendas of social change and inclusion must be heeded. Nor is the academy always justified in its conservatism. It is generally true that, with age, people and institutions alike tend to fall into habits that are defended as institutional necessities when they are, in fact, personal preferences.[69]

If the interest of the academy generally is autonomy, the legal academy has particular reasons to be concerned with security, status and control. In continental Europe generally, the universities created the modern law of Europe, whereas in England it was created by the judiciary and the profession in the Inns of Court.[70] This history is said to have engendered a lack of academic confidence. In the mid 1800s a select committee urged the development of law in the universities, but identifiable law programmes, which at their best combined philosophy, theory, practice and reform, only emerged at Oxford, Cambridge and London towards the end of the nineteenth century.[71] The English approach to legal study was shaped in the nineteenth century by a largely Oxford-based elite, including Anson, Salmond, Dicey and Pollock. In this 'classical period' in the development of the 'black letter' law tradition,[72] between 1850 and 1907, the systematisation, exposition and analysis of legal doctrine was the priority.[73] The aim was to create an area of autonomy between the university, the profession and the state, and the organising concept of this domain was the rule of law.[74] This reification of doctrine at the expense of social, political or moral perspectives was the bedrock of English legal education, but for the English

[67] Ibid 29.

[68] Ibid 185.

[69] Ibid generally.

[70] B Hepple, 'The Renewal of the Liberal Law Degree' (1996) 55 *Cambridge Law Journal* 470; D Sugarman, '"A Hatred of Disorder": Legal Science, Liberalism and Imperialism' in P Fitzpatrick (ed), *Dangerous Supplements: Resistance and Renewal in Jurisprudence* (London, Pluto Press, 1991) 34, 60.

[71] M Partington, 'Academic Lawyers and "Legal Practice" in Britain: A Preliminary Reappraisal' (1988) 15 *Journal of Law and Society* 374.

[72] The term 'black letter law' derives from the presentation of basic legal principles in bold type in traditional texts. AC Hutchinson, 'Beyond Black-Letterism: Ethics in Law and Legal Education' (1999) 33 *Law Teacher* 301.

[73] Sugarman, n 70, 34.

[74] Ibid 36.

academy it was, as Sugarman says, a narrow ledge. In England, however, on their ledge '[l]aw dons were masters of the principles of law. To assert that law was principled and internally coherent seemed to require that facts and reality were kept at a safe distance'.[75] English practitioners remained masters of the relation between law and facts, whereas in the US, professors carved a significant role as critic, playing on the indeterminacy of law.[76]

In the period after 1907, academic lawyers were cemented in a conservative and static role, updating the canon created by their predecessors. When at the turn of the century Law emerged in provincial universities, the programmes were often developed in collaboration with local law societies and, being taught by local practitioners, reflected their practical approach.[77] In 1913 the Haldane Commission saw the ideal curriculum as combining theory and practice.[78] This approach to law, as a system of rules devoid of social, political or moral context, was ideological, so much a part of academic identity that it was unambiguously endorsed by the president of the Society of Public Teachers of Law in a post-Second World War review of legal education. In his view, legal education should reject subjects based on legislation rather than precedent. Criticising law and discussing law reform was dangerously like sociology which would, in his view, impinge on the objectivity necessary for legal study.[79] This was not the view of the whole academy. Gower, notably, argued for lawyers that knew of economics, political science and sociology as early as 1950.[80] Gradually, the orthodoxy came under sustained pressure. By the 1970s, the doctrinal pedagogy was identified with competitiveness, orthodoxy and conservatism, and blamed for turning students away from whatever public service orientations stimulated their interest in law.[81] This conservative and sterile positivism[82] fell out of favour with many academics from the 1960s onwards. Its legacy, however, was that legal academics were a largely undistinguished group, respected in neither the universities nor the profession.[83] The profession's willingness to add the statement that law should be taught

[75] Ibid 41.

[76] The US also developed a 'scientific method' under the influence of the Dean of Harvard Law School, Christopher Langdell, in the late nineteenth century. Under his 'Socratic method', students were expected to state the facts of the case, the outcome and whether it was 'good' law.

[77] B Abel-Smith and R Stevens, *Lawyers and the Courts* (London, Heinemann, 1967), 182.

[78] Hepple, n 70, 474.

[79] Partington, n 71, 377.

[80] LCB Gower, 'English Legal Training' (1950) 13 *Modern Law Review* 137.

[81] C Stanley, 'Training for the Hierarchy? Reflections on the British Experience of Legal Education' (1988) 22 *Law Teacher* 78; S Matambanadzo, 'Fumbling Toward a Critical Legal Pedagogy and Practice' (2006) 4 *Policy Futures in Education* 90.

[82] Hutchinson, n 72, 303.

[83] Abel-Smith and Stevens, n 77; Partington, n 71.

'in context' to the 1995 Joint Announcement on Qualifying Law Degrees[84] legitimised increasing multi- and inter-disciplinarity[85] This reflected a shift in legal scholarship that opened up possibilities for a new dialogue between academics and the legal professions.

The status of the academy began to change with the increase in scale brought about by the 1960s expansion and with the recruitment as academics of substantial numbers of qualified lawyers and, even, past practitioners. Perhaps the biggest influence, however, was the growth of socio-legal research in the universities, which escaped the 'black-letter' straightjacket. The new work of the academy constituted a form of knowledge that was not found in practice and was valuable in law reform, as evidenced by the establishment of the Law Commission in 1965.[86] Research on the profession formed a critique of legal ideologies and governments were interested in it as a springboard for reform. Through research, academics had new ways of building social capital. During this phase of the academy's development there was concern, even among academics, that their preoccupations were at the expense of the law curriculum and law teaching. MacAuslan, for example, was anxious that the professional bodies were more interested in, and knowledgeable about, new ideas in education than the academy.[87] Economides and Smallcombe commented that: 'Perhaps in the interests of preserving some spurious notion of academic autonomy, lawyers in higher education have on the whole shut themselves off from the needs of the legal profession and the clients they serve.'[88]

Whether or not the profession was aware of the drift towards multi-disciplinary research, and the profusion of research perspectives under the umbrella of socio-legal studies,[89] it would probably not have approved. This reflected a growing confidence in the legal academy, but was not unproblematic. If reflected in teaching, the new perspectives would take students further from the subject matter and narrow rule handling techniques in which older practitioners were trained, towards more analytical and critical perspectives on law. There was, in the academic community, some

[84] The text of the 1995 Announcement can be found appended to P Birks, 'Compulsory Subjects: Will the Seven Foundations ever Crumble?' (1995) *Web Journal of Current Legal Issues*, Issue 1, available at http://webjcli.ncl.ac.uk/articles1/birks1.html. The reference to social context was omitted from when current (1999) version was agreed—see www.sra.org.uk/documents/students/academic-stage/academicjointstate.pdf.

[85] Ormrod, n 11, para 109; ACLEC *First Report on Legal Education and Training* (London, ACLEC, 1996) at para 2.4.

[86] Partington, n 71, 385.

[87] P McAuslan, 'The Coming Crisis in Legal Education' (1989) 16 *Journal of Law and Society* 310.

[88] K Economides and J Smallcombe, *Preparatory Skills Training for Solicitors* (London, The Law Society, 1991) 4.

[89] A Boon, 'The Formalisation of Research Ethics' in R Banakar and M Travers (eds), *Theory and Method in Socio-Legal Research* (Oxford, Hart Publishing, 2005) 301.

anxiety about movement away from 'professionally useful' conceptions of knowledge.[90] Nevertheless, the direction was maintained and reinforced when the law panel for the 1991 RAE issued guidance that practitioner works would only be counted if they contained significant scholarly material, causing considerable doubt over submitting such work.[91] Young academics, increasingly, were recruited with PhDs rather than from practice. They often had no practical background, no interest in and little contact with the profession.[92] These cumulative changes served to weaken connections between academics and the legal profession. According to Cownie, law is 'a discipline in flux... moving away from its exclusive concern with doctrine and... closer to the heart of the academy'.[93]

The potential for academic drift in law teaching was not detected in the many reviews of legal education over the past forty years. The Ormrod,[94] Benson[95] and Marre[96] reports endorsed the universities' discrete role in professional preparation. Ormrod, the first of these, marked the beginning of a clear role for university legal education, out of the shadow of the profession, by embracing the Robbins vision of liberal education for the legal discipline. Yet it also desired greater integration of the whole of legal education and training, the contextual, the doctrinal and the practical. Consistent with this somewhat contradictory approach, Ormrod, and the later reports, stressed the importance of imbuing degree students with ethics and the ethos of public service.[97] The Lord Chancellor's Advisory Committee for Education and Conduct (ACLEC) followed this tradition in its 1996 report,[98] but offered a far more concrete path towards achieving the desired goal. It suggested that the degree should be charged with achieving broad outcomes, including an emphasis on ethics and public service, providing a stronger foundation for practice. For the profession, the sting in the tail was ACLEC's recommendation that it lose the right to stipulate the content of law degrees. Provided universities could show that the curriculum of their courses would achieve the outcomes, students would be given qualifying degrees.

[90] See Bradney, n 13, 125–26, discussing the views of Peter Birks and Harry Edwards.

[91] F Cownie, *Legal Academics: Culture and Identities* (Oxford, Hart Publishing, 2004), 200.

[92] Ibid 156–158.

[93] Ibid 199.

[94] Omrod, n 11.

[95] 'The Royal Commission on Legal Services, Final Report' (Cm 7648, London, HMSO, 1979).

[96] Marre Committee, n 16.

[97] A Boon, 'Ethics in Legal Education: Four Reports, Three Jurisdictions and a Prospectus' (2002) 5 *Legal Ethics* 34.

[98] ACLEC, n 85.

Suggesting that the professional stranglehold on law degrees should be removed was certainly not novel,[99] but the timing was surprising. Rising criticism of law graduates by employers seemed to support the case for closer collaboration between the profession and the academy. The success of the new vocational courses, most of which were run by universities, hinted that a better relationship was attainable and that it could be beneficial. The so-called integrated course run at the University of Northumbria, where the degree and Legal Practice and Bar Vocational courses were fused, was held up by many, particularly in the profession, as a model. This picture of increasing closeness and harmony was, however, somewhat illusory. The universities offering the LPC or BVC, with the exceptions of Cardiff, Sheffield and City, are former polytechnics.[100] The developing relationship between the new universities and the profession reflected the enduring vertical schism in the aspirations and orientations of the academy, and the 'old universities' perceived hostility to 'vocationalism' and a practical approach.[101] The view in the 'old' institutions tends to be that the profession's prescribed curriculum already overcrowds the degree, that many law students do not go into practice and it is the role of the liberal law degree, advocated by Ormrod, to educate rather than to train.[102] Intending practitioners are not the only concern, since not all law degree entrants plan to become lawyers.[103] Around 60 per cent of law graduates go into practice, although there is evidence that more wish to do so as a result of studying law.[104]

[99] In 1913, the Haldane Commission had opined that university law faculties would develop better outside the control of the profession. See Hepple, n 70, 474.

[100] There had originally been four pre-1992 universities validated to deliver the LPC from 1992; Bristol had offered the LPC but transferred the course and staff to the University of the West of England in the latter part of the 1990s, because of the possible impact on its research profile. From September 2006 the LPC at Exeter University similarly transferred to the University of Plymouth—also a new university. City acquired its vocational profile as a 'job lot' with the Inns of Court School of Law; integration is a work in progress.

[101] J Webb, 'Inventing the Good: A Prospectus for Clinical Education and the Teaching of Legal Ethics in England' (1996) 30:3 *The Law Teacher* 270, 271; see also n 4 and n 6. Today the academy is represented laterally across the sector by bodies such as the Committee of Heads of University Law Schools (CHULS), the Association of Law Teachers (ALT), Society of Legal Scholars (SLS—formerly the Society of Public Teachers of Law) and Socio-legal Studies Association (SLSA). Most institutions retain vestiges of their origins on either side of the binary divide. Originally the SLS and ALT represented (primarily) the interests of the pre- and post-1992 sectors respectively.

[102] The argument was succinctly put in response to an argument by Nigel Bastin, the then Chief Education Officer of the Bar, that the degree should pick up more of the burden of professional preparation so as to reduce the debt incurred by students in the vocational stage. N Wikeley, 'The Law Degree and the BVC' *The Reporter*, Spring 2004, 23.

[103] The Law Society cohort study found that more than 50% of home law students had, at age 16, seriously considered a career as a solicitor and thirty three per cent as a barrister. D Halpern, *Entry into the Legal Professions: The Law Student Cohort Study, Years 1 and 2* (London, The Law Society, 1994) ch 7.

[104] The cohort study also found that those thinking about being a solicitor had jumped to 75% of home undergraduates, while those considering the Bar had fallen to 14%. Halpern, ibid 46.

Twining considered that legal education and training was an uneasy compromise between the professional bodies and the university law schools, seeking to balance their role as 'service institutions' for the profession with finding acceptance in the academy and acting as 'engaged, critics and censors of law in society'.[105] This dilemma was recognised in ACLEC's first report in 1996, which had been based on considerable consultation. Following the Haldane and Ormrod committees, it proposed that the profession should be limited to checking university courses and licensing them if they met the broad goals suggested in the report. However, together with this significant nod to the academic lobby, ACLEC also proposed an end to what Bob Hepple, one of its leading members, called 'the false antithesis between the "academic" and the "vocational", which had been "legitimated and given an institutional basis" by the Ormrod committee'.[106] ACLEC, he said, favoured

> erosion of the traditional linear model of academic and vocational stages ending with qualification as a barrister or solicitors, and its replacement by the notion of lifelong personal development in the Law as a liberal and humane profession... a renewal of an older vision of Law as a liberal discipline which inspired such great Cambridge teachers as Andrew Amos and Frederick William Maitland.[107]

The partnership model had, for Hepple, two other abiding and baleful legacies; it separated the teachers of vocational law from the academy and led the profession to see itself 'as regulators of the law degree instead of facilitators and partners with the universities'.[108] Hepple envisaged a system providing 'flexibility, variety and diversity; multiple entry and exit points; an all-round preparation for a wide range of occupational destinations; intellectual rigour; and common professional education.'[109] Those legal employers who might fear they would be taking 'postmodern critical theorists who know little law' into their firms and chambers were invited to 'trust the universities and put their faith in the market'.[110]

Following the ACLEC report the legal profession stood in a weakened state against the government and the universities. Its own interest, seen as the maintenance of standards in universities, was regarded as a peripheral consideration when set against the more direct interests of the universities themselves, their students and the state, acting as the broker of these interests.[111] Since ACLEC had been created under the Courts and Legal Services

[105] W Twining, 'The Benson Report and Legal Education: A Personal View' in PA Thomas (ed), *Law in the Balance: Legal Services in the 1980s* (Oxford, Martin Robertson, 1982) 2.
[106] Hepple, n 70, 471.
[107] Ibid.
[108] Ibid 478.
[109] Ibid 481.
[110] Ibid 480.
[111] LRP Reavill, 'Quality Assessment, Total Quality Management and the Stakeholders in the UK Higher Education System' (1998) 8 *Managing Service Quality* 55, 61.

Act 1990 to advise the Lord Chancellor on the exercise of the responsibility under the Act for education and conduct, the report posed some threat to the profession's control of legal education. Initially, the legal profession went slowly down the route indicated by ACLEC. In 1998 the profession endorsed the ACLEC view that the law degree should stand as an independent liberal education not tied to any specific vocation,[112] a direction taken with the benchmarking of general transferable skills rather than legal skills for inclusion in all degrees.[113] The profession also endorsed ACLEC's position that students should acquire knowledge 'of the social, economic, political, historical, philosophical, moral, ethical, cultural and comparative contexts in which law operates'. While the Joint Announcement was amended to reflect this emphasis, no additional content was prescribed. It is therefore unknown, probably even within the professional bodies, whether most law degrees profess or have systematic coverage or assessment of these perspectives.

Since there were no moves to strip it of its power over the curriculum, and with the abolition of ACLEC, the Law Society launched a review of its Training Framework in 2001. From the start the Training Framework Review promised something iconoclastic, making knowledge, skills and ethics core elements of solicitors' education and training 'from the cradle to the grave'.[114] This approach was welcomed by most respondents to the first consultation[115] and the Law Society convened a group, the Training Framework Review Group (TFRG), to develop proposals. The TFRG began by identifying what a newly qualified solicitor should know and be able to do before proposing that regulation should focus on assessing these outcomes, rather than courses or other processes. Although the outcomes could be fitted to the existing framework of higher education,[116] they could also be met in a variety of other ways.[117] This relaxation of control over providers was to be balanced by the reintroduction of centralised assessment of some of the post-degree outcomes. The only course requirement would be an honours degree, the common currency of European education and

[112] The Law Society and the General Council of the Bar, *A Consultation Paper on the Revision of the Joint Announcement on Qualifying Law Degrees* (September 1998).

[113] J Bell, 'General Transferable Skills and the Law Curriculum' (1996) 2 *Contemporary Issues in Law* 1.

[114] Law Society, *Consultation: Training Framework Review* (London, Law Society, 2001).

[115] A Boon and J Webb, *Report to the Law Society on the Consultation and Interim Report on the Training Framework Review* (February 2002), on file with the authors.

[116] The first of four groups of outcomes comprised the intellectual, analytical and problem-solving skills delivered in honours degrees, together with a core of legal knowledge containing much of the 'seven foundations'. The second group, headed 'the ability to complete legal transactions and resolve disputes', map onto Legal Practice Course. The third group, 'practical understanding of the values, behaviours, attitudes and ethical requirements of being a solicitor' and the fourth group 'professional, personal management and client relationship skills', overlap the LPC and period of work based learning.

[117] Law Society Consultation, n 114, para 38.

professional entry under the Bologna Declaration[118] and a two-year period of work-based learning, completed under the supervision of a solicitor.

The proposals received a lukewarm response from parts of the profession and from the academy, with the most hostility, unsurprisingly, directed to those proposals closest to the homes of each.[119] The Law Society missed a considerable opportunity to court the academic lobby by clarifying the proposals in relation to the new substantive core.[120] Had it, for example, offered a reduction of the core this may have assuaged much academic anxiety. The potential for incorporation of the 'vocational stage' in three-year programmes may have been sufficient to make the proposals unattractive to many.[121] The proposals were initially defended by senior executives in the Law Society,[122] arguing that they would address rising criticism of access to the profession.[123] However, the regulatory revolution that took place in anticipation of the Clementi proposals, whereby committees were disbanded and reconstituted, and education and training came increasingly to be reconstructed as a regulatory matter, has not only slowed the rate of progress but created new opportunities for the now divided representative and regulatory bodies to treat the TFR as one of a number of political footballs.[124] Similarly, a recent report for the Law Society by Kim Economides and Justine Rogers,[125] recommending enhanced ethics education at both the academic and vocational stages well illustrates the increasingly fractured and fractionalised process of educational regulation and reform. The commissioning of the report can itself be seen as part of a process whereby

[118] J Hodgson, 'Bologna—How Far Have We Got?' (2004) 38 *Law Teacher* 341.

[119] The idea that students need not attend a vocational course before taking their vocational examinations threatened a source of considerable investment and income by institutions. See N Johnson, 'The Training Framework Review—What's All The Fuss About?' (2005) 155 *New Law Journal* 341; B Malkin, 'Market Slams Law Soc Plans to Abolish Vocational Training' *Lawyer 2B* February 2005, 1. It was feared that the training contract proposals would greatly increase the burdens on solicitors firms.

[120] J Webb and A Fancourt, 'The Law Society's Training Framework Review: On the Straight and Narrow or the Long and Winding Road' (2004) 38 *Law Teacher* 293.

[121] Wikeley, n 103.

[122] C Sanders, 'Profile: Janet Paraskeva, Chief Executive, Law Society' *Times Higher Education* (February 2005) 4.

[123] A Langlands, *Gateways to the Professions: A Consultation Paper* (Department for Education and Skills, January 2005); A Fuller and L Unwin, 'Vocational Guidance' *Education Guardian* (29 March 2005).

[124] Thus, in 2006, when Peter Williamson consulted on proposed amendments to the LPC, half the package bore no relation to the majority TFRG proposals. Yet, in a further twist, when the new Solicitors Regulation Authority's own consultation went public in February 2007, a number of the original TFRG objectives were re-established. For a fuller account of the proposals for the LPC up to January 2008, see A Boon and J Webb, 'Legal Education and Training in England and Wales: Back to the Future?' (2008) 58 *Journal of Legal Education* 79, 106–9.

[125] K Economides and J Rogers, *Preparatory Ethics Training for Future Solicitors* (London, The Law Society, 2009) available at www.lawsociety.org.uk/secure/file/179388/e:/teamsite-deployed/documents/templatedata/InternetDocuments/Non-governmentproposals/Documents/ethics_training_apr09.pdf.

the Law Society has sought to recapture the training initiative from the Solicitors Regulation Authority (SRA), and to resurrect a number of ideas that were originally mooted with the Ethics Education Forum that was chaired by Economides as part of the TFR. Nevertheless, if the recommendations of the report are to be progressed it will require the support of not just the Law Society Education and Training Committee, but the SRA as well. Its proposals for changes at the academic stage will also need to win over the JASB (discussed below), in consultation with the law schools. As pilots of the new, and controversial, work-based learning stage also progress, eight years after its launch, the ghost of the Training Framework Review lumbers on.

By contrast, the Bar, while under even greater pressure on the access issue,[126] limited its review very much to the vocational stage. An initial working party was constituted under the chairmanship of Cambridge academic Professor John Bell. This resulted in relatively little proposed change,[127] and in particular upheld the principle that the BVC should continue to provide a common platform of training for both civil and criminal work. Subsequently, in the light of the need to revalidate providers of the BVC and the changes to the regulatory structure, the Bar Standards Board instituted a further Working Group under the chairmanship of Derek Wood. This in turn reported in July 2008 and made a number of recommendations for a revised BVC, to be called the 'Bar Professional Training Course' (BPTC). Interestingly, again, the conclusions were markedly less radical than the SRA's, and showed relatively little departure from Bell, despite having been formulated in the shadow of a fairly radical report by the Neuberger Committee. The substantive course recommendations, accordingly, were largely at the level of detail, rather than signalling a substantial change in orientation or direction of the course.[128] The Wood Report, moreover, rejected Neuberger's proposal to impose a 2:i entry criterion, though it has proposed the development of a bespoke aptitude test for all applicants.

In many respects, then, this represents a continuation for the Bar of its established direction of travel: an emphasis on maintaining and, potentially,

[126] ie In terms of both the high cost of vocational training against a low chance of pupillage and tenancy, discussed above. The average fees for both courses now exceed £10,000 with the BVC tending to be slightly more expensive.

[127] A Boon, J Flood and J Webb, 'Postmodern Professions? The Fragmentation of Legal Education and the Legal Profession' (2005) 32 *Journal of Law and Society* 473.

[128] The main recommendations of the Wood Report were to introduce Professional Ethics and Conduct as a separately (as opposed to pervasively) taught and assessed subject; to omit Legal Research as a separately taught and assessed subject; to make various adjustments to Civil Litigation, Criminal Procedure and Evidence and Remedies and to focus more on the core elements of these subjects; to maintain the importance of written and oral advocacy and ensure that all advocacy trainers follow rigorously the so-called 'Hampel method' (based on the National Institute of Trial Advocacy method of training developed in the US); to lay greater emphasis on standards of written and oral English, and to introduce a new taught course on the Resolution of Disputes out of Court while abandoning the assessment of negotiation. It also proposed the introduction of centralised examinations.

enhancing its reputation as a high quality specialist referral advocacy profession, whilst seeking to establish legitimate mechanisms for re-establishing a greater degree of supply control. It is perhaps of particular note that both the training reviews for the solicitors' and barristers' professions have sought the introduction of an element of centralised assessment. While this has been presented as a matter of quality assurance, it is perhaps no coincidence that it offers a—perhaps now the only—means readily available to the professional bodies to re-establish themselves as educational gatekeepers for the profession.

A FUTURE FOR THE LEGAL PROFESSION AND THE ACADEMY?

The legal profession and the legal academy have both been subject to increasing pressures and changes, through the greater intervention of the state in their spheres of influence. This can be seen as an example of the ideological victory of private sector, or corporate professionals, over the public sector professions[129] played out particularly in the current schism within the Law Society between the corporate and high street firms. Finding an education regime that can meet the needs of both could make the difference for the Law Society between domination of the European legal market or further fragmentation and potential dissolution.[130] From the perspective of the academy, the question remains what the impact of such schisms may be. The recent training reviews demonstrate, potentially, not just widening gaps within the professions, but also between them. So far, however, this has not been reflected in the regulatory relationship between the professions and the academy. The main avenue of dialogue on the law degree has been through the Joint Academic Stage Board (JASB), a body established by the professions primarily to review the Joint Statement on Qualifying Law Degrees, and related matters, and keep it advised of any changes 'from time to time required'.[131] The relationship between the JASB and the academy can be a somewhat uneasy one. The academic subject associations engage with the JASB, but have no direct representation, and seem to desire no such representation upon the Board, so that academic members of JASB sit in a purely personal capacity. It is unclear whether this body has the muscle to make substantial reforms to, rather than incremental adjustments of the undergraduate curriculum. Even were it expected to do so, it may not be so inclined.[132]

[129] H Perkin, *The Rise of Professional Society: England Since 1880* (London, Routledge, 1989), ch 10.

[130] Boon, Flood and Webb, n 128, 490–91.

[131] *Agreement Between the Law Society of England and Wales* (2004) para 2.1.

[132] Though there is some feeling (anecdotally) within the academy that the JASB has been taking a more interventionist line, for example, by requiring clearer evidence at programme validations of the ways in which the Law Benchmarks are met, and by seeking to extend the 'guidance' (which supplements the Joint Statement) offered to law schools.

It currently has a membership tilted towards higher education providers, albeit that over half represent the vocational side, though this too may alter as the membership of the JASB is also about to change. Such changes, and any greater fragmentation of professional interest groups, may not be in the interest of the academy, which benefits from the professions channelling their combined demands through, and mediating them within, a single body. This suggests that the legal academy and the legal profession retain a common interest in preserving professional control in the sense, following Perkin, of their mutual control. Between the profession and the academy, however, there is suspicion of the other's desire to meddle in domestic affairs or, perhaps even, to take over functions. The failure of either, or both, to secure their area of competence could lead to further erosion of autonomy by inviting government (or regulatory) intervention. Government pressure may have set the academy and profession against the other, yet continuing stalemate supports the currently orthodox theory of professional regulatory incompetence.

While the main challenge for the legal profession is reconciling the needs of increasingly diverse constituencies, change in the universities goes to the heart of academic endeavour. Many legal academics are attracted by the original vision of universities as entities bound by collegial exploration for truths. The realisation of this vision seems increasingly remote. Whereas academic working lives and careers were often largely defined by research and publication, although more so in the old universities,[133] there is increasing sensitivity about the place of research and even concern about speaking truth to power.[134] Today, research takes a place among other activities in a highly competitive market for students. Academics perceive that their institutions see scholarship as 'a commercial overhead'.[135] The pay-off for universities lies in the esteem generated by good ratings and the income produced by the Research Assessment Exercise (RAE) and, for academics, highly rated research is a key determinant of career advancement. We speculate that growing pressure on academics from increasing student numbers, and the demand from institutions to publish, has increased resentment of demands on time and energy caused by the intrusion of 'external' institutions, like the professions, pressing their own agendas. The situation has probably been exacerbated by academic drift away from doctrinal scholarship, hastened by the RAE.

We should also acknowledge that academics are doing research, as well as teaching, with an eye to constituencies beyond the traditional legal profession. Legal academics are widely engaged in research, consultancy, 'knowledge transfer' and—even—practice for a wide range of organisations. A recent

[133] Cownie, n 92, 201.

[134] P Baty and J Shepherd, 'Ministers Vilify Researchers' *Times Higher Education Supplement* (1 December 2006) 1, 6, 7.

[135] Plender, *A Stake in the Future* (1997) 250.

AHRC/ESRC sector interaction study[136] has emphasised the extent to which legal academics are engaged in activities such as legal advice and lobbying activities for NGOs and pressure groups, policy advice and research for governmental and quasi-governmental bodies, and judicial training. Yet, the embedding of the vocational courses in many universities has not yet resulted in a renaissance of scholarship on the interface between the academic discipline of law and legal practice. Most of the vocational course teachers were recruited for their practice experience and their priority is to reflect contemporary practice. While some have produced practitioner and teaching texts, very few have aspired to entry in the Research Assessment Exercise. The vocational and academic course teachers remain consigned to their sides of an invisible intellectual divide within each law school. From the other direction, it is perhaps not surprising that engagement with legal practice itself by academics remains 'variable'.[137] In some settings, more notably the Bar, there are strong relationships, especially where chambers like Matrix, Doughty Street and Tooks Court actively support and encourage links with academia. In other areas, contact may actually be becoming more remote.

Equally, the world of higher education has also become more sophisticated. Educational debates may still seem to be fairly marginal to some of us within the law schools, but discussions about, for example, learning outcomes and learning processes, curriculum design, e-learning, experiential and work-based learning are carried on to a degree and with a sophistication that was unheard of even twenty years ago. This is a world that will be alien for many, if not most, practitioners,[138] and there are even fewer opportunities for practitioners to engage deeply with the law schools than vice versa. Law schools do not, for the most part, have visiting schemes for senior practitioners (in the way for example that some schools of education do) and few UK law firms encourage fee earners to take academic sabbaticals away from the office. In the absence of opportunities to cross over the

[136] Arts and Humanities Research Council/Economic and Social Research Council, *Report of the AHRC-ESRC Legal Professions Sector Interaction Study* (2005) (no longer available online; copy on file with the authors).

[137] Ibid 7.

[138] Only 79 responses were received by the Law Society in response to its first consultation on the TFR. Less than half of these were from solicitors' firms. Our analysis indicated, not surprisingly, that some the educational nuances were not properly understood either by respondents, or perhaps even those responsible for drafting the original consultation document. See Boon and Webb, *Report to the Law Society* (February 2002) paras 6.4–6.8, 7.18–7.20. An equally low response was achieved in respect of the latest (2006) consultation on the proposals for work-based learning. See www.lawsociety.org.uk/documents/downloads/becomingtfrconsultationwblanalysis.pdf. This obtained 71 responses, 23 of them (32.4%) from solicitors firms. While some of the non-response to these consultations may be accounted for by key players wishing to 'keep their powder dry', the extraordinarily low response rates suggest there may be large amounts of apathy and/or downright ignorance in the profession as regards issues of educational regulation and reform.

lines and share knowledge and experiences, it is likely that academics and professionals will continue to talk past each other.[139]

It is in this context that we must recognise that continuing failure to agree a way forward for legal education and training could result in intervention when the 'Clementi super-regulator', introduced under the Legal Services Act, finds its feet. In the past ten years there have been continuing invocations of the public interest to implement aspects of ACLEC's and the TFRG's proposals,[140] some of which would be consistent with international developments.[141] Nor is further distancing from one of its natural stakeholders a logical step by the academy. There is also a danger that the new regulatory arrangements, focused as they are on regulatory oversight, will increase rather than reduce the distance between the academy and the professional bodies. The initial composition of the new oversight regulator, the Legal Services Board, and of its Consumer Panel, have now been agreed, and concern has already been expressed that these lack current legal academic 'representation' or expertise.[142] Such concern has been heightened by uncertainty over the future of the Standing Conference on Legal Education, which has been seen as a way of ensuring that academic voices were heard on legal education policy matters.[143] It also remains to be seen whether changes to

[139] These are hardly new observations. See Partington n 71; see also J Webb, 'Looking to the Future: The Academy and the Profession' in J Macfarlane and J Chapman (eds), *Developments in Legal Education 1987–89: The Silver Jubilee Collection for the Law Teacher* (London, Sweet & Maxwell, 1990).

[140] Lord Justice Potter, for example, at an Anglo-American conference on ethics in legal education, proposed that the undergraduate curriculum should include both the ethics of law and the ethics of practising lawyers. See 'The Ethical Challenges Facing Lawyers in the Twenty-First Century' (2001) 4 *Legal Ethics* 23, 38–9.

[141] G Powles, 'Taking the Plunge: Integrating Legal Ethics in Australia' 33 *Law Teacher* 315; see also WM Sullivan and MS Rosin (eds), *A New Agenda for Higher Education: Shaping a Life of the Mind for Practice* (San Francisco, Jossey-Bass, 2008).

[142] See the UKCLE's *Directions in Legal Education* (Autumn 2008) 3, available at www.ukcle.ac.uk/directions/previous/issue17/autumn08.pdf. This is despite the fact that knowledge and understanding of legal education and training is a competence required of the Board by the Legal Services Act 2007 sch 1, para (3)(b).

[143] A Legal Services Consultative Panel was created under s 35 of the Access to Justice Act 1999 as a more limited replacement for ACLEC. Its functions have been to provide the Secretary of State with advice and assistance in the maintenance of standards of legal education and training. In fulfilling this function it has been supported by the Standing Conference on Legal Education, an ad hoc body organised by the Department of Constitutional Affairs/Ministry of Justice, involving an annual meeting of a relatively fluid group comprising the Consultative Panel itself, representatives of government, and of the academic and practising profession—both interest groups and regulatory bodies—together with a number of other academics with expertise in legal education matters. The Legal Services Act abolishes the Consultative Panel, and the fate of the Standing Conference is now in the hands of the Legal Services Board. See the speech by Bridget Prentice MP (Parliamentary Under-Secretary of State to the Ministry of Justice) to the Standing Conference on 21 November 2007, available at http://www.justice.gov.uk/news/sp211107a.htm. At the time of writing a further meeting of the Standing Conference has been called for November 2009, but it is still unclear whether or not this has been re-established as a one-off or continuing event.

the JASB, and the inclusion of academics among the 'lay' membership of the new committee structures of the Bar Standards Board and Solicitors Regulation Authority will provide any more substantial co-regulatory or dialogical structures. If they do, it will generally be on the basis of individual application for lay roles on committees. It is unknown whether the gradual inclusion of academics on committees will sufficiently enhance a stakeholding perspective among professionals or encourage academics to see themselves as empowered participants in professional formation and development.

There are also competitive threats that the academy must confront, including the prospect of more private institutions entering the market and increasing encroachment on the universities' turf. The hyper-specialisation of practice, particularly in the areas of high value transactional lawyering, and the growth in private law making and adjudication, has arguably opened up greater gaps between academic law and practice. Indeed, in some such areas, cutting edge knowledge is more likely to be produced and codified by practice than by academic scholarship.[144] The College of Law and BPP have strong relationships with employers through Continuing Professional Development programmes and through their customised vocational courses. They have also proven popular with students, who have paid higher fees for their vocational courses than those charged by universities, despite the fact that the private institutions have no 'academic' research profile. This popularity can be partly ascribed to the implied endorsement of the elite employment sector, but it also reflects a reputation for a culture that is student and customer focused.[145] The challenge of private institutions may intensify in future, as they combine their popularity with students with the market potential vested in their new degree awarding powers. This could bring competition directly to the old universities' backyards.

CONCLUSION

The legal profession and the legal academy have strong historical ties and an interest in preserving a strong relationship. Aspects of the relationship that are resented by the academy do offer some advantages to both sides, although there are often grounds for renegotiation. For example, oversight and renewal of the content of qualifying law degrees is valuable in building trust in law degrees, an independent legal profession and support for the rule

[144] See, eg J Flood and E Skordaki, 'Normative Bricolage: Informal Rule-Making by Accountants and Lawyers in Mega-Insolvencies' in G Teubner (ed), *Global Law Without the State* (Aldershot, Dartmouth, 1997); D Trubek et al, 'Global Restructuring and the Law: Studies of the Internationalization of Legal Fields and the Creation of Transnational Arenas' (1994) 44 *Case Western Reserve Law Review* 407.

[145] See Boon and Whyte, this volume.

of law, as jurisdictions that lack professional infrastructure attest.[146] Against this, the accountability of any institution must be finite. Endless consultation, auditing and justification are debilitating and the effort and time taken weakens enterprise. If it is conceded that the legal profession has a stake in legal education, the issue of its powers of prescription remains open. Unless this issue can be resolved, the risk is that another solution will be imposed on the profession and the academy, to their mutual disadvantage.

It is time to acknowledge that legal professions, on their own account, and as representatives of legal employers, have a claim to be stakeholders in the legal academy.[147] Although there is potential to translate this interest into collaboration over the desirable level of prescribed content of a first degree, the profession and the academy have found accord difficult. This is because, in England and Wales the relationship between the legal profession and the academy has been formalised in the division of educational responsibility into stages that are progressively vocational.[148] The profession's reliance on the academy for providing a substantial proportion of legal education is double edged. By transferring a significant regulatory responsibility to the academy, the profession has been hindered in its response to demands for greater flexibility and accessibility in the education and training regime. As the demands on professionals have grown, and as the profession's regulatory powers have come under threat, it has struggled to reclaim lost ground.

The academy has, as part of the post-Omrod consensus, negotiated itself into a position where it experiences a fairly light regulatory burden relative to that imposed by many other legal education systems. At the same time, the academy has also sought to recognise and regulate its commitments to other stakeholders in its enterprise—undergraduate students who will not enter the profession, postgraduates pursuing further academic qualifications, and the commissioners and users of research and consultancy—and, to a degree, use these as a bulwark against professional encroachment. For its part, the legal academy desires more freedom to develop law as a discipline, moving away from its doctrinal roots. This is understandable and desirable for the intellectual growth of the discipline. It might also be argued that it is desirable for the profession if the universities are properly to fulfil their role as the profession's 'house of intellect'[149] and an

[146] E Mytton and G Meladze, 'Legal Education in Transition: A Study from Georgia' (2006) *Web Journal of Current Legal Issues*. Issue 3, http://webjcli.ncl.ac.uk/2006/issue3/mytton-meladze3.html.

[147] See Boon and Whyte, this volume.

[148] RA Barnett, RA Becher and NM Cork, 'Models of Professional Preparation: Pharmacy, Nursing and Teacher Education' (1987) 12 *Studies in Higher Education* 51, 61.

[149] N Savage and G Watt, 'A "House of Intellect" for the Profession' in P Birks (ed), *Pressing Problems in the Law Vol II: What are Law Schools For?* (Oxford, Oxford University Press, 1996) 45.

appropriately critical friend.[150] But it too must be careful. Pragmatically speaking, the academy benefits hugely from the fact that most entrants to law degrees at least start with an aspiration to legal work. The demand for law degrees would be nowhere near as significant if this were not the case. If a case can be made that law degrees, by ceasing to serve the profession's purpose, are no longer sufficiently serving the public interest, they may no longer be accepted as the standard for entry to the profession. Intellectually speaking, too, we should stop to ask whether the academy will suffer if the distance from its conceptual and cultural roots in the practice of law becomes too great.

The academy may feel secure that the Bologna process will ensure that European professions will be graduate-entry only. But if the law content of law degrees is too diffuse, idiosyncratic and unreliable, if the only benchmarks were the ACLEC outcomes for example, the profession may well attempt to sideline the law degree and impose its requirements later, for example, by insisting that everyone passes an entry test for the vocational stage. It could be a mistake in this context to look at the SRA and BSB review processes simply as evidence of the academy's relative insulation from further review. The more radical thinking of the TFR suggests that, given the right incentives and context, another such process could spawn new conversion or foundation courses, significantly affecting the demand for law degrees and bringing about an even more substantial shift in the academy. Institutions and their teachers might have to choose between shorter 'preparation' courses or the law degree. Old divisions between academic and vocational institutions could re-emerge, or more flexible, market-responsive private providers could seize the initiative away from the university sector.[151] Either way, the result could presage the demise of a robust and powerful legal academy. This would not be in the public interest. It might well result in a decline in the scale of university legal education, to the detriment of legal scholarship and research and at the expense of the development of our understanding of law.

[150] The need for critical distance was well made in the Canadian Arthurs Report, thus: '[T]he scholarly enterprise of law can flourish neither divorced from the profession, nor in its close embrace, nor in hand-to-hand combat with it. Its best prospect for growth and development is therefore to take up a position within the law faculties as a distinct and separate endeavour, with its own goals, standards and basis of legitimacy. Only such a stance will at once stimulate energies, promote sensible interdisciplinary cooperation and provide a free and equal basis for exchange between scholars and practitioners.' Social Science and Humanities Research Council of Canada, *Law and Learning: Report of the Consultative Group on Research and Education in Law* (Ottawa, SSHRCC, 1983) 140. See also J Webb, 'The "Ambitious Modesty" of Harry Arthur's Humane Professionalism' (2006) 44 *Osgoode Hall Law Journal* 119, 124–9.

[151] The recent moves by the College of Law and BPP to obtain degree awarding powers, discussed above, and the move by Kaplan, the American training giant, into the UK vocational course market certainly suggest that private providers may already be preparing for a new and more aggressive phase of development in legal education.

4

South Africa: Legal Education in a Transitional Society

ROB MIDGLEY

INTRODUCTION[1]

AS IS THE case elsewhere, South African law faculties do not have sole prerogative over legal education and curriculum issues. As much as academics would like to proclaim academic freedom as a constitutional right, the reality is that academic freedom in South Africa has a particular history and its context is now informed by the country's foundational values: in particular, 'the achievement of equality and the advancement of human rights and freedoms', 'non-racialism and non-sexism', 'supremacy of the constitution and the rule of law' and 'accountability, responsiveness and openness' in the governance and management of public institutions.[2] There is a drive to achieve equality and to rid the country of the iniquities of the past, and so academic institutions are not free to articulate an ivory tower vision, but are instead called upon to play their part in building a just society.[3] Academic freedom has taken on a particular form: one has the

[1] This review has a strong personal element to it. It draws heavily on my experiences and participation in national and institutional debates, and on my particular educational environment—a small, rural English liberal arts institution in one of the poorest provinces in South Africa. I have, where possible, used examples from other institutions, but naturally most of the examples are drawn from my own institution.

[2] Constitution of the Republic of South Africa 1996 s 1.

[3] In *The Investigating Directorate: Serious Economic Offences v Hyundai Motor Distributors (Pty) Ltd* 2001 (1) SA 545 (CC), (2000) 10 BCLR 1079 (CC) at para 21 the court said, 'The Constitution is located in a history which involves a transition from a society based on division, injustice and exclusion from the democratic process to one which respects the dignity of all citizens, and includes all in the process of governance,' while in *Holomisa v Khumalo* 2002 (3) SA 38 (T) at para55 the court noted that the constitutional order created by the interim Constitution (The Constitution of the Republic of South Africa Act 200 1993) 'was a bridge from the past to the future, an attempt to break away from the evils of the apartheid years.'

freedom to think what one likes, and to be creative; but within societal and institutional constraints.[4]

This contribution focuses on stakeholders that are external to universities and their influence on South African legal education. Internal stakeholders—the faculties themselves, their staff, their students, their senates and institutional management, as well as representative organisations like the South African Law Deans' Association (SALDA) and the Society of Law Teachers of Southern Africa (SLTSA)—are by definition excluded from receiving specific attention and analysis, but their views and interests have not been ignored entirely. Wherever relevant, the manner in which universities have interacted and responded to external interests has also been recorded.

THE EDUCATIONAL ENVIRONMENT PRE-1994

Academic Institutions

Academic teaching of law in South Africa started in April 1859 at what is now the University of Cape Town (UCT),[5] but the first faculty of law came into being at UCT only in 1918.[6] Apartheid ideology provided the educational framework after 1948. In 1959 university education was formally structured along ethnic and racial lines,[7] and later, with the development of the apartheid government's homeland policy, several universities were

[4] For detailed analysis and discussion of this topic see www.che.ac.za, and especially Council on Higher Education 'Overview of Recent and Current Debates in South African Higher Education: Academic Freedom, Institutional Autonomy and Public Accountability' (2005) www.che.ac.za/documents/d000118/index.php; K Bentley, A Habib and S Morrow, 'Academic Freedom, Institutional Autonomy and the Corporatised University in Contemporary South Africa" (2006) www.che.ac.za/documents/d000136/index.php; S Friedman and O Edigheji, 'Eternal (and Internal) Tensions? Conceptualising Public Accountability in South African Higher Education' (2006) http://www.che.ac.za/documents/d000135/index.php; and R Jonathan, 'Academic Freedom, Institutional Autonomy and Public Accountability in Higher Education: A Framework for Analysis of the "State-Sector" Relationship in a Democratic South Africa' (2006) www.che.ac.za/documents/d000138/index.php.

[5] The Cape Parliament voted a salary of £300 to a professorship at the South African College. JH Brand, who was later to become President of the Orange Free State in 1863, was appointed the first professor of law in March 1859. For detail, see Cowen in D Cowen and D Visser, *The University of Cape Town Law Faculty, A History 1859–2004* SiberInk, Cape Town (2004) ch 1. Given that parliament also established the framework for legal education in the Cape (see n 13 below), it is clear that, from the inception of legal education in South Africa, the government was an important stakeholder.

[6] The Union Parliament had enacted Act 13 1916 and Act 14 1916, establishing the universities of Cape Town and Stellenbosch, but the faculties of law were established later: UCT in 1918 and Stellenbosch in 1921. See Cowen in Cowen and Visser, n 5, 22 and JR Midgley, 'Punching Beyond its Weight—The First Hundred Years of Rhodes University's Law Faculty' (2005) 19 *Speculum Juris* 246.

[7] With the enactment of The Extension of Universities Education Act 1959.

established in the so-called 'independent states'.[8] In 1994, when a constitutional state replaced the apartheid regime, there were twenty universities offering formative academic education that could lead to entry into legal practice at 24 teaching sites.[9]

Although generalisations might obfuscate the issue, in broad terms, universities in the apartheid era could be divided into three groups: the English liberal or open universities; the Afrikaans universities; and the black universities, many of which were located in the apartheid homelands.[10] Afrikaans universities were almost entirely closed to black people, while the English universities admitted black students in varying degrees and numbers, but always within constraints set by the apartheid government.[11] Only in the black universities could black people obtain legal qualifications in any significant numbers. And then their practice of law was restricted to the homeland and township areas.

Academic Qualifications

The first local practice qualification was the Law Certificate.[12] In 1874 the LLB degree was introduced, 'with quite a respectable curriculum,'[13] consisting of Roman Law, English Law, Dutch and Colonial Law, Law of Evidence and International Law, including Conflict of Laws.[14] Initially it was possible to obtain the degree in one year, but at UCT[15] it developed into a four-year

[8] See PF Iya, 'Legal System and Legal Education in Southern Africa: An Overview of Past Influences and Current Challenges' paper delivered at the Conference of International Legal Educators, Florence, Italy, 24–27 May 2000, available at www.aals.org/2000international/english/southafrica.htm.

[9] By 2006 these were reduced to 19 universities teaching at 21 sites. Registration of new students at Walter Sisulu University was suspended for a while, but the University is enrolling students once again.

[10] The University of Durban-Westville, the University of the Western Cape and later Vista University, were not 'homeland universities'.

[11] Black students graduated from Rhodes University in the 1950s and early 1960s, but in reality they were Fort Hare students, with Rhodes being the accrediting institution. English universities admitted black students in the 1960s, but government did not allow them to live in residence. UCT's Law Faculty admitted students of colour during the 1960s. See Visser in Cowen and Visser, n 5, 83–84. The Rhodes Law Faculty did not do so until the middle 1970s. See Midgley, n 6, 253.

[12] With Act 4 1858 the Cape Parliament established a Board of Public Examiners which was authorised to examine a certificate of the Higher Class in Law and Jurisprudence and admission of successful candidates to practice was made possible through Act 12 1858.

[13] Cowen in Cowen and Visser, n 5, 15.

[14] Ibid 16. Interestingly, few candidates graduated. The majority of admitted practitioners still obtained their legal qualifications abroad. Ibid 17.

[15] While there were curriculum and timing differences at other universities, the UCT experience reflects the broad trends.

undergraduate degree by 1918 and a five-year BA LLB route by 1926.[16] Initially legal curricula were practice-orientated, even those subjects like Roman Law and Roman-Dutch Law which formed part of the BA degree,[17] and often taught primarily by practising advocates, or academics who also practised at the Bar.[18] Essentially there were two schools of thought around the academic curriculum: one, mainly centred in the English universities, which followed a liberal arts approach and which emphasised the need for a broad education in other disciplines as well; and another, the 'Unisa[19] model' followed mainly by Afrikaans and black universities, which was packed with law courses and contained fewer non-law credits. These two approaches were pretty well entrenched and for many years, curriculum reform was placed on the back-burner.[20] However, universities did tinker with finding ways around the statutory practice requirements (compulsory credits in Latin, English and Afrikaans), despite strong opposition from the professions.[21]

The Law Certificate, in difference guises, continued to provide entry into legal practice,[22] even after the introduction of the LLB degree.[23] By the 1970s, however, three degrees had evolved.[24] The postgraduate LLB degree—a qualification route totalling five years in which one first obtained a BA or B Com degree with a law major or a B Juris degree (three years), followed by a two-year LLB degree—was the standard academic route for

[16] Cowen in Cowen and Visser, n 5, 17, 33–35. According to Cowen: 'Both the Lawrence Commission in 1914 and Mr GR Hofmeyr in 1917, stressed that the teaching of law in a university should not be geared solely to the technical needs of those studying law as a professional career.' Ibid 48. He also points out that Kotze J had similarly expressed preference for the BA LLB route in *Ex parte Van der Willigen* [1920] CPD 302. Ibid 34.

[17] Ibid 48.

[18] The first full-time professor of law was appointed at Rhodes University in 1905, 46 years after the first part-time professor was appointed at UCT. Even though faculties expanded their full-time complements considerably, they continued to rely on practitioners to assist them on a part-time basis. See also ibid 67–68.

[19] The University of South Africa.

[20] Cowen in Cowen and Visser, n 5, 5–66.

[21] While English and Afrikaans were dropped from the LLB curriculum at Rhodes in the 1960s, Latin remained a degree requirement until 1989. See Midgley, n 6, 250. However, a university credit in all three languages was a requirement for LLB graduates to enter the professions, even though these credits were not necessary in most LLB curricula. The language requirements for practice fell away with the promulgation of the Admission of Legal Practitioners Amendment Act 33 1995.

[22] It was an entry qualification for attorneys and for civil servants.

[23] Rhodes University offered two diplomas, the Diploma in Law and the Diploma in Law (Public Service) until 1972.

[24] Minimum entry qualifications were determined, for advocates, by s 3 of the Admission of Advocates Act 74 1974 (the LLB); for attorneys, by s 2 of the Attorneys Act 53 1979 (the LLB or B Proc); for regional court magistrates, by s 9(b) of the Magistrates Courts Act 32 1994 (the LLB); and for prosecutors and district magistrates, by policy directives of the Department of Justice (the B Juris).

most practitioners and was offered by all law faculties.[25] This route allowed one entry into any aspect of legal practice, whether as an advocate, attorney or as a participant in the criminal justice system, both in lower and higher courts. Most universities, but not all, also offered the B Proc degree, a four-year undergraduate qualification that had replaced the Diploma in Law and which was specific to the practice of law as an attorney, but which also provided entry into the civil service, for practice in the lower courts.[26] Yet a smaller cohort of faculties, mainly from Afrikaans and black universities, offered a third degree, the three-year undergraduate B Juris, which was the basic qualification for civil servants practising in the lower courts and which could also provide the necessary undergraduate requirement for entry into the LLB degree.[27]

Initially, to practise law, the LLB degree was sufficient. However, from 1934 attorneys were required to undertake articles of clerkship totalling two years,[28] followed by attorneys' admission examinations. Advocates also had to undergo practical training—pupillage—which gradually increased from three to six months, and from 1980, they had to write and pass Bar examinations. Civil servants (prosecutors, magistrates and state advocates) were not required to undertake formal apprenticeships and could be admitted upon obtaining the requisite academic qualification. They did attend in-house training courses at the Justice College in Pretoria, however.

Master's and PhD degrees in law were a rarity.[29] The purpose of legal education was to prepare lawyers for practice and, 'having regard to the smallness of our staff and the fact that there were many other pressing challenges to meet, the active promotion of post-LLB degrees would have to wait.'[30] What this meant, however, was that law as an academic discipline and the associated preparation of future legal academics were non-essential by-products of what happened at universities. Similarly, specialisation

[25] The LLB was actually a three-year postgraduate degree, the length of which could be reduced by one year if sufficient law credits were obtained in the preceding bachelor's degree (usually obtained by majoring in Roman-Dutch Law, Legal Studies or Legal Theory, the nomenclature depending upon the university).

[26] To practise in the higher courts, civil servants needed an LLB degree.

[27] Since the curricula for the B Juris LLB contained no arts (or non-law) courses apart from one-year courses in English, Afrikaans and Latin, those that followed this route did not have the 'liberal' education offered by the BA LLB or B Com LBB routes. It is more than likely that this had some impact later, when curriculum reform came under the spotlight.

[28] Attorneys, Notaries and Conveyancers Admission Act 23 1934. Alternatives to the two-year period were introduced after 1994.

[29] Interestingly, although the University of the Cape of Good Hope awarded its first PhD in 1899 (Cowen in Cowen and Visser, n 5, 17), Cowen recalls only one during his time at UCT (ibid 65). At Rhodes, the first Master's graduate was in 1984 and the first PhD in 1986 (Midgley, n 6, 252, 256).

[30] Cowen in Cowen and Visser, n 5, 65. This comment, referring to the UCT situation, applied to other faculties as well.

was not a priority and universities did not offer any taught (course-work) Master's degrees until the 1980s.[31]

Composition of the Professions

Although theoretically open to all, the practice of law was dominated by white males, both numerically and in terms of lucrative practice.[32] In the main, black lawyers had criminal law practices and later human rights practices, while women were generally in family law. The judiciary, even in the homeland areas, was overwhelmingly male, and white.[33] The position in the lower courts was not much different, although the homelands had more black practitioners, and the magistrates there were mostly black and male.

Academia reflected similar demographics. Although the percentage of women academics was higher than those in practice, white males still dominated, especially in senior positions. Black universities had a number of black academics, often reflecting the institutions' ethnic identities, and while some white institutions did make some effort in appointing black members of staff, black staff in those institutions were the exception rather than the rule.

POST-1994 DEVELOPMENTS IN LEGAL EDUCATION

Quite understandably, the majority black population did not trust the legal system, nor the professional bodies and the universities. Both the legal and educational systems were implements of the apartheid regime and not only were they dominated by whites and males, but there was also systemic discrimination in each of these areas that perpetuated the inequality. Blacks and women were not going to make much headway in a system in which white males would continue to dominate legal culture and legal practice, and so continue to hold the advantage.

In 1994, with a change of regime and South Africa becoming a constitutional democracy, a number of black lawyers either returned to, or came to, South Africa with qualifications from other countries, some of which had

[31] Visser in Cowen and Visser, n 5, 111.

[32] The government's policy was to have separate trading areas for white and black people. Black practitioners could open practices in the townships but could not practice in towns without government permits (www.bla.org.za, 'History'). In 1985 black attorneys numbered only 10% of all attorneys. Ibid.

[33] The South African Law reports indicate that in 1980 there were no black judges, even in the homeland courts, and only one female. By 1994 there were four black (two in the homeland areas) and two female judges.

systems quite foreign to that in South Africa. Some, mainly returning South Africans, found themselves in government; others, often from East and West Africa, were academic appointments. None of these lawyers qualified via the traditional route; many had three- or four-year qualifications that incorporated the practical professional components and which allowed them to enter practice in other countries immediately upon graduation. To them, the five-year 'liberal education' route was a luxury that South Africa could ill afford in transitional times. They themselves were living proof that a four-year qualification was a more than adequate preparation for practice, and their qualifications were in line with those in many countries throughout the world. A five-year programme was not only unnecessary, but being more expensive, also served to exclude poor, mainly back people, from entry into the legal professions.

Calls for transformation and a change in the composition and management of the judiciary and the legal professions soon came to the fore. Black lawyers, many of them members of the National Association of Democratic Lawyers (NADEL) and the Black Lawyers' Association (BLA), were increasingly being elevated to the bench or appointed to the civil service, and many found themselves in influential positions in the Department of Justice and Constitutional Affairs. Black lawyers, amongst others, considered the professions to be a closed club of white males who had designed strict professional examinations specifically to prevent other race groups from entering the profession. For them, governance of the professions was no different from the way in which the country had been governed. And the same accusations were being levelled at the law faculties, particularly those labelled 'historically white'.

Naturally, one of this new power group's priorities would be to address the imbalances in the legal professions, and its approach was multi-pronged: to reform the existing professional structures by including black lawyers in the governing committees; to replace the dual-bar (advocates/attorneys) system with one profession (legal practitioners); to address the way in which the professional entry examinations were being managed; and to address the basic academic entry qualifications, focussing on consolidating the various degrees into a uniform entry qualification for all legal practitioners and introducing a greater emphasis on practical skills.[34]

[34] The call for rationalisation was not entirely new. During October 1991 a national conference on legal education in Pretoria called for restructuring of the professional entry system. A working committee was appointed to look into the feasibility of a ladder system, in terms of which a B Juris graduate could practise as a prosecutor or criminal defender after three years and each additional year of study would improve the areas of practice—a B Proc after four years would entitle one to become a civil practitioner or a magistrate and the LLB after five years would enable practise in the higher courts. Nothing came of the committee's proposals, however.

Around this time law faculties were also facing pressure from a different source. Educational experts in South Africa were reviewing the manner in which universities provided education and concluded that the approach was too 'ivory tower' and not at all contextualised. The Department of National Education introduced and actively promoted outcomes-based education at schools and universities, the objectives of which were not too dissimilar to those of the professions, and the BLA and NADEL in particular. The policy makers contended that liberal arts education was too Euro-focused, too classical, and did not suit the milieu and needs of a modern South Africa which was in need of major reconstruction and transformation. Instead, the emphasis should be on what graduates could do with their education and curricula should focus on the improvement of practical skills.

Government took charge.[35] Following the establishment of a National Consultative Forum in 1994, the Department of Justice's Planning Unit published a strategic plan for transformation of the justice system in 1995.[36] Forums and meetings were held, ostensibly to deal with access and governance issues within the profession.[37] On the access front, the initial target was the professional examinations; but it soon became clear that the university law curricula would feature prominently in searching for solutions. Most black lawyers wanted to break the professions' hegemony and wanted the Bar and attorneys' examinations, which were seen to be protectionist instruments of exclusion, to be scrapped. The best way to improve access for black lawyers, it was strongly argued, was to follow the practice in other African countries and for universities to provide an all-encompassing entry qualification: a four-year undergraduate university qualification with

[35] More accurately, the Department of Justice took charge. A major feature of the negotiation process surrounding the LLB was the Department of National Education's lack of participation. The two government departments appeared to be driven by different policies and no attempts were made to reconcile them. The Department of National Education came into the process only at the very end, in August 1997, when it insisted that its policies be adhered to. In a letter to deans dated 28 August 1997, Cheryl Loots of the Department of Justice's Planning Unit noted that the new LLB had to be submitted to the University and Technikons Advisory Council (AUT) for approval. She noted that in terms of the Department's policy guidelines, '[a] Qualification Structure for Universities in South Africa... the old LLB was classified as an "Advanced Bachelor's Degree"' and '[t]he new LLB will be classified as a "Career-orientated Bachelor's Degree"'. She elaborated: 'Career-oriented Bachelor's Degrees require a minimum of three years of study. At least 50% of the credits should consist of basic and contextually basic subject contents, and at least half of the 50% should represent basic subject contents. Non-law courses and broad-based law courses, such as introduction to the study of law or constitutional law, would fall under "basic subject contents". Basic professional courses, such as contract and delict, would be contextual courses. Specialised, advanced and applied courses would fall into the third category "other".'

[36] *Justice Vision 2000—A Strategic Plan for the Transformation and Rationalisation of the Administration of Justice* (1995). See www.justice.gov.za/policy/misc/justice2000.htm.

[37] A National Forum was held on 26 and 27 November 1996, followed by a task group meeting on 15 and 16 April 1997. For a detailed discussion of the process see PF Iya, 'Reform of Legal Education in South Africa: Analysis of the New Challenge of Change' (1997) 31 (3) *The Law Teacher* 310.

a strong a practical component, thus entitling a graduate to practise law upon graduating from university without having to undertake pupillage or articles.

The response from the professions and from the universities was defensive and focused primarily on maintaining the status quo—under the guise of maintaining academic and professional standards, and thereby the status of the legal professions, and protecting the public from lawyers that were either incapable or inadequately prepared and who should not be offering legal services to the public. Both sectors were against the four-year LLB option, but the professions were more amenable to the introduction of skill-based curricula which was compatible with their need for better vocational training. The universities bemoaned the loss of academic time—the effective reduction of a five-year programme to three years, the loss of non-law subjects which many academics considered essential for a rounded legal education and the fact that they would have to provide practical professional training, which not only meant that they were being shouldered with a burden that properly belonged with the professions, but that their degrees would lose their academic integrity and standing and become training qualifications. Not all universities spoke with the same voice, however. The opposition came mainly from the English ('liberal arts') universities and some of the Afrikaans universities whose degrees were more academic and suited to the five-year qualification route. The Afrikaans and black universities, those that placed less emphasis on a classical or a liberal arts approach, took a more pragmatic view. They had always preferred the undergraduate three-year B Juris and four-year B Proc degrees as their main pre-LLB offerings and saw very little difference between these offerings and the proposed new four-year undergraduate LLB.

The outcome was a compromise. In reality, the more academic, postgraduate five-year route was an apartheid relic as far as those with political and financial influence and power were concerned, and there was enormous social pressure to abandon it. So in 1996 the universities accepted, with varying degrees of enthusiasm, the four-year undergraduate LLB option as the entry qualification for all legal practitioners, in private practice and in the civil service. And after government made the necessary legislative amendments,[38] the degree was offered for the first time in 1998.[39]

Universities also conceded that their curricula should reflect and emphasise the values of the new society and provide basic skills training to students. However, they differed on the extent of the exposure to practical

[38] Qualification of Legal Practitioners Amendment Act 78 1997.

[39] The other degrees had to be phased out as they would not provide entry into legal practice after 2004. A crucial factor, however, was that combinations with the LLB degree—BA LLB or B Com LLB, for example—were not prevented. So it was still possible to offer the five-year routes, but entry into the LLB was not restricted to postgraduates.

situations. Some believed that universities had the capacity to provide full practical legal education; others contended that the curriculum should remain primarily academic and merely expose students to some practical aspects—the context in which their knowledge would be applied.[40] In the end, issues such as the exact nature of the curriculum, outside accreditation, and the provision of practical training, were left in abeyance. The one-size-fits-all LLB curriculum that was advocated at some stage was rejected and each university retained the academic freedom to determine its own curriculum,[41] within its own institutional constraints.[42]

All universities introduced the four-year degree and incorporated practical aspects into their curricula, but the detail varied. The University of Fort Hare (and black universities generally), Potchefstroom University, the University of Port Elizabeth, the University of the Free State, University of Pretoria and Unisa, for example, devised curricula that primarily contained law courses and which, in line with what the attorneys' profession wanted, focused on practical aspects. The Rand Afrikaans University (RAU) continued to emphasise its more traditional academic approach, while Rhodes University, UCT, the University of the Witwatersrand, the University of Natal and Stellenbosch University devised curricula with strong 'non-law' components to them. UCT, Stellenbosch and Rhodes, while offering the undergraduate route, preferred and promoted a five-year combination route with the BA and B Com, along the lines of the previous five-year route. Gradually the market had its influence, and in time more and more universities included a five-year B Com LLB option among their offerings.[43]

Just under 10 years after the introduction of the four-year LLB, matters are not as rosy as anticipated. Attempts to consolidate the professions and to streamline their regulation have dragged on endlessly[44] and recently there have been numerous calls for reform. As was the case in 1994, the

[40] Philip Iya, then Dean of the Faculty of Law at the University of Fort Hare, was a strong proponent of the former position; I favoured the latter.

[41] However, among themselves, law faculties agreed on 26 core courses.

[42] Faculties are not autonomous. At Rhodes, the academic community, particularly the Faculty of Humanities, resisted the introduction of the new LLB. Other academic departments had a stake in the five-year programme, which not only enabled students to take a non-law major, but often also served as a postgraduate recruiting ground for such departments. And for some the non-law component of legal education was essential for their survival. (When the language requirements for the LLB were abolished, Classics departments throughout the country lost almost all their students, and many such departments disappeared, for the first-year course in Latin was their life-blood.)

[43] Interestingly, although many universities abandoned the B Juris degrees with gusto, the University of Port Elizabeth (now, after a merger with other institutions, Nelson Mandela Metropolitan University) made a strategic decision to retain the degree, arguing that it provided a suitable qualification for civil servants who do not wish to practise law, and also a convenient exit qualification for persons who are unable to complete the LLB degree.

[44] The Legal Practice Bill, the first draft of which appeared in August 2000 and which was supposed to be tabled in 2002, was again put on ice in 2006.

catalysts have been, on the one side, lack of meaningful reform towards black empowerment within the professions; and on the other, persons entering the professions with limited or unsuitable skills.[45] In October 2005 the professions hosted a summit on legal education and a task team consisting of SALDA representatives and representatives from the professions met on several occasions, but with limited, mainly cosmetic, results. All the while, the deadline for re-registering the LLB degree with the South African Qualifications Authority loomed, but some relief was obtained when it was extended for another year, to early 2008. Yet another round of negotiations took place in 2008. SALDA hosted a summit meeting of all stakeholders in Pretoria in June 2008. While the parties broadly recognised that the current legal education system was not producing graduates with the necessary literacy and numeracy skills for practice, there was little consensus on how to address the concerns. Outside stakeholders appeared to favour central intervention and the setting of a common, generic LLB curriculum, while academics insisted on protecting their autonomy in deciding curricula, favouring a less rigid system with each university having the ability to determine its own emphasis. The matter has not yet come to a head, however. The parties were given a reprieve, since further changes to the qualifications framework at national level meant that the generic LLB qualification which will become the benchmark for all law faculties need not be finalised before 2010. The next section will focus on the key external role players who are likely to influence the outcome.

THE EXTERNAL STAKEHOLDERS

Government

The Department of Justice

Since 1994 the Department of Justice has played an active role the education and training of legal practitioners. Under the leadership of the then Minister of Justice, Dullah Omar, the Department held legal forums, amongst them one on legal education.[46] At the end of 1995 the Department established a Planning Unit which drafted a strategic plan for the provision of legal services and the administration of justice for the country. Although the plan does not specifically address legal education, one of the plan's

[45] Professions, and the attorneys' profession in particular, bemoan the quality of law graduates, and highlight the lack of basic literacy and numeracy attributes, as well as poor vocational skills—computer skills, bookkeeping knowledge and practice management knowledge. Universities acknowledge some of the problems, but do not accept sole responsibility for the necessary remedial action.

[46] *Justice Vision*. www.justice.gov.za/policy/misc/justice2000.htm.

key result areas is: 'A well trained, broadly representative, accessible and evenly distributed legal profession.'[47] Later in the document, the strategy for achieving this is unpacked:

> Here we will deal with the transformation of the legal profession. We will change the way that people who go into the legal profession are educated and trained. We will make sure that the composition of the legal profession properly reflects all the different people in South Africa. We will make sure that the entire legal profession properly reflects all the different people in South Africa. We will make sure that all legal professionals have some understanding and appreciation of the many different people in South Africa particularly people who are different in terms of their race, gender, culture, disability, religion, language or sexual orientation. We will make sure that the legal profession can respond properly to the legal needs of all the people in the South African society. We will make sure that the legal profession is fully accountable to the public for the things that it does. We will focus particularly on four areas:
>
> (1) We will support training programmes for people, especially for historically disadvantaged people, so that they will be able to enter the legal profession, and to be promoted in it.
> (2) We will develop policies to make sure that legal services are evenly distributed in all areas, and to all people.
> (3) We will develop policies to make sure that people can afford to use legal services.
> (4) We will review the way that the legal profession works, and develop policies to protect people who use it and to make it more accountable to the public.[48]

A more recent departmental initiative is the Legal Services Charter,[49] a product of a National Indaba[50] held at the Sandton Conference Centre on 17 and 18 August 2006. The Indaba was itself the culmination of a drafting process that had been approved by Cabinet in July 2005. First a reference group was established, followed by the appointment of a Steering Committee in January 2006 which advised the minister. The Steering Committee's Drafting Team compiled the initial drafts. Three academics were part of the initial drafting process[51] and while SLTSA was represented on the Steering Committee, SALDA was not. A second and third draft were undertaken before the final version was published on 4 December 2007.

The Charter's focus is on the sector that is engaged in the practice of law.[52] Institutions that provide legal education are not included among

[47] Chapter 1: The Guiding Principles. Legal education gets no specific mention in the Department's Mission statement.

[48] Chapter 2: The Strategies, item 6. www.doj.gov.za/policy/misc/justice2000.htm.

[49] The final document is available at www.doj.gov.za/LSC/legal_charter.htm.

[50] 'Indaba' is a isiXhosa and isiZulu word for a meeting or conference.

[51] Professors Alberteyn, Gutto and Schlemmer.

[52] There is ample reference to 'the legal services sector' in the Charter and the implicit assumption in the draft versions that faculties and schools of law fall within that sector is not replicated in the final version.

those to whom it is to apply,[53] although universities, and particularly their law faculties and legal aid clinics, are listed separately as stakeholders.[54] The principal objectives of the Charter centre around meaningful transformation in the legal services sector and the promotion of access to justice and the creation of 'an affirming and enabling environment.'[55] Among the challenges to equitable entry into the legal professions that the Charter lists,[56] one (the availability of quality legal education to historically disadvantaged individuals) impacts on universities directly, while the other two (the availability of continued legal education and training and providing quality learnership opportunities) might do so less directly.

Chapter Two of the Charter deals with access to justice, of which access to the legal profession is naturally a part. Such access, according to the Charter, requires improving the quality of legal services, amongst others, by monitoring and evaluating academic qualifications.[57] This is a clear indication that in future the proposed Legal Services Sector Charter Council will become another stakeholder in legal education, even though the more specific provisions contained in the third draft have now fallen away.[58]

The creation of a unified legal profession is the overt goal of Chapter Three of the Charter and it mentions that 'standards of education and training' and 'qualification criteria for admission to the profession' need to be addressed.[59] Chapter Four addresses the empowerment of historically disadvantaged individuals. Save for a suggestion in Chapter Four that faculties and schools of law should promote participation of such persons in managerial and leadership structures, the neither chapter sets out specific commitments.[60]

[53] See art 1.2.2 of the Charter. Art 5.2 proposes the establishment of a Legal Services Sector Charter Council and universities may nominate a representative to be appointed as a member of the Council. This is an improvement from the first draft in which 'legal academics' were grouped together with prosecutors, state law advisors, the judiciary, paralegals, arbitrators and insolvency practitioners who collectively had one representative on the Council. The Council's function will be to oversee compliance with the Charter's provisions and commitments (art 5.4), which would include some of the aspects involving universities.

[54] Art 1.2.2.v.

[55] Art 1.1.

[56] Art 1.1.1.iv.

[57] Art 2.1.v.

[58] The third draft enjoined universities to promote access to the profession by providing 'accessible legal education and training to prospective legal practitioners' (art 2.5.2) and to promote access to legal services by undertaking to 'provide legal education in communities through street law and other outreach programmes' and to 'provide paralegal training where appropriate, provide primary legal advice through law clinics and work with government in realizing community legal services' (art 2.2.2).

[59] Art 3.2.iii. The final version no longer contains the detailed, possibly controversial, professional entry provisions that were set out in the first draft.

[60] Art 4.1.v.b. Again, the detailed employment equity and economic empowerment provisions of the first draft as they related to universities have been omitted; as are the controversial suggestions that faculties had to consider implementing compulsory community service for graduates.

The final version is tidier than the original draft[61] and, unlike the first three versions, does not contain any specific undertakings on behalf of universities. Nonetheless, the undertakings originally suggested in the drafting process provide some indication towards the Department's thinking in respect of legal education. The draft versions, which committed universities to a number of onerous obligations, were drafted without formal input from SALDA or university administrations[62] and while their gist was not problematic, they indicated that the Department was not aware of the tension between its more vocational interests and the interests of its counterpart in the education sector, whose focus is on the provision of formative education.[63] (For example, according to the Department of National Education, paralegal training is not the purview of all higher education institutions.[64]) Fortunately, the final product is far more focused and the possible tension areas with the educational sector have been eliminated. The only worrying aspect is the Department's initial disregard for meaningful consultation with the university sector and its seeming willingness to impose undertakings upon universities without consideration of competing interests.

In the post-apartheid era, the Department of Justice has been the leading and most influential external stakeholder and is likely to maintain this position for the foreseeable future. As its approach to the Legal Services Charter shows, legal education is not its prime focus, however: education is but a sub-component of the Department's oversight of the entire justice system. The driving force is the Department's vision for the system as a whole and educational institutions are, in the broader context, merely part of the herd.

[61] A detailed discussion of the provisions of the first draft can be found in R Midgley, 'South Africa: Legal Education in a Transitional Society', a paper presented at the Joint Meeting of the Law and Society Association and the Research Committee on the Sociology of Law of the International Sociological Association, Humboldt University, Berlin, 28 July 2007.

[62] As noted below, SALDA objected to its exclusion and was then invited to be part of the process. The Department's attitude appears to have been that the process was open to all interested parties and that SALDA did not take advantage of the opportunity to provide input. See the letter of the Director-General: Justice and Constitutional Development (20 December 2006). SALDA then elected a representative, and informed the Department, but it again had no input into the subsequent drafts. The representative reported that he had not been informed of or consulted in the process, except for one occasion where he had been requested to attend a meeting at the eleventh hour, and he did not receive any documentation. The President of SLTSA reported that although she had been appointed to the Steering Committee she, too, had not been informed of progress and, because of the lack of consultation, she withdrew from the process. See the minutes of a SALDA meeting (8 November 2007).

[63] The proposals also show a disregard of the resource implications for universities and a lack of awareness concerning the philosophical, but important, distinction between community outreach and community engagement programmes.

[64] Rhodes University's Legal Aid Clinic has a vibrant paralegal training and support programme servicing advice offices in rural areas throughout the Eastern Cape Province; yet, when it applied to have the training programme accredited, the South African Qualifications Authority (a component of the DoE) turned down the application as not being appropriate for the type of educational institution that Rhodes professes to be.

The Department of National Education (DoE)

In February 2001 Cabinet approved a National Plan for Higher Education, the overall goal of which was to transform the higher education system, ie redressing past inequalities, increasing access, promoting diversity in the system and ensuring that graduates have skills that are aligned to societal needs. Since then, the DoE has actively driven transformation in a number of ways, amongst others, by restructuring the institutional landscape, merging institutions, reconstituting university councils and rationalising existing educational programmes while restricting the introduction of new ones; by drafting a National Qualifications Framework, including a programme and qualifications mix for universities; by requiring institutions to conduct strategic planning regarding their size and shape and to submit three-year strategic rolling plans; by releasing a language policy for higher education; by investigating the feasibility of introducing a national, central application bureau and ways of regulating private higher education institutions; by instituting a new funding framework for universities; by requiring institutions to have quality assurance and capacity development systems in place; and by conducting a number of institutional audits and review of specific educational programmes.

The National Plan has had an enormous impact on the *size and shape* of the tertiary education system. In December 2002 the DoE ordered several institutions to merge (with effect from 1 January 2004), resulting in a reduction of the number of tertiary institutions from 36 to 21, the incorporation of some universities and technikons[65] into other institutions and the creation of new, larger, universities.[66] Those that seemingly were unaffected by the merger process still had to consider internal adjustments as their institutions adapted to the changing educational playing field.[67]

Law faculties were not unaffected. Vista University's faculty, which taught law at various sites around the country, was split and incorporated into the faculties of the Universities of Pretoria, Johannesburg (formerly RAU) and the Free State (formerly the Orange Free State), and the Nelson Mandela Metropolitan University (formerly University of Port Elizabeth). The Potchefstroom University and the University of Boputhatswana merged

[65] Technikons were tertiary institutions providing a more technical education at diploma and degree levels. Their hierarchal status resembled that of the former polytechnics in the UK.

[66] Following a report of a Size and Shape Task Team (7 April 2002), the then Minister of Education, Kader Asmal, made the initial announcement in June 2002. See 'The Transformation and Restructuring: A New Institutional Landscape for Higher Education' available at www.polity.org.za/article/asmal-transformation-amp-reconstruction-of-higher-education-system-09122002-2002-12-09 After considering representations, Cabinet approved the restructuring in December 2002.

[67] Eg government indicated that the balance in enrolments had to shift in the medium term from 49% to 40% in the humanities; from 26% to 30% in commerce; and from 25% to 30% in science, engineering and technology.

under the umbrella of the Northwest University, but the two law faculties continue to operate autonomously on the two campuses. The faculties of the University of Natal and the University of Durban-Westville merged, offering tuition, as the University of KwaZulu-Natal, at two sites (Pietermaritzburg and Durban) instead of the previous three; and the teaching of law on Rhodes' East London campus was taken over by the University of Fort Hare. Unisa, the University of the Free State and Nelson Mandela Metropolitan University also had to absorb staff and students from technikons. The following law faculties were left unscathed: UCT, Stellenbosch, Rhodes,[68] and the Universities of the Western Cape, Zululand, Limpopo and Venda.

The DoE also subsidises university activities. For 20 years, universities were funded in terms of the SAPSE formula,[69] but a new *funding framework* for higher education was published in August 2003. Unlike the old market-driven formula, the new one is intended to be a steering mechanism—'a goal-directed, distributive mechanism which relates government funds to academic activity and output'—and funds will be allocated, amongst others, according to government's policy priorities and academic activity which leads to 'improvements in the social and economic conditions of the country.'[70]

The system, as could be expected, focuses on teaching and research 'inputs and outputs'. Of immediate relevance to law faculties is the fact that teaching subsidies are now allocated in terms of a funding grid, or ladder system, with four levels—and law faculties have been placed on the lowest rung. Law teaching, therefore, receives one unit of funding, whereas others receive up to four times the amount for equivalent outputs, depending upon the level at which they were placed. The categories, universities were informed, reflected the costs involved in teaching each discipline as well as the need to attract students to particular fields, especially those where human resources are scarce. Law, being essentially 'chalk and talk', is a low-cost activity, and a popular vocational choice, and so the DoE's financial incentives are directed elsewhere.

The Regulatory Network

In managing higher education, the DoE is advised and assisted by an interrelated network of governmental institutions, the South African Qualifications Authority (SAQA) and the Council for Higher Education (CHE) and its committee, the Higher Education Quality Committee (HEQC).

[68] The excising of its East London campus had little impact on the university's main campus in Grahamstown.

[69] South African Post-Secondary Education funding formula.

[70] See Anonymous, 'Government Funding of Public Higher Education (August 2003) available at www.ukzn.ac.za/dmi/downloads/gov%20gazette%20aug%202003.doc. See also Government Notice 1791, GG 25824 (9 December 2003).

The South African Qualifications Authority (SAQA)

SAQA is a statutory regulatory authority[71] whose members are appointed by the Ministers of Education and Labour. Its primary purpose is to develop and implement a National Qualifications Framework (NQF), to register education and training qualifications, and monitor and audit educational programmes in terms of set standards.[72]

The NQF's purpose is transformation and arises out of 'discontent with the nature and quality of education and training in South Africa,' including issues such as equity and redress, productivity and economic competitiveness, and promotion of quality in learning.[73] Its primary objective is 'to create an integrated national framework for learning,' but quality assurance, access, mobility and progression are also key.[74]

SAQA's operations are best described in its own words:

> In 1998 SAQA published the National Standards Bodies (NSB) Regulations whereby provision was made for the registration of National Standards Bodies and Standards Generating Bodies. These bodies will be responsible for the generation and recommendation of qualifications and standards or registration on the NQF. The Education and Training Quality Assurance (ETQA) regulations were also published in 1998 and provided for the accreditation of Education and Training Quality Assurance bodies. These bodies will be responsible for accrediting providers of education and training standards and qualifications registered on the NQF, monitoring provision, evaluating assessment and facilitating moderation across providers, and registering assessors.[75]

Within the NQF, legal *qualifications* fall under the auspices of National Standards Body Organising Field Number 8[76]—for Law, Military Science and Security. Within that organising field is a sub-field, Justice and Society[77] and within that sub-field one finds a Standards Generating Body (SGB) for Legal Education and Training.[78] The SGB is closest to the coalface, and it is responsible for setting the standard for the LLB degree.[79] In 1997, when

[71] Established in terms of the South African Qualifications Authority Act 58 1995.

[72] www.saqa.org.za, 'About SAQA'. See also *SAQA Bulletin* Volume 1 number 1 (May/June 1997) www.saqa.org.za, 'Promotional Material, 'SAQA Bulletins' 4–5.

[73] *SAQA Bulletin* 2.

[74] *SAQA Bulletin* 5.

[75] www.saqa.org.za/structure/nqf/overview01.html.

[76] NSB 08 Law, Military Science and Security. There are 12 such organising fields.

[77] The other two are 'Safety in Society' and 'Sovereignty of the State'.

[78] NSBs and SGBs are registered in terms of s 5(1)(a)(ii) of the South African Qualifications Authority Act 58 1995.

[79] Five of its 23 members, including the chairperson, were either nominated or endorsed by the SLTSA (SALDA did not exit at the time of nomination in 1999). Other members were nominated by the LSSA, General Council of the Bar, Justice College, Independent Association of Advocates, BLA, NADEL, Department of Justice, Committee of Technikon Principals, Lawyers for Human Rights, National Para-legal Institute, AULAI (the Association of Legal Aid Institutions), Midrand University (a private university), and LIPCO (the Legally

the four-year undergraduate LLB was introduced, each university had to apply separately to the University and Technikons Advisory Council (AUT) for permission to offer the new degree.[80] The AUT's function was taken over by the CHE in January 1999. When SAQA became operational soon thereafter, universities had to re-submit their degrees for registration, on an interim basis before 30 June 2000, so that the degrees could be placed on the correct NQF level.[81] However, after consultation with stakeholders, SAQA registered a generic LLB degree, which is the standard to which all current LLB qualifications must comply. The generic LLB appears to have been no more than window-dressing, however, because each university's LLB was also registered separately, and so there was no need to comply with the generic criteria. The generic LLB registration was to have expired in February 2007, but SAQA agreed to a one-year re-registration. It indicated, however, that only a generic LLB would be recognised in future and the extension was granted[82] (after a request from SALDA) to enable the universities and the professions to consult further on the matter.

Whereas in the past *assessment* of student learning has been unregulated, SAQA has now set out criteria for registration of assessors.[83] The HEQC is the registering authority, but it has delegated this function to each university. Provided that they have proper quality management and monitoring systems, universities will be able to register their own staff as assessors.[84] These systems are in turn assessed during the HEQC's institutional audits. To comply with these requirements, Rhodes, for example, offers an assessment course, a Postgraduate Diploma in Higher Education, which new staff members are required to complete as part of their probationary

Independent People's Corporation). See www.saqa.org.za. While this representation might seem rather diverse, it must be borne in mind that the SGB is not solely concerned with the LLB qualification, but also for all 'law and justice' degrees, diplomas and certificates. The SGB's brief is set out at www.saqa.org.za.

[80] C Loots' letter to law deans (28 August 1997).

[81] The NQF is a set of education and training levels across three broad bands: general, further and higher education and training. For some time there was great confusion as to the appropriate levels for university degrees. Initially it appeared that ordinary Bachelor's degrees would be placed on level 6 and professional bachelor's degrees at level 7, but in some instances levels 7 and 8 were used. A minimum number of credit points (120 per annum), and the levels at which they were to be obtained, was also stipulated. (Based on a 40-hour week and a 30-week working year, a notional study year is equal to 1200 notional study hours, or 120 credits. See South African Universities' Vice-Chancellors' Association (SAUVCA) *SAQA Action Group Facilitatory Handbook on The Interim Registration of Whole University Qualifications by June 2000* (May 1999), SAUVCA, Pretoria 48.

[82] After a request from SALDA in October 2006.

[83] An assessor is 'the person who is registered by the relevant Education and Training Quality Assurance Body in accordance with criteria established for this purpose by a Standards Generating Body to measure the achievement of specified National Qualifications Framework standards of qualifications. SAQA Regulations (8 September 1998). See SAUVCA *Facilitatory Handbook* 50.

[84] SAUVCA *Facilitatory Handbook* 51.

requirements, and which tenured staff are encouraged, but not obliged, to complete. Some other universities, but not all, have similar programmes. Those that do not, will be required to comply or face de-accreditation.

The Council on Higher Education (CHE)

The CHE is a statutory body established in terms of the Higher Education Act[85] and has a permanent subcommittee, the Higher Education Quality Committee (HEQC). The HEQC operates within the South African Qualifications Authority Act[86] and its regulations and has executive responsibility for quality assurance in higher education, amongst others, by accrediting educational programmes and by institutional audits.[87] While SAQA registers learning programmes that lead to a qualification on the NQF, the HEQC evaluates and accredits those programmes and also the institutions that offer them.[88] In doing so, the HEQC has a strong inclination towards a quality assurance system based on fitness for purpose of an institution within a national framework and in pursuit of national goals and priorities.[89] It liaises with other accreditation agencies and professional councils, but essentially focuses on providers of educational programmes that SAQA has accredited, and assesses whether or not their programmes meet the necessary quality standards for (continued) accreditation.[90]

A key commitment in the National Plan was the *programme and qualification mix* (PQM) exercise, which was finalised in 2003. Each university had to submit its PQM to the Department as well as delivery sites and government then approved what qualifications each university could offer, and where, based on its 'current programme profile, its location and

[85] Act 101 1997.

[86] Act 58 1995.

[87] www.che.ac.za/heqc/heqc.php. See also www.che.ac.za/heqc_ac/accreditation.php and www.che.ac.za/heqc_ae/audit.php. See also Higher Education Quality Committee *Framework for Programme Accreditation* (November 2004) 4–5. See www.che.ac.za/documents/d000080/Programme_Accreditation_Framework_Nov2004.pdf.

[88] *Framework for Programme Accreditation* 5, 7.

[89] www.che.ac.za/heqc/heqc.php. The HEQC's document, *Framework for Programme Accreditation*, states at 6: 'Specific quality-related goals facing the South African higher education sector include increased access and equity opportunities for previously marginalised groups, especially women and black students and staff; greater responsiveness to local, regional and national needs in and through teaching and research; improved institutional efficiencies, leading to increased throughput, retention and graduation rates in academic programmes; and increasing the pool of black and women researchers, and the pool of basic and applied knowledge, to enhance understanding and social application. The mergers and incorporations, and the development of universities of technology and comprehensive institutions in public higher education, bring the additional challenge of developing new institutions, the academic functions and products of which are characterised by improved quality and standards.'

[90] If the audit requirements are satisfied, an institution may be granted self-accreditation status in respect of educational programmes for a period of six years. *Framework for Programme Accreditation* 7.

context, its responsiveness to regional and national priorities, as well as the demonstrated capacity to add new programmes to its profile.'[91] The effect of this approach is that government is in a position to ensure an overall balance to the educational programmes on offer in the country and avoid unnecessary competition among universities.[92] In addition, the PQM would determine what programmes the government would subsidise. At first universities were at liberty to offer new programmes of their choice, but unless they receive governmental approval through inclusion in the PQM, new programmes will not be subsidised. Since the latter part of 2004, however, no new programme, including unsubsidised ones, can be offered without CHE approval. Should a university wish to introduce a new programme, it would have to satisfy government that the programme would add value to the overall educational need in the country and that it would not undermine existing programmes.

The PQM exercise resulted in government withdrawing permission to offer certain programmes at some institutions. No law faculty was immediately affected, and most were given permission to offer LLB, Master's (by course-work and thesis) and PhDs by thesis, as well as various diploma offerings. In April 2006, however, government used its extraordinary power to close down programmes that it considered to be unviable, when the Minister of Education informed the Vice-Chancellor of Walter Sisulu University (WSU) that she did 'not support the continuation of the LLB degree... at WSU under the current conditions.'[93] As a result, WSU did not register new law students in 2007, although it continued its commitments to existing students. This restriction was subsequently lifted.

The HEQC has also undertaken specific reviews of providers of the MBA and M Ed degrees, accrediting some institutions and de-accrediting others. Members of the legal profession requested that a similar process be instituted in respect of LLB providers, but this seems to have fallen by the wayside after the HEQC indicated that the professions and the universities should discuss the matter first. This interaction was behind the scenes and this directive may well have been the catalyst for the current round of negotiations between SALDA and the professions.

Institutional audits are one step removed from programme reviews. Audits are comprehensive reviews of entire institutions, both public and private, and not only particular programme providers within the institutions, and

[91] cl 7.2 of the Ministry of Education's *National Plan for Higher Education in South Africa* (2001) www.education.gov.za/Documents/policies/NationalPlanHE2001.pdf.

[92] Universities were instructed to rationalise their offerings on a regional basis. Although every university offers the LLB, to the best my knowledge, no region considered rationalising law faculties.

[93] Letter dated 17 April 2006. The conditions referred to appear to be that, in the Minister's opinion, the Faculty of Law did not have the human resources and delivery capacity to offer the LLB.

audit teams look into all aspects of the institution's academic, administrative and social involvement.[94] Although audits can result in far-reaching recommendations that impact on the way students are admitted and educational services are provided, by and large these recommendations focus on the institutional milieu and institutional policies instead of on particular programmes. Nonetheless, a recommendation regarding external examining, or administration of short courses, might well impact directly on particular educational services on offer.

The National Research Foundation (NRF)

The role of the NRF is to support and promote academic research in South Africa. Its strategy is to improve the quality of research by encouraging researchers to form partnerships and publish in the international arena. As with all public institutions, it has a strong capacity building focus, and its funding is often geared to projects that focus on equity and redressing past imbalances, ie developing back and women researchers.[95] The Foundation not only provides funding for research projects but also operates a voluntary rating system for researchers.

For many years, from 1984 to 2001, the NRF's rating system focused on research in science and engineering, but in 2002 it extended its remit to the humanities and social sciences. Some universities have responded enthusiastically, but there is also a fair deal of scepticism, not only regarding the need for a rating system, but also regarding the process. SLTSA and SALDA have had several meetings with NRF delegations regarding their concerns and in January 2004, supported by some members of the NRF's Rating Panel for Law, submitted documentation to the NRF suggesting improvements to the rating criteria. Since then, the NRF has consulted further, but, despite recommendations from other quarters that the rating system should be reviewed,[96] no changes have been made. While the suggestions for change have not yet been rejected, there is substantial resistance to change within the organisation.

Even though the rating system for law researchers has been in place for less than five years, and irrespective of its merits, there is a discernable impact—not necessarily on the quality of legal research, but definitely on the way in which legal academics plan and conduct their research, and where they publish. Academics, especially from those universities that

[94] During an audit the institution's 'policies, systems, strategies and resources for quality management of the core functions of teaching and learning, research and community engagement' are evaluated. *Framework for Programme Accreditation* 7.

[95] www.nrf.ac.za/profile.

[96] Similar recommendations came from the NRF's institutional review and from a workshop that the NRF convened on 31 January and 1 February 2006, which included local and overseas 'outsiders'.

have bought into the rating system,[97] now concentrate far more on their international profiles and faculties are less inward-looking than before and encourage contact with sister institutions around the world. This has begun to break the isolation and insular thinking that characterised the apartheid years and it may well encourage more theoretical, discipline-orientated research over more practice-orientated approaches. However, while it is necessary that researchers do operate in the international academic arena, and while international research collaboration and publication is to be encouraged, the NRF's current rating criteria might well compromise its obligation to promote research that impacts on South African society. A system that rewards international standing and impact above inherent quality and local impact could encourage researchers to 'go global' and to ignore issues that would improve local quality of life.

The Department of Science and Technology (DST) and Academy of Science of South Africa (ASSAf)

In December 2001 the DST contracted ASSAf to conduct research into a strategic framework for South African research journals. The objectives included promoting and enhancing the standing and effectiveness of local journals, nationally and elsewhere and ensuring that research findings were made known beyond the research community.[98] The research considered all academic journals, including law journals, and its recommendations included the establishment of an accreditation system and quality audits (in five-year cycles).[99] If the gist of ASSAf's recommendations is to be implemented, then ASSAf will be responsible for the quality assurance, which in turn will make it an important stakeholder in academia.

There is no doubt that this journal accreditation will impact on legal research. For many years the system has been uncoordinated and there is a proliferation of law journals in South Africa, several of them, as the ASSAf research shows, no more than in-house, non-refereed, institutional journals in which faculty members publish articles that attract government subsidy. Law researchers have been prolific. There are approximately 25 law journals in South Africa, 12 of which account for 27.35 per cent of the articles published in 'arts and humanities' journals, while of these, three account

[97] Not all have. My impression is that the administrations of Stellenbosch, UCT and the University of the North West actively encourage their academics to apply for rating, and law faculties have obliged. At other institutions the approach appears to be more low-key, leaving it to individuals to decide. The system has not found universal favour among researchers in the humanities and social sciences, and some law researchers have refused to participate.

[98] Academy of Science of South Africa, *Report on a Strategic Approach to Research Publishing in South Africa* (March 2006) vii. See www.assaf.org.za/strat_report.html.

[99] Ibid viii–ix.

for 11 per cent of all articles.[100] Of the 10 South African journals with the highest single institutional contribution, four are law journals, with three of them being in-house.[101]

The message that government is sending out at present, through the DoE, the DST and the NRF, is that the system is unacceptable, as the subsidy-accreditation system, which encourages a proliferation of publications, impacts negatively on research quality. If undeserving research is subsidised, the system is also financially wasteful. So in recent years the DoE has requested journal editors to supply details of their quality assurance mechanisms if they wish to remain accredited.[102] As a result, every law journal has established a peer review system of some sort and articles submitted for publication are now rejected more frequently than before. And, in anticipation of further changes—there is a real likelihood that the number of accredited law journals will decrease—journals are similarly applying to be included on international citation indices to improve their international visibility and standing.

Professions

The General Council of the Bar of South Africa (GCB)

The GCB is a federal governing structure for advocates with 10 constituent Bars from across the country.[103] It lists as its first objective considering, promoting and dealing with 'all matters concerning the teaching and practice of law and the administration of justice.'[104] In practice, however, its other objectives—to deal with matters affecting the profession, and to uphold the interests of advocates[105]—have taken precedence. Nonetheless, GCB representatives have participated in liaison meetings, forums and working groups that government departments and the attorneys' profession have organised. Constituent Bar representatives also sit on university faculty boards.

While the GCB is currently not as active as the Law Society of South Africa in trying to change LLB curricula at universities, it certainly has the ability to do so. For some time since the late 1970s universities were offering

[100] Ibid 38.

[101] Ibid 45–48.

[102] To be accredited for subsidy purposes, the DoE requires that the purpose of the journal is to disseminate research results and the content must support high-level learning, teaching and research in the subject area; an International Standard Serial Number; regular and frequent publication; an editorial board with appropriate expertise in the subject area and with research standing; a peer-review mechanism for articles that have been submitted; and distribution beyond a single institution. Ibid 29.

[103] cl 3 Constitution of the General Council of the Bar of South Africa www.sabar.co.za/about.html.

[104] Ibid cl 2(a).

[105] Ibid cls 2(b) and (c).

Latin courses (often called 'Latin Special' or something similar) to law students who had not taken Latin at school. In the 1980s some of them sought to have these courses declared suitable to meet the Latin language requirement for professional practice. Bar Associations across the country successfully opposed the court applications,[106] which certainly impacted on the basic education required for legal practice. So, when they choose to exercise their powers, the GCB and its constituent Bars can be powerful stakeholders in university educational matters.

The Law Society of South Africa (LSSA)

The LSSA, through its educational arm, LEAD,[107] concentrates mainly on providing practical legal education to attorneys, specifically by managing the various legal practice schools,[108] candidate attorneys' courses and conveyancing and notarial practice courses, and providing continuing legal education for attorneys.[109] It maintains close links with academia, however, and has substantial influence in moulding curricula. LSSA coordinates and finances an annual Liaison Meeting between stakeholders in legal education, its representatives sit on some faculty boards, it has been invited to attend SALDA meetings as an observer, and it conducts joint courses with some universities.[110] It also participates actively in the Attorneys Fidelity Fund's educational committees. LSSA's primary focus is to improve the practical skills of attorneys and prospective attorneys and it lobbies extensively for the inclusion of more practical and professional skills training in university curricula. It also promotes extra-curricula events that focus on improving practical skills, such as the Client Counselling Competition.[111]

The LSSA exerts a prominent and direct influence on legal education. Its approach is hands-on, establishing contact with the influential roleplayers and negotiating cleverly both publicly and behind the scenes, to promote its views and interests. It is probably the most active of all stakeholders in this regard. For example, the LSSA is campaigning extensively for the inclusion of numeracy and literacy skills, and practice management

[106] See, eg *University of Cape Town v Cape Bar Council and Another* 1986 (4) SA 903 (A) and *Ex parte Lynn and Others* 1987 (1) SA 797 (N).

[107] Legal Education and Development.

[108] Attorneys provide practical professional training at 10 Schools for Legal Practice; some separate from, others in conjunction with, universities.

[109] See www.lssalead.org.za.

[110] Certificates in Corporate Law and Deceased Estates with the University of South Africa (Unisa), a certificate in Insolvency Litigation and Administration with the University of Pretoria, a certificate in Tax Practice with the University of KwaZulu-Natal and a diploma in Labour Law with the University of the North-West (Potchefstroom). www.lssalead.org.za/d_e.htm.

[111] Originally a competition that involved teams from South African universities and practical legal training schools and linked with an international competition in the United States, it now is a regional competition for teams from SADC countries.

in the LLB curriculum. It operates at various levels. Initially it reported perceived shortcomings in legal graduates to SALDA and to the Liaison Committee and asked that these be addressed by including practical courses in the LLB curriculum. Some, but not all, universities obliged. As an incentive, the Attorneys Fidelity Fund's policy towards funding university projects changed and projects that did not serve the objectives of the attorneys profession stood little chance, if any, of receiving financial assistance. Attempts to improve numeracy, for example, were generously funded. But these initiatives were also not as successful as the LSSA would have liked. So the LSSA conducted investigations into the various LLB curricula in South Africa, highlighting where, at what level and to what extent practical skills were being addressed and proposing a set of outcomes for the LLB. In October 2004 it arranged a summit meeting on the competency of aspirant legal practitioners. The summit generated some debate, resulting in universities undertaking to consider the ways of remedying the shortcomings that the professions identified[112] while a joint university/professions task team drafts a joint position paper.

Most law graduates in South Africa enter the attorneys' profession and the LSSA is an active and influential stakeholder in legal education. Its main concern is to ensure that graduates have the core skills for attorneys' practice and in recent years LSSA has been a vocal critic of the LLB curriculum. Without any doubt, it will lobby hard for the inclusion of practical components in the generic LLB curriculum.[113]

[112] Focusing on:

6.1 High quality skills training pertaining to oral and written communication, research, problem solving, numeracy and the use of computers;
6.2 The formulation by SALDA of uniform minimum outcomes for such skills training and the sharing of expertise and materials among law schools and faculties in the interests of the national improvement of the skills of law graduates, and
6.3 Achievement of the exit level outcomes and assessment criteria of the LLB programme as provided for in the SAQA framework.

Joint Statement on Legal Education by the Liaison Meeting between the Legal Professions and the South African Law Deans Association, Johannesburg International Airport (13 October 2006).

[113] The LSSA's position appears anomalous, however. While it has correctly identified the shortcomings in many LLB graduates, its proposed solution is one that militates against improving the situation, for it addresses symptoms, not causes. In my view, the reason for graduates not having numeracy, literacy and organisational skills is a lack of basic formative education, not a lack of specific skills training. No amount of training will improve the situation if the foundations are not in place. If there is a decline in the quality of graduates the problem should be addressed at source: broaden the basic, generic skills that are on offer, improve students' insights by expanding the non-law components of the curriculum, and lengthen, instead of shortening, the academic education for lawyers. The result would be that graduates have core generic skills upon which the professions can build. For example, a course in accounting, which the LSSA advocates, would serve no purpose if students do not have basic numeracy skills. So, too, is there no point in providing a course in practice management to people who have no experience of practice and no context in which to locate their learning. These are courses that more properly belong in professional training courses: the task of

The Attorneys Fidelity Fund (AFF)

The AFF serves to protect the public from losses resulting from theft of trust funds by practitioners.[114] The AFF's link to legal education is primarily financial: it provides funds to the LSSA for its practical legal training and educational development programmes, to the BLA for its Legal Education Centre, and to the universities, to assist with legal aid clinic salaries, with library holdings and with projects that could enhance practical skills of students.[115] It also has an extensive bursary scheme for LLB students[116] and in the past made significant contributions towards funding the All Africa Moot Competition.

The AFF's funding policy is to consider projects that have the following objectives:

Academic excellence, with particular reference to capacity building at historically disadvantaged universities.

Practical and legal skills training.

Continuing legal education programmes.

Human rights and constitutional programmes.

Community service (other than law clinics and advice bureaux).

Active involvement and academic empowerment of students.

Promotion of African jurisprudence.

Improvement of students' literacy and legal skills.[117]

And the criteria for assessing particular projects are:

Relevance within the context of current developments in South Africa.

The potential for sharing resources, expertise and results between law faculties and other institutions.

The potential for providing or enhancing training in the following practical skills of students: literacy, communication, computer use, research, analytical and research-based problem solving.

The incorporation of, or emphasis on, principles of accounting and management, ethics and professional conduct.

The availability of other funding and resources.[118]

universities is to ensure that their graduates have the necessary foundational competencies for the professions to build upon.

114 www.fidfund.co.za/pages/nature_text2.htm.
115 www.fidfund.co.za/pages/legal_edu_text2.htm.
116 www.fidfund.co.za/pages/bursaries_text2.htm.
117 www.fidfund.co.za/pages/legal_edu_text2.htm.
118 www.fidfund.co.za/pages/legal_edu_text2.htm.

The Fund's influence on legal education is subtle. Its professed involvement is financial but there is no doubt that funding can influence educational emphases and direction. Although an independent entity, the AFF tends to work in tandem with the LSSA and its funding objectives are biased towards the needs of the attorneys profession.

Black Lawyers Association (BLA) and National Association of Democratic Lawyers (NADEL)

The BLA was formally constituted in 1980. Its forerunner, the Black Lawyers' Discussion Group, was formed in 1977 to respond to problems that were peculiar to black lawyers stemming from various pieces of apartheid legislation.[119] NADEL grew out of the BLA and was designed to be accessible to a broader group of people. It was launched in 1987 but soon after, in January 1998, BLA members broke away and continued a separate existence.[120]

One of the objectives of the BLA is to provide continuing legal education to black lawyers and it has run trial advocacy programmes for black lawyers since 1986. It has also run programmes on constitutional litigation, immigration and refugee law, and commercial law.[121] Its educational flagship programme is the Legal Education Centre which 'is aimed at building capacity and making the study of law accessible to all aspirant Black legal practitioners.'[122] NADEL used to operate a Human Rights Advocacy Project and still makes representations to government regarding legislation;[123] but, while its representatives sit on liaison and AFF committees and so indirectly contribute to university legal education in that way, it is uncertain whether the organisation has any other educational or training interests.

For a number of years BLA and NADEL voiced the views of black and progressive lawyers. The organisations were outsiders in regard to the formulation of government policy, to professional governance and to educational issues. In the transition era, however, these organisations asserted substantial influence and at present, even though their members have become more involved in mainstream governance of the professions, they continue to provide back-up support for transformation initiatives. In future, as transformation occurs, their role is likely to diminish.

[119] http://www.bla.org.za, 'History'.
[120] http://www.bla.org.za, 'Training'.
[121] Ibid.
[122] www.fidfund.co.za/pages/legal_edu_text2.htm.
[123] See, eg www.pmg.org.za/odb/Nadel.htm.

CONCLUSION

South African law faculties not only operate within the higher education landscape, but they also have to take cognisance of the needs of the justice system and of the professions. It would be a mistake to consider outsider involvement in legal education as a recent phenomenon, though. It is not recent, for government was involved in legal education from the outset in 1859 and the professions played a major role in maintaining the professional practice language requirements as essential components of the LLB curriculum. If anything, the reason for the scant outside governmental interference prior to 1994, was simply that the structures and objectives of legal education in the main suited the government of the day and law faculties produced graduates who met the needs of the dominant external stakeholders, the advocates and the attorneys.

The situation changed after 1994. The organised legal professions no longer held the high ground, and the Department of Justice became the lead stakeholder, with formerly marginalised structures, the BLA and NADEL, in support. The Department was and continues to be totally committed to its transformation agenda and to diluting the control and influence of pre-1994 elites. And to the extent that faculties of law were out of step with that agenda, they needed to respond. Equity issues are at the forefront, as the proposed Legal Services Charter indicates, and until internal faculty structures and the nature of law graduates change to reflect the needs of the dominant stakeholders, law faculties' autonomy of yesteryear is unlikely to return. While there is no doubt that government became more active after 1994 and that faculties have had to align their programmes with governmental policies, in reality transformation would not have occurred without a revision of the system itself.

Transformation has its price, however, and sometimes equity and quality may be incompatible. As much as some would wish to deny it, the quality of legal education varies enormously, often, although not entirely, along formerly-advantaged and formerly-disadvantaged institutional lines. In my view, the Department, in pursuing its objectives, did not pay sufficient attention to core educational issues, and where these are raised, they are often perceived as attempts to resist societal transformation. The reality, however, is that the Department has not liaised with another important government stakeholder, the DoE, which is pursuing a similar transformation agenda in the education sector, but which is also faced with the problem of ensuring that higher educational institutions have the capacity to produce quality graduates. Even though they are pursuing the same objectives, the two government stakeholders appear to have been talking past each other and they have failed to ensure that their approaches are compatible.

Quality is certainly the motivation for the increased involvement of the legal professions in legal education. When it comes to curriculum issues there is constant tension between the educational objectives and professional requirements. In this regard, universities are not autonomous and in the past 10 years curricula have been shaped away from theory towards practice.

It would also be a mistake to suggest that lines should be drawn between law faculties and internal stakeholders on the one hand, and external stakeholders on the other. The milieu is multi-faceted: in some instances, as with the choice between a four-year and five-year LLB curriculum, universities are not unanimous, and nor are the professions; and in others, for example, the need for universities to provide professional skills training, the difference is ostensibly between internal and external stakeholders, but there is also a marked difference in approach between the Department of Justice and the DoE and its regulatory institutions. And when it comes to defining quality, the points of departure vary enormously.

Whether the involvement of outside stakeholders amounts to an unwarranted interference with academic freedom is a complex issue, and beyond the scope of this contribution. Suffice it to note that the nature of academic freedom in South Africa has for some reason not been at the forefront of the legal education debate, despite academic freedom being a constitutional right.

5

Students as Stakeholders in Legal Education: Gaining Admission to Law School

BENJAMIN J RICHARDSON

INTRODUCTION

WITHOUT STUDENTS, LAW schools as we know them would cease. Virtually no law school anywhere in the world operates purely as a research institution. The seemingly insatiable demand for legal education however has sometimes caused faculties to underestimate their dependence on students. The number of law schools in some jurisdictions, particularly in Australia and the UK, has exploded in recent years.[1] In these countries, the law degree (LLB) is possibly supplanting the Arts degree (BA) as the general degree of higher education.[2]

This chapter considers students as stakeholders in relation to the policies and procedures that govern admission to law school. It focuses on admission to Bachelor's degrees or equivalent law programmes, rather than graduate legal education such as LLM and PhD programmes.[3] The chapter considers the experiences of the major common law jurisdictions, specifically the US, Canada, UK, Australia and New Zealand. The primary issue examined is the tensions between policies to widen access to achieve a more diverse student body representative of society, and the traditional methods of selecting students based on academic grades and test scores. Further, the chapter considers how the rising cost of legal education, principally because of tuition fees, affects the above policy goals. The aim is clarify and deepen readers'

[1] For information on law schools in these jurisdictions, see Australian Council of Law Deans www.cald.asn.au, and the UK's Association of Law Teachers www.lawteacher.ac.uk.

[2] See generally J Goldring, C Sampford and R Simmonds (eds), *New Foundations in Legal Education* (Sydney, Cavendish, 1998).

[3] For further information on admissions policy at graduate level, see SS Anand, 'Canadian Graduate Legal Education: Past, Present and Future' (2004) 27(Spring) *Dalhousie Law Journal* 55.

understanding of these issues, in the hope that future reforms to law school admission policies will be better informed.

SYNOPSIS OF LAW SCHOOL ADMISSION PROCESSES

Law school admission policies are diverse. They differ not only internationally, but also among schools within a single jurisdiction. One primary distinction exists between those countries where legal education is effectively a graduate programme, with admission based on completion of undergraduate studies (as in the US and Canada), and other jurisdictions where the study of law is a Bachelor's degree with entry normally directly from secondary school (in Australia and the UK) or after a preliminary single year of university study (in New Zealand).[4]

New Zealand has six law schools, all public institutions (the sixth was launched in 2009 at the Auckland University of Technology). Most students complete a combined degree programme, in which the LLB degree is studied with another degree over a five-year period (eg in Arts, Economics or Science). The majority of institutions also offer a straight four-year law degree. Admission to New Zealand law schools is generally an internal university process that occurs after the first undergraduate year. This process is competitive, based upon students' performance in an introductory legal systems course and other first year units studied at each university. The initial law course is generally open to most entering undergraduates.

The New Zealand law school admissions system has the advantage of giving students the opportunity to take an introductory law course, and those students admitted to law school will have demonstrated some competence in legal studies. Admissions decision-makers in this system are thus largely spared the trouble of having to infer applicants' aptitude for legal education from grades of uncertain merit achieved in courses of possibly only tangential relevance to law.

Australian and British law schools share similar admission standards, normally admitting students directly from secondary school based on their final year school qualifications. They also, like in New Zealand universities, set aside places for mature age applicants who have been in the work force for some time.

[4] For information regarding the structure of legal education in some jurisdictions, see UK Centre for Legal Education www.ukcle.ac.uk, American Association of Law Schools www.aals.org, New Zealand Council of Legal Education www.nzcle.org.nz, Council of Australian Law Deans www.cald.asn.au/slia/Legal.htm and Council of Canadian Law Deans www.ccld-cdfdc.ca.

Australia has a plethora of law schools for a country of only 21 million people.[5] In 1988, it had 12 faculties of law. That ballooned to 24 by 1993, and has since risen further to 31 as of December 2008.[6] All but two are public institutions.[7] Canada, with approximately 34 million people, presently has just 22 law schools by contrast (in 2008 new law schools were proposed in Ontario, but their establishment was deferred).[8] Canada's first new school in several decades was launched in 2009 at Thompson Rivers University, in British Columbia. As in New Zealand, virtually all the Australian law schools offer a combined five-year degree programme or the option of a straight four-year LLB degree. Entry into law school is competitive, based primarily on secondary school termination examinations. Significantly, in 2008 the University of Melbourne made its law programme available only as a graduate degree (Juris Doctor, JD), with students having to complete a three year Bachelor's degree before being eligble for admission.[9] Since then, a number of other Australian law schools have also introduced the JD degree, although they have retained the LLB option for students wishing to commence legal studies immediately after high school. In another variation, the University of Tasmania uses the New Zealand model to admit some students into its legal programme, taking into account applicants' performance in their first year of undergraduate studies for those persons ineligible for direct entry.[10]

The UK has at least 80 law schools, with significant institutional growth since the early 1990s.[11] They are nearly all public institutions, except for the University of Buckingham's law school and the BPP Law School, the latter being operated by a private European provider of professional education.[12] More such private institutions will likely be established, in line with current UK government policy.[13] Entrance to the British LLB programmes is typically based on students' performance in the 'A level'

[5] S Parker, 'A Global Legal Odyssey: Legal Education in Australia: The Perfect Storm?' (2002) 43 *South Texas Law Review* 535, 537; for an historical perspective, see D Pearce, E Campbell and D Harding, *Australian Law Schools: A Discipline Assessment for the Commonwealth Tertiary Education Commission* (4 volumes), (Canberra, AGPS, 1987).

[6] J Hatchard (ed), *Directory of Commonwealth Law Schools 2003-2004* (Routledge-Cavendish, London, 2002); for the latest numbers, see Australian Council of Law Deans www.cald.asn.au.

[7] Bond University was the first private university in Australia, and opened a law school in 1989. The University of Notre Dame later open a second private law school.

[8] The average enrolment numbers of Australian and Canadian law schools are broadly similar, with approximately 150 to 200 students admitted into each first year class (although there is wide variation from school to school, with some admitting about 300 students).

[9] www.law.unimelb.edu.au.

[10] www.law.utas.edu.au/.

[11] See the list of law schools maintained by the UK Centre for Legal Education www.ukcle.ac.uk/directory/index.html.

[12] See www.bpplawschool.com.

[13] C Sanders, 'Private Law Schools Push into the Degree Market' *The Times* (London 18 Oct 2005).

final examinations. Admission committees may also consider applicants' personal statements and letters of reference. Some law schools, such as at Cambridge and Oxford Universities, also interview short-listed applicants. In 2004 an important change occurred with the introduction of the National Admissions Test for Law. Modelled on a similar test used in North America, it is a standard test that supposedly measures applicants' aptitude for studying law. At least 10 institutions presently use this test as a supplementary admission-screening tool.[14]

The US has by far the largest and most diverse legal education sector.[15] As of late 2008, 200 law schools were approved by the American Bar Association (ABA), in addition to scores of other unaccredited institutions.[16] Of the ABA-accredited law schools, approximately 55 per cent are private institutions. In most states, a law graduate cannot take the Bar exam without having graduated from an ABA-approved school.

Competition for places in the elite US law schools is intense.[17] They select applicants primarily upon their undergraduate grade point average (GPA), personal statements, letters of recommendation and scores in the nationwide Law School Admissions Test (LSAT). Other factors such as ethnic diversity often play a part too. In practice, the applicant pool is initially ranked on the basis of a composite score derived from each applicant's GPA and LSAT score. Usually only applicants in the top tier of the pool proceed to have the other information in their files considered by admission committees in a more individualised, nuanced fashion.

Similar practices apply in Canada's common law faculties.[18] They initially screen the applicant pool on the basis of GPA and LSAT scores before undertaking, if at all, a closer review of the top applicants' work experience, extra curricular activities, letters of reference and other sundry information. As in the US, some law schools set aside places or use additional criteria to recruit students from designated disadvantaged backgrounds, as well as to admit mature age students. The Quebec civil law schools do not require prior undergraduate studies or completion of the LSAT for admission. Rather, they select students primarily on the basis of their performance in a collège d'enseignement général et professionnel (Cégep), the colleges forming the first tier of post-secondary school.

[14] www.lnat.ac.uk.

[15] By way of introduction, see RB Stevens, *Law School: Legal Education in America from the 1850s to the 1980s* (Chapel Hill, University of North Carolina Press, 2001).

[16] www.abanet.org/legaled/approvedlawschools/approved.html.

[17] Evident for example by the plethora of literature advising applicants. Eg R Montauk, *How to Get Into the Top Law Schools* (Upper Saddle River, New Jersey, Prentice Hall Press, 2006); CL Wright, *The Ultimate Guide to Law School Admission: Insider Secrets for Getting a 'Big Envelope' With Your Acceptance to Law School!* (Center Valley, Pennsylvania, Marriwell Publishing, 2003).

[18] Law School Admission Council, 'Official Guide to Canadian Law Schools' www.lsac.org/canadianCFC/template2.asp?url=HowApplicantsSelected.htm.

NUMERICAL INDICATORS OF MERIT

Introduction

Students become stakeholders in legal education when they seek admission to law school. The admission policies and procedures of law schools profoundly affect an individual's chances of admission and, thereby, entry into the legal profession. Because demand for places usually greatly exceeds the places available, especially in the prestigious law schools, admission policies are highly contentious. Often, law schools make choices among individuals who are virtually all well qualified and likely able to successfully complete law studies. Rarely is it simply a choice between those that can succeed and those unqualified.

Traditionally, all applicants to law school were judged virtually solely on their academic records. Such records supposedly allowed for 'objective' comparison of applicants' academic abilities considered relevant to success at law school. In Australian and British law schools, 'merit' meant excellent secondary school grades. In North America, merit was based on pre-law university GPA and LSAT scores. Apart from their supposed reliability as indicators of scholarly abilities, law schools favoured numerical indicators for their ease of assessment. The premium placed on efficiency of time and administrative resources in law school admissions decision making arguably skewed policies to a narrowly conceived notion of merit. From the perspective of students, such policies are controversial because they can lead to places in law school being rationed without sufficient regard to the individual qualities and suitability of each applicant for eventual success in the law profession or other endeavours.

Academic Grades

North American law schools are virtually unique in requiring applicants to have completed a programme of university study, preferably a Bachelor's degree. In other common law jurisdictions, students generally enter law school directly from secondary school or a first year of undergraduate study. Such law schools rely on final year school qualifications or first year undergraduate grades to assess applicants.

In most cases, where GPA or other numerical indicators serve to rank applicants, admissions committees usually do not differentiate courses and programmes on their academic content or quality, although some studies perhaps provide better preparation for law school than others. In 1972, a report of the Law Society of Upper Canada unfavourably contrasted 'lawyers… with a fairly narrow range of pre-law experience' with lawyers who 'have taken degrees in commerce and engineering [or have] qualifications as chartered accountants or graduate economists [whose] diverse skills are needed to deal with many of the problems created by the complexity of modern society'.[19]

University GPA or secondary school qualifications may poorly reflect an applicant's ability to succeed at law school. Grades mask differences in the rigour of academic programmes, methods of assessment and their relevance to future legal education (and practice). A qualitative rather than a quantitative assessment may thus be necessary to look behind the academic transcript for such factors as trends in an applicant's grades, discrepancies among the grades, difficulty of coursework and course load, class rank and time commitments while attending college. And, as preparation for law school, preference could be given to those who took courses that develop skills and competencies most relevant to the study of law. However, while we know that pertinent differences exist between courses and universities, and some programmes are harder or easier than others, the difficulty is to formulate consistent ways to compensate for those differences.

Apart from weaknesses in properly capturing student academic performance, grades may also hide applicants' disparate life experiences. Those with family care responsibilities or part-time work to financially support themselves or others may commit less time to their studies and consequently suffer academically.[20] Mazer, who served on the University of Windsor's law school admission committee for many years, contends that what is important 'is not the grade-point average but rather the individual's characteristics in light of his/her personal situation and the extent to which that achievement can provide an indicator for the potential to succeed in law school study'.[21] Individuals who have overcome adversity and barriers to educational opportunities may display traits relevant to success at law school and the profession, and other vocations, such as determination and industriousness.

The principal means by which law schools have compensated for weaknesses in the integrity of academic grades is to differentiate candidates on

[19] Law Society of Upper Canada, *Report of the Law Society of Upper Canada Special Committee on Legal Education* (under the chairmanship of BJ MacKinnon) (Toronto, Law Society of Upper Canada, October 1972) 21.

[20] The 12 years of pre-university schooling (K-12) have a formative influence on one's prospects for access to and success at higher education. Considerable inequality of educational provision in the K-12 years exists, not merely between private and public schools, but also among public schools. A system that funds education from municipal property taxes, as in Canada and the US, may lead to disparities in the financial resources for schools in wealthy and poor communities. A Venezia, MW Kirst and AJ Antonio, *Betraying the College Dream: How Disconnected K-12 and Post-Secondary Education Systems Undermine Students' Aspirations* (Stanford, California, Stanford Institute for Higher Education Research, 2003); JW Guthrie et al, *Modern Education Finance and Policy* (Boston, Allyn and Bacon, 2006).

[21] BM Mazer, 'Access to Legal Education and the Profession in Canada' in R Dhavan et al. (eds), *Access to Legal Education and the Legal Profession* (London, Butterworths, 1989) 119.

the basis of their scores in special law school entrance tests. From the perspective of students, these test scores can be just as problematic as reliance on GPA for admission to law school.

Law School Admission Test (LSAT)

Standardised tests for admission to higher education are used extensively worldwide.[22] In the context of legal education, the leading example is the Law School Admission Test (LSAT). Developed in 1948 and administered by the Law School Admission Council (LSAC), the LSAT assesses some basic competencies considered relevant to the successful study of law.[23] The LSAT includes multiple choice and essay components, which assess reasoning skills, logical aptitude and reading comprehension.

Most US law schools revere LSAT. They treat high LSAT scores as indicative of a talented student body.[24] A law school's students' aggregate LSAT scores is one seminal criterion behind the law school rankings formulated by *US News & World Report*.[25] Law schools' reliance on LSAT also owes to a requirement of the ABA.[26]

Much of the controversy over LSAT concerns the social science that informs it, particularly whether the test accurately predicts students' success in law school and its possible discriminatory impact on some groups such as ethnic minorities. There is no well-developed theory of what legal 'aptitude' involves.[27] A related concern is the relative weight that should be placed on LSAT and university GPA. Most US law schools assign more weight to LSAT, while Canadian law schools tend to weigh them equally or to prefer GPA.

[22] L Scott Miller, *An American Imperative: Accelerating Minority Educational Achievement* (New Haven, Connecticut, Yale University Press, 1996); R Zwick, *Fair Game? The Use of Standardized Admission Tests in Higher Education* (New York, Routledge, 2002); E Rule, 'The Use of Objective Testing for Law School Admissions' (1990) 24(1) *Law Teacher* 37.

[23] www.lsac.org/LSAT/about-the-lsat.asp.

[24] For a critique of these rankings, see PE Hobbs, 'Noblesse Oblige: Four Ways the "Top Five" Law Schools Can Improve Legal Education' (2001) 33 *University of Toledo Law Review* 85, 86–87.

[25] W Henderson and A Morriss, 'Student Quality as Measured by LSAT Scores: Migration Patterns in the U.S. News Rankings Era' (2006) 81 *Indiana Law Journal* 163.

[26] The ABA standard, however, did not mandate the *extent* to which law schools rely on LSAT, among other criteria. Interestingly, the ABA approved a change to its Standard 503, which requires law schools to use 'a valid and reliable test' in their admissions decisions. Prior to August 2003, the LSAT was mentioned specifically in this Standard. Since then, the possibility exists for law schools to use different tests, although there is an obligation on a law school to 'establish that such other test is a valid and reliable test to assist the school in assessing an applicant's capability to satisfactorily complete the school's educational program'. *ABA Standards Approval of Law Schools*, Interpretation 503-1 (August 2003).

[27] D Kaye, 'Searching for the Truth About Testing' (1980) 90 *Yale Law Journal* 431, 445.

While favouring GPA might seem justified if university grades capture more information about a student's determination, creativity, and intellectual curiosity than LSAT does, some correlation studies suggest otherwise. LSAC's research suggests that the LSAT is generally a better predictor of first year performance in law school (although, in combination, LSAT and GPA have a better predictive value than either score alone).[28] However, the LSAT's predictive success might owe precisely to a bias in the way law schools examine students' performance. Heavy reliance on administratively-convenient final examinations as the basis for the entire evaluation of students' learning in the first year tends to replicate the conditions of LSAT. This statistical correlation may be weaker in the upper years, where courses enrolling smaller classes are more often assessed by diverse methods such as research essays and class participation.[29] The uniformity of first year curricula and methods of assessment in law schools may seem to promote more statistically reliable correlations, but students have different learning styles. The 'one-size-fits-all approach to student learning' disadvantages some individuals.[30] Statistical correlation studies that only consider first year law grades may also fail to account for 'late bloomers', especially students from disadvantaged backgrounds who need more time to settle into law school.[31]

Ironically, LSAC—the very body that devises and administers the LSAT—has become one of the most vocal critics of law schools' emphasis on the numbers. It has acknowledged that 'the modest size of the correlations suggests that a substantial amount of the variance in outcomes is left unexplained by the two measures'.[32] In other words, neither LSAT nor GPA appears very useful at predicting success at law school, let alone success afterwards. LSAC concedes that LSAT scores 'have never come close to accounting for all the factors that contribute to an individual student's performance'.[33] Expert testimony in the *Grutter* case, involving a challenge to the admissions policy of the University of Michigan Law School, suggested a correlation between LSAT scores and first year law school grades of 'only 16–20%, which is to say that 80–84% of first year law school grades are not predicted by the

[28] Eg LA Stilwell, SP. Dalessandro and LM Reese, *Predictive Validity of the LSAT: A National Summary of the 2001–2002 Correlation Studies* (Newtown, Pennsylvania, Law School Admission Council, 2002).

[29] The correlation studies on cumulative law school performance have been somewhat inconclusive. See, eg LF Wightman, *Beyond FYA: Analysis of the Utility of LSAT Scores and UGPA for Predicting Academic Success in Law School* (Newtown, Pennsylvania, Law School Admission Council, 2000), arguing that LSAT retains its validity in predicting a student's cumulative law school performance; JC Hathaway, 'The Mythical Meritocracy of Law School Admissions' (1984) 34 *Journal of Legal Education* 86, 93, arguing against such a correlation.

[30] D Tong and WW Pue, 'The Best and the Brightest? Canadian Law School Admissions' (1999) 4 *Osgoode Hall Law Journal* 843, 849.

[31] Ibid 865–66.

[32] Ibid.

[33] PD Shelton, *The LSAT: Good—But Not that Good* (Newtown, Pennsylvania, Law School Admission Council, Law Services Report, October 1997).

LSAT'.[34] Yet, the LSAC still maintains there is no other measurement that 'comes close to matching the predictive qualities of the LSAT'.[35]

LSAC, along with many individual commentators, advocate that law schools should use LSAT in combination with other information about applicants.[36] The test does not measure other factors relevant to success at law school or beyond, such as an individual's industriousness, motivation, judgement, creativity, courage, personality, verbal skills, organisational ability, among other characteristics.[37] Some of these traits for success at law school, and the legal profession, can be demonstrated through an applicant's extracurricular activities and work experience. To assess these factors requires qualitative methods of assessment, involving interviewing applicants and reviewing their resumes, references and other qualitative information.

Discriminatory Impact of LSAT

During the 1970s, a debate began in the US legal education community regarding whether LSAT is culturally and ethnically discriminatory. The criticism concerning test bias did not allege discrimination in the sense of disparate treatment. Rather, some critics argued that LSAT has a disparate impact on minority and disadvantaged applicants in two specific ways. First, the phrasing and content of LSAT questions supposedly discriminates against applicants from non-English-speaking backgrounds.[38] Second, LSAT score disparities were said to reflect differences in educational achievement, which in turn reflect social inequities.[39] The LSAC research data generally indicates that minorities (eg African-American, Latino, and Indigenous) perform poorer on the LSAT compared to Caucasian students. But LSAC maintains the LSAT does as well for minorities as it does for other students in forecasting who will succeed in law school.[40] In other words, applicants

[34] *Grutter v Bollinger et al*, 137 F Supp 2d at 860; and 539 US 306 (2003).

[35] PD Shelton, 'Admissions Tests: Not Perfect, Just the Best Measures We Have' (6 July, 2001) *Chronicle of Higher Education* B15.

[36] See, eg D White, 'An Investigation Into the Validity and Cultural Bias of the Law School Admission Test' in D White (ed.), Towards a Diversified Legal Profession (New York, National Conference of Black Lawyers, 1981) 66; Allan Nairn, *The Reign of ETS. The Corporation that Makes Up Minds: The Ralph Nader Report on the Educational Testing Service* (Washington DC, Allan Nairn and Associates, 1980).

[37] P Liacouras, 'Toward a Fair and Sensible Policy: Professional School Admission' (1978) 1 *Cross Reference* 155, 161.

[38] Kaye, n 27.

[39] See, eg O Milton, H Pollio and J Eison, *Making Sense of College Grades* (San Francisco, Jossey-Bass, 1986); WC Kidder, 'Does the LSAT Mirror or Magnify Racial and Ethnic Differences in Educational Attainment? A Study of Equally Achieving "Elite" College Students' (2001) 89 *California Law Review* 1055.

[40] LC Anthony and M Liu, *Analysis of Differential Prediction of Law School Performance by Racial/Ethnic Subgroups Based on the 1996–1998 Entering Law School Classes* (Newtown, Pennsylvania, Law School Admission Council, 2003).

who score low on LSAT tend to subsequently perform below par at law school, according to the LSAC. Yet, heavy reliance on LSAT scores for these groups will result in their under-representation in law school and, subsequently, the law profession.

Concerns among academics and students regarding the discriminatory affect of LSAT have also aired in Canada.[41] The US higher education sector is much more diverse than Canada's, featuring many private universities. Therefore, the need to place greater reliance on a standardised test to compensate for the greater diversity in the quality of undergraduate programmes is less compelling for Canadian law schools.[42] As in the US, the LSAT has been the subject of litigation in Canada. In 1998, a rejected law school applicant, Selwyn Pieters, unsuccessfully challenged the legality of Ontario law schools' reliance on LSAT, alleging it violated the province's human rights legislation.[43]

LSAC has gradually come to accept the legitimacy of some of these reservations about its test. It has explored techniques for increasing minorities' access to legal education (particularly through the work of its Minority Affairs Committee). LSAC has issued 'Cautionary Policies Concerning LSAT Scores and Related Services', and in 1999 published a paper to assist law schools interested in experimenting with alternative admissions models.[44] These initiatives demonstrate the increasing sensitivity to the position of students as stakeholders in legal education.

Admissions Testing in Other Jurisdictions

Elsewhere, some law schools also, on a less extensive basis, rely on LSAT-type examinations as an additional tool to assist in admissions decisions.

The Australian Law Schools Entrance Test (ALSET) is used by an increasing number of Australian law faculties for special categories of applicants. Prepared by the Australian Council for Educational Research (ACER), the ALSET contains questions similar to those in some parts of the LSAT.[45] According to ACER:

> ALSET is designed to provide an opportunity for those candidates who have not completed a recent or standard university entrance qualification to demonstrate

[41] Canadian Bar Association, *Gender Equality in the Legal Profession* (Ottawa, Canadian Bar Association, 1993).

[42] Tong and Pue, n 30.

[43] D Gambrill, 'OHRC Report Questions Validity of LSAT' *The Law Times* (27 November 2000).

[44] Law School Admission Council, *New Models to Assure Diversity, Fairness, and Appropriate Test Use in Law School Admissions* (Newtown, Pennsylvania, Law School Admission Council, 1999).

[45] See www.acer.edu.au/news/index.html.

> an ability to cope with tertiary studies in Law. ALSET thus provides a degree of access to, and equity for, places in Law Schools for a significant group of special category applicants.[46]

Presently, only a small number of students fall into this situation, and it does not yet act as a general filter for the bulk of applicants to Australian law schools. However, the Melbourne Law School has decided to make more extensive use of standardised testing, and has borrowed the LSAT as a selection tool for its new JD programme.

In the UK, a consortium of eight law schools in 2004 adopted the National Admissions Test for Law (known in brief as the LNAT) for use alongside secondary school grades and other existing selection mechanisms.[47] The LNAT is modelled on LSAT, but is shorter. The 10 law schools currently participating in the LNAT as of September 2009 include the elite institutions at University College London and Oxford University. However, the University of Cambridge Faculty of Law decided in late 2008 to abandon use of the LNAT, 'based on its own assessment of the usefulness of the test in the context of Cambridge's admissions process, which is distinctively different from those of other universities'.[48] The LNAT was introduced primarily because 'the growing number of candidates with top scores at GCSE and A-level has made it increasingly difficult for the most competitive law schools in the country to rank their applicants satisfactorily'.[49] Contrary to the objections against LSAT, the participating UK law schools do not view LNAT as a barrier to widening access. Indeed, they see it as a tool for widening access. For instance, University College London's Faculty of Laws explains that the test: 'is intended to improve the selection process and to make it fairer to all candidates, whatever their educational background' such as by 'providing objective evaluations of candidates from a wide range of social and educational backgrounds by assessing essential general intellectual skills of comprehension, analysis, logic and judgment'.[50] Despite some contrary fears that LNAT would in fact discriminate against government school candidates who might be less well prepared, some preliminary evidence suggests negligible differences in the average test scores of applicants from the different UK educational sectors.[51]

[46] www.acer.edu.au/alset/.

[47] www.lnat.ac.uk.

[48] University of Cambridge, Faculty of Law, 'LNAT To Be Phased Out of Law Admissions at Cambridge' (3 September 2008), www.law.cam.ac.uk/press/news/2008/09/lnat-to-be-phased-out-of-law-admissions-at-cambridge/712.

[49] Quoting Tim Kaye, undergraduate law admissions dean, University of Birmingham School of Law, in 'New Entry Test for Law Students' *BBC News Online* (2 February 2004) news.bbc.co.uk/2/hi/uk_news/education/3451897.stm.

[50] University College London, Faculty of Laws, 'National Admissions Test for Law (LNAT)' www.ucl.ac.uk/laws/prospective/undergraduate/index.shtml?entry_lnat.

[51] Discussed in L Lightfoot, 'Would-be Lawyers Flop in Essay Test' *The Daily Telegraph* (London 3 February 2006).

WIDENING ACCESS TO LEGAL EDUCATION

Rethinking 'Merit'

Widening access to legal education for visible minorities and disadvantaged groups has become an issue of public debate, and of particular concern to students of course.[52] This has created additional challenges to law schools' admissions policy-makers, forcing some to rethink their traditional understandings of 'merit'. Students and other stakeholders expect transparent and accountable admission policies and procedures. The *Grutter* and *Gratz* decisions[53] of the US Supreme Court, involving challenges to the admissions process at the University of Michigan, highlighted several characteristics a defensible admissions policy should contain. These include: identifying desired educational outcomes; linking admissions decisions to identified outcomes; considering ethnic/race neutral alternatives; making the policy and process reasonably transparent; considering the effects of the policy on the broader society; and evaluating admission policies over time.

Some research doubts that reliance on academic grades and test scores alone meet these attributes of a defensible admissions policy. As Tong explains:

> [M]erit, in an ideal sense, is typically associated with *achieved* characteristics rather than *ascribed* characteristics. The achieved characteristics which constitute merit, however, are affected by and linked to ascribed characteristics such as race, gender and age. As a result, the traditional administration of the meritocratic order has worked to the disadvantage of members of minority groups.[54]

Lacking objectivity to some, merit is perceived 'as a malleable concept determined not by immanent, preexisting standards but rather by the perceived needs of society'.[55] Thus, if we value having an ethnically diverse law student body, and law profession, then ethnicity can be conceived as a key criterion of merit in admissions decisions. Law schools' historic reliance on a slender range of academic criteria produced a student population that tended to be young, upper middle class, relatively unvaried in ethnicity and

[52] M Tzannes, 'Strategies for the Selection of Students to Law Courses in the 21st Century: Issues and Options for Admissions Policy Makers' (1995) 29(1) *Law Teacher* 43.

[53] *Grutter v Bollinger* 539 US 306 (2003); *Gratz v Bollinger* 539 US 244 (2003); for analysis, see P Aka, 'The Supreme Court and Affirmative Action in Public Education, with Special Reference to the Michigan Cases' (2006) *Brigham Young University Education and Law Journal* 1.

[54] D Tong, 'Gatekeeping in Canadian Law Schools: A History of Exclusion, The Rule of "Merit", and a Challenge to Contemporary Practices' (LLM thesis, University of British Columbia, 1996) 29, my emphasis.

[55] R Kennedy, 'Persuasion and Distrust: A Comment on the Affirmative Action Debate' (1986) 99 *Harvard Law Review* 1327, 1333.

unrepresentative of society as a whole. Thus, Delgado condemns 'merit' as a fig-leaf for maintaining the status quo: 'merit sounds like white people's affirmative action... A way of keeping their own deficiencies neatly hidden while assuring that only people like them get in'.[56] Such criticisms of course do not in themselves provide answers to formulating criteria for determining who should be admitted to law school.

Rationales of Widening Access

Since the 1970s, many law schools, beginning in Canada and the US, have sought to widen access to legal education to visible minorities, disabled persons and other groups who have historically suffered barriers to education. Today, the majority of law students are female, and relatively more come from ethnic and socio-economic constituencies once under-represented in law school. Such changes in the composition of law school student bodies perhaps indicate that some of the criticisms of law schools' reliance on LSAT and other hard numerical criteria for admission have been overstated.

There are three compelling rationales for widening access to legal education. First, it enriches the educational experience of all students. A diverse student body has pedagogic value through the broader range of opinions and perspectives in the classroom. LSAC, in its report on *New Models to Assure Diversity, Fairness, and Appropriate Test Use in Law School Admissions*, explained:

> Perspectives and prior experiences are key elements in this exchange of ideas. For example, a discussion of search-and-seizure law taught by a learned academic to a class of very bright, upper-middle class students who grew up in white suburbs could be a very engaging intellectual exercise. Consider, however, the impact on that discussion of introducing into the class the perspective of a student who, prior to law school, had spent ten years as a police officer in a big city police department. Add to that discussion the voices of inner city black males whose personal histories might include being stopped for no apparent reason, and it becomes more relevant and takes on a new dimension for every student in the classroom. Law schools have long recognized the value of all kinds of dynamic diversity within the educational setting.[57]

A second rationale for diversity is that it fosters empathetic lawyers who should be more understanding and caring of clients from diverse backgrounds with varied problems. Students with cross-cultural dialogue skills

[56] R Delgado, 'Rodrigo's Chronicle' (1992) 101 *Yale Law Journal* 1357, 1364.

[57] Law School Admission Council, *New Models to Assure Diversity, Fairness, and Appropriate Test Use in Law School Admissions* (Newtown, Pennsylvania, Law School Admission Council, 1999) 3.

should appeal to employers. Those who can communicate and work with people of diverse ethnic and cultural backgrounds should be more accomplished lawyers. Inevitably, the character, quality and effectiveness of the legal system depend greatly on the type of people who receive a formal legal education.

Third, widening access promotes representation of all groups in a heterogeneous society in positions of authority, including the law profession, government, business and other domains employing lawyers. Equitable admission policies further law schools' commitment to social justice through legal education. As a powerful and privileged profession, the legal community surely must include members of minority and disadvantaged groups in society. As attorneys, judges, professors, civil servants and legislators, legally-trained persons control or materially influence numerous policy decisions and law-making processes in society. Many law graduates also pursue careers in non-traditional occupational fields, such as business, journalism and education, thereby widening the legal community's sphere of influence. Thus, access to formal legal education is an important determinant of political, social, and economic reality.

Some of these arguments were acknowledged in the seminal *Grutter* case.[58] The US Supreme Court held that diversity is a compelling interest in higher education, and that race is one of several factors that law schools may consider to achieve the educational benefits of a diverse student body. The majority in *Grutter* reasoned that diversity offers various educational benefits, including 'cross-racial understanding' and the breaking down of racial stereotypes. The Court cited social science research showing that 'student body diversity promotes learning outcomes... better prepares students for an increasingly diverse workforce and society, and better prepares them as professionals'.[59] It also acknowledged that, 'major American businesses have made clear that the skills needed in today's increasingly global marketplace can only be developed through exposure to widely diverse people, cultures, ideas and viewpoints'.[60]

But what do we actually mean by 'diversity'? Like the fuzzy concept of 'merit', diversity is relatively plastic. It may encompass ethnicity, gender, sexual orientation, religion, class, geography, as well as physical and intellectual impairment. An individual student rarely if ever falls neatly into any of these seemingly monolithic categories. More commonly, a student displays several of these characteristics, spanning ethnicity, culture and class. Pigeon-holing a student into a single admission category box may not capture this complexity. For example, among US colleges and universities there has been a rise in enrolments of Afro-Americans; but when gender is

[58] *Grutter v Bollinger* 539 US 306 (2003).
[59] Ibid 330.
[60] Ibid 330–31.

taken into account, the data shows that many more black women rather than black men have enrolled.[61] It is challenging to compare the significance of different characteristics considered relevant to the goal of a diverse student campus.

Some commentators emphasise another type of diversity, namely intellectual diversity.[62] Students of varied political and philosophical outlooks may inject creativity and vibrancy into the classroom. Yet, what of individuals who espouse racist, sexist or otherwise intolerant and seemingly extreme views? Should they too be the beneficiaries of widening access policies? Arguably they should not; persons should not benefit from diversity policies if their presence at law school would hinder the educational experience of other students (ie individuals whose views intimidate or are hostile to other students).

Ultimately, diversity should not be defined so broadly that it covers all students' characteristics, as thereby it loses its heuristic significance and so defines nothing concretely. Among the selection criteria that could inform a student diversity policy are: (1) persons from groups that have suffered a history of discrimination; (2) persons from groups that are underrepresented in the legal profession; (3) persons who are motivated to help represent and empower minority or underrepresented communities; and (4) persons from backgrounds who can help enhance the educational experience of all students.

What kind of policies can recruit such persons? Policies to widen access are notoriously difficult to implement and controversial even for the intended beneficiaries. Such policies may be viewed by students as unfairly denying admission to better-qualified applicants. Delgado also surmises that special admission policies might actually perpetuate the dominant culture's attitude of how members of ethnic minorities can enhance the academic experiences of the dominant culture. He argues:

> In law school admissions, for example, majority persons may be admitted as a matter of right, while minorities are admitted because their presence will contribute to the majority... The assumption is that such diversity is educationally valuable to the majority. But such an admissions program may well be perceived as treating the minority culture as an ornament, a curiosity, one who brings an element of the piquant to the lives of white professors and students.[63]

[61] BL Bridglall, 'Meeting The Challenge of Grutter—Affirmative Action in Twenty-Five Years: A Misguided Debate About Affirmative Action?' (2006) 67 *Ohio State Law Journal* 15, 22.

[62] The rationale of intellectual diversity was emphasized in the *Grutter* case. *Grutter v Bollinger* 539 US 306 (2003), 334.

[63] R Delgado, 'The Imperial Scholar: Reflections on a Review of Civil Rights Literature' (1984) 132 *University of Pennsylvania Law Review* 561, 570, fn 46.

Similarly concerned, Brooks and Newborn argue that affirmative action policies may simply ensure that 'not too many minorities will be selected, for that would be terrifying, nor too few, for that would be destabilizing'.[64]

The next section reviews the types of policies adopted by law schools to achieve more diverse student bodies.

Policies to Widen Access

Beginning in the early 1970s, law school admissions committees in North America began to pay more attention to the racial and socio-economic diversity of their student population.[65] In the US, the accreditation standard required all ABA-approved law schools to take concrete steps to increase the number of lawyers from minority communities entering the profession.[66] In 1991, the Association of American Law Schools (AALS) advised law schools to avoid sole reliance on conventional quantitative measures like LSAT and GPA.[67]

Admission policies to widen access typically entail reduced reliance on academic grades and test scores, and creation of special admission streams for designated groups (e.g Indigenous, mature age, disabled). Between 10 to 30 per cent of a first year class may be admitted through such categories.

For example, Osgoode Hall Law School in Canada adopted in the late 1980s the following criteria for its 'Access' category of admission:

(1) Individuals who due to economic pressures entered the work force at or before graduation from high school, rather than continuing through the academic stream into university;
(2) Individuals who entered university but were forced through economic circumstances to work more than casually to support themselves or their families, as a result of which their academic performance suffered;
(3) Individuals who through family obligation or circumstances were prevented from either pursuing academic studies or entering the work force, but who have demonstrated abilities in some other way; and
(4) Individuals who because of their membership in ethnic minority groups have had problems of integration into Canadian society, which have resulted in their being less attractive to law school and their preponderant

[64] RL Brooks and MJ Newtown, 'Critical Race Theory and Classical-Liberal Civil Rights Scholarship: A Distinction without a Difference?' (1994) 82 *California Law Review* 787, 821.

[65] H Ramsey Jr, 'Affirmative Action at American Bar Association Approved Law Schools: 1979–1980' (1980) 30 *Journal of Legal Education* 377.

[66] American Bar Association Commission on Racial and Ethnic Diversity in the Profession www.abanet.org/minorities.

[67] 'AALS Issues Joint Press Release Addressing LSAT Concerns and Misconceptions' Association of American Law Schools Newsletter (August 1991).

> emphasis on grade point average and LSAT score for a limited number of law school positions.[68]

Some law faculties reject the dichotomy between 'regular' and 'special' admission categories, and favour a single basket of admissions criteria (eg the law faculties of Windsor University in Canada and City University of New York).[69] This approach often incorporates non-traditional admission criteria, which are weighed and considered in a discretionary, holistic decision making process. Windsor's admission policy for example includes these criteria:

> Community Involvement
>
> Contribution to the community (city/town; university; religious; etc.) will be assessed for indications of commitment to the community. Factors examined include the nature of the applicant's participation in service clubs, community service organizations, religious, athletic, and social organizations.
>
> Personal Accomplishments
>
> Factors can include extracurricular activities, hobbies and special accomplishments; artistic and athletic accomplishments; communication skills and languages spoken.
>
> Personal Considerations
>
> Personal factors affecting the applicant are recognized in this section. Any personal factors such as illness, bereavement, unusual family responsibilities or other such circumstances which may have some bearing on the applicant's qualifications will be noted.[70]

In this approach, academic grades and test scores still count, but ostensibly carry less weight.

These policies however have been controversial and not always accepted by students or other stakeholders. When the Law Society of Upper Canada in 1973 recommended that Ontario law schools admit Aboriginal and mature age students without the usual academic prerequisites, the Ontario law firm, Tisdall, Sinclair, Murakami and Loney, objected in the following terms:

> The concept of allowing mature students and native Canadians into law schools without compliance with ordinary admission standards is unacceptable. This

[68] Osgoode Hall Law School, *LLB Guide* (Toronto, Osgoode Hall Law School, 1987) 3. In 2007 Osgoode Hall adopted a new LLB admissions policy which abolished the Access category in a move towards a more uniform admissions selection system. www.osgoode.yorku.ca/llb.

[69] D Blonde et al, 'The Impact of Law School Admission Criteria: Evaluating the Broad-Based Admission Policy at the University of Windsor Faculty of Law' (1998) 61 *Saskatchewan Law Review* 529; City University of New York School of Law, 'Admissions & Aid' www.law.cuny.edu/admissions.html.

[70] Faculty of Law, 'Admission Information 2007–2008' (Windsor, Ontario, University of Windsor, Faculty of Law, 2006) 2.

> type of paternalism should be discouraged in the strongest way. Admission to law school should be based solely on merit and not founded on sympathy or ill-defined motives.[71]

It is also said that 'the temptation for admissions committees to view them as imperfect images of the "regular" stream is strong'.[72] Tension between academic criteria and non-academic criteria arises where an applicant has strength in one set of criteria but not the other. The qualitative and discretionary nature of admissions decision making can mask continuing discrimination against applicants lacking the traditional indicia of 'merit'. A University of Manitoba law school study 'concluded that letters of reference, interviews, and the like cannot be reliably built into law school admissions processes because there are no effective controls for interviewer bias or dishonesty by referees or candidates'.[73] The administrative burden of considering such information is also a reason why qualitative assessments are not favoured more widely.[74]

The University of Alberta's Faculty of Law also expressed concern about reliance on letters of reference. In abolishing their use in 2001, it explained that the 'uniformity of the content of the reference letters that were received made it extremely difficult to make a fair judgment on a potential applicant'.[75] Moreover, the fact that students could obtain access to such letters through freedom of information laws made it 'highly unlikely that references will be as objective as they might have been before the implementation of the legislation'.[76]

Canadian law schools enjoy greater latitude than US law schools to implement special admission policies. Canadian human rights codes tolerate race conscious affirmative action measures. Constitutional law provisions in the US interpreted to prohibit strict quotas for minorities tend to restrict equivalent admission policies in US law schools.[77] Conversely, Canada's Charter of Rights and Freedoms explicitly allows 'any law, program or activity that has as its object the amelioration of conditions of

[71] Tisdall, Sinclair, Murakami and Loney, 'Letter to the Secretary of the Law Society of Upper Canada' (7 February 1973).

[72] Tong and Pue, n 30, 849.

[73] Ibid 861, citing B Browning, 'A Walk Through the Black Forest or a Study of Criteria Effectively Available for the Selection of Students to Faculties of Law' in RJ Matas and DJ McCawley (eds), *Legal Education in Canada: Reports and Background Papers of a National Conference on Legal Education* (Ottawa, Federation of Law Societies of Canada, 1987).

[74] The US Supreme Court in *Grutter* rejected administrative burden as a valid excuse for adoption of a mechanical admissions policy that judges applicants on the basis of quantitative factors such as LSAT and GPA alone. *Grutter v Bollinger* 539 US 306 (2003).

[75] University of Alberta Faculty of Law, *Admissions Policy Research Project* (Edmonton, University of Alberta, Faculty of Law, 2003) 1.

[76] Ibid.

[77] RH Sander, 'A Systemic Analysis of Affirmative Action in American Law Schools' (2004) 57 *Stanford Law Review* 367.

disadvantaged individuals'.[78] Thus, Ontario's Human Rights Code 1990 permits special programmes to relieve hardship or economic disadvantage or to assist disadvantaged persons or groups to achieve equal opportunity.[79] Canadian law schools set aside some 10 to 30 per cent of places for students recruited through special admission programmes. Many law schools have placed special attention on recruitment of Indigenous students. The Program of Legal Studies for Native People at the University of Saskatchewan has since 1973 helped prepare such students academically and culturally for the rigours of law school by running a summer school where students receive instruction in basic legal skills.[80]

Law schools (and universities generally) in Australia, New Zealand and the UK appear to have been slower to widen access to higher education, although efforts have stepped up significantly since the late 1990s. New Zealand law schools typically set aside a limited number of admission places for Maori and Pacific Islander students. The University of Auckland's Faculty of Law has a 'special quota' for applicants from these backgrounds; they can be admitted with academic grades below the usual standard and on completion of an interview.[81] It also has places for mature age and disabled applicants. The University of Waikato's School of Law, with approximately 40 per cent of its students of Maori or Pacific Islander background, explains in its policy:

> Applicants will be considered for Special Admission on a case by case basis, having regard to their academic preparedness for University study. Factors such as any previous study interests and expertise, experience and skills, gained through employment and/or community involvement. Applicants are required to provide full information, and supporting documentation with their personal written or typed statement of application.[82]

Competition for places in Australian law faculties has traditionally favoured students from the elite private secondary schools.[83] The result is that law faculties in their socio-economic and ethnic composition have probably not been representative of the Australian population.[84] Some institutions have been slow to widen access beyond discrete arrangements whereby a

[78] s 15(2). See also Peter W. Hogg, *Constitutional Law of Canada* (Toronto, Thomson Canada Limited, 2003) 1062–3.

[79] s 14.

[80] www.usask.ca/nativelaw/programs. See also Law Society of British Columbia, *Addressing Discriminatory Barriers Facing Aboriginal Law Students and Lawyers* (Vancouver, Law Society of British Columbia, April 2000) s II.B.

[81] University of Auckland Faculty of Law, *2010 Undergraduate Prospectus* (Auckland, Faculty of Law, 2009) 5.

[82] www.waikato.ac.nz/law/prospectus/admission.shtml.

[83] R Nankivell, 'Legal Education in Australia' (1992) 72(Winter) *Oregon Law Review* 983, 985.

[84] Ibid 986–87.

few places are saved for Indigenous, mature age or disabled students. The historic lack of Indigenous law students is particularly notable;[85] proactive measures to *recruit* such students are not common. The University of Western Australia law faculty's admission policy of 2006 appears to be typical of the approach:

> In 2006 a number of places in addition to the University's Admissions and Quota Policy may be offered to Aboriginal students who have applied for admission but who do not meet the standard admission requirements for entry under Groups A, B or C.
>
> Aboriginal students who intend seeking selection to the Law School in 2006 and who wish to be considered for a place in the Aboriginal Student Quota for Law should contact the Head of the School of Indigenous Studies.
>
> Provided places are available, successful completion of the Aboriginal Pre-Law Programme will be an acceptable method of admission.[86]

Among the more ambitious attempts to widen access, the Melbourne Law School participates in a university-wide scheme called 'Access Melbourne'. It professes to facilitate admission of students, including provision of scholarships, who satisfy one or more of the following criteria:

> Indigenous Australians
>
> Experience difficult family circumstances
>
> Suffer hardship caused by socio-economic circumstances
>
> Have a disability/long-term illness
>
> Come from a non-English speaking background
>
> Have undertaken Year 12 at a Victorian School that is under-represented in the tertiary sector
>
> Have completed school in a rural or isolated area.[87]

In the UK higher education sector, the widening access debate has focused on socio-economic class.[88] Not enough students from working-class communities and government comprehensive schools enter university, including law school.[89] The British government has sponsored many studies and

[85] H Douglas, 'The Participation of Indigenous Australians in Legal Education 1991–2000' (2001) 24 *University of New South Wales Law Journal* 485; D Lavery, 'The Participation of Indigenous Australians in Legal Education' (1993) 4 *Legal Education Review* 177.

[86] See www.law.uwa.edu.au/courses/applying/selection_policy.

[87] University of Melbourne, 'Access Melbourne' www.futurestudents.unimelb.edu.au/ugrad/accessmelb/.

[88] Department for Education and Skills, *Widening Participation in Higher Education* (Department for Education and Skills, London, 2003).

[89] LS Bibbings, 'Widening Participation and Higher Education' (2006) 33(1) *Journal of Law and Society* 74; S Schwartz, P Lampl and P Ramsey, *Improving Access to UK Universities*

canvassed policy options to make higher education more inclusive for these stakeholders.[90] Among various initiatives, it has offered financial bonuses to universities that recruit more students from designated poverty post-codes.[91] Other initiatives include pre-university summer schools for school students from disadvantaged backgrounds,[92] academic mentoring programmes in local schools for potential university students, and organised campus visits.[93] These initiatives apparently increase the chances of an individual being offered a place at that university. One government report noted that 'there is much work being done to improve and develop routes into [higher education], particularly for those who do not hold traditional qualifications, or who have been outside mainstream education for a considerable time'.[94]

Among UK law schools specifically, the University of Bristol's school is one institution experimenting with innovative ways to widen access. In recent years it has offered admission to some applicants from government schools with slightly lower secondary school qualifications than normally expected, on the assumption that these students' abilities are not fully reflected in their academic grades owing to differential access to educational opportunities.[95] Bristol's 2006 admission policy explained that, when interpreting grades, it takes account of

> 'exceptional circumstances' [that] have had an impact on the applicant's ability to study or perform to capacity in examinations. Examples of 'exceptional circumstances' include disability or illness, caring duties within the family, a disruptive home life and significant problems with their teaching and learning environment (eg teacher's illness). Consideration of such factors is undertaken on an individual basis. In particular, in the case of disability, the score is based upon the individual circumstances of the particular candidate. Further information is sought where this is deemed appropriate.[96]

(Special Schools Trust, London, 2003). The latter comments that 'a child of a professional is five times more likely [to go to university] than his or her blue-collar counterpart' (1).

90 See Universities UK, *Fair Enough? Widening Access to University by Identifying Potential to Succeed* (London, Universities UK, 2003); Higher Education Funding Council for England, *Widening Participation: A Review. Report to the Minister of State for Higher Education and Lifelong Learning by the Higher Education Funding Council for England* (Bristol, Higher Education Funding Council for England, 2006).

91 Higher Education Funding Council for England, 'Widening access for students from disadvantaged backgrounds' www.hefce.ac.uk/widen/fund/postcode.htm.

92 Sutton Trust, 'Summer Schools' www.suttontrust.com/applyingtouniversitysummerschools.asp.

93 Higher Education Funding Council for England, *Widening Participation* (2006) 33–34.

94 Ibid 37.

95 Interview conducted by author with the Admissions Tutor, University of Bristol School of Law (10 September 2002).

96 School of Law, 'Admissions Policy Statement 2006–2007' (Bristol, University of Bristol, School of Law, 2006) 3.

Such initiatives recognise that students can be wrongly treated as an undifferentiated stakeholder with uniform social and economic characteristics.

Impact of Widening Access Reforms

Have reforms to widen access worked? Most research suggests that the composition of law schools has changed significantly in the past three decades. The greatest transformation is the surge in female enrolments (and among faculty members too). Women now comprise a clear majority of law students in nearly all jurisdictions.[97] For instance, in 2004 the ratio of women to men in Ontario law schools was 55.9 to 44.1.[98]

The proportion of visible minorities has also increased.[99] A 2004 study of Ontario law schools found that 'law students appear quite similar to the Ontario and Canadian residents aged 20 to 29 years in terms of their distribution within the specified ethnocultural categories."[100] This report also noted that 'Arab, Chinese, Korean and South Asian students are slightly overrepresented at law schools compared to the Ontario population, while Aboriginal students (Métis and North American Indian) are underrepresented'.[101] Some other Canadian law schools have reported relatively high enrolments of Aboriginal students.[102]

However, research also suggests law students are more likely to still come from relatively wealthy households and families with well-educated parents. The study of Ontario law schools showed that law students are more than twice as likely as Ontario residents generally to come from homes where the father and/or mother has a university education.[103] It also found that the 'household income of law school students tends to be much higher than that observed for Canadian families'.[104]

[97] BM Mazer, 'An Analysis of Gender in Admission to the Canadian Common Law Schools from 1985–86 to 1994–95' (1997) 20 *Dalhousie Law Journal* 135.

[98] AJC King, WK Warren and SR Miklas, *Study of Accessibility to Ontario Law Schools* (Kingston Ontario, Social Program Evaluation Group, Queen's University, October 2004) 83.

[99] S Nueman, *Provost's Study of Accessibility and Career Choice in the Faculty of Law* (Toronto, University of Toronto, Faculty of Law, February 2003) 13, showing that the percentage of visible minorities registered at the University of Toronto Faculty of Law increased from 21 per cent to almost 30 per cent from 1995 to 2003.

[100] King, Warren and Miklas, n 98.

[101] Ibid.

[102] J Vandstone, *Legal Education Access Report* (Victoria, University of Victoria, Faculty of Law, 2005) 37, noting that Aboriginal students constitute nine per cent of the Victoria law school's population, while Aboriginal people comprise four per cent of the population of British Columbia.

[103] King, Warren and Miklas, n 98, 88, noting that 43% of mothers and 53.9% of fathers had a Bachelor's or an advanced degree.

[104] Ibid 89.

Similar trends in the composition of law schools have occurred in the US. In 1980, 66 per cent of law students were male and 34 per cent were female, and ethnic minorities comprised eight per cent of law students in 1980. In 2004, about half of law students were women, and 22 per cent were from ethnic and other minorities.[105] Yet, some minorities have faired better than others; there has been a surge in Asian-American enrolments in recent decades and corresponding falls in Afro-American and Indigenous students.[106]

What of the impact of widening access reforms on the legal profession itself? This effect is harder to ascertain. In Ontario, according to statistics from the Law Society of Upper Canada: 53 per cent of students who took the Bar Admission Course in 2002 were women, compared to 48.7 per cent in 1998; 16.5 per cent self-identified themselves as persons of colour, compared to 14.9 per cent in 1998 (17.5 per cent of the population comprises people of colour, according to the 1996 Canadian Census); 1.7 per cent of students were Aboriginal compared to 1.3 per cent in 1998 (1.4 per cent of the population is Aboriginal according to the Census).[107] More such research on such trends in other jurisdictions is needed.

While the Ontarian evidence suggests that the Canadian law profession is becoming more diverse and representative of society as a whole, there is no compelling evidence that the influx of lawyers from minorities or other disadvantaged groups is preferring careers that emphasise charitable, community or other public interest objectives. The University of Windsor law faculty, which professes to have one of the most equitable admission policies in Canada, has researched the career choices of its alumni.

Its alumni study of 1993 concluded disappointedly that 'no dramatic differences exist... to suggest that non-traditional admittees... are more likely to choose non-traditional career paths'.[108] The study explained that, 'the lure of the traditional legal market place is undoubtedly strong for most graduates... Our interviews uncovered a general impression by graduates that they had few real options when choosing their career paths'.[109] In other words, the structure of the legal job market, and the dominant role of the law profession in serving business, apparently leaves few opportunities for law graduates interested in social justice and public interest careers. Windsor's research, however, found that some of its graduates had cultivated a socially responsible ethos, and 'the interviews provided some evidence of restlessness and a desire by some graduates to work in a less

[105] NW Hines, 'Ten Major Changes in Legal Education Over the Past 25 Years' (August-September 2004) Association of American Law Schools Newsletter, www.aals.org/services_newsletter_presNov05.php.

[106] Ibid.

[107] Law Society of Upper Canada, 'Fact Sheet: Equity and Diversity in the Legal Profession' www.lsuc.on.ca/latest-news/b/fact/fact-equity.

[108] Mazer, n 97.

[109] Ibid.

traditional context'.[110] On the other hand, the Windsor study also noted that 'lawyers from non-traditional backgrounds often argue that they should not be expected to be radically different from traditional law graduates who view the legal profession, at least in part, as a means of personal status advancement'.[111]

In another, smaller study, of the careers of Osgoode Hall law graduates previously admitted in its mature-age category, the highest percentage (32.5 per cent) found employment in small firms, followed by government (20.6 per cent) and then large firms (14.7 per cent).[112] These statistics show higher levels of employment in government service than is common for Canadian law graduates generally.

TUITION FEES

The Issues

Getting admitted to law school is not just a matter of good grades and test scores. Students must also pay for the cost of their legal education. Judging by the issues that students are mostly likely to voice concern about, tuition fees are of the greatest importance.[113] While policies for educational equity and the enhancement of access to legal education have become prevalent, the concomitant escalation of tuition fees in many law schools has likely created new barriers to legal education. The Canadian Bar Association's report, *Racial Equality in the Canadian Legal Profession*, noted that the financial barriers to law school 'fall more heavily on students from disadvantaged socio-economic backgrounds'.[114]

The cost of legal education worldwide has soared in recent years, outstripping the rate of inflation and increases in average household income. The US law schools, particularly the private institutions, have long charged the highest tuition fees. Tuition fees for legal education in Australia, Canada and New Zealand began to be deregulated in the 1990s in the wake of declining state funding. Their governments have increasingly subjected universities to the same sort of market-oriented restructuring that much of the rest of society has already undergone. In Australia, paradoxically, at the very moment the government exerted pressure on universities to increase

[110] Ibid.

[111] Ibid 550.

[112] Justice S Chapnik, *A Journey Taken: The Mature Student in Law School: A Retrospective Study* (Toronto, Osgoode Hall School of Law, September 2001) 23–24.

[113] Eg protests in Canada. See 'College & University Students Protest High Tuition Costs' CityNews (7 February 2007) www.citynews.ca/news/news_7621.aspx.

[114] Working Group on Racial Equality in the Legal Profession, *Racial Equality in the Canadian Legal Profession* (Canadian Bar Association, Ottawa, 1999) 4.

their student intake, the per capita funding of higher education places was curtailed.[115] Pressures to run legal education on the cheap have been reported in other jurisdictions.[116] Most Canadian provinces in the 1990s began to allow universities to set their own tuition fees in professional programmes (eg law, dentistry, medicine and business), although there has been some governmental re-regulation in recent years in the wake of some hefty fee increases. Still, the result has been substantial rises in tuition fees for these courses.[117]

The UK has followed suit to some extent; in 2004, the Labour Government introduced a new financing arrangement for British universities that allows universities to phase-in 'top-up' tuition fees for courses and programmes.[118] Until then, domestic students in English law schools paid only about £1000 per year, though some 40 per cent of students paid no fees based on their own or their parents' income falling below designated poverty thresholds. In all of these jurisdictions, tuition fees for non-domestic students were never subsidised and consequently remain much higher.[119]

Public-sector law schools are thus mired in an uneasy financial squeeze. They suffer gradual reduction of government subsidies, which must be replaced by higher tuition fees and other sources of revenue such as donations. Concomitantly, however, students resent hefty tuition increases and will often organise resistance to further significant increases. While governments are deregulating tuition fees, they sometimes also place restrictions on fee-raising or offer incentives to ensure student aid reaches needy applicants.

There is much debate as to the extent tuition fees have discouraged students from lower income backgrounds or from minority groups to apply to or stay at law school.[120] The increased earning capacity acquired with a law degree does not provide immediate income to pay for tuition. The real

[115] C McInnis and S Marginson, *Australian Law Schools After the 1987 Pearce Report* (Australian Government Publishing Service, 1994) 14–19; Christine Parker and Andrew Goldsmith, '"Failed Sociologists" in the Market Place: Law Schools in Australia' (1998) 25(1) *Journal of Law and Society* 33.

[116] See B Hepple, 'Some Concluding Reflections' in P Birks (ed), *Reviewing Legal Education* (Oxford, Oxford University Press, 1994) 110; H Arthurs, 'The State We're In: Legal Education in Canada's New Political Economy' (2001) 20 *Windsor Yearbook of Access to Justice* 35, 49.

[117] M Frenette, *The Impact of Tuition Fees on University Access: Evidence from a Large-scale Price Deregulation in Professional Programs* (Ottawa, Statistics Canada, 2005).

[118] BBC Online, 'Blair Wins Key Top-Up Fees Vote' (27 January 2004) news.bbc.co.uk/2/hi/uk_news/politics/3434329.stm, discussing the Higher Education Act 2004.

[119] For instance, in 2006, the University of Auckland Faculty of Law charged domestic LLB students NZ$4416 per year and most international students NZ$19,686 per year. www.law.auckland.ac.nz/uoa/law/for/undergraduate/prospectus/how_to_apply.cfm.

[120] JR Kramer, 'Will Legal Education Remain Affordable, by Whom and How?' (April 1987) *Duke Law Journal* 240; LE Zubrow, 'Is Loan Forgiveness Divine? Another View' (1991) 59 *George Washington Law Review* 451; KA Tongue, 'Law Degrees on Credit: Today's Law School Students are Graduating with Record Levels of Debt' (1995) 56 *Oregon State Bar Bulletin* 9.

financial burden of attending law school is much higher if one factors in students' cost of living and their potential income had they been working full time. Moreover, the poorer the student is, the more reluctant he or she may be to assume a large debt load to fund acquisition of a degree. Without extensive financial assistance, students from low-income families may be deterred from entering university.

Some research, however, casts doubt on the impact of tuition fees on some aspects of student diversity. The 2004 *Study of Accessibility to Ontario Law Schools* noted:

> Although it is true that law schools enrol disproportionately high numbers of students from middle- and upper-class homes, there has only been slight change in the socioeconomic characteristics of law school students over the past seven years... At the five law schools, members of visible minority groups, except for Aboriginal students, are represented proportionately to their distribution within Ontario society, and the trend since tuition deregulation has been towards an increase rather than a decrease in visible minority representation.[121]

Another consideration is that while legal education is expensive, arguably those who reap the most benefit should contribute to some of this cost. While society as a whole benefits from an educated population, the greatest direct benefit of a law degree, like other university qualifications, is reaped by the student.[122] The law graduate acquires a significant earning capacity, as well as benefiting from personal intellectual growth. It could thus be appropriate to expect lawyers to bear some, perhaps a significant portion, of the cost of their training.

Apart from the debate about the extent to which tuition fees create barriers to legal education, and to what extent society should subsidise this education, there is the question of whether some graduates may forsake preferred career paths because of significant debt, to their own detriment and that of society. In the US, considerable public attention was given to the 2002 report, *From Paper Chase to Money Chase*.[123] It presented data to support the contention that debt load has an impact on law graduates' career choices, encouraging more graduates to seek lucrative private sector careers over lower paid public interest legal work. Some Canadian research also suggests a correlation between student debt and career choices.[124]

[121] King, Warren and Miklas, n 98, 172.

[122] F Vaillancourt, 'The Private and Total Returns to Education in Canada, 1985' (1995) 28 *Canadian Journal of Economics* 532.

[123] Equal Justice Works, *From Paper Chase to Money Chase: Law School Debt Diverts Road to Public Service* (Washington DC, Equal Justice Works, 2002).

[124] HP Beyer, 'Law Society of Upper Canada Examining How to Approach Issue of Soaring Tuition Fees' *The Lawyers Weekly* (5 April 2002).

Student Aid

Students typically finance their legal education from a mix of sources: parental contributions, personal savings, income earned during their education, scholarships and loans. In all countries surveyed in this chapter there has been a sharp increase in the debt burden of law students and the proportion of law school costs financed through loans.[125]

In the US, the largest source of financial aid for students attending most graduate and professional schools is the Federal Student Aid programme.[126] To receive such aid, students must meet extensive criteria, including: qualify for financial need; meet minimum educational qualifications; maintain satisfactory academic progress once in university; and not be in default of a federal student loan.[127] Other student financial aid schemes vary from state to state and school to school. Financial aid by individual law schools is often considerable. The goal of Harvard Law School's financial aid programme is stated as: 'to always provide enough funding to meet any gap that may exist between our annual cost of attendance (our student budget) and every student's family resources'.[128] Harvard's programme considers the ability of students to pay tuition and living expenses to determine entitlement to aid.[129] More than a third of the law school's operating budget comes from non-tuition sources such as endowments and donations from alumni. This money is used in part to fund the financial aid programme.

Since tuition fees at Canadian law schools were substantially deregulated in the late 1990s, students have been paying ever-increasing sums for their education.[130] Canadian provincial governments, however, commonly require the increases in tuition fees for professional programmes to be partially offset by setting aside some revenue for student financial assistance, and most now put a cap on the size of any annual tuition fee increases.[131] The Ontario provincial government also operates a system of student loans

[125] LA Kornhauser and RL Revesz, 'Legal Education and Entry into the Legal Profession: The Role of Race, Gender, and Educational Debt' (1995) 70 *New York University Law Review* 829, 877; J-A Pickel, 'What Will Rising Law School Tuition Fees Mean for Law and Learning?' (2003) 18 *Canadian Journal of Law and Society* 67; 'Tuition Fees: The Higher Cost of Higher Education, *CBCNews.ca* (Ottawa, 28 August 2008), www.cbc.ca/money/story/2008/05/15/f-highereducation-tuitionfees.html.

[126] Federal Student Aid, 'Graduate and Professional Students' studentaid.ed.gov/PORTALSWebApp/students/english/gradstudent.jsp.

[127] Federal Student Aid, 'Student Aid Eligibility' studentaid.ed.gov/PORTALSWebApp/students/english/aideligibility.jsp?tab=funding.

[128] Harvard Law School, Financial Aid, 'Determination of Financial Need' www.law.harvard.edu/current/sfs/policy/need.html.

[129] Ibid.

[130] L Brown, 'Law School Fee Hike Sparks Anger' *The Toronto Star* (Toronto 9 March 2004).

[131] In Ontario, the required minimum of 30% of new tuition revenues is set aside for student financial assistance. See further AM Boggs, 'Ontario's University Tuition Framework: A History and Current Policy Issues' (2009) 39(1) *The Canadian Journal of Higher Education* 73.

through the Ontario Student Assistance Program (OSAP).[132] However, the OSAP loans are too low to cover the full cost of tuition fees and other expenses at law school.

Canadian law schools have introduced a miscellany of additional measures to assuage the impact of rising fees. Many law school students have been grandfathered at the tuition rate of their entering first year. In addition, some law schools maintain debt relief programmes. Osgoode Hall Law School has prided itself on exceeding the Ontario government's standard by recycling 38 per cent of its tuition fees to student financial aid. Osgoode also has an agreement with the Royal Bank of Canada that allows students to receive up to C$50,000 in the form of a low interest line of credit.

Is there anything else that the governments or law schools should do to alleviate financial barriers to legal education, short of returning to greater public subsidises for higher education? Seeking higher levels of funding from private donors brings with it the usual quandary that the person who pays the piper calls the tune. Educational priorities may be influenced by the exigencies of fund-raising.

One plausible option is income-contingent loans.[133] Under this scheme, the extent of the obligation to repay the loan varies with level of income. The graduate would agree to pay to the government in each future year a specified percentage of his or her earnings in excess of a specified sum. This option frames the problem as not one of high tuition fees, but their timing: law students should not be compelled to pay for their education before they are financially able to do so. Income-contingent loans are used in the Australian and New Zealand higher education sectors, and among some US law schools.[134]

A related option proposed is income-contingent tuition fees.[135] Under this proposal, the extent of the financial obligation varies with level of income. But this model differs in that the financial sponsor is the university, and not the government, and the student does not pay interest. Law schools would make a financial investment in their students by providing legal education at reduced up-front cost, and in return they would be entitled to some of the future income of the lawyers they educated. Admitted students would have to promise to pay their school a certain percentage of their employment income for a given period following graduation. Pardy argues that, 'for students, this is a risk-free approach that reduces the economic

[132] Ontario Student Assistance Program, 'How Loan Amounts are Determined' osap.gov.on.ca/eng/not_secure/funds.htm#Types%20of%20assistance.

[133] DB Johnstone, *New Patterns for College Lending: Income-Contingent Loans* (New York, Columbia University Press, 1972).

[134] V Rateau, *Action: Creating Law School Loan Repayment Assistance and Public Interest Scholarship Programs* (Washington DC, National Association for Public Interest Law, 2000).

[135] B Pardy, 'Poor Students, Well-Paid Lawyers: Post-Graduation Income-Contingent Tuition Fees for Law Schools' (2004) 29(Spring) *Queen's Law Journal* 848.

disincentives to attend law school'.[136] And, for law schools, 'it would provide a source of income that is more secure, predictable, and generous than current sources'.[137] Further, graduates would presumably be more willing to make career choices not motivated by the need to repay huge debt after graduation.

CONCLUSION

Law schools in the major common law jurisdictions have implemented profound changes to their student admission and tuition policies in recent decades. Students, as stakeholders in legal education, have mostly been the recipients of, rather than participants in the making of, these changes. The reforms have benefited some types of students, while hurting others.

On the one hand, admission to law school is generally less reliant on simple numerical indicators of academic merit. Law schools, especially in North America, increasingly seek to evaluate students against a basket of criteria, and are more attentive to the impact of social and economic barriers to access to legal education. Consequently, law schools have become more socially diverse, enrolling many more women, as well as more ethnic minorities and other disadvantaged groups.

Yet, rising tuition fees that have paralleled these reforms have engendered new barriers to legal education. As legal education has become more expensive, economic barriers have perhaps become as great as the traditional social barriers once were. Student aid schemes have helped to mitigate these financial obstacles, though they tend to benefit the neediest while possibly excluding many middle-class students. In an era of declining public financial support for universities, there are no simple solutions to the challenges of maintaining high quality legal education while minimising barriers to student access to that education. The law profession itself will likely be increasingly pressured to shoulder a greater burden of these costs. In considering future reforms, it is crucial that students be recognised as key stakeholders entitled to greater participation in policy-making and law school governance.

136 Ibid.
137 Ibid.

6

The Value of Practice in Legal Education[1]

ANDREW GOLDSMITH AND DAVID BAMFORD

INTRODUCTION

COMPARED WITH A generation ago, Australian law students are spending more time working and engaged in extracurricular activities.[2] Financial pressures, as well as employer expectations, are playing a major part in shaping the law student learning environment. Their significance as stakeholders in legal education has however, if anything, *increased* rather than diminished in this changing climate. A more instrumental approach towards university education is now apparent.[3] The popularity of on-line lecture notes and intensively taught vacation topics has contributed to the declining attraction of traditional classroom-based education. Classes tend now also to be larger, with fewer staff per student. There is greater reliance placed upon casual teachers. Another factor however helps to explain the fading allure of traditional classroom-based legal education: *many students enrolled in university law undergraduate degrees express a clear preference for practice-oriented opportunities within the curriculum and during the law school years, while demonstrating a growing impatience with conventional law school curricula and teaching methods.* While students are expected to pay more for their legal education, and many are predictably concerned about getting jobs at the end of their university

[1] The authors would like to thank their colleague, Rachel Spencer, for reading and commenting on an earlier draft of this chapter.

[2] Universities Australia, *A National Internship Scheme: Discussion Paper* (2007) www.universitiesaustralia.edu.au. See also R Johnstone and S Vignaendra, *Learning Outcomes and Curriculum Development in Law: A Report Commissioned by the Australian Universities Teaching Committee* (Canberra, Department of Education, Science and Training, 2003); J Campbell, '15 Lessons from Law school' *Australian Law Students' Association (ALSA) Reporter* (Winter 2006) 18; C McInnes and R Hartley, *Managing Study and Work: The Impact of Full-Time Study and Paid Work on the Undergraduate Experience in Australian Universities* (Canberra, Department of Education, Science and Training, 2002).

[3] McInnes and Hartley, above n 2.

courses, they are being largely denied experiential and practically focused opportunities within the structure of the law curriculum, commensurate with the level of demand.[4] These experiential educational forms of legal education, while widely regarded as resource-intensive and hence expensive to mount, have been linked to high levels of student motivation.[5]

For some commentators, this shift has been viewed as largely negative, signalling the ascendancy of vocationalism[6], or the defeat of a liberal or radical model of legal education.[7] We take a different, more hopeful view. In this chapter, we will argue that universities and governments have not responded appropriately to the implications of this state of affairs. In particular, we shall suggest that 'practice' within legal education needs to be re-evaluated and more clearly engaged with during the university law degree both to reflect student interest and to explore the nature of law in a more grounded, yet also ethical, sense. As will be seen, we are suggesting the need for further engagement with practice, in the field as well as the classroom, but not in ways that can be reduced to (or dismissed as) legal vocationalism or an uncritical assimilation of practical orthodoxy. While becoming more cognisant of the expectations around practice coming from students and other law school stakeholders, we offer a pathway whereby 'practice' can be more deeply understood and subjected to criticism, as well as ultimately practiced.

While relatively low levels of federal government funding for legal education has contributed to poor staff-student ratios and inadequate numbers of internship and clinical law placement opportunities, law academics themselves have also played a part in bringing about this disjuncture between the academy and practice. They have been cautious, conservative, and indeed wilfully blind in some instances in their responses to the 'demand for relevance' emerging from the legal profession and law students. However, the 'demand' is real and cannot be ignored. In the UK, a study conducted for the Law Society of England and Wales in the 1990s by the Policy Studies Institute (PSI)[8] discovered that 'undergraduates were much more likely to stress the importance of the practical and instrumental aspects of the degree, while law teachers were more likely to stress the importance of the more global aspects of the degree.'[9] In Australia, while no systematic study exists of law student attitudes to the perceived 'academic' and 'vocational'

[4] See above n 2.
[5] J Hillyer, 'From Theory of Practice Into Practice' (2000) 7(3) *International Journal of the Legal Profession* 261, 263.
[6] N James, 'Why has Vocationalism Propagated so Successfully Within Australian Law Schools?' (2004) 6 *University of Notre Dame Australia Law Review* 41.
[7] M Thornton, 'The Idea of the University and the Contemporary Legal Academy' (2004) 26 *Sydney Law Review* 481.
[8] D Halpern, *Entry Into the Legal Professions: The Law Student Cohort Study, Years 1 and 2, Research Study 15, Summary* (London, Law Society, 1994).
[9] Ibid at vi–vii.

elements of the law degree, the pressures on students to 'get jobs' and the perceived need to have 'relevant experience' before the completion of the law degree are familiar to, if often ignored, or poorly managed by, legal academics already working under more onerous employment conditions than a decade or two ago.[10]

The discrepancy in question however cannot be readily dismissed. There is no 'real' legal education that exists independently of student interests and tastes. As 'consumers' of education, students now have an even greater stake in defining what law schools offer and judging the respective merits of different offerings.[11] As Hillyer has argued in the UK context, legal academics need to take sufficient account of contemporary student *motivations* for studying law:

> Legal education has to find a way of working with the vocational orientation of its student rather than against it, without compromising breadth of vision or appearing to ignore the large numbers of law graduates who will not qualify as solicitors or barristers in the traditional way. This is not to take a simplistic approach to the student as consumer of educational services, but rather to suggest that the issue of motivation should be given proper attention.[12]

'Taking account,' in our view, does not imply the suppression or the subversion of such motivations. Nor does it equate to an embrace, or even acceptance of vocationalism, defined by James as 'the set of statements about legal education produced by law schools and by legal scholars which emphasise the importance of the teaching of legal skills and prioritise employability as an objective of legal education'.[13] Rather, we propose a constructive engagement between the practical realm and the goals of 'breadth of vision' and social criticism more commonly associated with academic knowledge and learning.[14] In short, the kind of engagement with practice we advocate is one that challenges the instrumentalist, performance-based approaches to experiential learning commonly found within higher education in the professions.[15]

In what follows, we first examine the factors making a realistic response to student interest in practice opportunities an inevitable one for law academics. Then, turning to the notion of practice itself, we consider how it is

[10] T Winefield, C Boyd, J Saebel and S Pignata, *Job Stress in University Staff: An Australian Research Study* (Brisbane, Australian Academic Press, 2008).

[11] V Brand, 'Decline in the Reform of Law Teaching? The Impact of Policy Reforms in Tertiary Education' (1999) 10 *Legal Education Review* 110.

[12] See Hillyer, above n 5, at 263.

[13] See James, above n 6, at 44.

[14] P Jones, 'Theory and Practice in Professional Legal Education' (2000) 7(3) *International Journal of the Legal Profession* 239.

[15] R Barnett, *Higher Education: A Critical Business* (Buckingham, Open University Press, 1997). See also D Boud, R Cohen, D Walker (eds), *Using Experience for Learning* (Buckingham, Open University Press, 1993).

and should be construed in the context of a *university-based* professional education. Third, we examine how a range of stakeholders (law students, legal professional bodies, employers of law graduates, and law schools) are contributing to, and coping with, this environment. Finally, we propose the elements of a *work-related learning* approach to professional legal education that would permit the retention of critical, reflective learning while acknowledging the changing nature of student and other stakeholder demands upon legal education.

THE NEED TO GET REAL ABOUT PRACTICE

A renewed student interest in 'practical' opportunities within the law degree should scarcely surprise anyone. There is considerable evidence that this particular group of stakeholders has tended to have a strong focus on their intention to pursue a legal career. Firstly, the history of legal education in common law countries has largely been one based upon the apprenticeship model, in which universities played no or only a limited part.[16] The 'academic' phase of legal education in most common law countries is of relatively recent provenance, constituting a modern interlude in an otherwise longstanding 'practical' pattern of professional training.[17] Ongoing interest by the profession and legal employers in legal education, primarily through exercising control over admission requirements and hence the law school curriculum, has meant that the profession's view of 'relevance for practice' has been kept clearly in view, a fact hardly lost on law students seeking admission to professional practice. When denied opportunities for actual practice within the law degree, students devote much energy nevertheless to determining and doing those classroom-taught topics perceived as most relevant to practice.[18] Surveys over the last decade have indicated that most law students still intend to qualify for practice as lawyers, even if their longer-term career aspirations and destinations are more diverse or unclear.[19]

The view that a clear distinction exists between 'theory' and 'practice' within professional education has few subscribers these days, except perhaps

[16] Australian Law Reform Commission, *Managing Justice*, Report no 89 (Sydney, Australian Law Reform Commission, 2000).

[17] L Martin, 'From Apprenticeship to Law School: A Social History of Legal Education in Nineteenth Century New South Wales (1986) 9 *University of New South Wales Law Review* 111.

[18] See Thornton, above n 7 at 481.

[19] R Johnstone and S Vignaendra, *Learning Outcomes and Curriculum Development in Law: A Report Commissioned by the Australian Universities Teaching Committee* (Canberra, Department of Education, Science and Training, 2003). See also D Halpern, *Entry Into the Legal Professions* (1994); S Vignaendra, *Australian Law Graduates' Career Destinations* (Canberra, Department of Employment, Education, Training and Youth Affairs, 1998).

within sections of the legal academy. Professional disciplines such as social work and education traditionally have included significant practicums as part of the formal requirements for graduation. This is increasingly true of other university courses as well. A decade ago, it was estimated that 60 per cent of Australian university courses included some form of workplace-based learning.[20] Since then, this pattern has extended to the humanities and social sciences. Abbott has described a 'shift from legitimacy of character to the legitimacy of technique' within twentieth-century professional education.[21] Here he points to moves away from grounding professional activity through social selection and transmission of traditional forms of professional knowledge to reliance upon achievements demonstrable in terms of the values of science and efficiency.[22] One example of this shift may be found in moves to develop competence-based approaches to professional education.[23]

In the UK,[24] the US[25] and Australia,[26] in-depth inquiries into professional legal education have called into question the idea of a purely 'academic' phase of legal education followed by a vocational phase. Some form of integrated legal education is broadly endorsed in which procedural as well as propositional knowledge forms part of the university stage of professional development. Insisting on a theory/practice divide has become even more difficult in light of developments in educational theory. Concepts of 'experiential learning' (Kolb) and 'the reflective practitioner' (Schon) permeate much of current educational literature on adult learning and professional development.[27] As Boud et al state, experience in a learning context is 'not just an observation, a passive undergoing of something, but an active engagement with the environment of which the learner is an important part.'[28] These notions imply a set of steps in the development of professional knowledge that requires active as well as passive forms of

[20] E Martin, 'Conceptions of Work Place University Education' (1998) 17 *Higher Education Research and Development Journal* 191.

[21] A Abbott, *The System of Professions* (Chicago, University of Chicago Press, 1998), 190.

[22] Ibid at 195.

[23] R Barnett, *The Limits of Competence* (Milton Keynes, Open University Press, 1994). See also n 6, at 239.

[24] Advisory Committee on Legal Education and Conduct, *First Report on Legal Education and Training* (London, Advisory Committee on Legal Education and Conduct, 1996).

[25] R McCrate, *Legal Education and Professional Development—An Educational Continuum: Report of the Task Force on Law Schools and the Professions: Narrowing the Gap* (Chicago, ABA, 1992). See also W Sullivan, A Colby, J Wegner, L Bond and L Shulman, *Educating Lawyers: Preparation for the Profession of Law* (San Francisco, Jossey Bass, 2007).

[26] D Pearce, E Campbell and D Harding, *Australian Law Schools: A Disciplinary Assessment for the Commonwealth Tertiary Education Commission: A Summary* (Canberra, AGPS, 1987).

[27] See, eg G Maudsley and J Scrivens, 'Promoting Professional Knowledge, Experiential Learning and Critical Thinking for Medical Students' (2000) 34 *Medical Education* 535.

[28] See Boud, Cohen & Walker (eds), above n 15.

learning, concrete as well as reflective experiences, as crucial elements of the learning process.

Broader changes are also pertinent to the (re) evaluation of the place of practice within universities, as concerns about 'skills' development[29] and the 'employability' of graduates have recently become focal concerns of higher education policy in Australia and the UK.[30] The Coopers and Lybrand (UK) report, *Skills Development in Higher Education*,[31] provides a good example of recent policy direction. Everyone concerned, law teachers, students, employers, government and the profession, in one way or another, has reason then to accept that legal education, as professional education, remains 'necessarily about practice'.[32] This remains true despite recent championing of the idea in the UK of the law degree as providing a liberal education.[33]

Resistance to the message about the value of practice among law teachers is likely nonetheless. A number of cherished assumptions and shibboleths about legal education and scholarship are at stake. These relate to how law is taught and researched, as well as to how it is funded. In terms of teaching and research, law academics have long accorded primacy to the *written word* or *text*, making its mastery central to the ends of the law degree.[34] It has meant that the classroom and the library have been the cornerstones of legal education.[35] This focus upon case law and statutes has tended to insulate legal scholarship from an understanding of, or interest in, the needs of legal (but not judicial) practice. This is discussed further below.

The textual, 'black-letter' orientation within mainstream legal education and scholarship has also allowed university administrators and government departments of higher education to view legal education as a 'cheap' (yet prestigious) option, compared to areas such as medicine, nursing and visual arts.[36] The portrayal of legal education as text-based has reinforced the abstract, 'academic' image of the field of law, distancing it from developments in educational theory as well as disadvantaging it in government

[29] See Barnett, above n 23.

[30] JM Hills, G Robertson, R Walker, M Adey and I Nixon, I, 'Bridging the Gap Between Degree Programme Curricula and Employability Through Implementation of Work-Related Learning' (2003) 8(2) *Teaching in Higher Education*' 211.

[31] Coopers and Lybrand, *Skills Development in Higher Education* (London, Coopers and Lybrand, 1998).

[32] See Jones, above n 14, at 239.

[33] C Gallivan and R Scragg, 'The Value of an LLB: Comparative Perspectives Between New Zealand and England and Wales' (2006) 4 *Journal of Commonwealth Law and Legal Education* 123. See also A Bradney, 'Liberalising Legal Education' in Cownie (ed), *The Law School—Global Issues, Local Questions* (Aldershot, Ashgate, 1999).

[34] See Bradney, above n 33, at 123.

[35] M Keyes and R Johnstone, 'Changing Legal Education: Rhetoric, Reality and Prospects for the Future' (2004) 26 *Sydney Law Review* 537.

[36] A Goldsmith, 'Why Should Law Matter? Towards a Clinical Model of Legal Education' (2002) 25(3) *University of New South Wales Law Journal* 721.

and university funding terms. In terms of government policy, two ironies are visible. The first is that students of law in Australia in recent years have been charged a contribution tax at the highest level under the present contribution system, on a par with medicine, dentistry, and veterinary science. Given the low per capita funding for law students returned to the universities by government, law has become a kind of 'cash cow'.[37] However, for the reasons indicated, the capacity of law schools to offer practical experience to their students has declined overall, despite federal government calls simultaneously for improved graduate 'employability.[38]

THE CONCEPT OF 'PRACTICE'

The significance of calls to 'get practical' in legal education depend upon the conception of practice in question. Here, by referring to 'practice', we mean to include a range of concepts that refer to learning opportunities that arise in the realm of *action*, rather than to those whose focus is principally in the realms of cognition and/or emotion. In this sense, our conception of 'practice' may be more sophisticated than that of some of the stakeholders who would like to see a more 'practical' approach in legal education. Thus, diverse activities such as simulated practice situations (eg interviews, negotiations, drafting), field visits, field placements, clinical legal education and externships fall within our concept of practice. What largely distinguishes these activities from those associated with traditional legal education are (1) their experiential, externally-oriented focus; and (2) their explicit, direct orientation to the world of legal professional work. Legal work may occur in law firms, the courts, private and public organisations, among community groups or indeed in simulated work settings, but in all relevant cases, it relates in some way directly or indirectly to the mobilisation of law. It may involve the actions of legally qualified individuals but it may also refer to the spheres of life in which law plays a significant part, involving people organising their affairs 'in the shadow' of the law, or who by choice or not become involved in legal processes of various kinds. The idea of work-related learning in law school will be developed with respect to this notion of 'practice.' It will be *highly cognisant of*, but not *dominated by*, existing forms of practice of a legal character. It is important in this regard not simply to equate 'practice' or 'work' with what lawyers currently do, what Thornton,[39] drawing on the work of Jaspers, refers to as 'frozen knowledge,' but rather to see it as an evolving field of activities and particular practices with political, social,

[37] See Keyes and Johnstone, above n 35, at 537.
[38] See Goldsmith, above n 36, at 721.
[39] See above n 7, at 501.

economic and ethical consequences.[40] In order to see practice as broader and more reflexive than *technique*, we propose an understanding of practice that connects the aspirations of law students with legal professional ideals (justice, service, fairness) and the goals of a university-based professional education. Values and attitudes, making up *ethico-practical dispositions*, are crucial elements of this notion of practice; it is *not* just a matter of legal technique and knowledge of legal doctrine.

PROCEDURAL AND PROPOSITIONAL KNOWLEDGE

'Theory,' as distinct from 'practice,' is frequently thought of as *propositional knowledge*—the abstract or generalised representation of knowledge, by implication at least suggesting a systematic approach to knowledge. 'Practice' in turn is commonly characterised as *procedural knowledge*—a more concrete form of knowledge intimately related to the practical accomplishment of specific tasks. This explanation fits well with the often-drawn distinction between 'knowing that' and 'know-how'.[41] The latter relates directly to the realm of action and experience. It implies a less structured, even unstructured, process of learning in which there is an acquisition of non-formal knowledge, sometimes referred to as *tacit knowledge*, 'that body of personal knowledge that is implicit in a professional's patterns of action and their "feel" for the stuff with which they work.'[42] This knowledge usually eludes specification, and is messy and imprecise by comparison with formal knowledge, because it emerges and develops *in action*. It is a realm that the practitioner-in-development often finds very strange, especially at the novice stage. While there is debate about the extent to which one can render tacit knowledge explicit and hence teachable to others, there is clearly a limit to developing a 'feel' for a subject without active experimentation through a range of concrete experiences (that is, without actual 'touch'). Professional education that excludes opportunities for active engagement as part of acquiring procedural knowledge withholds the chance for students to actively develop their repertoires of practical skills. It does very little in terms of producing 'employable' graduates, whether by this term we refer to the acquisition of particular generic skills (eg interpersonal skills, team-working, action planning, networking, decision-making and so on) or to a broader capability conception.[43] It also denies the contexts to 'feedback' experiences from the active/experimental phases

[40] See above n 36, at 737.

[41] G Ryle, *Concept of Mind* (London, Hutchinson's University Library, 1949).

[42] See above n 14, at 246.

[43] P Knight and M Yorke, 'Employability and Good Learning in Higher Education' (2003) 8 *Teaching in Higher Education*, 6.

of learning to the conceptualisation/reflection phases identified in Kolb's experiential learning cycle[44] and other accounts of experiential learning.[45]

This position we take does not deny that the ability to practise a skill in a particular setting necessarily presupposes a fund of propositional knowledge related to the area of practice. For example, one cannot play tennis without a grasp of the rules of the game. While a grasp of rules alone is hardly sufficient to ensure the skilful application of that knowledge, it nonetheless provides a framework or set of guidelines for the practical task at hand. Equally, propositional knowledge can relate to the manner of execution of the task, as well as to the goals or objectives behind the activity. The laws of civil and criminal procedure are two prime examples. Both provide relatively explicit direction of a *necessary but not sufficient* kind in terms of the relevant steps involved in instituting and prosecuting legal proceedings. In terms of legal education then, it is possible to propose a spectrum of legal knowledge, with doctrine at the formal/propositional end, tacit knowledge at the informal/procedural end, with procedural rules and forms of consciously acquired 'know-how' to be found somewhere in-between.

INSERTING THE ETHICAL INTO THE PRACTICAL

Abbott's comment about the 'legitimacy of technique'[46] and Lyotard's focus on 'performativity'[47] in modern education suggest a critique of the moral and political vacuity viewed as being behind the promotion of practical knowledge within professional education. As one example, the competence-based approach to higher education and employability has caused consternation among commentators such as Barnett.[48] Others have found the 'skills' movement to lack notions of reflection and self-awareness.[49] The thrust of this critique is that practice should not be viewed or taught except with regard to the *context* in which it occurs and to the wider *consequences* of those practical actions.[50] Even adding an element of reflection to competency requirements or skills training is not enough. As Barnett argues:

> Such reflection will hold students at the lower performative levels of criticality unless those reflections situate the action in the wider world of social arrangements,

[44] See Maudsley and Scrivens, above n 27, at 535.

[45] See above n 15.

[46] See Abbott, above n 21, at 190.

[47] J Lyotard, *The Postmodern Condition: A Report on Knowledge* (Manchester, Manchester University Press, 1984), especially at 47–53.

[48] See above n 23.

[49] See Knight and Yorke, above n 43, at 3.

[50] A Goldsmith, 'An Unruly Conjunction?: Social Thought and Legal Action in Clinical Legal Education' (1993) 43 *Journal of Legal Education* 415.

> policies and public interests, and students are invited to envisage alternative structures, systems and possibilities for collective action. Unless reflection rises to these higher levels of reflection, the student's reflection would amount to decisionism and operationalism.[51]

Aristotle's notion of *praxis* is suggestive for our argument. This notion cannot be equated with practice, for the former contained an intrinsic concern with the goodness of the outcome, rather than purely being of instrumental significance.[52] Thus, while issuing a civil action on a client's behalf would constitute practice in the instrumental sense, in order for such an action to become *praxis*, there would also need to be reflection upon the likely ends and impacts of that action, consideration of alternative courses of action and monitoring of the actual effects. Closer to current instrumental notions of practice is Aristotle's notion of *poiesis*, often described as productive thinking. This conception of practical knowledge is much narrower in its outcome focus than *praxis*. Finding a place for this kind of knowledge in the university setting is obviously more difficult if evaluated against traditional liberal educational criteria such as disinterested inquiry and disputation of ends and means. Relying upon this distinction, the importance of procedural knowledge within legal education remains clear. However it does so in a form that is more akin to *praxis* than to *poiesis*.

PUTTING THEORY INTO PRACTICE

Universities' modern role has principally been associated with the discovery and promulgation of propositional knowledge. Considerations of an ethical nature have also loomed large in the university mission. However in the field of law, the effective translation of research findings into practical settings has very often proved impossible, or has not even been attempted.[53] While universities have long been prone to being criticised in some quarters for their presumed 'ivory tower' remoteness from the 'real world,' it is undoubtedly the case the field of legal scholarship has long lacked an empirical, real-world orientation relative to other disciplines.[54] In law, to the extent that academic researchers have failed to engage the realm of practice through their choice of research topics and methods, they have helped to maintain the gap between the academy and the 'real world' of practice as imagined or known by law students. They have, in other words,

[51] See above n 15, at 104.

[52] G Squires, *Teaching as a Professional Discipline* (London, Falmer, 1999), at 112–113.

[53] N Fox, 'Practice-Based Evidence: Towards Collaborative and Transgressive Research' (2003) 37 *Sociology* 81.

[54] A Goldsmith, 'Standing at the Crossroads: Law Schools, Universities, Markets and the Future of Legal Scholarship' in F Cownie (ed), *The Law School: Global Issues, Local Questions* (Aldershot, Dartmouth, 1999), at 92–93.

relinquished the chance to add insight to their law teaching that draws upon experiential and activity-based practice moments. This amounts to a refusal through research as well as teaching to respond to the powerful practice-oriented motivations of many of their students, described earlier. Developing a richer concept of procedural knowledge, one that embraces *praxis* as well as *poeisis*, is crucial if law academics are to actively develop a work-related learning environment that befits a university. The kinds of research that they do lend will also affect the value as well as the credibility of what they offer to students and other stakeholders.

CURRENT VALUATIONS OF PRACTICE IN AUSTRALIAN LEGAL EDUCATION

In analysing how practice is valued in Australian legal education the question of *from whose perspective must be addressed.* While there is a wide range of perspectives, we have chosen to illustrate this by examining what law schools are doing, what law students appear to be seeking and what admission authorities want law schools to produce. From this we illustrate not only how practice is valued and thus affecting the nature of legal education but also the content of the concept of 'practice'.

The Structural Context

We begin with an overview of developments in Australian legal education over the last two decades. This decade has seen a major transformation in Australian legal education—both in numbers of law schools, staff and students, and in the content of legal education. Before the mid-1980s the dominant paradigm of legal education reflected the English model where legal education was predominantly the preserve of the 'old' universities (often described as the 'sandstones' after the preferred university building medium of the late nineteenth century) operating with a trichotomy based on academic education at university-based law school, practical legal training courses and/or work experience and continuing legal education after admission. By 1987 there were 12 Australian law schools, predominantly in 'old' universities.

In 1987 a comprehensive picture of the state of Australian legal education was provided by the Pearce Report,[55] produced following a national discipline review set up by the federal government as part of its drive for accountability and the desire to assess the needs of legal education.

[55] See Pearce, Campbell and Harding, above n 26.

Contemporaneous with the Pearce Report was the federal government's restructuring of the tertiary education system as part of its aim to increase the knowledge and skills base of the nation. The pre-1987 model of universities, Colleges of Advanced Education and Institutes of Technology was abandoned and a flattened model adopted whereby the latter two types of institutions were recreated after a series of amalgamations as universities. This expansion in the number of universities between 1987 and 1992 was accompanied by requests from a number of these new universities to be allowed to offer law degrees. Whether it was because it was seen as raising the status of the new universities or because it attracted a 'better' quality of student, a law school was seen as desirable. Furthermore, prevailing pedagogical practice meant law courses involved significantly less cost for universities that almost all other disciplines. By 2001 there were some 29 law schools offering law degrees across Australia, a doubling in just over 10 years. By 2008, that number had increased to 32. Not only were new law schools expanding the legal education sector but the existing law schools also increased their intakes.[56] Table 1 shows the growth in law school enrolments.

Along with the growth in law school and law student numbers has been a change in the financing of law schools. In 1987 the era of free tertiary tuition came to an end with the introduction of the Higher Education Contribution Scheme (HECS)—a deferred payment scheme where fees are recovered as a tax surcharge once the former student obtains a prescribed level of earnings. Law students pay the top band of $8333 per annum and commence paying this charge when their income reaches $39,824. As the student contribution to the costs of their tertiary education increased, the

Table 1 Student Enrolments 1987, 1991, 2000

Year	Law/legal studies (% of total students)	Total students
1987	11,345 (2.9%)	393,734
1991	16,310 (3.1%)	534,510
2000	36,331 (5.2%)	695,485

(Higher Education Students Time Series Tables 2000).[57]

[56] C McInnes and S Marginson, *Australian Law Schools After the 1987 Pearce Report* (Canberra, AGPS, 1994).

[57] Department of Education, Training and Youth Affairs, *Higher Education Students Time Series Tables 2000* (Canberra, Department of Education, Training and Youth Affairs, 2000) Table 7, 18.

Australian government reduced its contribution from general revenue.[58] Associated with the change in public funding was the lifting of the prohibition on charging domestic students upfront fees. These changes encouraged the creation of a competitive market in legal education with the commensurate need to meet market demands. Not only have law schools had to develop a range of entrepreneurial and marketing skills but these changes have changed the nature of the student/school relationship with students transformed into paying consumers.[59] It has also changed the content of legal education with law schools and students retreating from the broad liberal curriculum, preferring 'trade' subjects that are thought to be more attractive to prospective employers and re-introducing stand alone law degrees for school leavers.[60]

The funding changes have also increased pressure on law schools to seek financial or corporate support from the legal profession. Ranging from sponsorship of academic positions through to fundraising, law schools are looking for ways to engage with and attract the support of the legal profession. The effect of all these developments is to renew the influence legal practice and the legal profession have had on legal education.

We now turn to the transformation in the content of legal education. The Pearce Report suggested that the content of legal education at law schools was excessively doctrinal and it recommended that 'law schools examine the adequacy of their attention to theoretical and critical perspectives, including the study of law in operation and the relations between law and other forces'.[61] Allied with this pedagogical approach was the growth in 'skills' education both as a means of operationalising law and breaking down the theory/practice distinction. In addition, as McInnes and Marginson note, as for higher education as a whole, law schools were influenced by the increasing emphasis given to vocational preparation as a key outcome for tertiary education.[62] The major constraint on the content of legal education was a set of national standards adopted by admission authorities in each Australian jurisdiction outlining areas of knowledge required for admission. The required curriculum closely reflects the traditional doctrinal fields of knowledge. These became the compulsory core of a law degree, leaving approximately one third of the curriculum available for law school and student choice.

Underpinning the liberal education model in law schools were the concepts of the inquiring mind and minimising narrow technical learning. Law

[58] Department of Education, Science and Training. *Rationalising Responsibility for Higher Education in Australia: Issues Paper* (Canberra, Department of Education, Science and Training, 2000), 9.

[59] See above n 35, at 554.

[60] See above n 7, at 483. See also n 35, at 548–50.

[61] See above n 26, 113.

[62] See McInnes and Marginson, above n 56, 25.

schools were not simply factories for the production of lawyers but rather the law degree would provide a range of knowledge and (for those law schools offering skills teaching) generic or transferable skills that would be valued in a wide range of occupations. The growth of double degree students was seen as a means of providing students with breadth of knowledge outside the confines of the law course—the Law degree was said to be the new Arts degree which would enable graduates to enter the corporate world, public service and the diplomatic corps. This vision of the law school was used to assuage the legal profession who became concerned when they discovered by the mid-1990s that there were as many law students as legal practitioners. The fact that many law graduates may not enter the legal profession should not disguise the fact that most law students enter law school intending to qualify for legal practice and in graduating students, law schools are certifying that the students have met the requisite standard for admission to legal practice. As Webber notes: 'Law schools do seek to educate students, above all, for legal practice'.[63]

All this would suggest the weakening of the role of the profession and the influence of legal practice in legal education but acting against this are the powerful drivers of student preferences in a competitive market, an unchanging core curriculum and the legal profession's desire to 'exercise a greater degree of control'.[64]

MEASURING THE NEXUS BETWEEN PRACTICE AND LEGAL EDUCATION

Having identified the main drivers of change over the last two decades, we can see more clearly what value is being given to practice in Australian university legal education. In this fluid environment, law schools have adopted a number of strategies that bring law school closer to the profession and practice. In analysing these changes to illustrate the relationship between practice and legal education we have, by necessity, had to treat the perspectives of different stakeholders as fairly monolithic. In reality, within each of the stakeholder groups, views about these changes can vary. For the profession, the prospect of a flood of law graduates has caused concern. For students and legal academics, both the pedagogical and resource implications of these changes has caused disquiet if not opposition in some places. Indeed some of the major stresses within the legal academy result from the tension between maintaining a broad liberal academic education in the face of student- and profession-driven vocationalism, and increasing closer ties

[63] J Webber, 'Legal Research, the Law Schools and the Profession' (2004) 26(4) *Sydney Law Review* 565.

[64] See above n 35, at 555.

with the profession, which is both a funding source and a market for the product.

So what criteria are we using to plot the relationship between practice and legal education? The main areas we will examine are (1) curriculum developments in law degrees, (2) the types of new programmes law schools have introduced, and (3) changing admission standards. In analysing changes in legal education over the last decade we find a closer nexus between practice and law schools. We illustrate this by looking at developments in law school curriculum and programmes, looking at the impact on both law students and academics of these changes, and the legal profession's response to these developments.

Curriculum Developments

Following the Pearce Report, a study McInnes and Marginson released in 1994 found that there had been significant attempts to broaden the curriculum to encompass teaching of theoretical perspectives and contextual frameworks, particularly by the new law schools established post 1987.[65] Contextualising legal doctrine provides an opportunity for increased attention to the way in which law is practiced and the role of the lawyer. While evidence to demonstrate whether this has happened is not easily available, it is reasonable to surmise that the increased focus on context and critical perspectives that McInnes and Marginson established has been accompanied by an increase in the study of the profession and practice.

More easily established has been the growth in skills teaching in law schools. While law schools have always taught research, analysis and legal writing (along with 'thinking like lawyers'), there has been a significant increase in the number of law schools teaching a broader range of skills.[66] Many of the newer universities, especially those established in the last 15 years or so, have an explicit commitment to the teaching of generic skills within the law degree. In the new managerial age of mission statements, references to skills teaching are increasingly common.[67] These skills move beyond the traditional to include the interpersonal skills of interviewing, negotiating, mediating and oral advocacy. Flinders University Law School is an example of the extent to which this new approach has been adopted. All students are required to take a subject called Lawyering in the first year in which the range of skills is introduced and then each skill is followed up in a structured skills programme incorporated within a compulsory topic later in the degree (eg interviewing in Administrative Law, drafting in Corporate

[65] See above n 56.
[66] See above n 35, at 550.
[67] See above n 6, at 41.

Law, negotiation in Civil Litigation). Student evaluations of these topics often mention the skills programme as one of the best things about the subject. The extent of these skills programmes varies from law school to law school but the trend is clearly toward introducing generic skills programmes that extend beyond legal research, analysis and writing.

There has also been a modest growth in clinical legal education.[68] Pioneered by Monash University and the University of New South Wales who received funding to set up community legal centres in the 1970s,[69] clinical legal education has expanded in the last 15 years. Resource constraints meant that for most of the period, the model of clinical legal education has been the development of externship programmes. Programmes range from placement with legal aid authorities (La Trobe University), placement with community legal centres (Griffith University), placement with the wider range of law related services (Adelaide University) to assisting unrepresented defendants in criminal appeals (University of Western Australia). By 2003, 23 of the then 29 Australian law schools were offering some form of clinical legal education.[70]

A further measure of the increased interest in clinical legal education has been a higher level of interest in and activity by the Clinical Legal Education Association. The Association is open to those involved or interested in clinical education and has now organised several national conferences. An obvious consequence of the development of legal education is a change both in the experience of law students of legal practice and, perhaps more importantly, the sorts of skills and knowledge needed and now found within the academic staff of law schools.

A new stimulus for law school activity in clinical legal education has come out of the current drive to promote *pro bono* legal services.[71] In 2000 the Australian Law Reform Commission, in its report into federal civil litigation, not only recommended encouraging *pro bono* work on the part of the profession but also that 'to enhance appreciation of ethical standards and professional responsibility, law students should be encouraged and provided with the opportunity to undertake pro bono work as part of their academic or practical legal training requirements'.[72] The Australian

[68] J Boersig, J Marshall and G Seaton, 'Teaching Law and Legal Practice in a Live Client Clinic' (2002) 6 *Newcastle Law Review*, 51.

[69] A Copeland, 'Clinical Legal Education within a Community Legal Centre' (2003) *Murdoch University Electronic Journal of Law* www.murdoch.edu.au/elaw/issues/v10n3/copeland103.html.

[70] Kingsford Legal Centre, *Clinical Legal Education Guide 2007/8* (Sydney, Kingsford Legal Centre, 2007). See also National Pro Bono Resource Centre, *Pro Bono and Clinical Legal Education Programmes in Australian Law Schools* (Sydney, National Pro Bono Resource Centre, 2004).

[71] J Corker, 'How Does Pro Bono Students Australia Fit With Clinical Legal Education in Australia' 8th Australian Clinical Legal Education Conference, Melbourne, 2005.

[72] See above n 16, 29.

Government has in the last four years been attempting to minimise its contribution to legal aid schemes. *Pro bono* work has been seen by the government as an alternative. In addition to sponsoring national conferences on *pro bono* work, the Australian Attorney-General funded a national taskforce that has developed a national *pro bono* strategy and the National Pro Bono Resource Centre. The Centre has, as one of its early projects, surveyed law schools on their *pro bono* and clinical legal education activities and investigated some of the key issues around developing and maintaining such programmes.[73]

One of the interesting questions that we cannot definitively answer here is the way in which practice is influencing the range of options or electives available to students. At any point in time, the range of electives available is affected by the academic expertise available and student demand. In times of resource scarcity, the ability of law schools to offer electives is particularly affected by student demand. Experience within Flinders University confirms the observation made by Thornton that the further the elective is from student perceptions of what is required for practice the more likely it is to struggle to maintain its viability.[74] One useful research study that would shed light on the way in which practice is valued would be to examine the range of electives on offer and the pattern of student enrolments in those subjects.

Law School Programmes

Not only is practice influencing the content of the curriculum within law degrees, practice is also influencing what other programmes or degrees law schools offer. To illustrate this, we focus on two developments: (1) the growth in practical training programmes; and (2) the continuing emphasis in law school in the postgraduate area on the development of practice-related course work programmes.

Practical Legal Training

The dominant model of legal education in Australia adopts the distinction made between academic and practical training. Since the 1960s the model has formally been that of a broad liberal academic education (that was the role of law schools), followed by a period of practical training (either provided by articles or a vocational training course offered by the equivalent of technical colleges). In the 1970s there was a move away from articles

[73] National Pro Bono Resource Centre, *Pro Bono and Clinical Legal Education Programmes* (2004).

[74] See above n 7, at 495.

of clerkship (now no longer available in most Australian jurisdictions) to tertiary training courses located outside law schools (eg the College of Law in Sydney and the Leo Cussen Institute in Melbourne). In 1990 almost no law school offered a practical training course, but by 2007 some 12 of the 30 Australian law schools offered a programme that satisfied the practical training requirements for admission to legal practice.

Two types of course have evolved. The first, and most common, maintains the separation of the academic programme from practical training by offering a postgraduate diploma course or its equivalent. The popularity of this model lies in the fact that it avoids having to resolve all the issues, both philosophical and practical, that are created by merging academic and practical training. As a postgraduate course, the law schools are also able to charge tuition fees, and most do.

An even closer relationship with legal practice is being formed with a new development in this type of stand-alone practical legal training course. Responding to the overtures of large commercial law firms, the Australian National University offered a version of its practical training course in house for the major commercial law firm Blake Dawson Waldron in 2000. Targeted towards the practice needs of large commercial forms, the law school staff visit the law firm and teach by a combination of flexible delivery and traditional small group teaching. Within a year a number of other major law firms followed suit.[75]

The second type is the integrated academic/practical training model. Only three law schools have proceeded down this path at the undergraduate level: Newcastle University, University of Technology Sydney and Flinders University.[76] Flinders University offers a Bachelor of Laws and Legal Practice as well as Bachelor of Laws that enables a Flinders graduate to apply for admission to practice on graduation without further requirements. The University of Technology Sydney has extended this model to its Juris Doctor programme that commenced in 2008 so that non-law graduates are able to combine their academic and practical legal training courses.

The different types of practical legal training courses have significant implications for the definitions of legal knowledge. The first type maintains the traditional theory/practice divide with the separate add-on practical legal training course and fails to take the opportunity of using practice to inform theory. Indeed it reinforces an unthinking, conventional approach to practice. It bears the character, for the most part, of *poesis* rather than of *praxis*. The second type, the integrated approach, has the potential to operationalise 'academic' learning and to subject 'practical' learning to academic

[75] Lawyers Weekly, 'The PLT Revolution' *Lawyers Weekly* (17 July 2004).

[76] R Spencer, 'Teaching Legal Skills at Flinders—an Integrated Practical Legal Training Programme' (2003) 6 *Flinders Journal of Law Reform*, 219.

inquiry. The challenge lies for those law schools adopting the integrated approach to demonstrate that they are doing more than importing the old practice course approach into undergraduate courses. This requires further evaluation.

Postgraduate Courses

The 1990s has seen the continued development in the range of coursework programmes aimed at meeting the needs of the practising profession. While the number of research higher degree completions between 1993 and 2000 rose from 31 to 61 for Law and Legal Studies the numbers of coursework postgraduate students rose from 1539 to 1848 in the same period.[77] In 2003 the Graduate Careers Council of Australia reported that up to 25 per cent of undergraduates go on to further study. Many of the postgraduate programmes in law are intended to enhance specialist knowledge and skills for legal practitioners. Melbourne University, for example, in 2008 offered 33 coursework Master's degrees across 23 specialist areas. In 2006 it was estimated that 16 per cent of the lawyers at an unspecified major commercial firm were undertaking postgraduate courses. The firm thought the courses particularly useful where they linked 'pure' law with the business of the student's clients.[78]

The introduction of mandatory continuing legal education in some Australian jurisdictions has led to some of the larger law schools developing significant commercial arms to satisfy this market. Accreditation schemes for specialist practitioners have also created a market for law school programmes. Some law schools provide tailor-made courses to meet particular practice needs. These have become so successful that some law schools have established centres for continuing legal education within law schools to meet this market (eg the University of New South Wales). The various coursework postgraduate courses may also satisfy continuing legal education requirements.

Changing Admission Requirements

Admission authorities play a central role in determining the importance of practice in Australian legal education. In Australia the regulation of the legal profession including admission to practice is a matter for individual jurisdictions. However, the difficulty of operating nine separate jurisdictions has led to de facto national standards. Legislation has led to mutual

[77] Department of Education, Science and Training, Higher Education Report for Triennium 2002–04 (Canberra, Department of Education, Science and Training, 2004).

[78] Lawyers Weekly, 'Advancing by Degree: Postgraduate Legal Study' *Lawyers Weekly* (12 January, 2005a).

recognition of qualifications and rights to practice. Concerns about differing admission standards led to the formation of the Legal Admission Consultative Committee with representatives from all jurisdictions. The Committee made recommendations as to what applicants for admission to practice would have to satisfy, which have been adopted by all the admission authorities. Known as the Priestly 11 and Priestly 12, they set out 11 content areas which law school were required to provide and a further 12 areas of practical legal training. Expressed in very broad terms they provided the basis for the structure of almost all Australian law degrees. The Priestly 11 remains the compulsory core of the law degree.

Legal academics have criticized the narrowness of the Priestly 11 with its traditional focus on torts, contract, property, equity, public law, crime and corporate law. However future directions lie not in the areas legal academics suggest—international law, jurisprudence, legal history. Reflecting the importance of practice in legal education, in 2008, prompted by the concerns expressed by some of Australia's senior judges, the Legal Admission Consultative Committee began actively considering whether statutory interpretation should be added as an required knowledge to the requirements for admission to legal practice. The Legal Admission Consultative Committee's consideration goes further and sets a new precedent by suggesting how statutory interpretation should be taught—as a stand-alone subject. In so doing the admission authorities, who in this context, constitute 'practice' have moved beyond their traditional role of prescribing the content of the core curriculum to prescribing how that content should be taught.

The practical legal training requirements have also been changed significantly in the last five years. The Legal Admissions Consultative Committee has replaced the original Priestly 12 requirements with a set of competency requirements developed by the Australasian Professional Legal Education Council (APLEC). Drafted in conformity with National Training Board Standards these outline descriptors and performance criteria down to very specific tasks. The new practical legal training requirements suffer from all the disadvantages that the considerable literature on the use of competencies discusses.

The model of legal practice adopted remains that of a generalist private practitioner engaged in the tasks of practice that were routine ten or twenty years ago. That is not to say those tasks are no longer relevant or useful but it does not allow for new concepts of practice and professional organisation, and life. While the competencies include the range of the usual skills—lawyer's skills, problem solving, work management and business skills, trust and office accounting—they also include ethics and professional responsibility. For the most part, these requirements reflect practice-related knowledge of a *poeisis* nature. The process by which these were arrived at was not one of evaluation of modern practice needs but rather a building on the original Priestly areas of practice along with APLEC's own assessment of practice needs (but not based on any empirical research or widespread consultation).

This approach to reformulating the practical legal training requirements for admission to legal practice has led to considerable debate over the changes that made criminal practice and probate practice optional requirements, with the only compulsory practice areas being civil litigation, commercial and corporate practice, and property law practice. This decision does not appear to have been based on any research or wide consultation over what the needs of contemporary practice are. One can read into the new proposals a diminishing role being given to meeting the needs of individuals and an increasing emphasis given to meeting the needs of the corporate bodies.

Impact on Law Students and Staff

As noted earlier, the value law students give to practice has existed for some time.[79] This has continued and has been enhanced during and since the 1990s. This challenges one of the justifications for the major increase in Australian law schools and student numbers—that law courses were no longer aimed at reproducing legal practitioners but that students and employers saw law courses as good preparation for a wide range of careers. Both the Roper study and the subsequent study by Vignaendra have showed that not only do the overwhelming proportion of law students wish to qualify for admission to practice but that large proportions are admitted.[80] Vignaendra's survey of the 1991 and 1995 cohorts of law graduates showed that around half of the graduates were engaged in private practice with around 18 per cent engaged in the public service. 'Only 11% of graduates in the 95 cohort, and 12% of graduates in the 91 cohort, were known to be in non-legal positions'.[81]

We have already suggested that there may be a change in the sorts of electives student are choosing while at law school. The challenge for those seeking to encourage a well informed, critical understanding of law and the legal system is not only to ensure that a broad range of electives is maintained but that those electives more closely related to practice are taught with a contextual and critical approach. While no doubt this may often be done, the extent to which it is accepted by students as central to their study of the law remains open to question and is certainly not evident generally

[79] See discussion commencing at n 16 above.

[80] S Vignaendra, *Australian Law Graduates' Career Destinations* (Canberra, Department of Employment, Education, Training and Youth Affairs, 1998) www.deetya.gov.au/archive/highered/eippubs/eip98-9/execsum.htm.

[81] See above n 82, at 2.

speaking from a perusal of the key teaching texts used in Australian law schools in 2008.[82]

The attractiveness of practice-oriented subjects has been enhanced by changes in the recruiting practices of the major law firms. The perception of law students is that the way to the highly paid, highly prestigious positions in the major law firms is through the individual law firm's clerkship programmes. More recently the perception is increasingly becoming reality. This 'shift in favour of vacation or seasonal clerkships as the primary source of recruits, [means] the pressure is on for students to start thinking about where they want to practice by at least their penultimate year'.[83] Each year enormous effort is made by law students to make the interviews for these clerkships. The law firms are thought to recruit from the pool of clerks they have employed in the later years of the law degree. Not only are students choosing what they study with this in mind, but they are also gaining knowledge of a type of legal practice that is very different to most legal work. The clerkship programmes tend to be found amongst the larger firms and government departments with an over-representation in corporate and commercial law.

The combination of curriculum and programme developments referred to above has had significant consequences for both the academic profile of law schools and the activities of staff members. Law schools are required to attract staff who are able to teach skills, teach in practical training courses and teach in postgraduate courses aimed at legal practitioners in a very competitive market. For those law schools maintaining a separation between academic practice and practical training, the issue of avoiding caste systems that have developed whereby those engaged in practical training/clinical legal education are treated as 'lesser' academics is challenging. In the integrated programmes the issue is perhaps less problematic. Adding to the difficulty for law schools is the ongoing lack of a sufficient pool of academics having both academic strength and professional experience or standing. Those with both these attributes are highly sought after by private practice, and in order to attract them some universities have had to offer better conditions than those enjoyed by traditional law academics.

The creations of professorial positions that are practice related give some indication of the value of legal practice in legal education. La Trobe University now has, for example, a post that combines a professorial post with the directorship of the Programme for the Study of Legal Practice and the Professions. One of the primary tasks for the professor was to oversee the setting up and development of 'links with the professions and the public

[82] On a personal note, experience of teaching in a very practice-related subject like procedure or litigation has shown that when students are given the option of assessment schemes that enable recognition of broader contextual analysis only a quarter will take up the option (often to reduce reliance on examinations).

[83] Lawyers Weekly, 'Try Before You Buy' *Lawyers Weekly* (19 August 2005b).

and private sectors, and to establish a funding base through the generation of enterprise income'. Monash University appointed a retired Supreme Court judge to be a full-time Professor of Advocacy and Trial Practice, the first of its kind in Australia.

GETTING BACK ON TRACK

Thus, while there has been a move towards greater vocationalism in Australian law schools in the last decade or so, to the regret of many liberal and more critical commentators in the legal academy,[84] it remains the case that little work has been done to try to find a balance between calls for 'relevance' through a focus on practice and wider appeals for law to remain within the ideals of the university system. The latter goal has never really been institutionally dominant in the vast majority of law schools, and the current constellation of professional, university, student and government pressures upon law schools is largely set upon keeping things this way. Rather than retreating into an actual 'ivory tower' of sorts, liberal or critical legal academics need to take a more pro-active approach in order to limit the sway of unchecked legal vocationalism in universities.

'Our Students Are Not Us'

Who we are as legal academics cannot be separated wholly from who our students are. Becker et al's study over 40 years ago of American medical students and their teachers identified an all too familiar dilemma faced by many law teachers today:

> The phrase 'give it to us straight' favourably used in an earlier example, is the student counterpart of the derogatory word 'spoon-feeding', used by the faculty. In our interviews with faculty members, those who oppose spoon-feeding the students or do it unwillingly often complain that students are too pragmatic, impatient of everything imprecise; they want only hard facts… They worry about what kind of physicians students will become if they accept only facts as material for learning and are uncritical of these facts in a rapidly changing discipline. They ask the perennial question of elders: Why aren't they more like us?.[85]

Work-hungry or experience-demanding students tend to reflect different priorities from many of today's law academics. These priorities are often taken from the field he or she wishes to enter, or at least from their own socialised conceptions of what that field is and demands, rather than

[84] See, eg, above n 6, at 41. See also, above n 7, at 481.

[85] H Becker, B Geer, E Hughes, A Strauss, *Boys in White: Student Culture in Medical School* (Chicago, University of Chicago Press, 1961), at 173.

mirroring or adopting the values and priorities of their teachers. Candy and Crebert describe this often stark difference as follows:

> The driving interest for the professional is much more oriented towards status, power, and profit than it is with self-fulfilment and the acquisition of knowledge that motivate the scholar. Likewise, projects that may be feasible in one context simply do not translate to the other. Thus, the profit-oriented, practical solutions of the manager have no correlative in the abstract philosophies of the professor who values theoretical coherence.[86]

Ways of accommodating differences in orientation around 'practice' are needed if law academics are to retain a sense of practical engagement in their professional discipline while simultaneously promoting broader, more ethically critical understandings of the practice of law.

Developing Work-Related Learning

It is clear to many already in legal education that something more than substantive and procedural knowledge is essential to the development of legal education in universities. For example, the Australian Law Reform Commission noted in 2000: 'In addition to the study of core areas of substantive law, university legal education in Australia should involve the development of high level professional skills and a deep appreciation of ethical standards and professional responsibility.'[87]

Calls for greater focus upon professional values reiterate the ongoing centrality of some kind of practice focus within legal education, which is reinforced by the law schools' various stakeholders.[88] Law schools' responsiveness to their students will of necessity demand closer integration of the goals of higher education with the practical needs and demands of prospective employers. Against this background, Law's future as a classical or liberal discipline, measured in curriculum terms, is inevitably constrained but certainly no more than it has been by requirements such as the Priestley 11, and potentially less so if our expanded understanding of practice is embraced.

The notion of practice must encompass new possibilities as well as address and critique current conventions in practice. The adaptive, experimental elements of learning about law cannot develop in the straightjacket provided by current orthodoxy, though it will inevitably remain a significant point of orientation and departure for pedagogical purposes. While scarcely suggesting law schools should abandon propositional knowledge, procedural

[86] P Candy and G Crebert, 'Ivory Tower to Concrete Jungle: The Difficult Transition from the Academy to the Workplace as Learning Environments' (1991) 62 *Journal of Higher Education* 576.

[87] See above n 16, Recommendation no 2.

[88] See, eg above n 25.

or process knowledge must play an enhanced role in the law curriculum. Process knowledge of the law 'in action' will assist in facilitating the exploration and transmission of value perspectives on practice consistent with the furtherance of justice and the provision of service. This will probably require a reduction in the 'bulk' of legal propositions taught in the curriculum. This will require reorientation of the admission authorities, in particular that they set their standards by reference to this broader, less technical conception of legal knowledge and accept that professional development requires ongoing educational opportunities. The 'one and only chance' mentality towards professional legal education must cease. Educationalists insist, and the rapidly changing environment in which we live and work dictates, that university graduates in any discipline must become 'life-long learners.'

Law teachers and their students need to reorient themselves towards the practice of law. Their approach should be neither that of the abstract critic nor the unreflective athlete-practitioner.[89] What is required is a balance between critical distance and the ability to be aware and function within legal environments. There must be something more required than Candy and Crebert's notion of the 'visiting anthropologist':

> However, it is both possible and desirable to smooth the transition from one environment to another; at the very least graduates should be equipped with skills and insights that allow them, like visiting anthropologists, to understand the culture of the workplace. But beyond mere understanding, graduates must have the capability to function in the new environment. In this sense they are much more like immigrants than tourists.[90]

University centres of legal education must be encouraged to develop and maintain the kind of 'connected critic' attitude towards law, legal institutions and lawyers.[91] Such a critical position is internal to the roles played by lawyers and legal workers, grasping the 'logic of appropriateness' shared within these legal communities, yet remaining conscious also of the 'logic of consequences', enabling the simultaneous practice of a critical stance of current conceptions of professional appropriateness in legal practice.[92] While law schools can undoubtedly do more to produce graduates more skillfully

[89] This concept refers to practitioners who see their role purely or predominantly as a matter of technical proficiency. It is discussed in some detail in Goldsmith, 'Is There Any Backbone in this Fish? Interpretive Communities, Social Criticism, and Transgressive Legal Practice' (1998) 23 *Law & Social Inquiry* 373, at 401–02.

[90] See Candy and Crebert, above n 86, at 576.

[91] See above n 89, at 384.

[92] I am using these terms somewhat differently from their original meanings (see James March and Johan Olsen, *Rediscovering Institutions: The Organizational Basis of Politics*, Stanford UP 1989). Here, I am distinguishing between the habituated conventional realm of practice, in which normative and practical issues are largely settled and familiar (appropriateness), and the task of critique of that realm, focusing upon the material and other outcomes of particular established practices and related values (consequences).

attuned to the demands of the workplace, they should not abandon their university-founded stewardship of the responsibility to be sceptical towards current practices, and to seek and promote wider values of justice, equity, access and truth within the wide variety of practices of the law.

The recent concern with values, and their perceived neglect in the past, is already setting the scene for a more fundamental questioning of what constitutes the relevant professional knowledge base for education. The need for a broader understanding of legal practice is implicit in recipes such as Timothy Floyd's for preparing good lawyers:

(1) focusing on what lawyers do
(2) dealing as much with people as with rules
(3) teaching more of the analytical tools lawyers actually use
(4) teaching more of the interpersonal aspects of lawyering
(5) emphasizing learning by doing
(6) attending more to real-world law
(7) rewarding teachers who focus on practice issues
(8) basing admission decisions on more than LSAT and GPA scores
(9) emphasizing the delivery of legal services
(10) making students focus on broader issues of their professional 'calling'.[93]

Another trend within professional education, the recognition of the central place of decision-making and judgement,[94] a space beyond propositional knowledge, also plays an important part in moving understandings of what appropriate practice-related education should look like.

In Table 2, we outline two models of legal education. The models draw partly upon earlier work by Andrew Goldsmith and Guy Powles.[95] The first, the *replicative*, in our view approximates the orthodox position, while the second, the *transformative*, reflects the kinds of attitudes towards professional knowledge, and particularly the conception of practice, that we deem preferable on academic as well as democratic and market-driven grounds. Clearly, the second model is more demanding of students and may be seen as threatening by some mainstream legal practitioners. Hopefully however, the second has the potential to be more interesting for students, enabling them to engage in a wider range of legal practice settings than those associated with legal vocationalism. The second model also requires a more empirical as well as critical disposition among law educators; while exacting in new ways for some of them, it offers a way of balancing or incorporating a focus on the practice domain with the liberal ideals of university education.

[93] TW Floyd, 'Legal Education and the Vision Thing' (1997) 31 *Georgia Law Review* 856.
[94] See Squires, above n 52, at 26.
[95] A Goldsmith and G Powles, 'Lawyers Behaving Badly: Where Now in Legal Education for Acting Responsibly in Australia' in K Economides (ed), *Legal Education for Ethical Conduct* (Oxford, Hart Publishing, 1998).

Table 2 Two Models of Legal Education

	Replicative/Poesis	Transformative/Praxis
Concept of knowledge	Operational/specific	Critical/generic
Knowledge-type	Know-how ('frozen')	Know-why/that/how ('adaptive')
Object of evaluation	Performance	Meaningful action
Criteria of evaluation	What works?	What are you up to?
Relevant field	Client, court, profession	Client, court, profession + community, society
Ethical orientation	Neutral partisanship	Reflective engagement
Relationship with 'real world'	Mute/subordinate/ passive formalism	Dialogical/dialectical/ active empiricism
Pedagogical focus	Content-driven	Process-focused

CONCLUSION

In this chapter, we have suggested that re-focusing legal education on the domains of practice is not the same as capitulating to the 'immediate goals of commerce'[96] or a singular focus on employability.[97] It is possible to contemplate legal education focusing on the development and transmission of an understanding of professionally-relevant practical knowledge that does not simply replicate current 'best practice' as conveyed directly or indirectly from the extant practising legal community.[98] Through thinking about the practice of law as *praxis*, rather than *poeisis*, it is possible to think more deeply about practice contexts, drawing upon the two logics of 'appropriateness' and of 'consequences' as we have used these terms here.

This perspective requires a willingness and disposition by law educators to engage with a variety of theoretical and empirical understandings of legal practice in the broad sense employed here so as to consider *consequences* of particular practices from a variety of viewpoints, while remaining attentive to the 'internal' perspectives of those engaged in the practice of law (the idea of *appropriateness*). Despite the persistence of perspectives that remain sympathetic to the goals of a liberal law school, a new path is required, one that is indeed 'liberal' in its attitude to student demands as well as to academic preferences. While some work has already been done,[99] that path requires further thought and specification regarding the place of practice

[96] See above n 21, at 211.
[97] See Goldsmith and Powles, above 95.
[98] See above n 89, at 413–21.
[99] See, eg Goldsmith and Powles, above n 95.

within legal education, beyond the modest justification and beginnings outlined here. Given that students are already working in legal and other environments during law school, the choice is clear. Legal educators can either meet the challenge of engaging the realm of practice, thereby helping not just to shape the doctrinal content of the law but also the ways in which it is practised, and the ends being pursued. Or they can relinquish their influence and authority over these issues by leaving them to 'market' and other (typically) uncritical stakeholder forces. The latter course, in our view, is unconscionable. It would be to relinquish a valuable learning opportunity demanded by the overall goals of a university-based education.

7

Will there be Blood? Students as Stakeholders in the Legal Academy

ANDREW BOON AND AVIS WHYTE

INTRODUCTION

IN 1866 WILLIAM Robertson Smith,[1] a student, wrote to his friend, Archibald McDonald, on life at Edinburgh University:

> My Dear Archibald,
>
> One of the most disagreeable features of the Hall here is that a good deal of writing is required. A natural reaction leads me to shirk epistolary correspondence... I hope [this will] serve as my excuse for not writing to you sooner.
>
> The Classes here are conducted in a very loose and irregular manner compared with those in Aberdeen. The professor seldom enters the room till ten minutes after the hour and it took a month to get the roll made up. I do not know my place in it yet, for the professors do not take the trouble to arrange it alphabetically...
>
> [Professor] Duns' Class (Nat. Hist.) is, you will be sorry to hear, so conducted as to be an unmitigated nuisance. In the first place it is impossible as a rule to find out what the lecture is about. Then the specimens never accompany the lecture but are given out a few days before or the day after. In the next place the spelling on the board is execrable, and the lectures are full of technicalities that are never written down or explained. To crown it all we have popular lectures on a Thursday crowded with bad metaphors & quotations from Tennyson, Ruskin &c.[2]

[1] Hereinafter WRS, one of the leading Scottish intellects of his generation. WRS enrolled at Aberdeen University just before his fifteenth birthday to study theology and subsequently entered New College, Edinburgh to prepare for the ministry. He had a spectacular academic career and was appointed to the Chair of Hebrew at Aberdeen Free Church College in 1870 aged just 24. See www.gkbenterprises.fsnet.co.uk/wrs.htm.

[2] WRS to his friend Archibald McDonald, letter dated 10 Dec, 1866 at www.gkbenterprises.fsnet.co.uk/letters/1866-12-10.html.

> I believe I shall never recover from the dislike to Nat. Hist. that Duns' lectures have inspired me with. I now make it a point of honour never to listen to the lectures & to absent myself from the class pretty often.
>
> The man is always stupid and superficial, generally talks nonsense and is occasionally profane. I have some rich specimens of his lectures which I must tell you when I see you next.[3]

More recently, a first year law student was asked to recount his experience of university by a news team following up a story about the low levels of teaching time undergraduates receive. He responded:

> We're at Uni six hours a week… that works out… three grand a year, that works out to about £120.00 for six hours, that's like £20.00 an hour. I'm good at maths. At this Uni I'll probably get a two one and someone like me, I'm expected to get the best degrees the best jobs. I would easily accept a two one from Cambridge rather than a one point one from here. I don't know why. Cambridge, that's just a prestige University. I'd rather go there than go here. It's plain and simple really.[4]

It could be concluded, simply, that frustration with the university experience is timeless, but, though similar, these different messages suggest that much has changed. Until relatively recently, universities housed a very small proportion of the population. They were places where the very privileged or the very intelligent were educated with a view to becoming, or remaining, leading and influential members of society.[5] The government's agenda to 'widen participation' has changed this, not only because the background of the students entering Higher Education (HE) has changed, but because their experience often does not prepare them for a 'traditional university experience'. The evidence of this is often found in poor attendance and preparation. It is also, sometimes, reflected in the kinds of relationship that students expect with the faculty. For example, a colleague recently received this email from a student:

> HI SIR ITS ROLAND FORM GROUP 12.
>
> I WAS SUPOSED TO HAND IN MY WORK TO YOU TODAY BUT I ARRIVED AT 12.50 (THINKING YOU WUD STILL BE THER) BUT YOU HAD ALREADY LEFT.
>
> BECAUSE TOMOROW IS THE LAST DAY TO GET IT ALL SIGNED OFF, AM ATACHING THE TASKS WHICH YOU HAVE NOT MARKED YET SO YOU CAN DO IT FOR TOMOROW (WE HAVE YOU AT 11 AM)

[3] Letter dated 6 Feb, 1867 at www.gkbenterprises.fsnet.co.uk/letters/1867-02-06.html#edn3#edn3.

[4] Video link to article 'Good Degrees, Poor Education' *The Daily Telegraph*, 31 Oct 2006 at www.telegraph.co.uk/news/main.jhtml?xml=/news/2006/10/31/nuni31.xml. R Hancock, 'They Teach you for 20 Minutes Then Say "See you next week"' *The Daily Telegraph*, 31 Oct, 2006 at www.telegraph.co.uk/news/uknews/1532845/They-teach-you-for-20-minutes-then-say-See-you-next-week.html.

[5] B Barrett, 'What is the Function of a University? Ivory Tower or Trade School for Plumbers?' (1998) 6(3) *Quality Assurance in Education* 145.

YOU PROBABLY HAVE OTHER THINGS TO GET ON WITH BUT IT AINT MY FAULT. YOU SHUD HAVE STAYED IN THAT ROOM TIL 1 PM (AS IT SAID ON BLACKBOARD)

ANYWAYS. SEE YOU TOMOROW SIR, AND ENJOY THE MARKIN. DATS WAT YOU GET PAID TO DO.

ROLAND[6]

Roland probably would not have entered university 30 years ago; he is of the first generation in his family to do so. His attitude and expectations may be attributed to this and, it is sometimes suggested, to his financial sacrifice made for HE. His demands, however, add to the increasing demands on many HE institutions. The new student body have more diverse educational needs than the traditional student population and yet their introduction to the system coincides with a declining ratio of staff to students. Roland, therefore, 'enjoys' a mass HE system with mass communication the medium; he belongs to a cohort of students over 300 strong, he contacts his tutor by email using text speak and receives notices via a virtual learning environment, Blackboard.

The scale and nature of the HE undertaking also has consequences for relationships, particularly between the academy and its students. Whereas William shared his complaints with Archibald, today's student is primed to share his complaints with the world. Therefore, when, albeit indirectly by means of a welter of surveys and league tables, they declare their experience as 'execrable', or similar, the world listens. The focus of our story, however, concerns the implications of the emerging academic market in law for the academy, specifically for its relationship to its students. It is a cliché that students are ever more demanding than their predecessors and some may perceive that they are less congenial.[7] We do not subscribe to either view, but students like Roland do represent a new challenge and, while they may yet be unfamiliar to some academics, most will be familiar with their mindset. While these may not seem like the best of times for law, worse may be to come. The prospective demographic of the university age group, intra-institutional competition and changes in the legal services market may soon lead to a reduction in the number of law providers.

In this chapter we explore the interests, expectations, desires and aspirations of HE law students, drawing primarily on experience and data from England and Wales. Some, as in the case of Roland, draws on our own experience. Other data has been collected more formally through research

[6] This was from a first year law degree student. The recipient had been in the designated room long after the stipulated time. Roland, not the student's real name, had possibly gone to the wrong room.

[7] For further exploration of issues surrounding student conduct, see S Wallace, *Managing Behaviour and Motivating Students in Further Education* (Exeter, Learning Matters, 2002); B Rodgers, *Cracking the Hard Class* (London, Sage Publications, 2006 and D Lee, *University Students Behaving Badly* (Staffordshire, Trentham Books, 2006).

projects we have conducted. Finally, we have also relied on data collected by other agencies. Part I of the chapter is a statistical overview of the legal education and legal services market many law students aspire to enter. In Parts II and III we look at the nature of the academy and the change in conception of the HE student, arguing that the two are interlinked. Part IV considers students' aspirations in relation to both legal education and a legal career. Part V assesses the impact of student voice on the academy. We conclude by exploring how increased concern with students' best interests has important implications for the way in which the relationship of students to the academy is conceived and the way that the academy both *is*, and is perceived.

HE AND THE LEGAL SERVICES MARKET

Legal education and training has been an expanding market for many years, as evidenced by increases in total numbers of graduates, vocational course students and entrants to the professions (see Table 1).

Table 1 Number of Law Degree Acceptances and Graduations, LPC Enrolments and Passes and Registration of Training Contracts[8]

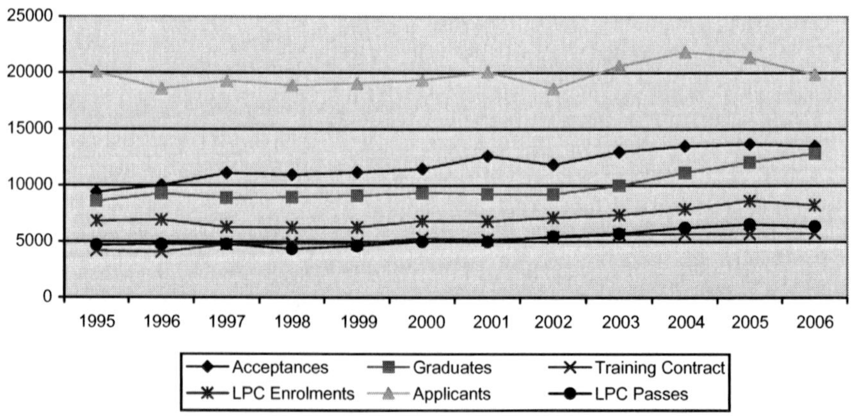

[8] All figures are taken from the Law Society's Annual Statistical Reports, *Trends in the Solicitors' Profession*. The legend denotes the following: 'Applicants' and 'Acceptances': the number of applicants and acceptances for undergraduate places at university full-time law degree courses, including overseas students. 'Graduates': the number of students graduating in law from universities in England and Wales. 'LPC Enrolments': the number of students who enrolled on an LPC course in England and Wales. 'LPC Passes': the total number of passes on the LPC course.

Universities have followed the market by expanding law places as demand for other disciplines has waned. Yet, from application to study law, to acceptance and graduation, from enrolment on the Legal Practice Course (LPC) to pass and registration of training contract, there is steady attrition. For example, in 2006 a total of 19,863 students applied to study law at undergraduate level,[9] 13,499 were accepted,[10] 12,858 graduated (a 39 per cent increase since 2001) and 8262 went on to enrol for the LPC, of which 6376 passed and 5751 registered their training contract.[11] While these figures do not consistently track the same cohort, a rough calculation shows that only 30 per cent of those originally applying to study law, and less than half who started a degree, finally become trainee solicitors. Nevertheless, relentless expansion of the profession has become the norm, beginning in 1970 when there were merely 24,407 practising solicitors; increasing to 37,832 in 1980, 54,734 in 1990; 82,769 in 2000;[12] and currently reaching 108,407.[13] Indeed as Table 2 illustrates, the profession has expanded by approximately 50 per cent every 10 years for the past three decades.

Table 2 Number of Solicitors Holding Practice Certificates[14]

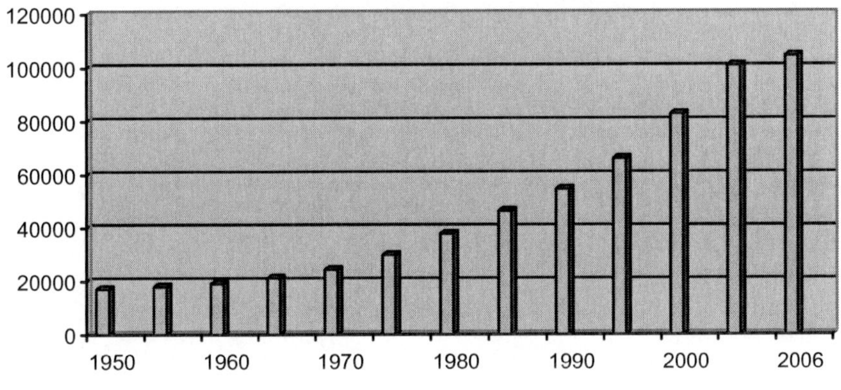

[9] Applicants are counted only once irrespective of the number of applications made on the UCAS form.

[10] An acceptance is defined is defined as a formal acceptance of a university place offered through the UCAS scheme.

[11] All figures are taken from B Cole, *Trends in the Solicitors Profession Annual Statistical Report 2007* (London, Law Society, 2008) 35.

[12] Law Society, "Number of Solicitors on the Roll and Practising Certificate Holders Since 1950: Law Society Fact Sheet Information Series' (no date) at www.lawsociety.org.uk/secure/file/167083/e:/teamsite-deployed/documents/templatedata/Publications/Research%20fact%20sheet/Documents/numsol_v7.pdf.

[13] As of 31 July 2007, 108, 407 solicitors have practising certificates and 134, 378 were on the roll. Cole, above n 11.

[14] Cole, above n 11.

As in the US,[15] expansion of the profession in England and Wales has led to demographic change, towards a profession that is more youthful,[16] more feminine[17] and more ethnically diverse.[18] There is also more competition in the legal services market, with two established branches of the profession, the Bar and the solicitors, vying with ambitious newcomers like The Institute of Legal Executives and The Council for Licensed Conveyancers. Within each group there are diverse modes of practice. For example, the solicitors' branch embraces large City firms, niche practitioners, 'generalist' High Street practices, sole practitioners and a growing number practising as 'employed' lawyers (see Chart 1).

Rose predicts that, if these trends continue, by the year 2055, 'barring the introduction of instant on-line justice and virtual lawyers', there will be a million solicitors on the roll, the profession will 'be dominated by women, with a larger representation of minorities than is reflected in the general

Chart 1 Practising Certificate Holders by Category of Employment as at 31 July 2007[19]

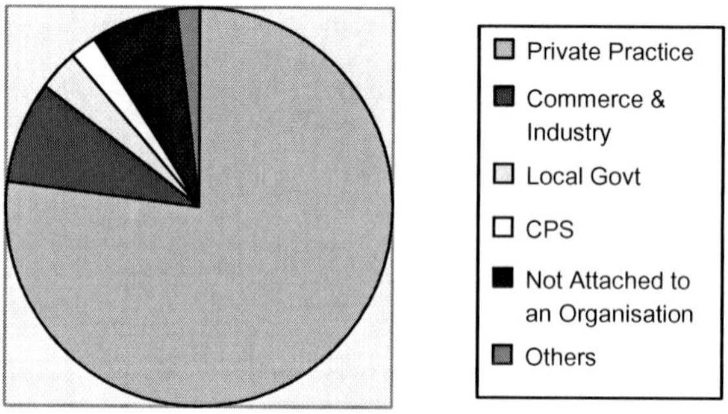

[15] M Galanter. 'Old and in the Way: The Coming Demographic Transformation of the Legal Profession and its Implications for the Provision of Legal Services" (1999) *Wisconsin Law Review* 1081 at http://marcgalanter.net/Documents/papers/ComingDemographicTransformation.pdf.

[16] 53.8% of solicitors are aged 40 or under, Cole above n 11, 12.

[17] It was not until 1957 that female solicitors began to hold practising certificates but in 2007, 43.4% of all certificates were held by women, Cole above n 11, 12.

[18] Around 9.5% of practising certificate holders come from minority ethnic groups compared to 4% in 1994 (Cole, above n 11, 10). Note that the 2001 census identified the size of the minority ethnic population in England and Wales at 7.9%.

[19] In total, 76.2% of the profession is in private practice. Commerce and industry is the next most popular category of employment (9.1%), followed by local government (3.7%) and the Crown Prosecution Service (2.2%) (Cole, above n 11, 14).

population' and most solicitors will work in large firms.[20] Moreover, these lawyers will face increasing competitive demands, with corresponding pressure for entrepreneurialism, specialisation and diverse skills. While the Legal Services Act 2007 will bring further and probably unpredicted changes to this market, the most significant division in legal work,[21] between corporate and private plight clients, will remain. In the US, it has been said that legal education mirrors this bifurcation, in the divide between the elite schools and the local 'trade' schools. Indeed, Jonakait argues that meaningful legal education cannot be fashioned without understanding this 'sharp and unbridgeable chasm'.[22]

There is, of course, an English version of the unbridgeable chasm in the division between Oxbridge[23] and, to a lesser extent, the Russell group[24] on one side and the rest, including the 'new' universities[25] on the other.[26] Rolfe and Anderson call the system a 'two-track entry and training to the legal profession',[27] resulting in graduates from the elite institutions being 16 times more likely to be based in City firms.[28] More recent data in 2001 and 2003 confirm the preference for Graduate Diploma students and Oxbridge or Red

[20] N Rose, 'The Great Divide' *The Law Gazette* (19 June 2001) at www.lawgazette.co.uk/news/the-great-divide.

[21] The 'two hemispheres' cover services to corporate clients *or* personal services to individuals and small businesses. Lawyers from the two hemispheres seldom, if ever, cross the equator. J Heinz and E Laumann, *Chicago Lawyers: The Social Structure of the Bar* (New York, Russell Sage Foundation, 1982). A later survey found smaller clusters within the hemispheres, but two regions based on the nature of clients. J Heinz, R Nelson, R Sandefur and E Laumann, *Urban Lawyers: The New Social Structure of the Bar* (Chicago, University of Chicago Press, 2005). See also R Abel, *The Legal Profession in England and Wales* (Oxford, Blackwell, 1988); J Flood, 'Megalawyering in the Global Order: The Cultural, Social and Economic Transformation of Global Legal Practice' (1996) 3 *International Journal of the Legal Profession* 169 and J Flood, 'Megalaw in the UK: Professionalism or Corporatism? A Preliminary Report' (1989) 64 *Indiana Law Journal* 569.

[22] RN Jonakait, 'The Two Hemispheres of Legal Education and the Rise and Fall of Local Law Schools' (2007) *New York Law School Law Review* 1, www.ssrn.com/abstract=913084.

[23] The term used for the universities of Oxford and Cambridge.

[24] Arguably equivalent to the US 'Ivy League', the Russell Group is an association of 20 major research-intensive UK universities (including Oxford and Cambridge), formed in 1994 at a meeting convened in the Hotel Russell, London. See www.russellgroup.ac.uk.

[25] Typically post-1992 universities (ie old polytechnics). Most of these universities are represented by Million+, a university think tank-formerly CMU (Campaigning for Mainstream Universities). See www.millionplus.ac.uk.

[26] This is a simplistic division and there are many different ways of categorising UK universities (eg Ancient, Red Brick, Plate Glass, Modern/New universities and the Open University). Their reputation is predicated on history, longevity, research output and latterly their league table ranking (see, eg J O'Leary, *The Times Good University Guide 2010* (London, The Times, 2009) and http://extras.timesonline.co.uk/tol_gug/gooduniversityguide.php. The Times is arguably the most reputable of the league tables.

[27] H Rolfe and T Anderson, 'A Firm Decision: The Recruitment of Trainee Solicitors' (2003) 10(3) *International Journal of the Legal Profession* 315, 331.

[28] M Shiner, *Entry into the Legal Professions: The Law Student Cohort Study Year 4* (London, Law Society, 1997) 80.

Brick university graduates among large law firms,[29] a legacy of privilege further confirmed by the Sutton Trust.[30]

Similar bias exists at the Bar,[31] with significant correlation between graduating institution and pupillage.[32] At the other end of the scale, students from non-elite universities tend to practise in small firms or as sole practitioners many of which rely substantially on legal aid. However, cuts in public funding have reduced the opportunities to train in legal aid firms, so that government has had to sponsor firms' training contracts directly through a scheme operated by the Legal Services Commission.[33] The situation is one of considerable ambiguity. It is undoubtedly the case that the profession has a profound influence on law schools, through articulating the knowledge, skills and values requirements of legal practice, and requiring their study as a stage of entry to the profession. It may also be argued that this projects the structural problems of the profession onto a curriculum designed for general practice. While the common curriculum has largely withstood the pull of practice towards business and corporate law, future trends toward specialisation may be less easy to accommodate.

THE NATURE OF THE ACADEMY

It is pointless to generalise about 'the academy' without defining what is meant. While the legal academy may have many points of comparison, it is broadly dispersed in a wide array of institutional forms. Therefore, before discussing the nature of the legal academy, it is necessary to discuss the way that universities organise to achieve their purpose and the impact of the

[29] V Bermingham and J Hodgson, 'Desiderata: What Lawyers Want from their Recruits' (2001) 35 *Law Teacher* 1 and Rolfe and Anderson, above n 27.

[30] Its analysis of the educational background of top legal professionals found that 82% of barristers, 81% of judges and 53% of the partners in 'magic circle' law firms, had attended Oxford or Cambridge. Sutton Trust, *Briefing Note: The Educational Backgrounds of the UK's Top Solicitors, Barristers and Judges* (2005) at www.suttontrust.com/reports/Comparison_educational_backgrounds.pdf.

[31] Shiner found the highest percentage of graduates to be offered a BVC place studied at Oxbridge (94% and 97% for CPE students) and the lowest studied at new universities (73% and 60% for CPE students). M Shiner, *Entry Into the Legal Professions: The Law Student Cohort Study Year 4* (London, Law Society, 1997) 125.

[32] Oxbridge graduates constituted c 50% of pupillage applications but gained 82% of the pupillages available. Whereas new university students made twice the number of applications but only secured 37% of the available pupillages. M Shiner and T Newburn. *Entry into the Legal Professions: The Law Student Cohort Study Year 3* (London, Law Society, 1995) 122.

[33] S Bacquet, A Boon, L Webley and A Whyte, 'Making Legal Aid Solicitors? The Training Contracts Grant Scheme' in A Buck, P Pleasence and N Balmer (eds) *Reaching Further: Innovation, Access and Quality in Legal Services* (Norwich, The Stationery Office, 2009).

resulting structure on culture.[34] Of the various models on offer, most are versions of the collegium, the bureaucratic, the corporate and the enterprising university.[35] These ideal types have different foundations, assumptions and aspirations and may therefore have different expectations of their students and envisage different relations to their student bodies.

The collegium represents universities as institutions beyond utilitarian and professional agendas; free from external controls[36] and dedicated to learning for its own sake.[37] The collegial structure is associated with the 'ivory tower' university, valuing research and scholarship above all else, intended for a close, small community of scholars, including students who, by intellect and social status, are destined for leadership. It is characterised by belief in the inherent difficulty of academic study and the limited distribution of academic talent. Crucially, it depends on a personal relationship between teacher and student, both socialised into the collegial ethos of campus, and the particular discipline, acquiring skills and experience of lifelong relevance.[38] Collegial assumptions survive in academic conceptions of the university ideal[39] but, for most academics, the collegium faded after World War II, when HE became a political tool of social engineering.[40] Post-war HE history[41] shows that, through government manipulation of

[34] For example, Edgar Schein offered an apposite view of organisational culture. E Schein, *Organisational Culture and Leadership: A Dynamic View* (San Francisco, Jossey Bass, 1985) 9.

[35] I McNay, 'From the Collegial Academy to Corporate Enterprise: The Changing Cultures of Universities' in T Schuller (ed), *The Changing University*? (Buckingham, The Society for Research into Higher Education and Open University Press, 1995) 105. See generally WH Bergquist, *The Four Cultures of the Academy: Insights and Strategies for Improving Leadership in Collegiate Organisations* (San Francisco, Jossey Bass, 1992), suggesting the collegial, managerial, developmental and negotiating cultures.

[36] Initially the Church, now mainly government. McNay, above n 35, 106.

[37] See Newman, Cardinal John Henry *The Idea of a University* (New Haven, CT, and London, Yale University Press, 1996) [first published 1852]; M Arnold, *Culture and Anarchy* (Oxford, Oxford University Press, 2006) [first published 1869]; and PR Trowler, *Academics Responding to Change: New Higher Education Frameworks and Academic Cultures* (Buckingham, SRHE and Open University Press, Buckingham, 1998), who argues that the collegium university is 'rooted in a belief in the value of cultural and disciplinary heritage, of which academics are custodians' (67).

[38] Barrett, above n 5, 147.

[39] See, eg A Bradney, *Conversations, Choices and Chances: The Liberal Law School in the Twenty-First Century* (Oxford, Hart Publishing, 2003) *seriatim* discussing the influence of Newman particularly, but also Arnold and Houseman on conceptions of a liberal legal education. (Arnold, above n 37. AE Housman, 'Introductory Lecture' in AE Housman, *Selected Prose* (Cambridge, Cambridge University Press, 1961).

[40] Government aspiration was that, as a quid pro quo for state funding, universities play a greater role in arresting economic decline by training an ever-larger percentage of each age cohort and engaging more greatly with vocational subjects. Today, with the government's target of 50% of 18 to 30 year olds entering HE by 2010, the role of social engineering is one that universities are still expected to play, *The Times*, 'Lowering the Bar: Social Engineering Should be Left to Academic Theorists' *The Times* (London 21 November 2006).

[41] See, eg 1956 White Paper, *Technical Education*; The Anderson Report, *Grants to Students* (London, HMSO, 1960); The Robbins Report, *Higher Education* (London HMSO,

competition and funding,[42] UK universities assumed responsibility for wide ranging outcomes; economic competitiveness, income generation,[43] social inclusiveness, technology transfer and supporting regional economies. They pro-actively embraced this agenda, shaping their destinies and organisations to deliver effectively their new 'missions'.

The universities' initial reluctance to respond to demand for expansion and a more vocational orientation led to the creation of the polytechnics in the 1970s. These institutions were originally cast in a more bureaucratic mould[44] than the collegial universities, with extensive committee systems. They also had some corporate features, with permanent managers of the academic disciplines rather than rotating Heads of School, as was common in the 'old' institutions. Bureaucracy fitted with the mission to broaden the social and curriculum vistas of HE because it enabled standard procedures to be rolled out. The corporatist features were more consistent with efficiency and innovation because permanent managers were in a less insecure position and therefore more able to effect change.

A feature of the polytechnics' 'social service' mission was that it came at the expense of research, for which only the 'old' sector was funded, creating a 'teaching only' ethos in the polytechnic academy. After the transition of the polytechnics to universities in the early 1990s, they entered the 1992 Research Assessment Exercise (RAE), in competition with the old universities. Generally poor results across the polytechnic sector, particularly in law, and the resulting inability to claim significant recurrent revenue, caused a new emphasis on research. It also led to a confusion of values,[45] but 'mission drift' was not confined to the former polytechnics. Although many old universities did not have the pure collegial structures of the Oxbridge institutions, they appreciated the importance of competing for

1963); and Department of Education and Science, *A Plan for Polytechnics and Other Colleges* (London, HMSO, 1966).

[42] The traditional funding streams include the discretionary block grant for teaching, the discretionary block grant for research and third leg funding, represented by the Higher Education Innovation Fund (HEIF). These funding streams are used in order to support the different missions of the universities and to shape their behaviour. For example, the old universities are the main beneficiaries of the block grant for research. HEIF, worth £112m for 2008–09, is intended to encourage non research-intensive universities to work with employers locally, regionally and nationally in 'knowledge transfer' activity. See 'Higher Education Innovation Fund 4' at www.hefce.ac.uk/reachout/heif.

[43] Through research grants, services to industry and recruiting overseas students. McNay, above n 35, 111–112.

[44] This alternative model of bureaucratic hierarchy was linked with more vocational/professional programmes. See, eg T Becher and M Kogan, *Process and Structure in Higher Education* (London and New York, Routledge, 1992).

[45] S Schwartz, 'What are Universities For?' BBC News Education (2003) http://news.bbc.co.uk/1/hi/education/2968744.stm.

academics, students and research funds,[46] also becoming more corporate in the process.[47] All universities became more entrepreneurial, seeking more productive ways to structure and systems that would release initiative. This gradual institutional homogenisation has proceeded at a different pace in different institutions, resulting in overlay of the different models.[48] This is with the possible exception of some elite institutions, which, like universities on the continent,[49] appear to have bridged the collegial and entrepreneurial models in exploiting intellectual capital, without moving through the bureaucratic and corporate stages.[50]

The implications of organisational change for academic culture are, in theory, profound. The collegium embodies academic professionalism, whereby all academics accept responsibility for the health and governance of the institution. The traditional collegial institutions trade on social capital, built on academic reputations. Research is the common currency and the peer group the judge of value. The polytechnics, however, tended to value administrative and entrepreneurial skills, for example, managing staff and creating new courses, giving rise to hierarchies of academics taking their status from bureaucratic effectiveness. The academic view was incorporated through committees, but came with the considerable disadvantages of rigid, standard operating procedures, complex decision-making and political manipulation.[51] Corporate frameworks saw executive authority focused on vice-chancellors, with senior teams operating outside the disempowering committee structures. It is a short step from the corporate structure to the enterprising institution, which now appears to be the aspiration of most institutions outside the elite. Within it we find minimal peer control, individuals seeking out and negotiating business opportunities and resources going to successful departments.

Organisational change created a more competitive and insecure HE world and new concerns echoed, in an educational lexicon moving closer to business and the market place,[52] in terms such as variable tuition fees,[53]

[46] N Butler, 'What are Universities for?' speech at the Foundation for Science and Technology (25 October 2006) at www.foundation.org.uk/events/pdf/20061025_Butler.pdf.

[47] G Neave (ed), *The Universities' Responsibilities to Society* (Oxford, Elsevier Science, 2000).

[48] McNay, above n 35, 111.

[49] In Eastern Europe it is from collegial/corporatist to collegial/entrepreneurial. Ibid 111–112.

[50] Ibid.

[51] McNay, ibid 106–7.

[52] McNay, ibid 107.

[53] The Higher Education Act 2004 gave institutions in England and Wales power to introduce variable fees for full-time undergraduates from September 2006. For a brief history on the policy for top-up fees, see S Alley and M Smith, 'Timeline: Tuition Fees' *The Guardian* (London 27 January 2004).

student loans,[54] student debt,[55] learning contracts,[56] performance indicators, quality assurance and auditing.[57] It is unclear, however, how far these changes impacted on the deep structures, the values and purposes of the academy. One core issue that did change was who and what was taught and how it was done.[58] As the percentage of the age group participating in HE broadened, it was thought that the external and internal academic worlds were out of balance,[59] leading to an industry in teaching theories and methods.[60] Academics were forced, not only to articulate more clearly their teaching aims, but also to consider how these might relate to the aspirations of students. While there may still be more to HE than getting a job[61] the 'benchmark statements' incorporated into degrees, learning independently, keeping a critical and open mind and communicating effectively,[62] are relevant to, if not determined by, employment agendas.

A changing academic relationship with students was a reality for most academics. Those in the collegial institutions saw students 'as acolytes, junior members of the academic body in a relationship of dependency with their mentors, on whose professional altruism they must rely'.[63] The move to a mass system not only sacrificed the 'intimacy' that was the core experience of previous generations, including academics themselves,[64] it changed the parameters of the relationship. Under the bureaucratic model, students were mere statistics, then units of resource under the corporate

[54] See Education (Student Support) Regulations 2006.

[55] The average student will leave university owing £15,000, up 318% since 2000. N Bosanquet, B Gibbs, S Cumming and A Haldenby, *Class of 2006 A Lifebelt for the IPOD Generation* (REFORM, 2006) at www.reform.co.uk/Research/Economy/EconomyArticles/tabid/81/smid/378/ArticleID/613/reftab/70/Default.aspx. See also H Metcalf, 'Paying for University: The Impact of Increasing Costs on Student Employment, Debt and Satisfaction' (2005) 191 *National Institute Economic Review* 106.

[56] Eg Oxford, Bristol and Nottingham Trent universities ask new students to sign contracts to guarantee their 'diligent' behaviour at college. J Meikle, 'Students Told: Turn up or Face Expulsion: Union Condemns University Contracts' *The Guardian* (London 11 September 2006).

[57] E Lewis, 'Goodhart's Law and Performance Indicators in Higher Education' (2003) 18(1)&(2) *Evaluation and Research in Education* 120. See, eg N Jackson, 'Internal Academic Quality Audit in UK Higher Education: Part I Current Practice and Conceptual Frameworks' (1996) 4(4) *Quality Assurance in Education* 37.

[58] L Wagner, 'A Thirty-Year Perspective: From the Sixties to the Nineties' in Schuller, above n 35, 15.

[59] When *The Times* thundered that 'social engineering and increasing opportunity for those in low socio-economic groups is a desirable political goal; but it is not the function of a university', its editor almost certainly had the elite, research intensive universities in mind. *The Times* 'Lowering the Bar' (2006): above n 40 and see Wagner, ibid.

[60] See, eg DA Kolb, *Experiential Learning* (Englewood Cliffs, NJ, Prentice Hall, 1984).

[61] Schwartz, above n 45.

[62] E Elbaz, 'Universities and Social Development: Partners and Stakeholders' in Neave (ed), *The Universities' Responsibilities* (2000) Neave, above n 47, 92.

[63] Becher and Kogan, above n 44, 123–24.

[64] Wagner, above n 58, 21.

model, then customers in the enterprise.[65] These shifts inevitably influence the way 'outsiders' perceive the purpose of the academy and how it should operate. And, as insiders, students' relationships with the academy changed with perceptions of the role and culture of universities. The passing decades have, therefore, left considerable doubt about a common role and mission for the HE sector and, not least, the place of students within it.

The universality of the university mission continues to be contested. Some hold that a university educated population is more likely to be politically and communally active 'to uphold democratic values and institutions and to be tolerant of different social, ethnic and ideological groups', thereby contributing to strong civic culture.[66] Universities themselves are presented as 'part of civil society, buffer institutions between state and citizen, independent forums for contestation, dissent and experimentation.'[67] Government, however, appears reluctant to acknowledge 'the civic and cultural functions of autonomous universities',[68] casting doubt over the compatibility of the emerging priorities of economic performance and social development.[69] Following a recommendation of the Dearing Report[70] it has developed complex performance indicators to benchmark comparable institutions and measure every aspect of the university performance it values,[71] a step intended to exert extreme pressure on institutional priorities.

While, historically, the collegial university viewed social development with purely academic interest, its successors are accused of over-emphasising material concerns.[72] This inevitably affects the nature of the academy, although the extent of the impact of financial considerations, for example, is debatable. An obvious area is independence and autonomy; many academics fear that the economic imperative undermines the detachment formerly seen as the necessary pre-condition of academic life. Another is the rhetoric of equal standards; competition for the system's scarce resources favours 'the haves', with governments worldwide under pressure to ensure that their elite institutions cement their place in the global pantheon of

[65] McNay, above n 35, 109.

[66] I Crewe, 'What are Universities for?" Speech given at a seminar at Number 11 Downing Street (12 March 2003) at www.essex.ac.uk/vc/speeches/2003/No11DowningStMar03.shtm.

[67] Ibid.

[68] Ibid. See also Department for Education and Skills, 'The Future of Higher Education' (Cm 5735, 2003).

[69] E Edgar, 'Universities and Social Development: Partners and Stakeholders' in Neave, above n 47, 90.

[70] R Dearing, *National Committee of Inquiry into Higher Education* (London, HMSO, 1997) at www.leeds.ac.uk/educol/ncihe/.

[71] HEFCE Quality Assurance and Enhancement Committee, *Review of Performance Indicators: Outcomes and Decisions* (London, Higher Education Funding Council, 2007) at www.hefce.ac.uk/pubs/hefce/2007/07_14/07_14.pdf.

[72] Elbaz, above n 62, 89.

esteem.[73] The assumptions that one size fits all, that fees should be the same, that difference can be catered for or that all degrees are equal, has been undermined and will undoubtedly be further tested. Now, even elite sectors of HE are coming under pressure to forsake the Socratic tutorial in favour of 'production line methods of teaching'.[74] In general, however, there is concern that the traditional university orientation to the 'critical perspective' that traditionally defined university education, scepticism of authority, distinguishing evidence, is being marginalised by employability agendas offering just 'enough education to produce, as in the Industrial Revolution, efficient workers.'[75]

WIDER PARTICIPATION AND THE CONCEPTION OF THE STUDENTS

In societies built on diverse populations and social consensus, equality of opportunity and meritocracy are fundamental principles, the chance to attend university a human right.[76] The process of escalating university attendance began in the 1960s, beginning with expanding the proportion of the school leaver population. The polytechnics were conceived of as institutions offering opportunities to students beyond this conventional university intake, particularly mature students. With the further expansion of 'A' level students and an increasing proportion of the school leaver population going to university, UK attendance reached mass during the 1990s.[77]

Labour's manifesto pledge was to increase the participation rate to 50 per cent of school leavers by 2010. An expansion from 40 to 43 per cent since 2001 was achieved in a number of ways. Pressure on schools to improve the performance of students led to 'A' level teachers providing more and more individualised assistance to students. Pressure on universities to expand

[73] J Gill, 'Australian Sector Asks for Cash to Compete with US' *Times Higher Education* (London 10–16 January 2008) 15.

[74] M Newman, 'Critics See Threat to Tutorials in Oxford Shake-Up' *Times Higher Education* (London 28 February 2008) 11.

[75] C King, 'Pay as You Learn? Students in the Changing University' in Schuller, above n 35, 126. R Attwood 'Nurture Sceptics, Not Industry Fodder, Critics Say' *Times Higher Education* (London 24 January 2008) 6.

[76] 'The right to education is a human right referred to in article 26 of the Universal Declaration of Human Rights. The UN Convention on the Rights of the Child states that "higher education should be made, by every appropriate means, accessible to all, on the basis of capacity."' L Smith, 'Universities Social Transformation and Access to Knowledge' in Neave, above n 47, 178.

[77] 'Full-time student numbers increased by almost 70% between 1989 and 1995 and one in three young people now enter higher education, compared to one in six in 1989. The result has been to introduce mass higher education in to the UK and with this a change to a much more heterogeneous student body.' Eurydice, *Two Decades of Reform in Higher Education in Europe: 1980 Onwards* (Brussels, Eurydice European Unit, 2000) 491 at www.eric.ed.gov/ERICDocs/data/ericdocs2sql/content_storage_01/0000019b/80/16/67/f4.pdf.

numbers led to increasing acceptance of students without three high grade 'A' levels. This had a number of consequences. Many of those joining this expanding student body were not from wealthy backgrounds and combined paid work and study. One 'A' level teacher told us:

> 'Everywhere I go my students are working… Hennes, Gap, Waitrose. The research says that if they do over eight hours a week of paid work their academic work suffers, but the results say otherwise. The clever ones have lessons in the morning, do school work all afternoon and go to their part-time job between five and eight or nine, two, three nights a week and all weekend. These are majorly committed kids. They are very strategic. They may or may not get 'A' grades, but if they do succeed, it has been planned'.[78]

This is a pattern now maintained by many entering HE, as exemplified in one student's email to her tutor, Rose:

> Dear Rose,
>
> I am having some trouble with my new module, Property and People, which takes place on Wednesdays from 11–1 pm… My problem is that I have work commitments on a Wednesday, which I arranged last term when I did not have any lectures. I am working four days a week, and my employer is saying that if i can't work Wednesdays, then I will lose my job.
>
> The problem is, due to living expenses I cannot afford to be out of work. This is a huge problem for me. I have done all the work for all the lectures, and have been getting notes from my fellow students, it is just my attendence that is a problem.
>
> I was wondering if there was any way around this?…
>
> If you could look into this for me, it will be much appreciated.
>
> Many thanks,
> Jane[79]

Further, mature students were more likely to have responsibilities, including, like Kim, as carers:

> This is to inform you all that I do not think I will be able to attend lectures and tutorials for a few weeks.
>
> My elderly (severely demented) father has recently had a stroke and is currently hospitalised and as I am his next of kin this is taking up a lot of my spare time.

[78] 'A' level teacher at a London comprehensive school (January 2008).

[79] Email (7 March 2007) from a first year student to her personal tutor (Rose and Jane are not the parties' real names). See also H Metcalf, 'Increasing Inequality in Higher Education: The Role of Term-Time Working" (2003) 29(3) *Oxford Review of Education* 315; and Centre for Higher Education Research and Information, *Survey of Higher Education Students' Attitudes to Debt and Term-Time Working and Their Impact on Attainment: A Report to Universities UK and HEFCE by the Centre for Higher Education Research and Information and London South Bank University* (London, CHERI and London South Bank University, 2005) at www.hefce.ac.uk/Pubs/rdreports/2005/rd15_05/rd15_05.pdf.

Over the months of October to February my Mum too has been ill and in and out of hospital and this too has caused me to miss classes during those months. I am struggling to ensure that I make it into work at the moment and I am afraid it is a case that something has got to give as at the moment my health is starting to deteriorate as I have too much on my plate. I have every intention to make sure that I do not fall behind in the work and will do as much reading and work as I can to keep up and will try to email the relevant tutors any work that I do. Any comments, feedback or advice on my work from any tutors would be much appreciated, time allowing on their part of course.

I hope this is acceptable to everyone and hope to see you as soon as possible. In the meantime I will try my very best to make it to as many classes as possible here and there if I am able, but anticipate that my attendance will be very inconsistent for a while.

Regards
Kim[80]

The new reality is one that HE, still in an age when only part-time courses are for those who need regular paid work, struggles to accommodate. Growth has created a more heterogeneous student body with a wider range of ability and learning needs and preferences not met by traditional structures and teaching. With additional government investment over the past five years, universities have experimented with ways of improving progression through first degrees, with increased pastoral care and novel approaches.[81] Yet, despite wide anticipation that a more diverse demographic would present new challenges, the numbers leaving before the end of their programmes have remained constant at around 22 per cent,[82] provoking a storm of recrimination over the causes, and doubt cast on the quality and value of university education.[83] The phenomenon also has an impact on relationships with students, with sheer large numbers and the potential drop-out a disincentive to effort. Then, the circumstances of students, like the fact that many are continuing their pre-university lives by living at home, is a significant change from the 1960s and 1970s,[84] when

[80] Email (1 March 2007) from a second year part-time evening student to her subject tutors (Kim is not the student's real name).

[81] In our own School of Law, for example, a Summer School has been introduced to help prepare students failing June exams for resits. See also A Thomson, 'Why We Can't Turn Our Backs on the League-Table Generation' *Times Higher Education* (London 10 January 2008) 24.

[82] J Grimston, 'Student Dropouts Cost Taxpayer £1bn' *The Sunday Times* (London 17 February 2008) at www.timesonline.co.uk/tol/news/uk/education/article3382180.ece.

[83] T Rawstone, 'A Degree of Betrayal' *Daily Mail* (London 21 February 2008); D Hayes, 'Colleges Blamed as a Quarter of Students Drop Out' *The Evening Standard* (London 20 February 2008); and J Bakewell, 'A University Drop-Out is a Sign of a Wider Failure' *The Independent* (London 22 February 2008).

[84] Numbers planning to live with their own families while at university to minimise debt have increased from 18% in 1998 to 56% in 2008. P Curtis, 'Tuition Fees Favour the Rich-New Study' *The Guardian* (London 14 February 2008).

students left home during term time to go to university. Despite increased attention to the issue, many institutions struggle for fuller understanding of why relatively poor retention and progression of such students is such an intractable problem.[85]

In an international study of first generation HE students, Thomas and Quinn found that drop out is exacerbated by poor choice of subject and the inability of some students to make the transition from school to more 'adult' educational environments and methods, with the new emphasis on independent learning. Other expectations of HE that run counter to the experience of many students is the emphasis on their personal responsibility, the distant relationships with staff, the lack of feedback on progress and the need for them to ask questions.[86] Many of the problems students experience with these expectations are caused or exacerbated by their lack of skills[87] and social capital. Therefore, the most significant variable, and sensitive indicator of disadvantage, more so than socio-economic status, is their status as first generation HE students. One way in which this impacts is that their parents, even though positive towards HE, are unable to offer informed advice or help their children negotiate the system. The students themselves find it difficult to manage the transition from school, where attendance is required and the days filled with activity, to a system with lots of free time and little guidance. Living at home increases the possibility of social isolation in the HE situation while heightening family anxiety about the investment being made in time and money. Not only is support often lacking in the inevitable troughs of university experience, but the home peer group and part-time work sometimes seem a more satisfying alternative to attending university. Many students drift away from university rather than decide to stop attending.[88]

For universities, the problems generated by 'widening participation' include the conception of the student body, the changing nature of which has exacerbated uncertainty around obligations to students and, hence, the nature of the relationship with them.[89] As if to emphasise the obligations

[85] National Audit Office, *Staying the Course: The Retention of Students in Higher Education* (London, The Stationery Office, 2007) at www.nao.org.uk/publications/0607/student_retention_in_higher_ed.aspx.

[86] L Thomas and J Quinn, *First Generation Entry Into Higher Education: An International Study* (Maidenhead, Open University Press, 2007) 89.

[87] Informational skills, for example, are inculcated in childhood, with the result that many students, and perhaps particularly first generation HE students, are over reliant on web-based research and lacking developed critical faculties. M Reisz, 'Hits and Misses' *Times Higher Education* (London 5–12 June 2008) 32.

[88] Thomas and Quinn, above n 86, 97.

[89] See also T Conway, S Mackay and D Yorke, 'Strategic Planning in Higher Education: Who are the Customers?' (1994) 8(6) *International Journal of Educational Management* 29 at www.emeraldinsight.com/Insight/viewPDF.jsp?contentType=Article&Filename=html/Output/Published/EmeraldFullTextArticle/Pdf/0600080607.pdf.

on universities implicit in government funding of widening participation, they have been encouraged to conceive of students as customers. Indeed, the government's *Charter for Higher Education* (1993) confirmed that students and employers could expect 'standards of service' from universities and complain where they were not met.[90] The customer analogy not only chimes with the propensity of the enterprise model to treat academic relationships as a business transaction, but with escalating competition between universities for students. This requires that students are courted, by emphasising to them the advantages, benefits and facilities the university has to offer. Universities are thereby cast in the role of service providers,[91] their task to find means to meet optimally the demand for transfer of expert knowledge and skills,[92] the students their customers. The 'customer' conception is, however, contrary to two primary functions of the traditional role of universities; setting disciplinary standards and credentialing for the job market. This conflict is increasingly problematic[93] not least because the increasing investment by students, with the introduction of fees,[94] encourages the perception that they are not only 'customers'[95] but 'primary' customers,[96] in their own eyes and in the eyes of vice-chancellors.[97] It is hardly

[90] Eurydice, above n 77, 500.

[91] LRP Reavill, 'Quality Assessment, Total Quality Management and the Stakeholders in the UK Higher Education System' (1998) 8 *Managing Service Quality* 55 at www.emeraldinsight.com/Insight/ViewContentServlet?contentType=Article&Filename=Published/EmeraldFullTextArticle/Articles/1080080106.html. See also Conway, Mackay and Yorke, above n 89, 32.

[92] In university terms this may 'also be about a curriculum committed to serve diverse communities or to develop enterprise skills and competences'. A Wignall, 'You Have Passed Go. Pay £3,000' *The Guardian* (London 26 September 2006) at www.guardian.co.uk/money/2006/sep/26/education.students.

[93] For example, Roland's contemporaries responded to a high failure rate in one subject with a letter to one of the authors, in his role as Dean of School, pointing out that 'the university must bear in mind that the students have paid for the course and have a duty to provide the best possible service'. Email (2 April 2007) from second year law Student Representatives to the Dean of the Law School. See also M Newman, 'Fees "Do Not Buy" a Guaranteed Degree' *Times Higher Education* (London 10 January 2008) 14 at www.timeshighereducation.co.uk/story.asp?storyCode=400110&sectioncode=26.

[94] Since September 2006, instead of having to pay an annual tuition fee before the start of the academic year, new students in England and Northern Ireland are charged an upper limit of £3000 in tuition fees, for which they are only billed once they have completed their courses. Eurydice, above n 77; and S Coughlan, 'Rammell's Mission to Explain Fees' (3 June 2006) http://news.bbc.co.uk/1/hi/education/4304774.stm.

[95] Reavill, above n 91. See also Weaver, who identifies four parties as potential customers: the government, its administrators, teachers/academics and the actual consumers (the learners, their families, employers and society as a whole). T Weaver, 'What is the Good of Higher Education?' (1976) 8(3) *Higher Education Review* 3.

[96] Robinson and Long distinguish between primary, secondary and tertiary customers. They see primary customers as being the students, secondary customers as the paymasters, ie local education authorities, employers, etc and tertiary customers as validating bodies, ex-students, employers, parents, etc. As cited by Conway, Mackay and Yorke, above n 89, 31.

[97] Gemma Tumely, former president of the National Union of Students as quoted by Wignall, above n 92.

surprising that ensuring that students are satisfied and stay in the institution becomes the main priority of the university[98] or that the idea of 'customer service' has become so prevalent.

Applying the customer analogy to HE students is not satisfactory, either practically or theoretically, for several reasons.[99] For example, students do not have complete freedom of choice in a market place and they do not always comprehend their options.[100] Further, reliably grading students, so that employers can make informed recruitment decisions, remains one of the important functions of the university. Indeed, were this function to the fore, the appropriate analogy is manufacturing, with students seen as 'educated end products',[101] certified with the award of a degree classification,[102] and employers as customers.[103] This, however, is inconsistent with the more responsive role that successive governments have urged on HE. Yet, while the manufacturing analogy is outmoded, nor is the idea of HE as a trade for fees apposite. This is because many features of the student's position contradict the notion that they are customers of HE. Not only does the contact between universities and students have features of exchange, licensing and membership, but occasionally a vital element is missing, as when, for example, parents, not students, pay fees.

While impartial credentialing remains an important function of universities, the transformative role of education also lifts it beyond simple trade. There are few services where consumers are subject to criticism with a view to changing them,[104] but HE, through regular academic assessment, performs what Harvey and Green call 'cognitive transcendence', 'doing something to the

[98] McNay, above n 35, 111.

[99] See W Bennis, 'A Delicate Balance', *Cincinatti Horizons,* September (1975), as cited by Conway, Mackay and Yorke, above n 89, 31.

[100] A survey of over 2000 students at the Russell Group universities suggests that these students are unaware of many firms beyond the 'top' five and are unable to detect any material or cultural differences between many of the law firms particularly from the commercial field. Legal Week Intelligence, *Law Student Survey* (2009) at www.legalweek.com/img/5e5e1146-347e-4109-9d3e-3368f793d789.pdf.

[101] Though not 'inanimate raw material(s)' as they will influence the production process, Conway, Mackay, and Yorke, above n 89, 33. And 'those processing plants [universities] with greater popularity… are able to select higher quality input material', Reavill, above n 91.

[102] 'Litten uses the term 'quasi-product' to describe the student's relationship to an academic institution. The student is not seen as a product as such because, technically, the student is not something that the college produces for *direct* exchange in the marketplace. However, there is a production function of academic institutions for, unlike most service industries, colleges evaluate the student-product and certify his/her characteristics in a similar way to which other industries certify the performance characteristics of their products.' LH Litten, (1980) 'Marketing Higher Education: Benefits and Risks for the American Academic System' (1980) 51(1) *Journal of Higher Education* 40 as cited by Conway, Mackay and Yorke, above n 89, 33.

[103] See further, Reavill above n 91.

[104] L Lomas, 'Does the Development of Mass Education Necessarily Mean the End of Quality?' The Sixth QHE Seminar: The End of Quality, Birmingham (25–26 May 2001) at www.qualityresearchinternational.com/papers/lomas.pdf.

customer rather than just doing something for the customer'.[105] Meanwhile, although students exchange money for the university's services, the high levels of motivation and commitment required and provided on their own account[106] is also somewhat inconsistent with the notion of a trade. Finally, however, the customer relationship is destructive of the special relationship that should exist between the academy and its students.[107] In a recent letter to a national newspaper the NUS president decried the use of social network sites to bully lecturers and the 'consumer mentality' and the 'market orientated funding system' that he claimed encouraged it. But, he said, 'it does underpin the importance of providing accessible ways for students to shape their learning experience and that of others' and advocated that 'an active partnership between staff and students is the best way to enhance the experience for all'.[108] This is to assert the superiority of the stakeholding model over the consumer model for both academy and student.

If the behaviour of universities towards students occasionally sustains their status as customers, or even as products, neither conception is adequate or satisfactory. The inability to find an analogy for the relationship is reflected in much confusion surrounding the use of the new terminology. The Higher Education Funding Council (HEFCE) strategic plan for 2006–11 uses the terms 'customers' and 'stakeholders' interchangeably.[109] For example, in a section on 'Meeting Customer and Stakeholder Needs', the plan moves from discussing student expectations to those of employers or society without signalling a shift in discussion of customers and stakeholders.[110] Similarly, in a section entitled 'Needs of Stakeholders' it again discusses the expectations of students before referring to 'students, employers and other stakeholders'.[111] This usage may signal doubt or confusion about the continuing designation of students as customers or, perhaps, marks a transition between these terminologies. It is, however, compatible with a shift towards perceiving students' relation to the academy as interest-based rather than rights-based. In this sense, 'stakeholding' has the potential to resolve the dilemma posed by the need to recognise the special relationship of students to universities.

As a term 'stakeholding' has a rich history in a variety of contexts,[112] but it has recently, to coin Gladwell's phrase, 'passed the 'tipping point'

[105] L Harvey and D Green, 'Defining Quality' (1993) 18(1) *Assessment and Evaluation in Higher Education* 9, as quoted by Lomas, ibid.

[106] Lomas, above n 104.

[107] Roland's email to his tutor (see above n 6) is the perfect example of this.

[108] Letter by Wes Streeting to *The Guardian* (22 July 2008) 4.

[109] Higher Education Funding Council, *Strategic Plan 2006–11* (2007) at www.hefce.ac.uk/pubs/hefce/2007/07_09/07_09.pdf.

[110] Ibid, at 5–8.

[111] Ibid at 12.

[112] See Boon and Webb, this volume.

into common use.'[113] It has yet to command a common meaning in its new guise, although the various recent definitions[114] share features like paying for, benefiting from[115] or supporting the long-term viability of organisations.[116] For the universities, recognising students as holding 'stakes' in the academy is preferable to the exclusive focus required for customers. The weight attributed to stakes requires balancing the loyalty, attention and resources attached to a range of other stakeholders, rather than prioritising the interests of one group, like students, at the expense of others, like employers.[117] It is arguable that students are towards the top of a league of 12 potential stakeholders in HE[118] comprising (1) students, (2) employers, (3) the family and dependants of the student, (4) universities and their employees, (5) suppliers of goods and services to universities, (6) the secondary education sector, (7) other universities, (8) commerce and industry, (9) the nation, (10) the government, (11) taxpayers, national and local, and finally (12) professional bodies. It is difficult to assign positions to these groups in terms of relative importance or power, but there is a case for placing students above employers, for example, precisely because of their 'customer' status'.[119] The fact that students are primary[120] (without them universities cannot survive) and active[121] (they have the power to influence the way in which universities are deemed to be performing) and because their interests are calculated in strategic decision making[122] we expect the student voice to become loud and strong. The student is, in the jargon,

[113] M Gladwell, *The Tipping Point: How Little Things Can Make a Big Difference* (Boston, MA, Little Brown & Company, 2000).

[114] '"The Stanford Research Institute's definition is those groups without whose support the organisation would cease to exist"... Freeman's definition states that stakeholders are: "any group or individual, who can affect or is affected by the achievements of organisation's objectives."... Clarkson... defines stakeholders as "persons or groups that have, or claim ownership, rights or interests in a corporation and its activities, past present or future"'. E Jansson, 'The Stakeholder Model: The Influence of the Ownership and Governance Structures' (2005) 56 *Journal of Legal Ethics* 1, 5). Bryson defines stakeholders as 'persons, groups or organizations that must somehow be taken into account by leaders, managers and front line staff.' JM Bryson, 'What to do When Stakeholders Matter' (2004) 6(1) *Public Management Review* 21, 22.

[115] Reavill, above n 91.

[116] Bryson, above n 114, 23.

[117] M Nuti, 'Democracy and Economy: What Role for Stakeholders?' (1997) 8(2) *Business Strategy Review* 14; and M Rustin, 'Stakeholding and the Public Sector' in G Kelly, D Kelly and A Gamble (eds), *Stakeholder Capitalism* (Sheffield, Palgrave/Political Economy Research Centre, 1997) 75.

[118] Reavill, above n 91.

[119] RL Daft, *Organization Theory and Design* (St Paul, Minn, West Publishing Co, 1992).

[120] MBE Clarkson, 'A Stakeholder Framework for Analysing and Evaluating Corporate Social Performance' (1995) 20(1) *Academy of Management Review* 92; and Reavill, above n 91.

[121] A Cambell, 'Stakeholders: The Case in Favour' (1997) 30(3) *Long Range Planning* 446.

[122] P Nutt, *Why Decisions Fail: Avoiding the Blunders and Traps that Lead to Debacles*, (San Francisco, CA, Berrett-Koehler Publishers, 2002) as cited by Bryson, above n 114, 23.

becoming less of a *subject* (one who has an interest but little power) and more of a *player* (one who has both interest and power).[123]

WHAT DO STUDENTS WANT?

'He who pays the piper should know the tune'

By definition the learner is outside of the practice, or at best is a novice with respect to the practice, thus, it is not possible for the learner to understand in advance what it is she will learn when she learns to become a participant in the practice.[124]

The student voice is increasingly heard via survey instruments.[125] Asked about their priorities for the investment of their university fees, students in general manifest concern for teaching quality (reflected in a desire for smaller teaching groups, better library, laboratory or specialist academic facilities) rather than general environment.[126] Any immediate concern with quality of experience is probably overshadowed by the longer term, and particularly the return from attending university.[127] Conventional wisdom has projected a significant though contentious 'graduate earnings premium', latterly perceived to be in decline.[128] Nevertheless, as a general

[123] C Eden and F Ackermann, *Making Strategy: The Journey of Strategic Management* (London, Sage Publications, 1998) at 113–135.

[124] W Morrow, 'Scripture and Practices' (2001) 19(1) *Perspectives in Education* 87, 91.

[125] See, eg P Surridge, *National Student Survey 2006* (University of Bristol for HEFC, 2007); K Purcell and P Elias et al, *Applying for Higher Education: Career Choices and Plans* (Warwick Institute for Employment Research and Higher Education Careers Service Unit, 2007); and B Bekhradnia, *The Academic Experience of Students in English Universities 2009 Report* (Oxford, Higher Education Policy Institute, 2009) at www.hepi.ac.uk/files/40Theacademicexperienceofstudents2009.pdf.

[126] B Bekhradnia, C Whitnall and T Sastry, *The Academic Experience of Students in English Universities* (Oxford, Higher Education Policy Institute, 2006) paras 40–45 at www.hepi.ac.uk/files/27Academicexperienceofstudents.pdf. The 2007 HEPI survey (T Sastry and B Bekhradnia, *The Academic Experience of Students in English Universities*, (Oxford, Higher Education Policy Institute, 2007 at www.hepi.ac.uk/files/33TheacademicexperienceofstudentsinEnglishuniversities2007.pdf) used a revised list of priorities and students rated 'training of lecturers (which was not included in the 2006 options) much higher than smaller teaching groups suggesting that it is the quality of the teacher which concerns students more than the character of the teaching occasion' (para 41). The 2006 National Student Survey (NSS) also confirms that 'teaching and learning has by far the greatest impact on overall satisfaction, while learning resources has the weakest', (above n 125, 100). The 2007 NSS found 82% of students satisfied with teaching on their course and 81% satisfied with the course overall.

[127] This is generally accepted as resulting in earnings of £160,000 more than non-graduates over a working lifetime. Universities UK, *The Economic Benefits of a Degree* (London, Universities UK, 2007) at www.universitiesuk.ac.uk/Publications/Documents/research-gradprem.pdf.

[128] K Purcell, P Elias, R Davies and N Wilton, *Class of '99: A Study of the Early Labour Market Experiences of Recent Graduates*, DfES Research Report no 691 (University of Warwick and University of the West of England, 2005). The DfES study observes that graduate earnings seemingly have not kept pace with earnings increases found more generally in the

proposition, students expect higher incomes to result from graduate level employment. It is generally assumed that incurring financial burdens make students more aware of the investment of their time and their parents' resources, more single-minded and conscious of career prospects.[129] Even before funding changes began to rack up graduate debt, students were anxious about a 'good degree' because of its labour-market implications. This tends to confuse perceptions of what motivates students in HE, whether vocational concerns, or an intellectual interest in their subject,[130] or reasons of personal development.[131] Vocational subjects have, however, tended to increase in popularity, possibly at the expense of traditional favourites.[132]

There are a small number of UK studies,[133] which have included some consideration of students' motivations for studying law—both at the academic and vocational stages—and their motivations for proceeding to legal practice.[134] The obvious motivation, as Bell and Johnstone confirm, is the desire to obtain a legal qualification and enter the profession.[135] But they can be grouped together broadly using the conventional dyad, the 'altruistic'

economy. Furthermore, it's been found that not until graduates reach 33 will their total earnings exceed their contemporaries who completed education at A level stage. Gabbitas Research (April, 2006), as cited by Bosanquet et al, above n 55, 7.

[129] King, above n 75, 119.

[130] Beecher and Kogan, above n 44, 124. Although this must be contrasted with recent research finding that applicants are *equally* motivated by the financial implications of graduate status and the love of study for its own sake. J Crace, 'Tracking Influences: Tuition Fees: Students Set Sail on Choppy Waters: What factors Influence the Decision to Apply to University? New Research Aims to Find Out if Class is Still Key' *The Guardian,* (London 19 September 2006) *Guardian Education* section, 10.

[131] See A Lipsett, 'Call for More Holistic Approach to HE' *The Guardian* (London 8 February 2008) at www.guardian.co.uk/education/2008/feb/08/highereducation.uk.

[132] UCAS figures show large rises in applicant numbers for nursing, social work, pharmacology and maths. See www.news.bbc.co.uk/1/hi/education/4719222.stm.

[133] More work has been done in the US. See, eg R Stevens, 'Law Schools and Law Students' (1973) 59 *Virginia Law Review* 551; HS Erlanger and DA Klegon, 'Socialisation Affects of Professional School: The Law School Experience and Student Orientations to Public Interest Concerns' (1976) 13 *Law and Society Review* 11; A Sarat and W Felstiner, 'Law and Social Relations: Vocabularies of Motive in Lawyer/Client Inter-actions (1988) 22(4) *Law and Society Review* 737; CW Mills, (1940) 'Situated Actions and Vocabularies of Motive' (1940) 5 *American Sociological Review* 904; and R Sennett, *The Corrosion of Character: The Personal Consequences of Work in the New Capitalism* (New York and London, WW Norton & Company, 2000).

[134] A Boon, 'From Public Service to Service Industry: The Impact of Socialisation and Work on the Motivation and Values of Lawyers' (2005) 12(2) *International Journal of the Legal Profession* 229; A Sherr and J Webb, 'Law Students, the External Market, and Socialisation: Do we Make Theme Turn to the City?' (1989) 16(2) *Journal of Law and Society* 225; N Fletcher, *Equality, Diversity and the Legal Practice Course Research Study* 49 (London, The Law Society, 2004). R Moorhead and F Boyle, 'Quality of Life and Trainee Solicitors: A Survey' (1995) 2(2)&(3) *International Journal of the Legal Profession* 217; P McDonald, 'The Class of "81"—A Glance at the Social Class Composition of Recruits to the Legal Profession' (1982) 9(2) *Journal of Law and Society* 267.

[135] J Bell and J Johnstone, *General Transferable Skills in the Law Curriculum* Report for the Department for Education and Employment (1998) at www.ukcle.ac.uk/resources/ldn/index.

versus the 'selfish'.[136] Thus, for instance, a selection of the drivers identified by Fletcher for study of the LPC: love of the work, the impact of its execution and the ability to help people, fall into the field of altruism; whereas money, job security, status/kudos and as the means to some other ends, are more 'selfish'.[137] In reality, of course, motivation is usually complex and it changes as student exposure to and experience of the law builds.

Both McDonald's[138] survey in the early 1980s and the Law Society's cohort studies[139] over 10 years later, highlight the strong influence family has on students' choice to study law. Fletcher's[140] survey, though not designed to investigate motivational issues in detail, also indicates the strong influence of family desire on students' choice to study law. McDonald, and the cohort study, use the Royal Commission on Legal Services'[141] findings as a baseline comparator and confirm its conclusions that law students continue to be drawn from principally middle class backgrounds.[142] Moreover the recent 2005 National Institute Economic Review states that having a graduate parent is one of the greatest influences on going to university at all.[143] Indeed, William's parents were both teachers and he fulfilled their expectations by gaining a bursary to the University of Aberdeen.[144] Roland,

html. Their evidence suggests a fairly high level of aspiration to enter the professions, eg 90% of final year undergraduates at the universities of Leeds and Sheffield.

[136] Boon, above n 134, at 231. And see, eg G Mungham and PA Thomas, 'Solicitors and Clients: Altruism or Self Interest?' in R Dingwall and P Lewis (eds), *The Sociology of the Professions* (Basingstoke, Hampshire, The MacMillan Press, 1983) 31.

[137] See also Fletcher, above n 134, 45.

[138] Above n 134.

[139] Hereinafter, 'the cohort study'. D Halpern, *Entry Into the Legal Professions: The Law Student Cohort Study Years 1 and 2* (London, Law Society, 1994); M Shiner and T Newburn, *Entry Into the Legal Professions: The Law Student Cohort Study Year 3* (London, Law Society, 1995); M Shiner, *Entry Into the Legal Professions: The Law Student Cohort Study Year 4* (London, Law Society, 1997); M Shiner, *Entry Into the Legal Professions: The Law Student Cohort Study Year 5* (London, Law Society, 1999); and L Duff, M Shiner, A Boon and A Whyte, *Entry Into the Legal Professions: The Law Student Cohort Study Year 6* (London, Law Society, 2000).

[140] Fletcher classed parental desire as 'encouragement', 'hard influence' or having family members as lawyers and clearly identified this desire as a phenomenon not dependant on ethnicity, above n 134, 44–45. Moreover, Halpern (ibid 24) found that the probability of a young person studying law is 10 to 15 times higher than expected by chance if one of their parents is already a lawyer. In addition Boon found that family wishes and traditions have strong underlying and sometimes residual impact, above n 134, 236.

[141] H Benson, 'Report on the Royal Commission on Legal Services' (Cm 7648, 1979).

[142] The Commission found 54% of university law students had professional or managerial fathers compared to just 16% with working-class fathers. Benson, ibid at 59. Of MacDonald's 'class of 81', a total 70% of members had father's with middle-class occupations and, in finding that just 18% of law students' fathers had working-class occupations, the cohort study figures are closely proximate to the Commission's. Halpern, above n 139.

[143] Metcalf, above n 55.

[144] www.william-robertson-smith.net/en/e040childhoodlessstudEN.htm.

however, is the first in his family to attend university and falls within the 16 to 18 per cent of students with working-class fathers.[145]

Beyond the influence of class it is difficult to generalise about student motivation. Indeed, the research usually presents the issue in different ways. Fletcher, on questioning student interviewees as to the influence on their choice to study law, grouped the results into parental desire and other non-family motivation, primarily the media and especially TV. Based on qualitative data, Boon argued that choice is usually ambiguous and media influence pervasive, identifying family wishes, autonomous decision making (perhaps as a result of experience in the field) and employment considerations as the main drivers.[146] This is somewhat consistent with studies, like McDonald's, which put security of income at the top followed by prospects and the satisfaction of helping people with their problems. In turn, this is similar to Sherr and Webb's findings from their survey of University of Warwick students, where interest in subject matter, desire for intellectual stimulation and desire for professional training were top ranking motivations. These 'selfish' reasons correspond with the cohort study's ranking of objectives by penultimate year law undergraduates, the top three reasons for taking a law degree being to acquire legal knowledge, to develop general intellectual skills and as preparation for legal practice.[147] Both the Warwick and the cohort studies rank 'altruistic' reasons towards or at the bottom of their scales.[148]

The various studies of law students suggest that motivation shifts at different points in their academic, vocational and newly qualified careers due to reconsideration and reassessment of options. Much of this change responds to external circumstances, such as debt, lack of access to social and support networks and discrimination (including age, sex, ethnicity and educational background).[149] Therefore, while most law students want to practice, they

[145] See above n 141 and n 142. Bill Rammell, Higher Education Minister, has stated 'if you come from the top two socio-economic groups, you've an 80 per cent chance of going to university. If you come from the bottom two, it's only 20 per cent. In the fourth richest economy in the world in the 21st century, this is unacceptable'. P Curtis, 'End "Social Divide" in HE, Says Rammell' *The Guardian* (London 16 November 2005).

[146] Elsewhere we have found that respondents frequently cite television programmes as an early motivation towards legal careers. A Boon and A Whyte, 'Looking Back: Analysing Experiences of Legal Education and Training' (2007) 41(2) *The Law Teacher* 169. See also C Sharp, 'Scarlet Letter or Chastity Belt? What Legal Dramas of the Twenty-First Century are "Telling" Law Students About a Career in Law (2002) 5(1) *Legal Ethics* 90.

[147] Halpern, above n 139, 39.

[148] For Halpern the least important objectives of taking a law degree were (10) the development of an understanding of the social context of the law, (11) the encouragement of a responsibility for law reform and (12) preparation as a future policy-maker. Ibid.

[149] See, eg R Rothwell, 'Black and Asian Lawyers Call for City Quotas' 101.33(1) *Law Society Gazette* (2 September 2004); L Duff and L Webley, *Equality and Diversity: Women Solicitors* Research Study 48, Volume II Law Society Research Study Series (London, Law Society, 2004); above n 27; and Sutton Trust, above n 30.

begin to see qualification as a risky venture, particularly at the Bar. Despite a rising number of places available on the BVC course[150] demand for places outstrips supply and the number of BVC graduates also regularly and substantially outstrips the number of pupillages available.[151] Students hear that with declining work[152] and numbers of pupillages, fewer than one in five make it into chambers to train[153] and that many young barristers struggle financially in the early years of practice, perhaps only receiving instructions sporadically. They will also appreciate that offsetting debt once careers as 'fat cat lawyers' begin, is a prospect only for those entering elite sectors of the profession,[154] that, despite the introduction of funded pupillage,[155] it may still be too costly for those from disadvantaged backgrounds to qualify at the Bar.[156] They may also justifiably fear that the surplus of BVC graduates from which chambers can choose works to the detriment of ethnic minorities.[157]

Appreciation of the difficulty of entering the Bar, together with larger minimum training salaries,[158] may explain the shifting aspirations of law students towards qualification as solicitors.[159] They may yet notice that

[150] Eg 1403 places were available in 2000/01 rising to 1594 between 2004/05. C Grimshaw, 'Bar Special: Pupillage Numbers Hit All-Time Low' *Legal Week Student* (26 October 2004).

[151] Annually there are approximately four times more BVC graduates than available pupillages. The Neuberger Report *Entry to the Bar Working Party: Final Report* (2007) para 37, at www.cms.barcouncil.rroom.net/assets/documents/FinalReportNeuberger.pdf. See also Grimshaw, ibid.

[152] Eg the 1999 Woolf reforms lead to a 50% deduction in traditional litigation work.

[153] General Council of the Bar, *Bar Council BVC Student Survey on Aspirations for Practice at the Bar* (London, ERS Market Research for the General Council of the Bar, 2006).

[154] Thus, while some of the commercial sets pay pupil barristers £40,000, most can expect the minimum £10,000 required by the Bar Council.

[155] The Bar Council resolved, from 31st Dec 2002, to introduce a policy for the compulsory funding of pupillage, see *The Bar Code of Conduct*, 'Funding of Pupillage and Duties of Heads of Chambers', paragraphs 404.2(c) and 404.3. Today the direct cost to the practising Bar of supporting trainees through the BVC and pupillage is in excess of £11 million. See N Duncan, (2004) 'Gatekeepers Training Hurdlers: The Training and Accreditation of Lawyers in England and Wales' (2004) 20 *Georgia State University Law Review* 911, at 922; and The Neuberger Report, above n 151.

[156] The former Bar Council chairman, Geoffrey Vos, called for funding methods to be overhauled to counter allegations that the Bar remains elitist and exclusive. *The Times*, (2007) 'Barristers Guilty of Being Posh' *The Times* 8 Jan 2007 at 22. Also, Neuberger looked into access and diversity issues at the Bar, above n 151.

[157] Many train as solicitors, or opt out of the legal profession completely. The Bar Access Group, *The Bar Access Group: At What Price the Cost of Legal Education*? (2005) at www.lawbore.net/articles/Bar_Access_GroupFinal.pdf.

[158] Over two years, trainee solicitors can expect a minimum (as of 01 Aug 2009) of £18,590 (in Central London) or £16,650 (outside London) at www.sra.org.uk/sra/news/2972.article. Though many commercial law firms start on considerably more, eg over £40,000 in some US law firms and over £37,00 in Central London 'magic circle' firms. H Begum, 'Training as a Solicitor' *Lawyer 2B* 02 Oct 2009 at http://l2b.thelawyer.com/training-as-a-solicitor/134652.article.

[159] According to one estimate 90% of law students want to be solicitors. F Gibb, 'Searching for Excitement, Adventure? Be a Lawyer' *The Times* 17 Oct 2006 at http://business.timesonline.co.uk/tol/business/law/student/article600461.ece.

the number of LPC graduates without training contracts rises each year.[160] Depending on their characteristics, some will particularly note that those from minority ethnic groups take longer to find training contracts compared to white British students,[161] that black African and black Caribbean people are slightly under represented in the profession and fewer women than men achieve partnership, whether or not they have elite educational backgrounds.[162] While career destinations of lawyers are difficult to track because of the gap between graduation and employment the latest data show that over 18 per cent of the 2005/06 cohort entered legal employment of some kind[163] and, although many subsequently improve their employment destination,[164] a substantial minority were in non-graduate employment.[165]

Those who progress in their legal careers may appreciate that unrealised aspirations are not the only reason for dissatisfaction among law students.[166] All will begin to realise, for example, that the high salaries of corporate practice have a price of long hours and, therefore, come at some cost to social and private lives.[167] Considering the quality of life of trainee and newly qualified solicitors, Moorhead and Boyle[168] found generally encouraging results (contentment with the quality of working life and an appreciation of the range of experiences it offered), but they also found 'indications of some considerable levels of dissatisfaction'. For all respondents the most

[160] The gap is often in excess of 1000 contracts annually. In 2005/06, 5751 trainee solicitors started their training contracts yet, having passed the LPC in July 2006, 6376 students were eligible to do so. See Table 1.

[161] Solicitors Regulation Authority, *Education, Training and Development for Solicitors: The Way Ahead* (2007) 6, at www.sra.org.uk/securedownload/file/1202.

[162] Eg in 2007, 49.2% of female solicitors with 10–19 years post qualification experience had achieved partnership compared with 77.8% of male solicitors in the same category. Cole above n 11, 16.

[163] As legal advisers in non-law firms (1.2%), legal executives and paralegals (12%), other legal professionals (1.9%) and solicitors (3.1%). Higher Education Careers Services Unit and the Education Liaison Task Group of the Association of Graduate Careers Advisory Services, *What do Graduates Do 2008? Career Planning for Higher Education and Beyond* (2007) 43, at www.prospects.ac.uk/downloads/documents/HECSU/Reports/WDGD%20_2008.pdf.

[164] Eg Purcell et al tracked a cohort of university students graduating in 1999 and found though approximately 50% of respondents initially took non-graduate jobs, within four years just 15% were still carrying this type of work. K Purcell, P Elias, R Davies and N Wilton, *The Class of '99: A Study of the Early Labour Market Experience of Recent Graduates* (London: DfES, 2005) at 117–18.

[165] The majority of law graduates entered into clerical and secretarial occupations (21.9%), followed by retail, catering, waiting and bar staff (12%). Prospectus *What did 2005 Graduates Do?* at www.prospects.ac.uk/cms/ShowPage/Home_page/What_did_2005_graduates_do_/charts_and_tables_pages/p!elkbpbj?subject_id=18.

[166] For further details on current levels of job satisfaction in the solicitors' profession, see Law Society, *Working Lives Survey 2005–06* (London, Law Society, 2006).

[167] Students expect to work long hours to improve their career prospects, but many also expect to achieve 'work-life' balance. Gibb, above n 159.

[168] Above n 134, 234.

prominent of these were concern over job security, debt[169] and dissatisfaction with formal (courses, internal seminars etc) as well as informal training (on the job training, supervision etc). The issue of training was, the authors found, 'perhaps the most disquieting',[170] with respondents in very large firms and those with sole practitioners much more positive about formal training than those in smaller firms.[171] Both branches of the profession remain committed to 'work based learning', while accepting that experience is uneven and sometimes unsatisfactory.[172] Studies of legal workplaces suggest that dissatisfaction often continues beyond training, with high numbers considering changes of direction, or even career. Although the causes are varied, Boon comments that:

> Intrinsic work motivation is predicted by challenging task characteristics, emotional exhaustion by high workload and lack of social support, and turnover intention is often predicted by unmet career expectations. Depending on context, each of these factors appears to play a role in determining the participants' level of career satisfaction and future intentions.[173]

Future prospects do not affect students' contemporaneous experience of the academy, but contemplation of the future does affect relationships, sometimes in a direct way. A legal education and training is expensive in time and money[174] and the prospect that its implicit promise—a secure and lucrative legal career[175]—will not be honoured, is chastening. The discovery that a 2:1 is a minimum requirement for the disadvantaged to bridge the gap to employability has, for many years, increased the anxiety of law students in general. It may even have contributed to the fact that 2:1 has

[169] Both of these concerns were felt by over half the study sample (54% for job security and 51% for debt). Moorhead and Boyle, above n 134, 234.

[170] Ibid 218.

[171] Ibid 227. This finding was confirmed by our own research. Boon and Whyte, above n 146.

[172] Current proposals from the Solicitors Regulation Authority (SRA) would go some way towards addressing a number of the issues raised by these research projects. In September 2008 the SRA launched a two-year pilot programme which tests alternative routes for work based learning (the training contract period). SRA, *Moving Forward With a New Framework for Work Based Learning* Oct, 2007 at www.sra.org.uk/securedownload/file/332; SRA, *Education, Training and Development for Solicitors: The Way Ahead*, Feb, 2007, above n 161; and P Williamson, 'Learning the Ropes' *Law Society Gazette* 17 Jan, 2008 at www.lawgazette.co.uk/features/learning-ropes.

[173] Boon, above n 134, 254.

[174] The time element, three years' undergraduate study (or one year Graduate Diploma in Law) and one year postgraduate study for both professions, followed by a period of training or pupillage, two years for solicitors and one for barristers, is substantial. The lawyers' vocational year adds to the average graduate debt of £20,000, particularly because of the scale of course fees for the BVC and LPC. Eg a LPC at City University cost £3000 in 2001, the same LPC in 2004/05 cost £5650; and a BVC at the Inns of Court School of Law cost £2875 in 1999/2, £5200 in 1995/6 and £11,360 in 2005/6. See *The Bar Access Group*, above n 157.

[175] See the literature quoted in Boon, above n 134. See also The Law Society Gazette, 'Learned in Law' *The Law Society Gazette* 23 July, 1986, at www.lawgazette.co.uk/news/learned-law.

replaced 2:2 as the largest degree classification.[176] This trend will undoubtedly continue if the Bar, responding to the massive oversubscription to the BVC, adopts a suggestion by one of its committees that it imposes a 2:1 as an entry requirement of the BVC.[177] Often the realisation of limitations on aspirations towards law dawns only during the course of legal study.

Although the aspirations of students are often towards practice, law as an undergraduate discipline is something of an anomaly when it comes to the curriculum and careers. The oldest university institutions are the most popular destinations for first degree students, despite the unpopularity of their more theoretical, less practical, approach with law students.[178] Their appeal is undoubtedly boosted by indicators such as the recruitment decisions of elite solicitors' firms and barristers' chambers. Another apparent anomaly is that elite employers, or solicitors at least, also prefer conversion course graduates to law graduates, perhaps because it expands the pool of those from the old institutions with 'good' degrees. Students who come to study the law with aspirations to high salary, and who are able to do so, therefore choose the most prestigious university for their degree, irrespective of discipline chosen.

Law applicants are at best sketchy about some of the above issues and their implications. There is mismatch between expectations of what a legal career involves and the reality[179] and the gaps are often appreciated only with hindsight. We quote in full the assessment of a participant in previous research who, having thought carefully about his experience of legal work and legal education, emailed us with his analysis of educational gaps:

> There were two key gaps—the first was 'career choice' based and the second 'day-to-day work' based. It would have been useful to have someone explain to me what it would be like to work as a barrister or a solicitor, and if as a solicitor, in a high street firm, a large commercial, but regional practice or in the city. For example, and even though I had undertaken several holiday placements, when I chose my training contract and made my first moves on qualification, I realise now that I had little idea how different these positions could be.
>
> I worked in a high street firm—there were funding difficulties within the firm, because turnover was low. I therefore had to do a lot of admin, as well as fee earning. The work was of a lower quality and often outside my areas of expertise or interest. The clients were often legally aided or just above the threshold limits. This meant that funding for cases was often a problem. My salary was lower as a result. These factors all lead to low job satisfaction for me. In many small high

[176] BBC News, 'Doubts Over Improved Degrees' 9 June, 2003, at http://news.bbc.co.uk/1/hi/education/2974454.stm.

[177] Neuberger Report, above n 151.

[178] Halpern blamed this for lower levels of student satisfaction with the curriculum in the old universities, particularly Oxbridge. Halpern, above n 139, 35.

[179] Boon, above n 134, 240–51 and Boon and Whyte, above n 146, 178–83.

street firms there is also the added pressure of a heavy work-load with few legal and admin resources for support. I had a very low workload in this particular firm, but I suspect that that is unusual. There are also specialisation issues. The law is vast and changing rapidly. You are often up against people who specialise. It is very difficult to have a broad enough knowledge of the law to really be a general participant any more.

In a larger firm, there is much better admin support, but you specialise. I think that is better but it does not suit everyone. There is much greater pressure to bill a certain number of hours and a certain amount of fees. There is also considerable pressure to develop the practice by marketing—something which is often difficult or impossible, depending on the type of work you do and the reputation of the firm.

I worked for insurers so there were no funding issues—at least the client could pay. However, the pressures were still there—internally, there are significant issues between departments because some types of client/work pay far better than others. This can mean that it is difficult to hit billing targets in some specialisations. These factors lead to significant competition between solicitors within a firm (for the best work, the best chance to shine and be promoted etc) and between firms. This can be stressful. However, I had good support in terms of admin and legal resources. I also worked with other very able people and this helped me to develop. Finally, I had much better quality of work.

I am now in-house. The billing, time recording and marketing aspects have gone, but others stresses have arisen. Typically, for this type of work, I have more reasonable hours so that my work/life balance is much better than it was in private practice, but my salary will probably fall significantly behind private practice rates going forward. Finally, moving in-house and moving back can be difficult.

Students need to know about all of these issues so that they can choose the right firm for them at an early stage. The profession is still quite staid in terms of commitment perception. People are expected to make only two or three firms changes in their career and they are not expected to change specialism more than once, if at all. There is therefore enormous pressure to get these choices right first time—something which can be difficult, if not impossible. There is also a significant snob value between types of firm and types of work within firm. This can help inter-firm moves, or hinder, depending on what you want to do and where you want to go. All of these things mean that the training contract casts a significant shadow over potential earnings and job satisfaction going forward. It is therefore important that students have a thorough understanding of these issues before making a commitment. If they do, this may help to reduce the significant number of people leaving the profession. (Incidentally, I don't know very many happy lawyers!)

As regards once you are in the job, PC skills are important—it would be well worth learning to touch type, word process, use PC based legal research tools and the Internet. It would also be useful if people were told about the politics within firms and how to handle them. An explanation of the various firm structures would help, eg what is lock step? (I still have little idea). Time and stress management training

> would be useful and training on what to do if you find something that has gone wrong (whether your mistake or someone else's). Who can you call? Who should you tell? How to protect yourself? People need to know about protecting their reputations and avoiding claims etc. Training on CV development, CV drafting and job interview skills is also likely to be useful.
>
> Finally—the sacred cow of marketing has become so significant in most firms that some training on how to market oneself within a firm (without arrogance etc) and how to market the firm and oneself to outsiders would inevitably help career choice and career/practice development.[180]

As this demonstrates, and as earlier research suggests, students' high expectations of the benefits of studying law sometimes lead to disappointment. Many students have little understanding of the profession they enter,[181] are unaware of what 'real' legal work involves and don't appreciate the significance of the wide divergence between types of firms, not least in terms of work, culture and politics.[182] This low level of understanding of legal work clearly impacts on choice of legal career, reinforcing the argument for further and better learning about 'being a lawyer' in earlier stages of legal education.[183] Students are paying the piper but they are often unaware of the tune.

The relative resistance of the academy to reflecting the needs and aspirations of students is reflected in the standard responses to the widening participation agenda. Thomas and Quinn identify three.[184] The academic approach regards first generation students as deficient, in awareness, aspirations and skills, leading to initiatives targeted at remedying the deficits, including strategies to attract talented first generation HE students and enable them to fit in to HE. The utilitarian approach sees the problem as adapting the HE sector to the economy, with employability and work placement modules and similar. The transformative approach envisages a more fundamental overhaul of the processes of knowledge production and transfer, of power and of decision making, so as to better meet a wider range of expectations, values and experiences. First generation students may need courses providing flexible study options, for example, supported distance learning, drop-out drop-in facilities, and better integration with families and communities. It is fair to say that some sections of the legal academy are grappling with the first two of these responses, but there are

[180] Email sent after project interviews by PM10. A Boon and A Whyte, *Legal Education as Vocational Preparation?: Perspectives of Newly Qualified Solicitors* (Coventry, UK Centre for Legal Education, 2002) at www.ukcle.ac.uk/research/projects/boon.rtf.

[181] For example, with regard to the implications of the Legal Services Act 2007, a survey of 1865 students by the College of Law for *The Times* newspaper heard one in three students say their knowledge of the Legal Services Bill 2006 proposals was 'non-existent' Gibb, above n 159.

[182] See Boon, above n 134, 240–51 and Boon and Whyte, above n 146, 178–83.

[183] Boon and Whyte, above n 146, 178–80.

[184] Above n 86, 129–31.

only isolated signs of the third. This raises the question how can students be the agents of the change they desire?

WHAT INFLUENCE DO LAW STUDENTS HAVE?

Direct action is a rare expression of student power,[185] a celebrated exception the 1960s student 'sit-in' leading to the creation of the Inns of Court School of Law and the reformation of training for the Bar.[186] The relative quiescence of law students is probably due to conditions and circumstances.[187] Smaller-scale victories are suggested by Arthurs' account of the Canadian experience.[188] As the academy gained control of the law curriculum from the legal profession in the 1960s, idiosyncratic interests filled the vacuum[189] with students prioritising teaching, community education and public advocacy over the academy's main priority, research. As part of their campaign, students resisted new critical scholarship and interdisciplinary courses, thereby constituting 'a political drag on the intellectual revolution in Canadian Law faculties'.[190] Arthurs does not explain how students pursued their goals, although it was probably through representations to faculty. The current scale of legal education means that contemporary modes of expression are more likely to be made via written or oral representations to government,[191] the press and universities, and via surveys.

Thomas, who observed the evolution of legal studies in England and Wales over a similar period to that covered by Arthurs, did not detect a student 'drag' on the development of law as a discipline. He notes that the socio-legal movement, which he did much to pioneer, was an engine for changing perceptions, specifically 'the belief that law is benign, neutral, objective and autonomous as presented by liberal legal idealogues'.[192]

[185] Eg the May 1968 international student revolt. T Pateman, '1968: Student Revolt and the Making of a Course-Critic' (2004) at www.selectedworks.co.uk/1968.rtf.

[186] In 1964, Bar students staged a 24-hour sit-in demanding the abolition of dinners, reduction in fees and changes in call requirements. E Cruikshank, 'Surviving Hard Times' 100 *Law Society's Gazette* (29 August 2003) 22.

[187] See also EE Robinson, '1966 and All That: A Revolution in Higher Education That is Yet Incomplete', public lecture delivered at the University of Central Lancashire, 19 Jan, 2007 at www.socialisteducation.org.uk/robinson_lecture_March07.htm.

[188] HW Arthurs, 'The Political Economy of Canadian Legal Education' (1998) 25 *Journal of Law and Society* 14.

[189] Ibid at 17.

[190] Ibid at 21.

[191] For example, the National Union of Students recently gave oral evidence to the government's Select Committee on Education and Skills with regard to student satisfaction and the student experience. HC (2007-2-19) 285(ii). And the Aldwych Group (comprised of the 20 Student's Unions of the Russell Group universities (see above n 24) campaigned against raising the £3000 cap on university tuition fees by handing in thousands of opposition 'Letters to Tony'. www.imperialcollegeunion.org/data/files/paper1-281-2806-839.pdf.

[192] P Thomas, 'Legal Education: Then and Now' (2006) 3 *The Law Teacher* 239.

Thomas conceives of law school academics as interpretative communities challenging the positivist approach that once characterised most law teaching. Although Cownie found that barely half of legal academics in her qualitative research took a positivist approach, teaching law in the traditional, doctrinal manner,[193] what we do not know is how pervasive and complete is the dissolution of common understanding in the academy about the nature and purpose of legal education. At a time when students are ever more concerned with the vocational, the academy approaches law from a multitude of 'radical and challenging ideological positions through their writing and teaching'.[194] Johnson points out that the sociological content in a socio-legal approach might be quite slight, yet still attract the label.[195] The danger is that this 'multidisciplinary edge' may yet be rather dull in terms of providing a rigorous intellectual or vocational platform, or, as Johnson colourfully puts it, 'garbage in, garbage out'.[196] Whether or not this matters, specifically in terms of a legal education fit for practice, may be moot, but the fact is that it probably does, or rather would, matter to law students, if it were clear to them.

Student opinion is better informed as a result of the range of data that is collected and made readily available, particularly through the web. A variety of organisations collect these data and for a wide range of purposes. Students sometimes conduct surveys themselves, usually with a view to bringing pressure to bear on institutions such as the professions.[197] More usually, however, institutions conduct surveys for reasons of their own, for instance, to aid analysis of criticised processes. An example of the latter includes the surveys conducted for the Bar and Law Society into student experiences of qualifying.[198] These reports highlight several areas of dissatisfaction, including with the quality of courses and their cost, the discouragement suffered by those from poorer backgrounds considering investing in the process[199] and the discrimination against ethnic minority and working-class students in the employment market.[200] By participating in such studies, students have

193 F Cownie, *Legal Academics: Culture and Identities* (Oxford, Hart Publishing, 2004) at 35–7.

194 Ibid at 245.

195 N Johnson, 'The Lecturer, the Law Student and the Transmission of Legal Culture' (2004) 40(2) *The Law Teacher* 117.

196 Ibid at 128.

197 See, eg The Bar Access Group survey, above n 157.

198 Such as J Shapland and A Sorsby, *Starting Practice: Work and Training at the Junior Bar* (Sheffield, Institute for the Study of the Legal Profession, 1995).

199 The accumulation of such concerns appears to have stimulated wider ranging reviews into the problems of those seeking admission to professions. A Langlands, *Gateways to the Professions: A Consultation Paper* (Department for Education and Skills, January 2005); A Fuller and L Unwin, 'Vocational Guidance: Students Won't Take the Vocational Route Unless They Can be Convinced That it Has Parity of Esteem' *The Guardian*, 29 Mar, 2005 at 13.

200 M Shiner, 'Young, Gifted and Blocked' in P Thomas (ed), *Discriminating Lawyers* (Oxford, Routledge Cavendish, 2000) at 87–120.

taken an admittedly weak form of direct action, by providing those in the professions arguing for change with ammunition. Among the results that can be partly attributed to them are salaries for pupil barristers[201] or the Solicitors Regulation Authority's current proposals for providing more flexible and quicker routes to qualification.[202] They may have also stimulated government interventions[203] to ensure that professional requirements do not artificially restrict the supply of lawyers and force up the cost of legal services.[204]

Student action also has direct impact when it takes the form of negotiation, whether with their institution or at a disciplinary level. The importance of 'the student experience' has become such an institutional preoccupation that student unions are potential partners in understanding and meeting student desires and supporting processes such as institutional audit. Consequently, student unions have become more active in academic structures, increasing the propensity for, and legitimacy of, challenges to the academy on a range of issues, including teaching. An apposite example of stakeholding at the disciplinary level are course committees, which usually include student representatives. Curiously, the role of such committees is said to have been stronger in the 1960s and 1970s, when students were regarded as 'partners in the enterprise'.[205] The weakening of these committees may reflect the loss of intimacy between the student body and faculty, leading to a focus on housekeeping issues rather than the curriculum or teaching. Our impression is that students are nowadays more inclined to try and bypass these formal avenues when they are unhappy about aspects of the delivery of course,[206] perhaps because raising an issue on a committee with staff present is too uncomfortable. The difficulty of voicing complaints through the formal quality assurance processes does not quite explain the growth of anonymous student surveys.

Questionnaires completed by students provide evidence used in quality assurance processes, but the impact depends on the capacity and willingness of staff to change, or the robustness of the university's mechanisms to ensure that they do. Failure to respond is punished by poor results in

[201] *The Bar Code of Conduct*, above n 155.

[202] SRA, *Moving Forward With a New Framework for Work Based Learning*, above n 172.

[203] Department of Constitutional Affairs Competition and Regulation in the Legal Services Market (CP(R2)07/02) July 2003; Sir David Clementi Review of the Regulatory Framework for Legal Services in England and Wales Final Report (December 2004) at www.legal-services-review.org.uk; Lord Falconer of Thoroton's speech to the Legal Services Reform Conference signalling the decision to widen providers in the will writing and estate management market (London 21 March 2005) at www.dca.gov.uk/speeches/2005/lc210305.htm.

[204] R Moorhead, A Sherr and A Paterson, 'Contesting Professionalism: Legal Aid and Non-Lawyers in England and Wales' (2003) 37 *Law and Society Review* 765, 797.

[205] Becher and Kogan, above n 44, 123–24.

[206] Certainly at our own institution, there appears to be an increase in *ad hoc* representations to management from students.

the National Student Survey (NSS), hailed by one of its champions as a 'national treasure', but a trove flawed in the picture it gives of HE providers.[207] The data from the NSS feeds into national league tables, comparing universities and courses, projecting anxiety about student satisfaction into the managerial levels of the university and back down into the disciplines.[208] Institutions have responded to negative results since the 2005 survey by providing new facilities, student support schemes, extended opening hours for libraries and other services, new assessment and feedback systems and more effective student consultation procedures.[209] Despite huge efforts to address particularly problematic areas there continue to be mismatched expectations. For example, the assessment and feedback section of the NSS is relatively poor across the sector. It has been suggested that long, written criticism of student work is misguided. It is often not collected and, when it is, it is not understood. More importantly what this tells us is that students want a dialogue, whereas traditional, written feedback is a monologue.[210] Again, the demands on the academy increase, while resources decline. Yet, the pressure on underperforming disciplines can be huge[211] leading to academics eschewing innovation in favour of inducing favourable survey responses.[212]

The existence of satisfaction surveys is great, but it is secondary to the most diffuse, but possibly the most effective, form of student pressure. The mechanism of the market, manifest in failure to choose law as a subject of study or to shun particular types of provision or providers, involves no interaction with institutions, disciplines or even pollsters. There is nothing

[207] Research into the NSS found that student profiles and characteristics affected responses so, for example, Asian students were generally less positive and older students more so. 'National Student Survey "a National Treasure"' (2006) 67 *Council Briefing* at 10.

[208] Many examples of attempts by HE staff to manipulate the NSS data by warning students that poor scores will devalue their degrees, (see, eg M Newman, 'Students Urged to Inflate National Survey Marks to Improve Job Options' *Times Higher Education*, 15 May 2008 at 7.

[209] For instance, according to Professor Arthur (VC University of Leeds, Chair of the NSS Steering Group) as a result of the NSS, his university improved its induction process for students, started a new peer mentoring scheme and underwent a major review of its internal learning and teaching processes; and the University of East Anglia increased the amount of its anonymous marking. Uncorrected transcript of oral evidence to the Select Committee on Education and Skills, Q134 HC (2007-2-19) 285(ii).

[210] O Wojtas, 'Lecturers' Feedback Efforts Misguided' *Times Higher Education* (24 January 2008 31 July 2008) 6. Although resources for this may be stretched, greater focus on self- and peer-assessment, examples of good previous essays could provide more interaction.

[211] In our own institution, Deans of School were required to produce papers outlining what steps have been taken to address issues raised in the survey.

[212] In the summer of 2007, HEFCE was obliged to examine allegations that NSS results had been distorted following the email sent by King's College London's President of the Student Law Society to students claiming it would be 'beneficial for any student looking to work in the legal profession to look kindly upon their university, as the more success King's has in the survey, the more employable King's graduates—that is you—become'. R Atwood, 'Undergraduates Give University the Big Thumbs-Up' *Times Higher Education* (10 August 2007) 2. See also R Attwood, 'Probe Ordered into "Manipulation"' *Times Higher Education* 28 Feb, 2008, at 5.

quite like the threat of extinction to change behaviour. Indications about likely student behaviour can be gleaned from the spate of surveys, for example on the cost to students of HE.[213] Some universities have responded by reducing fees or offering discounts or other incentives,[214] such as accelerated completion of programmes. Despite the perception that academic self-interest is the only impediment to such courses,[215] two-year honours degrees, incorporating 'burst mode' learning options and unconventional attendance patterns have definitely arrived.[216] Not all the degrees with work-related elements, or engaging subject matter, are, however, met with acclamation and most are derided in the media.[217] The result is a complex and confusing range of choices for students.

The difficulty of choosing between what universities and courses offer, may explain why the strongest demand continues to be for places at the institutions with cultural capital. This explains why they are also less responsive to the change agenda. The private institutions seem equipped to buck this trend. A good example is the University of Buckingham, for the past 30 years the UK's only private university.[218] It offers multiple start dates for courses, all year round tuition and claims to be the 'only British University which puts the student first.'[219] Although Buckingham has

[213] 16% of home students think that their course is poor value for money. Bekhradnia et al, above n 126, para 53. Wes Streeting, the vice president of the National Union of Students with responsibility for education, predicts that this 16% 'will grow and grow' if there were no improvement in the areas of the amount of contact time with staff or the facilities provided. As cited by D MacLeod and J Meikle, 'Report Reveals Teaching Gap Between Universities *Education Guardian* (31 October 2006) at www.education.guardian.co.uk/universityteachinginspection/story/0,1935806,00.html.

[214] Leeds Metropolitan broke with the sector norm of charging fees of £3000 per annum in 2006 to charge £2000 for all its courses, Gloucestershire University offered a 20% discount to any student who could afford to pay the total £9000 tuition fee up front and Anglia Ruskin University gave £2000 cash to all prospective full-time students who began a full-time course. I Pollock, 'New Students Face Future of Debts' BBC News (22 August 2006) at www.news.bbc.co.uk/1/hi/business/5274342.stm.

[215] Rammell recently opined that traditional degrees had been organised for the convenience of academics rather than students, adding that 'we live in a world where people expect that service providers will have scope to offer flexibility, not uniformity'. BBC News, 'Two-Year Honours Degrees Offered' (18 April 2006) at www.news.bbc.co.uk/1/hi/education/4918652.stm.

[216] Staffordshire, Derby, Leeds Metropolitan, Northampton and The Medway Partnership (Kent), BBC News, ibid.

[217] For example, degrees in physiotherapy and sports science, growth industries requiring high-tech skills, such as cinematics and animation, and courses that are the butt of newspaper jokes such as horse studies, golf course studies and accommodation management, Smith, above n 76, 180. Indeed, Chris Woodhead, whilst chief inspector of schools, claimed that universities were devaluing HE by providing a 'plethora of quasi-academic courses' through vacuous degrees in media studies, knitwear, beauty therapy and golf course management. R Smithers, 'Woodhead Attacks Vacuous Degrees' *The Guardian*, 14 Aug, 2000 at 9.

[218] The University College at Buckingham (UCB) was incorporated on 29 March 1973, in the form of a non-profit-making company registered as an educational charity. See www.buckingham.ac.uk/facts/history.

[219] Terence Kealey, vice-chancellor of the University of Buckingham. See www.buckingham.ac.uk/standingout/independent.

probably not been taken seriously by the public sector institutions, the fact that it topped the NSS[220] suggests fitness for the new conditions. In legal education, the closest parallels are the College of Law and, particularly, BPP, the latter building its success in law teaching on the Graduate Diploma in Law (GDL), formerly the Common Professional Exam (CPE). The GDL, a one-year full time conversion for non-law graduates, is the prototype of 'the law course students want'. It was pioneered by City University and our own institution, as the Polytechnic of Central London, at the behest of the Council of Legal Education, for entry to the Bar Vocational Course.

The CPE was recognised by the Law Society as an alternative route to the Law Society finals course in 1989 and offered by large numbers of universities. Subsequently, however, the course has been identified with the College of Law and BPP, which have incrementally increased their numbers each year until their entry figures dwarf those of any university.[221] Their relative success can be explained by a number of factors. First, because they lack degree courses, they have relatively few distractions and economies of scale. In marketing terms, size can be an advantage because it sends a positive message to students about the importance of a course to a provider. It may also be significant that such providers adopt a no-nonsense, doctrinal approach uncomplicated by multi-disciplinary perspectives. It is no surprise that Kaplan International and Bridgepoint Education, major US education companies, are aiming to become UK for-profit private universities.[222] An analogous development is the growth of in-house training operations eliding the line between the educational role of the university (basic research, general education) and of the company (applied research, job-specific training).[223] All of this is perhaps a warning to the rest of stiff competition to come. As universities are encouraged to generate more and more of their core funding from sources other than the government, the time when they could ignore the market may be ending.

Scale does not entirely explain why graduates choose relatively expensive private providers with no research profile and, therefore, none of the normal

[220] Along with the Open University, itself a distance-learning university. *National Student Satisfaction Survey* 2006, 2007 and 2008. The survey can be found at www.thestudentsurvey.com. The results of the surveys can be found at www.unistats.com.

[221] Though globally the total number of places offered in the first round of GDL applications has been decreasing since a high in 2003/04 of 4138 to 3731 offered in the 2007/08 round. Figures provided by the Legal Practice Course and CPE/Diploma in Law Courses Central Applications Board, on file with the authors. The latest data shows there are 5386 places, of which the College of Law offer 1600 and BPP 1584. In 2008/9 there were only 3878 enrolments in England and Wales. The private colleges did not make their numbers known, but the course of the largest university provider, Nottingham (400), was less than half full.

[222] D Turner, 'US Companies in UK Degree Plan' *The Financial Times* (London 12 October 2007) and J Boone, 'US Group Plans UK For-Profit University' *The Financial Times*, 20 Nov 2006.

[223] Disney offers an MBA programme not only for its own employees. Smith, above n 76, 177.

indicators of prestige that weigh so heavily in the university sector. Indeed, the lack of research focus of the private institutions means that they make 'student-satisfaction' their focus. The answer may be that the 'prestige gap' is filled in the minds of students by the close association the private colleges have with the world of legal work, first with the vocational courses, and second with employers, particularly the commercial firms. This relationship was initially grounded in the Continuing Professional Development (CPD) market, in which the private colleges have long been active. It developed, however, because they brought this flexibility to their other operations, for example, the bespoke LPC courses they developed with solicitors' firms.[224] This flexibility contributes a practical orientation to the ambience of these institutions that universities have not matched.

The legal services market itself will, of course, be changing radically as the new Legal Services Board begins to roll out the provisions of the Legal Services Act 2007. The re-alignment of lawyers within Legal Disciplinary Partnerships and the approval of Alternative Business Structures could reduce the scope for independent barristers and lawyer partners. It could also quicken the trend towards para-legals replacing the established professions in many legal operations. These changes come at a time when the Community Legal Service is experimenting with Legal Advice Networks, geared to dealing with client problems holistically, which could further weaken solicitors' engagement with the welfare law market.[225] Despite the traditional appeal of law as a subject, these trends may presage a slackening of demand for legal careers and for the familiar undergraduate and vocational courses. At the same time, increasing diversification of legal careers, and the potential for their assimilation into existing structures,[226] suggests potential for the diversification and proliferation of law and law-related courses. Both of these strands of change may ensure that an increasing number of law schools may need to adapt and change or grapple with the challenge of a more diverse student body.

CONCLUSION

The collegial setting of the traditional academy provided a context in which students in general, and certainly senior and exceptional students, were conceived of as participants or members. The sudden expansion of the HE

[224] See, eg G Charles, 'A Revolution in Legal Education' *The Lawyer* 22 Mar 2004 at www.thelawyer.com/a-revolution-in-legal-education/109190.article.

[225] For the background to this, see R Moorhead, 'Third way regulation? Community Legal Service Partnerships' (2001) 64(4) *Modern Law Review* 543. For details of the current state of the project (involving around 14 local authorities), visit the LSC website at www.legalservices.gov.uk/civil/community_legal_advice_centres_and_networks.asp.

[226] Eg the Law Society offering routes into the solicitors' profession for paralegals.

sector forced a move towards a mass heterogeneous student body causing individual relationships across the divide between lecturer and student to become more difficult, if not impossible. Large-scale lectures, the internet, email and distance-learning materials were new means of communicating knowledge.[227] Moreover, the increasing importance of recruiting and keeping students caused successive re-evaluations of the relationship between the academy and students. Under mass systems, students in general became subjects, products and then customers of, and, increasingly we argue, 'stakeholders' in their institution. This labelling is not idle or inconsequential. Students' occasionally inappropriate sense of entitlement, and institutions' ambivalent responses, may stem from sloppy analogies and metaphors.

Defining students as consumers assures them of an enhanced status as purchasers, free to choose an educational product,[228] and demonstrates that universities are responsive to their needs and accountable. Yet consumerist concepts put pressure on universities to satisfy students according to *students'* definition of what is valuable. Re-conceptualising students as stakeholders could have a transformative effect on the way that students, as well as universities, are perceived. Stakeholders are 'involved with an organisation, society, etc and therefore [have] responsibilities towards it and an interest in its success'.[229] The advantage of conceiving of students as stakeholders, rather than customers, is that they will be treated as such, with possible advantages for the curriculum and the quality of learning. Engagement is consistent with treating students as co-producers in their own learning, rather than mere consumers of an educational product. The stakeholding model conceives of the possibility of authentic dialogue between the university, its staff and its students, and the continuing active participation of the latter as members of the academy.

The alternative to such a development is that academic institutions will be increasingly ruled by indirect measures of student satisfaction. A significant problem for the league table culture is its unreliability as an indicator of quality, particularly of fitness for purpose. If students feel that they are progressing smoothly towards their goals, they are satisfied. If their first goal is qualification and their second goal a rewarding career, they are likely to be satisfied only if they perceive that they are on course. Otherwise they are likely to resent the time and money spent on education. Failure

227 Lomas, above n 104, 3.

228 See eg, L Morely, 'Reconstructing Students as Consumers' in L Morley, *Quality and Power in Higher Education* (Maidenhead, Open University Press and DHRE, 2003), at 129; T Pitman, 'Perception of Academics and Students as Customers: A Survey of Administrative Staff in Higher Education (2000) 22(2) *Journal of Higher Education Policy and Management* 165; and D Robertson, 'Students as Consumers: The Individualization of Competitive Advantage' in P Scott (ed), *Higher Education Reformed* (London, Falmer Pees, 2000) at 78.

229 Cambridge Dictionary. See www.dictionary.cambridge.org/define.asp?key=77370&dict=CALD.

to pass examinations, poor marks and gathering gloom about employment prospects is bad for student morale and bad for the satisfaction surveys of the institutions that take them. The fact that students' goals are defined and bounded by their institutions is both a source of power and a trap. The curriculum is irrelevant unless it offers the qualification students want, providing scope for disciplinary indulgence. However, there is also great pressure, particularly on institutions engaged in the widening participation agenda, to reduce demands on students and therefore to compromise standards.

To understand students' needs, and respect their position as stakeholders, the legal academy needs to engage with them, to understand their short-term requirements and expectations. Both short and long term, what national and local surveys, staff student committees, and end of course feedback questionnaires reveal, is a desire for quality, affordable education and appropriate career training leading to a well-paid and secure career in the law. Interpreting these desires into actions by the academy almost certainly implies a move to more individual or personalised programmes of learning. Re-imaging the student and university stakeholder relationship would, we suggest, see universities and vocational course providers re-evaluating their courses and also being more proactive in informing students' expectations. The academy needs to be more interested in what motivates students and more committed to informing them. Graduates should pursue a legal career with full knowledge of the field; ensuring they 'know the tune' is a basic requirement of their 'stake' having meaning.

8

Stakeholders in the University Law School: A Note in Dissent

ANTHONY BRADNEY

INTRODUCTION

THERE CAN BE no doubt that the term 'stakeholder' has entered into the vocabulary of both universities in general and university law schools in particular. Thus, for example, in the UK the Quality Assurance Agency intones, with almost ritual solemnity, that its institutional audit reviews have the task of ensuring that universities 'have appropriate quality assurance policies and procedures in place... [that] are sufficiently reliable to continue to provide stakeholders with the necessary assurances for the future'.[1]

The Strategic Plan for the Agency for 2003 to 2005 sets out the Agency's perception of its duties towards its stakeholders and states that the Agency works in partnership with, amongst others, stakeholders.[2] Similarly in 2004, in the US, the web site of the Thurgood Marshall School of Law at the Texas Southern University told us that '[t]he goal of the Department is to advance the brand of the School of Law by effectively and efficiently implementing marketing and communications strategies to articulate the mission of the School to its stakeholders'.[3]

In New Zealand the University of Auckland's website once had on it a list of stakeholders, a list that included the Auckland District Law Society and the Council of Legal Education, whilst at the University of Waikato

[1] See, eg Quality Assurance Agency Institutional Review Report, 'University of Aberdeen' (1998) para 2; and Quality Assurance Agency Institutional Review Report 'University of Abertay, Dundee' (2002) para 2.

[2] Quality Assurance Agency, 'Strategic plan 2003–05' (2004) http://www.qaa.ac.uk/aboutus/strategicplan/. Its more recent 'Strategic Plan 2006–11' continues to talk about 'students, potential students, universities and colleges and their staff, and other stakeholders in higher education' (Strategic Plan 2006–11 (2006) Quality Assurance Agency for Higher Education p1).

[3] http://www.tsulaw.edu/communication/index.asp. See similarly the School of Law's website at Howard University (http://www.law.howard.edu/18).

the Pro Vice-Chancellor (Public Affairs), Professor Shirley Leitch, has said that '[s]trong relationships with... stakeholder groups can shift the University from compliance mode, in which the University simply responds to policy, to proactive mode, in which the University drives policy and funding initiatives'.[4]

In Australia, at Monash University, '[s]taff and students are invited to attend stakeholder forums to have an opportunity to have input into the Research and Research Management Review'.[5] Finally, once again in the US, Kelsey and Mariger argue that section 102 of the Agricultural Research, Extension, and Education Reform Act 1998 is a mechanism for ensuring that 'stakeholder input must be collected when setting research, extension and education priorities' in land-grant universities.[6] The notion of the stakeholder is a concept that plainly has significance in many parts of the international academic community.

Notwithstanding the regularity with which the term is used in relation to higher education, the notion of the stakeholder is, nevertheless, not ubiquitous within either the academy or within university law schools. Thus, for example, whilst the last major enquiry into universities in the UK, the Dearing Report, referred to stakeholders in its analysis on a number of occasions, the Government's response to that report used the term only once.[7] Moreover, sometimes, when the concept is used, there appears to be a degree of hesitancy accompanying its employment. Barnett, for example, in making occasional reference to stakeholders in his analysis of the position of universities,[8] frequently puts the term in inverted commas. It seems that the stakeholder is a creature known to the academy but it is not clear that it is well-liked. The question thus arises, is the notion of the stakeholder a valuable concept whose use should be encouraged when writers seek to analyse the role and work of universities and their law schools or, instead,

[4] www.auckland.ac.nz (visited 2006). The list does not appear on the website as at October 2009. However the University's Charter states that '[e]ffective linkages with key stakeholders outside the teaching sector are a key element of the University's mission' ('University of Auckland Charter 2003' (http://www.auckland.ac.nz/uoa/home/about/the-university/official-publications/charter-2003)); 'Professor Appointed to Key University Role" (10 March 2003) http://www.waikato.ac.nz/news/index.shtml?article=224.

[5] www.monash.edu.au/research/review/session.html.

[6] K Kelsey and S Mariger, 'A Survey-Based Model for Collecting Stakeholder Input at a Land-Grant University' (2003) 41(5) *Journal of Extension* www.joe.org/joe/2003october/a3.shtml.

[7] The National Committee of Inquiry into Higher Education, 'Higher Education in the Learning Society" (The Dearing Report) (Her Majesty's Stationery Office, 1997). DfEE, 'Higher Education for the 21st Century: Response to the Dearing Report' (DfEE, 1997) para 4.4. Other government pronouncements on higher education have also made either no use or only limited use of the term stakeholder. See, eg 'The Development of Higher Education Into the 1990s' (Cm 9524, 1985) and 'The Future of Higher Education' (Cm 5735, 2003).

[8] R Barnett, 'Beyond All Reason: Living With Ideology in the University" (2003) *Society for Research into Higher Education and Open University Press* 3, 78, and 91.

does employment of the concept pose problems if one wants an accurate understanding of these institutions?

In one sense all the essays in this volume are an attempt to see whether or not the term stakeholder has utility when it is applied to university law schools. However, whilst the other essays in this book try to answer the question by looking at the position of particular putative stakeholders in the law school, in this essay I want to take a completely different approach. I will trace the history of the term stakeholder. In doing this I hope to show what the original intention was in introducing the term into analysis. Having done this I will then analyse the impact that the term has when it is used in the context of universities.[9]

THE ORIGINS OF STAKEHOLDING

The concept of the stakeholder in its modern form first arose in literature on business management and business ethics.[10] 'Stakeholders were originally identified as those without whom a business corporation could not survive, those in whom the business had a stake.'[11] Stakeholders included 'owners, employees, suppliers, industry and the community'.[12] From its very beginning central to the notion of who a stakeholder was, was the question of who the stakeholder was not. The stakeholder was somebody distinct from the shareholder or stockholder who conventional economic

[9] In any analysis of universities there must be an implicit or explicit concept of what a university is and how it should function. The premise for this essay is that universities are or should be vehicles for the pursuit of a liberal education. See also A Bradney, *Conversations, Chances and Choices: The Liberal Law School in the Twenty-First Century* (Oxford, Hart Publishing, 2003).

[10] According to Freeman the term was first used in 1963 'in an internal memorandum at the Stanford Research Institute'. RE Freeman, *Strategic Management: A Stakeholder Approach* (London, Pitman Publishing, 1984) 31. See also J Wang and H Dewhirst 'Boards of Directors and stakeholder orientation' (1992) 11 *Journal of Business Ethics* 115, 115. Hirst sees the origins of stakeholding as being in Berle and Means' book *The Modern Corporation and Private Property* which did not use the term stakeholding but did argue that '[n]either the claims of ownership [or companies] nor those of control can stand against the paramount interests of the community'. P Hirst, 'From the Economic to the Political' in G Kelly, D Kelly and A Gamble (eds), *Stakeholder Capitalism* (London, Macmillan Press, 1997) 65; A Berle and G Means, *The Modern Corporation and Private Property* (London, The Macmillan Company, 1932) 356. The Oxford English Dictionary traces the use of the term in the context of gambling back to the 16th century. The theory remains contentious. For a recent rejection of the theory see, eg A Black, P Wright and J Davies, *In Search of Shareholder Value* 2nd edn (London, Financial Times, Prentice Hall, 2001).

[11] E Sternberg, 'Stakeholder Theory: The Defective State It's In' in W Hutton et al (eds), *Stakeholding and Its Critics* (London, IEA Health and Welfare Unit, 1997) 71. See also Freeman's definition 'any group or individual who can affect, or is affected by, the achievement of a corporation's purpose'. Freeman, above n 10, vi.

[12] D Grace and S Cohen, *Business Ethics: Australian Problems and Cases* (Oxford, Oxford University Press, 1995) 70.

and business management theory saw as being central to business concerns. Thus, in an essay first published in 1970, Friedman had written 'a corporate executive... has direct responsibility to his employers... to conduct business in accordance with their desires, which generally will be to make as much money as possible while conforming to the basic rules of society'.[13]

By contrast stakeholder theory argued 'the modern organization—whether public or private—is beholden to, at the very least affected by, a larger set of forces than the three parties, stockholders, customers and the organization itself.'[14]

Conventional management theory understood the importance of a wide range of groups to businesses and was therefore willing to take account of these groups and even accepted the need for businesses to seek to satisfy them but only in so far as this was commensurate with and necessary for the overriding objective of the business, 'the maximization of shareholder value'.[15] The way that business treated other groups was thus merely a means to this end; business did not value other groups for themselves. '[S]takeholder theory purports that stakeholders should be considered as ends in themselves, rather than just means'.[16] Stakeholder theory thus sought to work to widen the gaze of business, forcing it first to accept that it had broad moral responsibilities to society at large as well as an economic duty to its shareholders and secondly making it take into account, in a Kantian fashion, the needs of a wider range of actors than it had previously considered.[17]

13 M Friedman, 'The Social Responsibility of Business to Increase Its Profits' in T Donaldson and P Werhane (eds), *Ethical Issues in Business: A Philosophical Approach* 2nd edn (Englewood Cliffs, NJ, Prentice Hall, 1983) 239. See also M Friedman, *Capitalism and Freedom* (Chicago, University of Chicago Press, 1962) 133–136.

14 I Mitroff, *Stakeholders of the Organizational Mind* (San Francisco, Josey-Bass Publishers, 1983) 21.

15 G Moore, 'Tinged Shareholder Theory: Or What's so Special About Stakeholders?' (1998) 8 *Business Ethics* 117, 118–119.

16 C Metcalfe, 'The Stakeholder Corporation' (1998) 7 *Business Ethics* 30, 31. See also Moore's comment that a common justification for the stakeholder approach 'is one based on Kant's second formulation of the Categorical Imperative'. Moore, above n 15, 121. The second formulation reads, '[a]ct in such a way that you always treat humanity, whether in your own person or the person of any other, never simply as a means, but always at the same time as an end. H Paton, *The Moral Law* (London, Hutchinson, 1948) 32. Hirst, in contrast, has argued that the foundations of the theory are democratic in their nature. 'The basic democratic principle is that the interests that are directly affected by the decisions of companies or under their authority should either have a proportionate voice in he making of those decisions or some other check upon the content and scope of such decisions'" Hirst above n 10, 63.

17 J Weiss, *Business Ethics: A Stakeholder and Issues Management Approach* (Fort Worth Texas, Harcourt and Brace, 1998) 44. However for a completely different approach see Jawahar and McLaughlin who argue that '[s]takeholder management is fundamentally a pragmatic concept' and that 'organizational needs vary with life cycle stages. The particular stakeholder or stakeholders with potential to meet these needs will be perceived as critical to organizational well-being and their concerns will be addressed proactively or at least accommodated'. I Jawahar and G McLaughlin, 'Towards a Descriptive Stakeholder Theory: An Organizational Life Cycle Approach' (2001) 26 *Academy of Management Review* 397 at 410.

WHO ARE STAKEHOLDERS?

Although, as seen above, early writing on stakeholder theory placed close limits on the notion of who might be a stakeholder the concept widened as the literature developed.[18] Thus by 1995 Calvert was writing that:

> A project's stakeholders can be identified as: 'all the people whose lives or environment are affected by the project, but who receive no direct benefit from it. These can include the project team's families, people made redundant by the changes introduced, people who buy the product produced by the facility, and the local community.'
>
> Stakeholders are also those people or groups who *believe* they are affected by the project or who have an *opinion* on the project or the changes that the project will create.[19]

Sternberg notes that '[t]errorists and competitors, vegetation, nameless sea creatures and generations yet unborn are amongst the many groups which are now seriously considered to be business stakeholders'.[20] Rather than stakeholders being those in whom business saw itself as having a stake the focus changed to those who might see themselves as having a stake in business.

Asking businesses to take account of those whom it saw itself saw as having a stake in it involved consideration of a greater number of people than the shareholders that traditional economic and management theory had directed business attention to. Changing the notion of the stakeholder to those who might see themselves as having a stake in a business still further increased the number of people or institutions that business needed to attend to. Thus, almost inevitably, the idea that stakeholders should be 'classified into meaningful groups' when businesses are looking at their stakeholders arises.[21] It is not just the number of stakeholders that is seen as being problematic for businesses when they are trying to develop future strategy but also the fact that 'different stakeholders do not generally share the same definition of an organization's "problems", and hence, they do not share the same "solutions".'[22]

Carroll, for example, suggests that businesses should divide their stakeholders into primary and secondary stakeholders: '[P]rimary stakeholders

[18] For a chronology of the different definitions of stakeholder, see R Mitchell, B Myle and D Wood, 'Toward a Theory of Stakeholder Identification and Salience: Defining the Principle of Who and What Really Counts" (1997) 22 *Academy of Management Review* 853 at 858.

[19] S Calvert, 'Managing Stakeholders' in J Rodney Turner (ed), *The Commercial Project Manager* (London, McGraw-Hill Book Company, 1995) 214, emphasis added.

[20] Sternberg n 11, 71. Weiss observes that '[s]takes and claims can be based on legal, economic, social, moral, technological, ecological, political, or power interests'. Weiss, n 17 30–31.

[21] J Harrison and C St John, *Strategic Management of Organizations and Stakeholders: Theory and Cases* (Minneapolis/St Paul, West Publishing Company, 1994) 20.

[22] Mitroff n 14, 5.

are seen as those that have a formal, official, or contractual relationship with the firm, and all others are classified as secondary stakeholders.'[23] However, whilst the idea of categorising stakeholders is common to many stakeholder theorists, the form that that categorisation should take is the subject of debate. Metcalfe, for example, observes that:

> Some commentators... argue that it is necessary to define 'Primary' or 'Participant' stakeholders who have a real interest in the company, such as investors, employees, and major customers and suppliers. These stakeholders should be viewed differently to 'Secondary' or 'Non-participant' stakeholders who have more remote or indirect interests, such as minor suppliers and customers, neighbours etc."[24]

The differences between various analyses are sometimes substantive rather than merely semantic. In the two schemes above, for example, whilst minor suppliers to a business, who therefore have a contractual relationship with the business, are primary stakeholders for Carroll, they are only secondary stakeholders for Metcalfe.

RESPONSIBILITY TO STAKEHOLDERS

Once stakeholders have been recognised, then stakeholder theory argues it is necessary

> to calculate the impact of an action or a practice on the stakeholders, and to figure into the overall calculation the effect of the practice or action on the stakeholders. Usually this is seen as a matter of calculating the utility or disutility of a proposed practice for the stakeholders, recognising that various stakeholders (groups of stakeholders) have different stakes in the possible outcomes of some activity.[25]

It is possible in some instances for businesses to calculate for themselves the impact of their proposed projects on stakeholders.[26] However, more normally, stakeholder theory, in keeping with its inclusive aspirations, emphasises the importance of businesses directly consulting stakeholders and making available to stakeholders the information they need to put forward their views on proposals that those businesses have. Indeed, stakeholder theory can go beyond this:

> Many stakeholder groups are not satisfied with simply being allocated some measure of organizational value; they want a say in how the organization creates this

[23] A Carroll, *Business and Society* (Cincinnati, Ohio, South-Western Publishing, 1989) 58.
[24] Metcalfe n 16 pp 32–33. Categorisation of stakeholders can be on a much more complex basis than either of the examples here. See, eg K Pajunen, 'Stakeholder Influences in Organizational Survival' (2006) 43 *Journal of Management Studies* 1261, at 1263–65.
[25] Grace and Cohen n 12, 72.
[26] Grace and Cohen n 12, 71–72.

> value. Perhaps not all, but many stakeholders want some voice in organization's decision making. Those who desire a voice should have it.[27]

In this type of stakeholder theory it is not just that stakeholder's interests are taken into account by business. Instead stakeholders are seen to 'acquire quasi-governance rights commensurate with the extent of their stake in the company'.[28] Stakeholders then need information at the requisite level to carry out this role and, indeed, they need to be part of the process of deciding what information it is that they need.[29]

One difficulty that this presents business with is that of looking at the needs and demands of such a large group of stakeholders. In this context categorising and prioritising stakeholders offers a way forward. However, although it is frequently argued that stakeholders have to be divided into different types by business, this is not to say that the idea of categorising them is unproblematic. If stakeholders are to be considered, in a Kantian sense, for themselves, then what difference does their category make and what purpose is there in carrying out the process of categorisation? The needs of stakeholders should be attended to, it would seem, whatever the nature of their connection with the business. Even distinguishing 'genuine stakeholders from those who have an officious interest' poses problems.[30] If stakeholders include 'those people or groups who *believe* they are affected by the project or who have an *opinion* on the project or the changes that the project will create' why are those with 'an officious interest' not genuine stakeholders?[31] Categorising stakeholders might, at best, be helpful in saying how different types of stakeholders with different types of needs should be dealt with. However, when it is argued, 'groups [of stakeholders] might be formed on the basis of their stakes in the organization and the type of influence over firm behaviour', the question of why stakeholders are being considered becomes potentially more complex than at first seemed to be the case.[32]

THE WIDER NOTION OF STAKEHOLDING

The use of the term stakeholding has now gone far beyond its original provenance. It has, for example, been argued that tenants should be seen as

[27] R Phillips, *Stakeholder Theory and Organizational Ethics* (San Francisco, Berrett-Kochler Publishers, 2003) 159.

[28] Metcalfe n 16, 34.

[29] R Roberts, 'A Stakeholder Approach to the Corporate Single Audit' (1989) 9 *Critical Perspectives on Accounting* 227 at 231.

[30] Grace and Cohen n 12, 71.

[31] Calvert n 19, 214, emphasis added.

[32] Harrison and St John, n 21, 20. See also the proposition 'stakeholders that are considered particularly important to the organization should be given ample attention during strategy formulation and implementation' (22).

stakeholders and a similar case has been made out for those who participate in pension schemes.[33] Even more widely than this, it has been suggested that citizens should be seen as having a stake in society. Ackerman and Alstott have argued for a specific stake for each American citizen; 'a one-time grant of eighty thousand dollars as he reaches early adulthood' to be used by that person in the way that they determined.[34] In the UK there have been two important contributions to the attempt to widen the notion of stakeholding. One is a relatively short flirtation that the Labour Party had with the use of the term as a potential 'big idea' in its political programme and the other is in Hutton's analysis of the economic, political and social condition of contemporary UK.[35]

The brief centrality that the term stakeholder had to the Labour Party's political agenda stemmed from a speech that Tony Blair made in Singapore in 1996 when he announced a commitment to stakeholder economics.[36] In this speech he attempted to weave '"stakeholding" together with three other established themes in New Labour political discourse—equality of opportunity, meritocracy, and social exclusion'.[37] Blair spoke of 'a stakeholder economy in which opportunity is available to all, advancement is through merit and from which no group or class is set apart or excluded'.[38] Commentators argued that:

> [M]any interest groups may be said to have a 'stake' in certain activities, not necessarily because they have a financial interest in them, but because they are affected by them. These stakes should be recognized by those whose actions may impinge upon them. Individuals should recognize that their behaviour can have repercussions upon society. They should act in a responsible way that does not damage others and also repay the costs expended by society on their behalf.[39]

The problem with New Labour's idea of a stakeholder society was that, beyond advancing the argument that all people should see themselves as having a stake in society, it was entirely unclear exactly what this might

[33] M Hood, 'Tenants as Stakeholders' in T Brown (ed), *Stakeholder Housing* (London, Pluto Press, 1999); F Field, *How to Pay for the Future: Building Stakeholder's Welfare* (London, Institute of Community Affairs, 1996). Stakeholder pension schemes are now defined under s 1 Welfare Reform and Pensions Act 1999.

[34] B Ackerman and A Alstott, *The Stakeholder Society* (New Haven, Connecticut, Yale University Press, 1999) 4.

[35] N Fairclough, *New Labour, New Language* (London, Routledge, 2000) 92; W Hutton, *The State We're In* (London, Vintage, 1996).

[36] This is not to say that Blair was the sole labour advocate of the stakeholder concept. See, eg Alistair Darling: 'Every individual ought to have a stake in the future of their country... To have such a stake is good for the individual and therefore good for society'. A Darling, 'A Political Perspective' in Kelly, Kelly and Gamble (eds), *Stakeholder Capitalism* (1997) 10.

[37] Fairclough, n 35, 89.

[38] Quoted in S Driver and L Martell, *New Labour Politics After Thatcherism* (Cambridge, Polity Press, 1998) 52.

[39] B Burkitt and F Ashton, 'The Birth of the Stakeholder Society' (1996) 16 *Critical Social Policy* 3, 10.

mean. Being susceptible to a huge range of contradictory interpretations, one of which was support for the corporatist states of Europe at a time when they were then perceived as beginning to fail economically, the idea did not take hold as a central organising concept within Labour Party discourse.[40] Because of this '[s]takeholding is now conspicuous by its absence from the vocabulary of general political discourse [in the UK]'.[41]

The failure of the concept of stakeholding in the development of Labour Party policy stemmed from a failure clearly to think out what the term might mean before it was first used. By way of contrast, Hutton's book, *The State We're In*, first published in 1995 and subsequently republished in a revised edition, attempted both a detailed analysis of what Hutton saw as the endemic political and social malaise in the UK and the way in which stakeholding and other allied notions could contribute to a new structure that would revitalise the country.

Central to Hutton's work is an argument that both those who are economically and socially successful in society and those who are marginalised fail to see themselves as being involved in any long-term project for the general improvement of society; the former because they are simply interested in short-term gains and the latter because they see no hope of success. In this context stakeholding is seen as a way of committing various parties and institutions in society to long-term relationships that are part of the process that will allow the UK 'to rethink its institutional structure and... be reoriented to longtermism, commitment and co-operation without losing the stimulus of competition'.[42] Thus, for example, Hutton argues that there should be '"stakeholder" unions, with formal rights of representation and even participation in decision-making [in businesses]'.[43] However, he sees the role of those trade unions not as being simply about the protection of their members' immediate interests, but rather as being one where they are committed to the continued prosperity of the business in which their members are employed even when their participation in decision-making means that they, for example, 'legitimise often painful programmes of job cuts and wage reductions'.[44] Balanced against this is the argument that institutional shareholders in businesses should not accrue voting rights simply by virtue of those shares, rights which they might use to drive businesses in directions that are of particular advantage to them because of their own

[40] Driver and Martell n 38 52. P Gould, *The Unfinished Revolution: How the Modernisers Saved the Labour Party* (London, Little, Brown and Company, 1998) 255.

[41] S Wheeler, *Corporations and the Third Way* (Oxford, Hart Publishing, 2002) 30. Although this does not mean that it has fallen out of government use entirely. See, eg Department for Constitutional Affairs, 'Increasing Diversity in the Judiciary' (Department of Constitutional Affairs, 2004) para 2.1.

[42] Hutton, n 35, 285.

[43] Hutton, n 35, 340.

[44] Hutton, n 35, 265, citing the German situation.

short-term needs, but that, instead, voting rights should be limited to those institutional shareholders who are represented on company boards, engaging 'in an ongoing dialogue with management about business strategy'.[45] Like Blair's statement, Hutton's account of the stakeholder society involves notions of much greater numbers of people being included in and engaged with society but provides much more detail about how that involvement and engagement will be achieved.[46]

THE STAKEHOLDER SOCIETY AND STAKEHOLDER BUSINESSES

The notion of the stakeholder society seen above is more than just a metaphorical application of the notion of the stakeholder business.[47] It involves one important theme that is common to the notion of the stakeholder as developed in business and management literature. In both instances the concept of the stakeholder involves trying to broaden of the vision of those to whom it is addressed. Just as businesses are enjoined to consider more than just the immediate interests of their shareholders so governments are exhorted actively to help 'individuals break out of exclusion and regain a stake in society'.[48] Moreover, institutions in society are encouraged to look beyond competitive and financial advantage and consider wider implications in the way in which they participate in decisions in society just as businesses are asked to look beyond immediate fiscal returns for their shareholders whilst individuals are urged consider how their participation in society can assist in improving the total good.

THE STAKEHOLDER IN THE UNIVERSITY

The main features of stakeholding in all its various forms having been established, it is now possible to go on and see how the term is used in the context of universities and university law schools.

The attempt to apply stakeholder notions to universities is perhaps almost inevitable. One of the reasons for using stakeholder concepts was because it was argued that there was 'a universal crisis of confidence... in business as an institution' and at the same time, it was said that 'educational... establishments around the world are all held in increasingly fragile esteem by

[45] Hutton, n 35, 302.

[46] For an attempt to reconceptualise the notion of capitalism in terms of stakeholding, see R Freeman, K Martin and B Parmar, 'Stakeholder Capitalism' (2007) 74 *Journal of Business Ethics* 303.

[47] Although the fact that it is a metaphorical application is also important. See A Barnett, 'Toward a Stakeholder Democracy' in Kelly, Kelly and Gamble (eds) above n 11, 82.

[48] Driver and Martell n 38, 56; Burkitt and Ashton n 39, 11.

ordinary citizens'; on this view stakeholder concepts are thus just as necessary in relation to universities as they are in the case of businesses.[49]

Asking universities to consider the needs of their stakeholders immediately raises three questions: who are stakeholders in universities?; what are their needs?; and how can those needs be taken into account? Answering each of these questions in turn reveals a series of more detailed issues.

Using any of the standard accounts of stakeholders found in management and business ethics literature, there are some very obvious groups who appear to be stakeholders in universities and thereby stakeholders in university law schools. The Dearing Report, for example, describes stakeholders in universities as being 'taxpayers, students and their families, graduates, employers and institutions themselves'.[50]

At even this early stage of drawing up a stakeholder map for a university it is clear that the nature of universities means that their maps are more complex than will typically be the case with businesses.[51] Universities are, for example, international in character, commonly drawing staff and students from outside whatever country they are located in. Equally, they have research projects and perhaps teaching schemes that stretch beyond their national borders. This is not just fortuitous. Fenwick observes that 'an international community is an essential element of any higher education institution' whilst Addison and Cownie note that '[f]or many academics in higher education institutions, the possibility of teaching and working with students from overseas is an important part of the academic enterprise'.[52] Universities are local in their setting but global in their reach.[53] UNESCO statistics suggest that in 2001/2002 there were nearly 2,000,000 foreign

[49] D Wheeler and M Sillanpan, *The Stakeholder Corporation: A Blueprint for Maximizing Stakeholder Value*" (London, Pitman Publishing, 1997) 3.

[50] The Dearing Report (1997) 263. Other Reports give slightly different and sometimes slightly vaguer definitions. Thus, for example, the Lambert Review talks about the university's stakeholders as being 'academics, students, funders and others' but also talks about the 'increased number' of stakeholders and the 'broad range' of stakeholders. R Lambert 'Lambert Review of Business-University Collaboration: Final Report' (HMSO, 2003) 14, 101, 102.

[51] For the concept of stakeholder maps, see Freeman n 10, 54–64.

[52] K Fenwick, 'Making the Most of Overseas Students' (1987) 41 *Higher Education Quarterly* 126, 137; W Addison and F Cownie, 'Overseas Law Students: Language Support and Responsible Recruitment' (1992) 19 *Journal of Law and Society* 467, 468. This is part of the history of universities. Thus, for example, in one of the earliest medieval universities, Paris, '[t]he renown of Abelard drew crowds of students from the remotest parts of Europe'. H Rashdall, *The Universities of Europe in the Middle Ages: Volume 1* (Oxford, Clarendon Press, 1936) 62.

[53] This is also true for some businesses but is not typical of businesses. Most of the top 100 British businesses operate abroad. J Parkinson, *Corporate Power and Responsibility* (Oxford, Clarendon Press, 1993) 7. However most businesses are small-scale. Parkinson, *Corporate Power* (1993) 4. They therefore tend to be local in character. Equally even where businesses appear to be global in their nature they sometimes try to divide their operations into separate, largely national elements. See, eg Union Carbide's description of its business in Bhopal. http://www.bhopal.com/ucs.htm. Universities, by contrast, tend to celebrate their international character.

students in universities world-wide with such students comprising 14 per cent of the total enrolment in Australia and 10 per cent of the total enrolment in the UK and Germany.[54] Thus, for UK universities, on this analysis, taxpayers are stakeholders. However, it is not just the British taxpayers, who in part fund the university, who are stakeholders, but also the taxpayers of other countries who are funding the education of students in the United Kingdom at undergraduate or postgraduate level. This is equally true for all the other examples of external stakeholders given by Dearing above.

The international character complicates universities stakeholder maps; so do other features of the universities' work. If stakeholders are, as Calvert suggests above, 'all the people whose lives or environment are affected by the project, but who receive no direct benefit from it' then anyone who may be affected, positively or adversely, by research done in the university is a stakeholder.[55] Given the way that research resulting from all disciplines permeates the world this plainly greatly extends each university's stakeholder map. Local communities are, of course, stakeholders in their universities but so are communities that are far distant, given that the research done by the university may impact on them. Equally, where, because of what they have learnt at universities, graduates directly or indirectly affect communities far-removed from the university it would appear that those communities have a right to see themselves as stakeholders in the university. Nor can stakeholding be limited to human beings. Given the ethical concerns that some have expressed about the use of animals in experiments in universities such animals might properly be regarded, using standard stakeholder concepts, as being stakeholders in the university.[56] Moreover stakeholders in universities are not just confined to the present generation. Given the long-term impact of what a university does, or what it elects not to do, future generations must also be considered. Indeed, in relation to any individual university, it is unclear who, and to some extent what, might justifiably be excluded from a place on the stakeholder map.[57]

The nature of the answer to the first question—who are stakeholders in the university?—determines the answer to the second question—what are the interests that these stakeholders have? The very large number of

[54] UNESCO Institute for Statistics, *Global Education Digest 2004* (2004) UNESCO Table 8. The US has the largest number of foreign students (582, 996) though they constitute only 4% of the total enrolment in higher education in that country (UNESCO) 110.

[55] S Calvert, 'Managing Stakeholders' in J Rodney Turner (ed), *The Commercial Project Manager* (London, McGraw-Hill Book Company, 1995) 214.

[56] The Scottish Society for the Prevention of Cruelty to Animals is part of the Scottish Executive's Animal Health and Welfare Stakeholder Group. www.scotland.gov.uk. whilst the drugs company Novo Nordisk regards the Danish Animal Welfare Society as being a stakeholder. www.novonordisk.com.

[57] Sternberg sees this argument as applying to all organisations. Sternberg n 11, 72.

stakeholders means that they are likely to have a diverse list of needs or interests. However finding out precisely what these needs are is more difficult. Looking at employer needs in one country is, for example, one thing. Looking at employer needs across a range of national borders is another. The first is difficult; the second begins to look like an overwhelming task. This is even more the case when it is arguably necessary to consider not just those employers who do employ a university's graduates but also those who might do so. Is an employer not as equally affected by the fact that they are unable to employ graduates, because, for example, the skills and knowledge those graduates have is not such as to make them useful employees, as is the employer who is able to employ the university's graduates? One employer has its pool of potential employees decreased; another has it enlarged. There are plainly practical, pragmatic problems whenever there is any attempt to work out what stakeholder needs are in any context. However, these problems take on a different scale when a university is the institution that is considering what its stakeholders want.

Stakeholder needs that are exceptionally large in number and diverse in kind because of the range of stakeholders that each university has, raises two different problems in answering the question, how does the university address those needs? One problem is simply what should they do? However the second problem, whilst not unique to universities, occurs at an altogether higher level of magnitude than in the case of other institutions having stakeholders; this is the question of what happens when stakeholders interests conflict? In the case of universities such conflicts seem to be not a possible but rather a necessary feature of the stakeholder map. Thus, to take an example that is currently important within the UK context, a government might see itself as having a stake in seeing that graduates are going to work in such a way as to enhance the economic well-being of its society.[58] However, each government that has graduates from a particular university amongst its nationals might equally well take the same position. To the degree that economic well-being is competitive, to the degree that it involves being better than another society, such needs are necessarily in conflict. British governments have a stake in seeing that British universities contribute to a thriving British economy, not to a thriving economy in the hundreds of countries that British universities draw their student population from. In stakeholder theory there is 'no clear decision-rule when attempting to adjudicate between rival claims of stakeholders'.[59] Such conflicts between stakeholders thus create a serious problem for universities.

[58] An approach first set out in the UK in the mid-1980s. 'The Development of Higher Education into the 1990s' (Cm 9524, 1985) para 1.2. And one that continues to the present day. DfEE, 'Higher Education in the 21st Century" (DfEE, 1997) 8.

[59] P Stiles, 'Corporate Governance and Ethics' in P Davis (ed), *Current Issues in Business Ethics* (London, Routledge, 1997) 45.

In practice many problems associated with the notion of the stakeholder in a university, whilst acknowledged, are capable of fairly simple solution. Using the approach in the literature on management and business ethics noted above it is possible to separate principal or primary stakeholders from other groups and to consider them when it comes to looking at who are stakeholders and at what needs those stakeholders have. Thus Dearing's description of stakeholders given above is said to be a description of 'principal stakeholders'.[60] Principal stakeholders are a fairly small group who are easy to identify, can have needs or desires more easily assessed and are less likely to make contradictory demands.[61] In this manner, in principle, it seems possible for universities to both identify and consider stakeholder needs. The University of Auckland's stakeholder list was lengthy, running to just over five pages, but it was manageable.

If universities can identify their principal stakeholders so can their law schools. Problems of detail remain; the Solicitors Regulation Authority and the Bar Standards Board, because of their regulatory responsibilities for solicitors and barristers, an occupational choice for many law graduates, are stakeholders for law schools in England and Wales but, given the fact that less than 50 per cent of law graduates from these law schools go into the legal profession, which other employers are also stakeholders? Questions like this, however, do not lead to the conclusion that it is impossible or undesirable to draw up a stakeholder map for the university law school. They merely indicate the intricate nature of the exercise.

At this stage a theoretical objection to the stakeholder exercise that was raised earlier in this essay now begins to take on considerable force. The need to identify who are the principal stakeholders in a university law school is justified by purely pragmatic considerations. Unless principal stakeholders can be separated from secondary stakeholders the stakeholder map is impossible to draw or make operational. However, some of those who become secondary stakeholders, and who therefore in practice are not considered by the law school, are not different in kind from those who are principal stakeholders. They are equally taxpayers, graduates, families and so forth. The nature of the stake that these principal and secondary stakeholders have in the law school is therefore precisely the same. The University of Auckland identified the Auckland District Law Society and the New Zealand Law Society as being stakeholders but did not mention any other local New Zealand District Law Society nor, despite the fact that it emphasised its international character on its web site, any foreign lawyers' association. What then justifies the law school focusing on the interests of one stakeholder and ignoring the interests of others?

[60] The Dearing Report, n 8, 263.

[61] Mace, however, observes that even these stakeholders are unlikely to agree. J Mace, 'The RAE and University Efficiency' (2000) 32 *Higher Education Review* 17, 31.

Principal stakeholders, as defined above, can be separated from secondary stakeholders by the fact that the latter can less easily have an impact upon the law school. Thus, for example, as foreign taxpayers they contribute very much less by way of financial support to a university or its law school, as foreign professional associations far fewer graduates are seeking their qualifications or as foreign families they are too far removed and there are too few of them to constitute a threat for the law school. Such a justification for separating principal from secondary stakeholders would receive support from the general literature on stakeholders. Freeman, for example, suggests that 'when we put the concept to practical tests we must be willing to ignore certain groups [who are stakeholders] who will have little or no impact on the corporation'.[62] Elsewhere he writes of 'a technique called "prioritized hierarchies" to actually quantify the importance of stakeholder groups and to check that resources are allocated in terms roughly equal to the importance of each group'.[63]

On this basis a law school is justified in considering the wishes or needs of law societies that are local to it and ignoring others that are geographically removed; domestic students and their families need consideration, those from overseas less so and so and so forth.[64] The difficulty with this approach, although it seems to be the only way of making the stakeholder notion operable in the context of universities, is that it subverts the intention that lies behind the application of stakeholder theory. If the strength of the stakeholder concept is Kantian in its form, stakeholders being considered for themselves, each stakeholder has an equal right to have its needs or desires considered. The impact that they have on the university is not of moment. In practice, however, stakeholding seems to suggest that universities behave in much the same manner that Friedman recommended to businesses; consider those, and only those, who might have a detrimental effect on you.[65]

In the context of both businesses and the notion of the stakeholder society the stakeholder concept widened the vision of those to whom it was applied, asking them to consider more than they had done previously. In the context of universities and their law schools the stakeholder concept serves

[62] Freeman, n 10, 52–53.

[63] Freeman, n 10, 159.

[64] At the more general level of the university the same argument is implicit in the Lambert Review's call for closer relationships between businesses and university in order to provide better economic performance. The Review uses stakeholder terminology with respect to universities but the only economy the Review is concerned with is the British economy. 'Lambert Review' (2003).

[65] Kelly, Kelly and Gamble note a similar criticism of stakeholding in general; that it is 'at its most intelligible when it refers to particular groups who have a common interest in the success of an enterprise' but that these groups' commitment assumes that others do not have the same commitment and that stakeholding is therefore exclusionary in its nature. G Kelly, D Kelly and A Gamble n 11, 247.

to narrow the gaze, counseling them that they need be concerned only by those who are immediately around them.

THE STAKEHOLDER'S ROLE IN UNIVERSITY LAW SCHOOLS

Although organisations may sometimes make their own decisions about the impact of their activities on their stakeholders it is, as is noted above, more usual in stakeholder theory to argue that stakeholders, having been supplied with the necessary information, should make their own voice known.[66] This is potentially problematic for university law schools.

Supplying stakeholders with the information that they need does not pose any problem of principle for the university law school. On the contrary, the enquiring nature of the law school, its habit of uncovering that which previously has been concealed, makes it difficult for it to justify refusing any appeal for information about itself. The law school is dependent on information about others for its work; information that it sometimes uses to the disadvantage of those that provide it; how then can it deny information to others, whatever the use that they might put it to? Notions of commercial confidentiality or similar considerations have limited currency within the academy. Historically, universities have concentrated on providing financial information in their annual reports; such data will not be sufficient for all stakeholders.[67] However they have also supplied a wide range of information in their other publications and in the publications of the academics who staff them. Providing stakeholders with more information creates problems for the university only when the staff costs or other costs arising because of the provision become disproportionate when compared with any benefit that results.[68]

If a university law school supplies information to stakeholders because the law schools accepts that they are stakeholders it creates a legitimate expectation on the part of those stakeholders that the law school will respond to their demands. It is at this point, however, that stakeholder theory poses some of the gravest problems for university law schools. Stakeholder theory does not just propose that stakeholders should have a voice; as we have seen above, it also makes suggestions about how that

[66] See, eg Grace and Cohen n 12, 72–73.

[67] D Coy, M Fischer and T Gordon, 'Public Accountability: A New Paradigm for College and University Annual Reports' (2001) 12 *Critical Perspectives on Accounting* 1, 10. Whilst this is a study of institutions in the US it seems unlikely that different results would be found in other countries.

[68] A complaint that has, for example, arisen in the UK in connection with supplying information for the Research Assessment Exercise. T Tapper and B Salter, 'Interpreting the Process of Change in Higher Education: The Case of the Research Assessment Exercises' (2003) 57 *Higher Education Quarterly* 4, 18. On the costs of audit, see also A Bradney, *Conversations* (Oxford, Hart Publishing Ltd, 2003) 180.

voice should be heard. 'According to stakeholder theory, the various groups who have an interest in the activities of an enterprise—workers, customers, communities etc—should acquire quasi-governance rights commensurate with the extent of their stake in the company.'[69]

To not give such rights is seen as being a denial of stakeholder status. Thus, for example, it is argued that '[t]enants have little real status as stakeholders. They do not have the same status as stakeholders in relation to their housing as that given to leaseholders.'[70] Such rights have to be given to stakeholders because it is said that they need to be 'actively engaged in the standard setting process' in an organisation; 'many stakeholders want some voice in organization's decision making'.[71] University law schools therefore need to consider how they can relate to stakeholders in such a position.

THE LAW SCHOOL'S RESPONSE TO STAKEHOLDERS

Some possible responses to stakeholder demands by law schools are obvious. For example, law schools may be able to respond positively to suggestions for changes to the curriculum or delivery of the curriculum made by students. Here there is a limited analogy to businesses responding to customer complaints, where such complaint 'yield an opportunity for understanding customer needs which ultimately translates into a good bottom line and satisfied stakeholders.'[72] Responding to students can be seen as improving the quality of the learning environment.[73] Similar analogous responses might be appropriate in the case of other stakeholders such as employers or government. All work done in universities is a good for society, the expansion of knowledge being always a desirable end in itself. However, often work will be of worth to particular groups or individuals. There can therefore be nothing wrong in principle in seeing whether changes to work, whether in teaching or research, can make that work more valuable to those groups or individuals. More than this, university law schools can 'use the information they collect from stakeholders to develop and modify their mission statements, goals, strategies, and implementation plans' as stakeholder theorists recommend to other organisations.[74]

There is, however, only a *limited* analogy between possible university law school responses to stakeholders above and the behaviour of businesses.

[69] Metcalfe, n 16, 34.

[70] Hood, n 33, 180.

[71] Roberts, n 29. R Phillips, *Stakeholder Theory and Organizational Ethics* (San Francisco, Berrett-Kochler Publishers, 2003) 159.

[72] Freeman, n 10, 71.

[73] P Ramsden, *Learning to Teach in Higher Education* 2nd edn, (London, RoutledgeFalmer, 2003) 221–23.

[74] Harrison and St John, n 21, 23.

On occasion law schools will see the wishes of stakeholders as being inappropriate to the law school mission and they will not be willing to yield to them. The UK provides a useful illustration of this phenomenon. In the UK the student view of the purpose of the law school and the dominant view of the staff are at odds. Students are largely pragmatic about their participation in the law school, seeing their education as being a vehicle to getting a good job.[75] Most academics, however, see the law school as having a wider purpose that fits broadly within the liberal notion that universities are there for the cultivation of the intellect and the increase of knowledge.[76] These two views can and sometimes do lead to a conflict between academic and student desires and, in such a situation, it seems likely that academics will insist on their view prevailing.[77] A student's participation in the law school is always voluntary—they are always free to pursue their life elsewhere—and they are not, even to the extent that they pay fees, customers who control the law school's product because academics do not view education as a commodity, with the university law school's interest being solely in its 'bottom line'.[78] Education, the development of the intellect and the expansion of knowledge, is perceived, rather, as a good in itself whose value remains the same whether or not anyone is willing to pay for it.[79]

The transformative and transgressive nature of a university law school's work may lead stakeholders to think that the law school is working against their desires and needs. Sometimes the law school will indeed be doing both. New knowledge and the development of the intellect within individual students is of value to society. It does not follow that it is of value to all groups within society nor does it follow that all societies at all times will benefit equally from that new knowledge. New knowledge may make old ways of living seem either inefficient or undesirable. Developing the intellect

[75] K Purcell and J Pitcher, *Great Expectations* (Manchester, Higher Education Careers Service, 1996) 11. This study found that law students were unusual in this respect with the majority of university students pursuing their studies because they found their subject interesting in itself.

[76] F Cownie, *Legal Academics: Culture and Identities* (Oxford, Hart Publishing, 2004) passim.

[77] Students might, of course take the view that since statistics indicate that British law graduates are more employable than graduates from most other disciplines they should accept the liberal education that they are being given even though they do not, unlike liberal educational theorists, see that education as being an end in itself. For statistics on employability, see A Smithers and P Robinson, *Trends in Higher Education* (London, The Council for Industry and Higher Education, 1995).

[78] 'A university is a place where ideas should be considered not for their cash value, but for their value to humanity'. M Tasker and D Packham, 'Government, Higher Education and the Industrial Ethic' (1994) 48 *Higher Education Quarterly* 182, 187. On the attempt to commodify education, see A Bradney, 'The Quality Assurance Agency and the Politics of Audit' (2001) 28 *Journal of Law and Society* 430.

[79] For a recent defence of the liberal concept of education in relation to university law schools, see M Thornton, 'The Idea of the University and the Contemporary Legal Academy' (2004) 26 *Sydney Law Review* 481.

and thus empowering students may mean that they are unwilling to accept some work environments that employers prefer. It is simply not possible for university law schools to accept that '[t]he good must be distributed with mutual consultation and so that no organizational stakeholders are complete losers while others are clear winners. Management must place a priority on the long term interests of all stakeholders'.[80]

Knowledge is what it is and both individual academics and individual students must follow their own freely chosen goals. Discoveries in the university both build new industries and destroy old ones. In the 1960s, partly because of the intellectual climate in the universities which was hostile to corporate America, large American law firms found that they had significant difficulties in attracting trainee lawyers.[81] Thus those who see themselves as being stakeholders in university law schools may justifiably not be enamoured with the work of the law school. Yet law schools may equally be justified, may indeed by their very nature be required, to reject any resultant complaints.[82] However, given that this is so, what is the nature of the 'quasi-governance rights' that stakeholders have acquired in the law school? What is their place in the 'standard setting process' and what role do they have in the 'organization's decision making'?

The notion of autonomy, at both the individual and the institutional level, has long been central to the work of the university.[83] These ideas continue to have contemporary significance. Thus Kogan has recently argued that '[u]niversities must be part of the working world, but that does not mean that they form part of a community with it except in very local and special senses.'[84] Similarly, Russell says of his 1993 book, *Academic Freedom*: 'The argument that universities know best how to manage their own business has been one of the central themes of this book.'[85] In the UK, '[w]hen asked what they liked most about being a legal academic, the factor identified

80 K Legge, 'Is HRM Ethical? Can HRM be Ethical' in M Parker (ed), *Ethics and Organizations* (London, Sage, 1998) 160. Similarly see Clarkson's suggestion that '[t]he economic and social purpose of the corporation is to create and distribute increased wealth for all its primary stakeholder groups, with out favoring one group at the expense of others'. M Clarkson, 'A Stakeholder Framework for Analyzing and Evaluating Corporate Social Performance' (1995) 20 *Academy of Management Review* 92 at 112.

81 M Galanter and T Palay, *Tournament of Lawyers* (Chicago, University of Chicago Press, 1991) 55–56.

82 Rejecting complaints is not, of course, the same thing as ignoring complaints. In a variety of ways, through web sites and publications, law schools constantly explain what they are doing.

83 See also A Bradney, 'Accountability, the University Law School and the Death of Socrates' (2002) 1 *Web Journal of Current Legal Issues* http http://webjcli.ncl.ac.uk./2002/issue1/bradney1.html.

84 M Kogan, 'Higher Education Communities and Academic Identity' (2000) 54 *Higher Education Quarterly* 207, 215.

85 C Russell, *Academic Freedom* (London, Routledge, 1993) 101.

most often... was autonomy'.[86] Yet the concept of autonomy sits uneasily with the idea of stakeholder participation in university law schools. By purporting to accept such participation those in law schools promise more than they can deliver, creating expectations that will never be fulfilled, because in practice they will not give up the autonomy that they personally prize and which is necessary for them to pursue their vocation.

POLITICS, LAW SCHOOLS AND LIBERAL EDUCATION

From the arguments above it would seem that the stakeholder concept can pose severe difficulties for universities and their law schools.[87] Yet it remains the case that the notion of the stakeholder enjoys a wide currency within higher education. This therefore raises the question why such a problematic idea continues to receive support?

In some cases it seems clear that the use made of stakeholder terminology in universities is one that conflicts with the theory of stakeholding outlined above. Thus, for example, the Pro Vice-Chancellor at Waikato, quoted at the beginning of this essay, who believes in '[s]trong relationships with stakeholder groups', does so because she sees this as being part of the way in which the university will be able 'to shape its own destiny'.[88] Stakeholders, seen in this way, are not valued for themselves but for what contact with them can do for the university.[89] Whether such an instrumentalist approach to stakeholders is good politics, producing the desired return, then becomes an important question. However what is clear is that such an approach does sit easily with the long-established notion of the autonomy of the university but does so at the cost of compatibility with all but the weakest forms of stakeholder theory. Here it is not so much that universities see some groups or institutions as stakeholders in the university but, rather, that they *say* they see them as stakeholders.[90] Such attitudes do not, however, account for all of the use that is made of stakeholder language in relation to universities.

[86] Cownie, n 76, 104.

[87] This is not to say that the use of stakeholder terminology always raises difficulties. In some instances, for example, the terminology seems to make no analytic contribution to debate and further seems not to be intended to make any such contribution. See, eg J Cook, D Holley and D Andrew 'A Stakeholder Approach to Implementing E-Learning in a University' (2007) 38 *British Journal of Educational Technology* 784.

[88] 'Professor Appointed to Key University Role' (10 March 2003) http://www.waikato.ac.nz/news/index.shtml?article=224.

[89] This approach is not just found in universities. Fransen and Kolk, for example, note the way in which businesses can 'manage" stakeholder contact for their own ends. L Fransen and A Kolk, 'Global Rule-Setting for Business: A Critical Analysis of Multi-Stakeholders Standards' (2007) 14 *Organization* 667, 671. See also A Zakhem, 'Stakeholder Management Capability: A Discourse-Theoretical Approach' (2008) 79 *Journal of Business Ethics* 395.

[90] This, of course, may be equally true of the behaviour of businesses that claim to subscribe to stakeholder ideals.

The use of stakeholder language in the context of higher education can be significant not because of any analytical merits that it possesses but because of the political imperatives that lie behind it. Stakeholder terminology, with its resonance of social inclusion, is a rhetorical device that potentially has particular power in the context of universities. It casts the university in a service role and appeals to notions that have deep emotional roots within the university.[91] Precisely because academics believe the academy to be 'the last good job' they are easily persuaded to assuage the guilt aroused by their perceptions of their own good fortune by doing things that are seen to be of direct benefit to those others who are not similarly fortunate; this is especially true for those with left/liberal leanings.[92] Attempts to persuade the academy to train workers rather than educate students are likely to fail fairly quickly.[93] Similarly efforts to set boundaries around what it is legitimate to research are quickly met with resistance.[94] If, however, the talk is of stakeholder needs then suggestions that in fact have the effect of training workers or determining the direction of research can take on a beguiling appeal.[95] A proposal that law schools should see themselves as being part of the human resource management arm of large law firms would immediately be dismissed by those in law schools. The proposition that large law firms

[91] 'All could agree that universities are "in the service" of the societies which nurture them". C Duke, 'The Learning University: Towards a New Paradigm?' (Buckingham, SRHE and Open University Press, 1992), 111. On the reasons why 'all' might not agree with this, see Bradney, 'Accountability' (2002).

[92] On the notion of the university as 'the last good job', see S Aronowitz, 'The Last Good Job in America' in R Martin (ed), *Chalk Lines: The Politics of Work in the Managed University* (Durham, Duke University Press, 1998). For a similar view of law schools, see D Weidener, 'The Crises of Legal Education: A Wake-Up Call for Faculty' (1997) 47 *Journal of Legal Education* 92. See also Cownie (2004) above n 76 ch 5. On the role of guilt, see the comment made by one academic about their reason for teaching: 'The kind of research we do here is parasitic on the public purse and if we are educating the younger generation, we are giving a little bit in return'. M Henkel, *Academic Identities and Policy Changes in Higher Education* (London, Jessica Kingsley Publishers, 2000) 184.

[93] See, eg, criticism of the Enterprise Learning Initiative in the UK, which sought to inculcate entrepreneurial skills in all students. Tasker and Packham, n 78, 186–88.

[94] See, eg, concerns about the possible effects of the Research Assessment Exercise in the UK. D Vick, A Murray, G Little and K Campbell, 'The Perceptions of Academic Lawyers Concerning the Effects of the United Kingdom Research Assessment Exercise' (1998) *Journal of Law and Society* 536, 556. Equally see the response to Carrington's suggestion that 'the nihilist who must profess that legal principle does not matter has an ethical duty to depart the law school'. P Carrington, 'Of Law and the River' (1984) 34 *Journal of Legal Education* 222; P Martin, '"Of Law and the River" and of Nihilism and Academic Freedom' (1985) 35 *Journal of Legal Education* 1.

[95] One obvious example of this phenomenon is the inclusion of teaching teamwork in the Law Benchmark that UK law schools have to conform to in order to be able to admit state-funded students. For details of this benchmark, see http://www.qaa.ac.uk/academicinfrastructure/benchmark/statements/law07.asp. On the ethical problems of teaching teamwork in a law school, see A Bradney, 'Elite Values in United Kingdom University Law Schools' (2008) 42 *The Law Teacher* 291.

are stakeholders in the law school is not so easily dismissed even though, in practice, the two statements amount to the same thing.

Stakeholder language, when used in the context of universities and university law schools, frequently fails to articulate its perception of the purpose of these institutions. Whilst this may be an intellectual weakness it can be rhetorically and thus politically expedient because it means that stakeholder arguments do not have to counter those accounts of the university's purpose that have suggested that the independence of the university is a necessary feature of its existence. Moreover stakeholder language can concentrate on the advantages that arise from stakeholder notions, the benefits that accrue to stakeholders, whilst being silent about the harm done both to those who are not primary or principal stakeholders and to the law school itself. 'Language has always been important in politics and government... Political differences have always been constituted as differences in language, political struggles have always been struggles over the dominant language.'[96]

The attempt to introduce stakeholder language into the law school can be seen as an attempt to radically change the focus of the law school not by arguing the merits for a new focus, such arguments having failed to attract support within law schools, but by altering the discourse that describes the law school. Were it to be successful, the result would be an impoverished law school reduced to servicing the immediate needs of those around it and less able to carry out its primary function of enquiring into the nature of law and reporting back its results.[97]

[96] Fairclough, n 35, 3.

[97] cf '[Legal academics should] study law and... teach students what they happen to discover'. O Fiss, 'Owen Fiss to Paul Carrington' in Martin, above n 94, 26.

Index